THE BEST OF

LOW-FAT
COOK BOOK

· ·

BY THE EDITORS OF SUNSET BOOKS

Sunset Publishing Corporation · Menlo Park, California

SUNSET BOOKS
President and Publisher:
    Susan J. Maruyama
Director, Finance and Business Affairs:
    Gary Loebner
Director, Manufacturing & Sales Service:
    Lorinda Reichert
Western Regional Sales Director:
    Richard A. Smeby
Eastern Regional Sales Director:
    Richard M. Miller
Editorial Director: Kenneth Winchester
Coordinating Editor: Cornelia Fogle
Research & Text: Cynthia Scheer
Copy Editor: Rebecca LaBrum
Editorial Assistant: Kevin Freeland
Design: Nina Bookbinder Design
Illustrations: Mary Haverfield

SUNSET PUBLISHING CORPORATION
Chairman: Robert L. Miller
President/Chief Executive Officer:
    Robin Wolaner
Chief Financial Officer: James E. Mitchell
Circulation Director: Robert I. Gursha
Editor, Sunset Magazine: William R. Marken
Senior Editor, Food & Entertaining:
    Jerry Anne Di Vecchio

Cover: Mediterranean Baked Chicken & Vege-
tables, page 100. Design by Jacqueline Jones
Design. Photography by Allan Rosenberg
and Allen V. Lott. Food and photo styling by
Sandra Griswold. Assistant food stylists:
Danielle DiSalvo and Elizabeth Ruegg.

Back cover photographers
Top row: No-sauce Pizza (page 193), Kevin San-
chez; Black Bean & Fresh Corn Nachos (page 10),
Nikolay Zurek; Raspberry-glazed Turkey Tender-
loins (page 111), Nikolay Zurek. Bottom row:
Baked Polenta with Veal Sauce (page 90), Kevin
Sanchez; Liqueur Pound Cake (page 199), Glenn
Christiansen; Black & White Soup (page 29),
Norman A. Plate.

First printing September 1994
Copyright © 1994 Sunset Publishing Corporation,
Menlo Park, CA 94025. First edition. All rights
reserved, including the right of reproduction in
whole or in part in any form.

ISBN 0-376-02654-5
Library of Congress Catalog Card Number: 94-66504
Printed in the United States.

♻ printed on recycled paper

DELICIOUS & HEALTHY!

For great flavor and good nutrition, *Sunset* has always relied on fresh, natural ingredients. Today, as always, superb taste is a requirement for all our recipes—but in recent years, we've added another goal. We aim to give you more for less: plenty of the tempting flavor you want, without the fat you'd rather avoid. In fact, each recipe in this book derives no more than 30% of its calories from fat.

In the *Best of Sunset Low-Fat Cook Book*, we've gathered hundreds of our favorite healthful dishes. A quick glance through these pages proves that lean, nutritious cooking can be delicious, attractive, and supremely satisfying. Besides recipes for everything from appetizers to desserts, you'll find short features on specific subjects—low-fat breakfasts and homemade broths, for example—and numerous tips covering all sorts of topics, from crisping greens to ripening too-firm fruit. And look for the special labels on some recipes; these tell you at a glance if a dish is a streamlined version of an old favorite, a choice that's naturally low in fat, or a selection you can prepare in under 30 minutes.

To help you in your meal planning, we provide complete nutritional information (see page 5) with each recipe.

All of the recipes in this book were developed and tested in the *Sunset* test kitchens. If you have comments or suggestions, please let us hear from you.
Write us at:
Sunset Books
Cook Book Editorial
80 Willow Road
Menlo Park, CA 94025

If you would like to order additional copies of any of our books, call us at 1-800-634-3095 or check with your local bookstore.

CONTENTS

A LETTER FROM SUNSET

Dear reader,

At Sunset, cooking light has become a delicious habit. No wonder, then, that we decided to put together this Best of Sunset Low-Fat Cook Book—*a wonderful collection of our (and your) favorite lean dishes. Here are ideas for every part of the meal, from appetizers through satisfying main dishes to tempting desserts.*

Our recipes prove something that many of you have already learned: light cooking doesn't mean deprivation dieting. In fact, to anyone with a healthy appetite, low-fat meals offer a grand bonus: larger portions and a fuller plate. As you reduce or omit fat, you save on calories, too—calories you can then spend on more generous helpings of all sorts of lean, filling foods. And of course, when you streamline a favorite dish, you can enjoy an ample serving worry-free. Take a look at our slimmed-down versions of beef Stroganoff (page 72), meat loaf (page 74), chicken-filled chimichangas (page 108), and chili mole (page 115); you'll be impressed, as we were, by the modest fat-and-calorie cost per portion.

As you browse through this volume, you'll see that we use a number of fat-reducing strategies. Two you'll come across often are braise-deglazing (see page 119) and sweating. The first is a way to "sauté" vegetables using water or other liquid in place of the usual oil or butter. Cooked by this method, onions and other vegetables brown and caramelize, developing marvelously rich flavor. Handsome Black & White Soup (page 29), Braised Chicken with Green Chile Sauce (page 105), and many other favorites start out with the braise-deglazing step. Sweating, too, substitutes liquid for fat: meat is browned in a little water or broth and its own juices. Besides being easier than messy flouring and frying, the sweating technique yields superb results; try Rich

Brown Braised Beef (page 70), for example. Other fat-reducing tactics include oven-browning instead of frying, as in Norwegian Meatballs (page 15), and roasting rather than sautéing, as in Roasted Tomato-Eggplant Crostini (page 8).

Perhaps the simplest way to eat well with less fat is to increase your consumption of grains, legumes, vegetables, and fruits. This book will give you dozens of ideas for presenting these foods deliciously, and that makes it easy to compose wonderful, bountiful—and healthful—meals for family and friends.

Think trim!

Jerry Anne DiVecchio
Senior Editor, Food and Entertaining

WHAT DOES "LOW-FAT" MEAN?

All of our recipes have been developed to conform to the American Heart Association (AHA) requirements for fat intake; in each, fat provides no more than 30% of the calories. In addition, we have used a special banner to designate recipes that are naturally low in fat (less than 2 grams of total fat and less than 1 gram of saturated fat per serving), those that are low-fat modifications of classic recipes or *Sunset* favorites, and those that can be prepared and cooked in 30 minutes or less.

A WORD ABOUT OUR NUTRITIONAL DATA

For each recipe, we provide a nutritional analysis prepared by Hill Nutrition Associates, Inc., of Florida. It states calorie count; percentage of calories from fat, carbohydrates, and protein; grams of total fat and saturated fat, carbohydrates, and protein; and milligrams of cholesterol and sodium. Generally the analysis applies to a single serving, based on the number of servings given for each recipe and the amount of each ingredient. If a range is given for the number of servings and/or the amount of an ingredient, the analysis is based on an average of the figures given.

The nutritional analysis does not include optional ingredients or those for which no specific amount is stated. If an ingredient is listed with a substitution, the information was calculated using the first choice.

APPETIZERS

*F*estive food adds to the fun of any happy occasion. And appetizers—crisp or creamy, hot or cold—begin such gatherings on a gracious note. When you select your appetizers, keep good nutrition in mind: guests will be doubly pleased with choices that are healthful as well as delicious. If you're looking for light bites, offer a platter of tempting fruit in season or a few dips made with vegetables or smooth, creamy yogurt. For heartier fare, try sizzling-hot chicken tidbits, spicy barbecued shrimp, or chunks of swordfish crowned with lemon relish. Or bring on a tray of vegetarian nachos— complete with fresh salsa and crunchy tortilla chips— or a big plate of warm-from-the-oven miniature calzones, plump with a filling of ham and spinach.

Yogurt Cheese & Tomato Torta

Preparation time: About 35 minutes
Soaking time: About 30 minutes
Chilling time: At least 13 hours

Bright colors and bold flavors combine in this irresistible appetizer. Pesto made from dried tomatoes is layered with soft, tangy yogurt cheese, then presented with crisp baguette slices or bite-size raw vegetables.

Yogurt Cheese (recipe follows)
Tomato Pesto (recipe follows)
Rosemary sprigs
Toasted French bread baguette slices or bite-size pieces of raw vegetables

Prepare Yogurt Cheese and Tomato Pesto.

Smoothly line a tall, wide-mouth 2-cup container (such as a bowl, a basket without finish or dye, or a clean new flowerpot) with muslin or a double layer of cheesecloth. Press a fourth of the Yogurt Cheese evenly into bottom of container. Evenly distribute a third of the Tomato Pesto over cheese. Repeat layers to use remaining cheese and pesto, finishing with cheese.

Fold edges of cloth over cheese. Press gently to compact. If using a basket or flowerpot, set it in a rimmed pan to catch liquid. Cover airtight and refrigerate for at least 1 hour or up to 6 hours; occasionally pour off liquid as it accumulates.

Fold back cloth; invert torta onto a serving plate. Lift off cloth. Garnish with rosemary sprigs. To eat, spread torta on toast slices. Makes about 2 cups (8 to 10 servings).

Yogurt Cheese. Line a fine strainer with muslin or a double layer of cheesecloth. Set strainer over a deep bowl (bottom of strainer should sit at least 2 inches above bottom of bowl). Spoon 4 cups **plain nonfat yogurt** into cloth. Cover airtight and refrigerate until yogurt is firm (at least 12 hours) or for up to 2 days; occasionally pour off liquid that drains into bowl. Gently press cheese to remove excess liquid.

Tomato Pesto. Soak 1 cup (about 2¼ oz.) **dried tomatoes** in **boiling water** to cover until soft (about 30 minutes). Drain; squeeze out excess liquid. Whirl tomatoes in a food processor or blender (or chop with a knife) until minced. Mix tomatoes with 2 tablespoons grated **Parmesan cheese,** 1 clove **garlic** (minced or pressed), and 1 teaspoon minced **fresh rosemary** or ½ teaspoon dry rosemary. Season to taste with **salt.**

Per serving: 64 calories (8% fat, 57% carbohydrates, 35% protein), 0.6 g total fat (0.2 g saturated fat), 9 g carbohydrates, 6 g protein, 0.9 mg cholesterol, 66 mg sodium

Curried Spinach Dip

Preparation time: About 15 minutes
Chilling time: At least 2 hours

Based on a blend of cottage cheese and skim milk, this emerald green dip goes beautifully with fresh vegetable spears—try red bell peppers, white jicama, or yellow summer squash. Or use the mixture as a filling for hollowed cherry tomatoes.

2	**cups low-fat cottage cheese**
¼	**cup nonfat milk**
2	**tablespoons lemon juice**
1	**package (about 10 oz.) frozen chopped spinach, thawed and squeezed dry**
3	**green onions, thinly sliced**
2	**teaspoons curry powder**
	Raw vegetable strips or spears

In a food processor or blender, combine cottage cheese, milk, and lemon juice. Whirl until smooth and glossy. Add spinach, onions, and curry powder; whirl until blended. Pour into a bowl; cover and refrigerate for at least 2 hours or up to 1 day. Serve with vegetables. Makes about 2¾ cups.

Per tablespoon: 12 calories (16% fat, 28% carbohydrates, 56% protein), 0.2 g total fat (0.1 g saturated fat), 0.8 g carbohydrates, 2 g protein, 0.8 mg cholesterol, 48 mg sodium

__Yogurt cheese__ plays a versatile role in low-fat cooking. On this page, it stars in a favorite Western appetizer, a handsome layered cheese torta. And in Berry Yogurt Cheese Pie (page 205), it's the base of a sweet, creamy filling.

Roasted Tomato-Eggplant Crostini

Preparation time: About 15 minutes
Baking time: About 50 minutes
Broiling time: About 4 minutes

Meals in Italy often begin with crostini—slices of bread or toast with a savory spread. The low-fat topping featured here combines red onion, tomatoes, and eggplant, baked until almost charred to caramelize the natural sugars. The vegetables need only the simplest of seasonings: salt, pepper, balsamic vinegar, and a minimum of oil.

> **Olive oil cooking spray**
> 1 **large red onion, cut into ½-inch-thick slices**
> 2 **tablespoons balsamic or red wine vinegar**
> 1½ **pounds firm-ripe pear-shaped (Roma-type) tomatoes, cut into ¼-inch-thick slices**
> 1 **medium-size eggplant (about 1 lb.), unpeeled, cut crosswise into ½-inch-thick slices**
> **Salt and pepper**
> 16 **slices crusty Italian or French bread (*each about 3½ inches wide, 5 inches long, and ½ inch thick*)**

Coat two 10- by 15-inch rimmed baking pans with cooking spray. Arrange onion slices in a single layer in one of the pans; drizzle with vinegar. Arrange tomato slices in same pan, overlapping slightly. Arrange eggplant slices in a single layer in second pan. Coat all vegetables lightly with cooking spray. Bake in a 450° oven until eggplant is browned and very soft when pressed (about 30 minutes) and tomatoes are well browned on edges (about 50 minutes).

Transfer all vegetables to a food processor or blender; whirl until coarsely puréed. Season to taste with salt and pepper. (At this point, you may cover and refrigerate for up to 3 days; bring to room temperature before serving.)

Place bread in a single layer on a baking sheet. Broil about 5 inches below heat, turning once, until golden on both sides (about 4 minutes).

To serve, spread toast with vegetable purée, using about 2 tablespoons purée for each slice. Makes 16 appetizers.

Per appetizer: 94 calories (15% fat, 72% carbohydrates, 13% protein), 2 g total fat (0.2 g saturated fat), 18 g carbohydrates, 3 g protein, 0 mg cholesterol, 152 mg sodium

Mushroom Pâté with Wheat Toast Points

30 MINUTES OR LESS

Preparation time: About 10 minutes
Broiling time: 2 to 3 minutes
Cooking time: 10 to 15 minutes

Smooth, rich pâté is a special treat, a perfect starter for an elegant meal. The traditional meat-based recipes tend to be high in fat and cholesterol, but you can make pâtés that are both richly flavored and lean by starting with vegetables. Our savory mushroom variation, seasoned with garlic and white pepper, is superb with crisp wheat toast.

> **Wheat Toast Points (recipe follows)**
> 2 **tablespoons butter or margarine**
> 1 **pound mushrooms, chopped**
> ¾ **cup chopped shallots**
> 1 **small carrot, chopped**
> 1 **clove garlic, minced or pressed**
> **Ground white pepper**
> **Chopped parsley**

Prepare Wheat Toast Points and set aside.

Melt butter in a wide frying pan over medium-high heat. Add mushrooms, shallots, carrot, and garlic. Cook, stirring often, until liquid has evaporated and mushrooms are browned (10 to 15 minutes). Transfer mixture to a food processor or blender and whirl until puréed. Season to taste with white pepper. Mound on a plate and sprinkle with parsley. Serve warm or at room temperature, surrounded by Wheat Toast Points. Makes 10 servings.

Wheat Toast Points. Stack 10 slices **whole wheat bread;** trim off crusts. Cut stack in half diagonally. Arrange triangles in a single layer on a baking sheet and broil about 5 inches below heat, turning once, until browned on both sides (2 to 3 minutes).

Per serving: 99 calories (29% fat, 58% carbohydrates, 13% protein), 3 g total fat (2 g saturated fat), 15 g carbohydrates, 4 g protein, 6 mg cholesterol, 148 mg sodium

Cherry Tomato Salsa

NATURALLY LOW IN FAT

Preparation time: About 20 minutes

Nippy with garlic and fresh jalapeños, this salsa tastes great with crisp cucumber slices or tortilla chips. For the prettiest presentation, use both red and yellow cherry tomatoes.

- 2 **cups (about 12 oz.) red or yellow cherry tomatoes (or use some of each)**
- 1 **clove garlic, minced or pressed**
- ⅓ **cup lightly packed cilantro leaves**
- 2 **fresh jalapeño chiles, seeded and finely chopped**
- 2 **tablespoons** *each* **thinly sliced green onion and lime juice**
  Salt and pepper
  About 3 cups cucumber slices
  Water-crisped Tortilla Chips (page 12) or purchased tortilla chips (optional)

Cut tomatoes into halves. In a food processor, combine tomatoes, garlic, cilantro, and chiles; whirl until tomatoes are coarsely chopped. (Or chop coarsely with a knife.) Transfer to a bowl and stir in onion and lime juice. Season to taste with salt and pepper.

Serve salsa with cucumber slices and, if desired, tortilla chips. Makes about 2 cups (6 servings).

Per serving: 23 calories (9% fat, 77% carbohydrates, 14% protein), 0.3 g total fat (0 g saturated fat), 5 g carbohydrates, 1 g protein, 0 mg cholesterol, 8 mg sodium

Layered Bean Dip

Preparation time: About 35 minutes
Baking time: 12 to 15 minutes

This multilevel dip starts with hummus, a smooth purée of chick peas and savory seasonings. Top the mixture with yogurt, cucumber, radishes, and feta cheese, then scoop up each bite with crunchy Pita Crisps.

Pita Crisps (recipe follows)
- 1 **can (about 15 oz.) garbanzo beans or 2 cups cooked garbanzo beans (page 149)**
- 3 **tablespoons tahini (sesame-seed paste)**
- ¼ **cup lemon juice**
- ½ **teaspoon ground cumin**
- 1 **clove garlic, minced or pressed**
- ½ **cup plain nonfat yogurt**
- 1 **tablespoon minced fresh mint**
- ½ **cup** *each* **thinly sliced cucumber and thinly sliced radishes**
- ¼ **cup crumbled feta cheese**

Prepare Pita Crisps; set aside.

Drain beans, reserving ¼ cup of the liquid; then rinse beans. In a food processor or blender, whirl beans, the reserved ¼ cup liquid, tahini, lemon juice, cumin, and garlic until smooth. Spoon mixture onto a large platter and spread out to make an 8-inch circle.

In a bowl, stir together yogurt and mint; spread over bean mixture. Sprinkle cucumber, radishes, and cheese over yogurt mixture. Tuck Pita Crisps around edge of bean mixture; scoop mixture onto crisps to eat. Makes 12 servings.

Pita Crisps. Split 6 **pita breads** (*each* about 6 inches in diameter) horizontally to make 12 rounds. In a small bowl, stir together 2 tablespoons **olive oil** and 1 clove **garlic** (minced or pressed). Brush split sides of bread with oil mixture, then sprinkle with **pepper.** Cut each round into 6 wedges. Arrange in a single layer on baking sheets. Bake in a 350° oven until crisp and golden (12 to 15 minutes). Serve at room temperature.

Per serving: 183 calories (28% fat, 59% carbohydrates, 13% protein), 6 g total fat (1 g saturated fat), 27 g carbohydrates, 6 g protein, 3 mg cholesterol, 312 mg sodium

Black Bean & Fresh Corn Nachos

. . . .

Preparation time: About 20 minutes
Cooking time: About 10 minutes
Baking time: About 10 minutes

Get a casual supper off to a satisfying start with this hot, hearty layered dip. You top seasoned black beans with fresh corn and creamy jalapeño jack cheese, then bake briefly and serve with chips and a tart tomatillo salsa.

Lime Salsa (recipe follows)
Savory Black Beans (recipe follows)

4   **cups cooked yellow or white corn kernels (from 4 large ears corn); or 2 packages (about 10 oz. *each*) frozen corn kernels, thawed**

1   **cup (about 4 oz.) shredded jalapeño jack cheese**
     About 12 cups Water-crisped Tortilla Chips (page 12) or purchased tortilla chips
     Cilantro sprigs or leaves

Prepare Lime Salsa and refrigerate.

Prepare Savory Black Beans. Spoon beans onto a large, ovenproof rimmed platter; spread out evenly to make an oval. Top beans evenly with corn, then sprinkle with cheese. Bake in a 400° oven until hot in center (about 10 minutes).

Remove bean mixture from oven. Tuck some of the tortilla chips around edge of platter; serve remaining chips alongside. Garnish with cilantro.

To serve, spoon bean mixture onto plates; top with some of the Lime Salsa. To eat, scoop bean mixture onto chips; add more salsa to taste. Makes 12 servings.

━━━

Fresh tomatillos *look like small green tomatoes with papery husks. Crisp in texture, tart and slightly fruity in flavor, they're a popular ingredient in Mexican and Southwestern-style sauces and salsas (see Lime Salsa, above, for example). To prepare tomatillos, remove the husks and stems; then rinse the fruit well to remove the sticky coating.*

Lime Salsa. In a bowl, stir together 1 medium-size ripe **red or yellow tomato** (about 6 oz.), finely diced; 4 medium-size **tomatillos** (about 4 oz. *total*), husked, rinsed, and chopped; 2 tablespoons minced **red or yellow bell pepper;** 1 tablespoon minced **red onion;** ½ teaspoon grated **lime peel;** and 1½ teaspoons **lime juice.** If made ahead, cover and refrigerate for up to 4 hours.

Savory Black Beans. Heat 1½ tablespoons **salad oil** in a wide frying pan over medium heat. Add 1 medium-size **onion,** coarsely chopped, and 1 clove **garlic,** minced or pressed. Cook, stirring often, until onion is soft and lightly browned (8 to 10 minutes). Drain 4 cups **cooked black beans** (page 149) or 2 cans (about 15 oz. *each*) black beans, reserving ½ cup of the liquid. Rinse beans; add to onion mixture along with the ½ cup reserved liquid and 1 tablespoon **distilled white vinegar.** Coarsely mash beans with a spoon. Season to taste with **salt.**

Per serving: 310 calories (23% fat, 61% carbohydrates, 16% protein), 13 g protein, 49 g carbohydrates, 8 g total fat (2 g saturated fat), 10 mg cholesterol, 242 mg sodium

White Bean Pâté

. . . .

NATURALLY LOW IN FAT

Preparation time: About 20 minutes
Cooking time: About 15 minutes

Piquant braised-deglazed onions enrich this creamy dip. Serve it with crisp vegetables.

1   **large onion, finely chopped**
2   **cloves garlic, minced or pressed**
     About ½ cup canned or homemade (page 41) vegetable broth or low-sodium chicken broth
¼   **cup sherry vinegar or 3 tablespoons white wine vinegar**
1   **can (about 15 oz.) cannellini (white kidney beans), drained and rinsed; or 2 cups cooked cannellini (page 149), drained and rinsed**
     Salt and pepper
     Red bell pepper strips and carrot slices

In a wide frying pan, combine onion, garlic, and ¼ cup of the broth. Cook over medium-high heat, stirring often, until liquid evaporates and onion begins to brown. To deglaze, add vinegar to pan and stir to scrape browned bits free. Continue to cook, stirring occasionally, until mixture begins to brown again. Repeat deglazing and browning steps 1 or 2 more times, using 2 tablespoons more broth each time; vegetables should be richly browned.

Add beans to onion mixture and mash coarsely with a spoon. If necessary, add a little more broth to give beans the texture of creamy mashed potatoes. Season to taste with salt and pepper. Mound in a bowl or on a plate. If made ahead, cover and refrigerate for up to 3 days.

Serve pâté warm or cool, with pepper strips and carrot slices. Makes about 1½ cups.

Per tablespoon: 17 calories (6% fat, 70% carbohydrates, 24% protein), 0.1 g total fat (0 g saturated fat), 3 g carbohydrates, 1 g protein, 0 mg cholesterol, 43 mg sodium

Smoky Tuna Spread

30 MINUTES OR LESS

Preparation time: About 10 minutes

When you're in a hurry, choose this appetizer: it's made with ingredients you probably have on hand, and it goes together in about 10 minutes. Serve the spread on baguette slices.

1	**can (about 9¼ oz.) water-packed albacore tuna, drained**
⅓	**cup low-fat cottage cheese**
3	**tablespoons lemon juice**
½	**teaspoon liquid smoke**
	Pepper
	About 1 tablespoon drained capers
	Parsley sprig and 1 thin strip of lemon peel
	French bread baguette slices

In a food processor, combine tuna, cottage cheese, lemon juice, and liquid smoke; whirl until very smooth (or beat with an electric mixer). Season to taste with pepper. Spoon mixture into a small bowl. If made ahead, cover and refrigerate for up to 1 day. Just before serving, garnish with capers, parsley sprig, and lemon peel. Serve with bread. Makes about 1⅓ cups.

Per tablespoon: 19 calories (17% fat, 5% carbohydrates, 78% protein), 0.3 g total fat (0.1 g saturated fat), 0.3 g carbohydrates, 4 g protein, 5 mg cholesterol, 71 mg sodium

Jicama & Fresh Fruit Platter

NATURALLY LOW IN FAT

Preparation time: About 30 minutes

Fruit and spice contrast deliciously in this eye-catching hors d'oeuvre. To assemble the dish, coat jicama slices and fresh fruit with lime juice, then sprinkle with chili powder and salt. For the fruit, we suggest using melon, oranges, and papaya; other good choices include mangoes, kiwis, and tart apples.

1	**small jicama (about 1 lb.)**
1	**large slice watermelon**
½	**small honeydew melon**
1	**small papaya (about 12 oz.)**
3	**medium-size oranges (1¼ to 1½ lbs. *total*)**
⅔	**cup lime juice**
½	**teaspoon salt**
1	**tablespoon chili powder**

Peel jicama; then rinse and cut in half lengthwise. Slice each half thinly. Remove rinds from watermelon and honeydew melon; cut fruit into chunks. Peel, seed, and slice papaya. Cut peel and all white membrane from oranges; then cut between membranes to release segments.

Coat jicama and fruit with lime juice; arrange in separate sections on a platter. (At this point, you may cover and refrigerate for up to 2 hours.)

To serve, combine salt and chili powder; sprinkle over jicama and fruit. Makes 8 servings.

Per serving: 100 calories (6% fat, 87% carbohydrates, 7% protein), 0.7 g total fat (0 g saturated fat), 24 g carbohydrates, 2 g protein, 0 mg cholesterol, 159 mg sodium

Corn Relish & Water-crisped Tortilla Chips

Preparation time: About 20 minutes
Baking time: About 6 minutes
Cooking time: About 5 minutes

Serve this green-and-gold relish as a dip for crisp corn or flour tortilla chips or as an accompaniment for grilled meat or chicken.

Water-crisped Tortilla Chips (recipe follows)

3	medium-size ears corn
½	cup finely chopped English cucumber
⅓	cup lime juice
¼	cup thinly sliced green onions
1	tablespoon grated orange peel
3	tablespoons orange juice
2	tablespoons chopped fresh mint or 1 teaspoon dry mint
1	teaspoon cumin seeds
1	or 2 fresh jalapeño chiles, seeded and finely chopped
	Salt

Prepare Water-crisped Tortilla Chips and set aside.

Remove and discard husks and silk from corn. In a 5- to 6-quart pan, bring about 3 quarts water to a boil over high heat. Add corn; cover and cook until hot (about 5 minutes). Drain and let cool.

Cut corn kernels from cobs and place corn in a medium-size bowl; add cucumber, lime juice, onions, orange peel, orange juice, mint, cumin seeds, and chiles. Stir to mix, then season to taste with salt. If made ahead, cover and refrigerate for up to 1 day. Serve with tortilla chips. Makes about 12 servings.

Water-crisped Tortilla Chips. You will need 12 **corn tortillas** (*each* about 6 inches in diameter) or 12 flour tortillas (*each* 7 to 9 inches in diameter). Dip tortillas, one at a time, in **water;** drain briefly. Season to taste with **salt.** Stack tortillas; cut stack into 6 or 8 wedges.

Arrange tortilla wedges in a single layer on large baking sheets. Bake in a 500° oven for 4 minutes. Turn tortilla wedges over and continue to bake until browned and crisp (about 2 more minutes). If made ahead, let cool; then store airtight at room temperature for up to 1 week. Makes about 8 cups corn chips, about 12 cups flour chips.

Per serving of relish: 36 calories (8% fat, 82% carbohydrates, 10% protein), 0.4 g total fat (0.1 g saturated fat), 8 g carbohydrates, 1 g protein, 0 mg cholesterol, 7 mg sodium

Per cup of corn chips: 55 calories (10% fat, 80% carbohydrates, 10% protein), 1 g total fat (0.1 g saturated fat), 12 g carbohydrates, 1 g protein, 0 mg cholesterol, 40 mg sodium

Per cup of flour chips: 114 calories (20% fat, 69% carbohydrates, 11% protein), 2 g total fat (0.4 g saturated fat), 19 g carbohydrates, 3 g protein, 0 mg cholesterol, 167 mg sodium

Quick Cuke Chips

NATURALLY LOW IN FAT

Preparation time: About 20 minutes
Standing time: At least 1 hour
Chilling time: At least 1 day

Sliced cucumbers and red bell pepper strips marinated in dill-flavored vinegar are attractive and addictive—and so easy to make that the pickle jar need never be empty. Serve them with sandwiches or cold sliced meats, or include them in a low-fat antipasto assortment.

3	large cucumbers
1	large red bell pepper (about 8 oz.), seeded and cut into ½-inch-wide strips
1	large onion, thinly sliced
1	tablespoon *each* salt and dill seeds
¾	cup sugar
½	cup white wine vinegar

Cut unpeeled cucumbers crosswise into ¼-inch-thick slices. In a large bowl, combine cucumbers, bell pepper, and onion. Add salt and dill seeds; stir well. Let stand, uncovered, for 1 to 2 hours; stir occasionally.

In a small bowl, combine sugar and vinegar; stir until sugar is dissolved. Pour over vegetables and mix gently. Spoon into glass or ceramic containers, cover, and refrigerate for at least 1 day or up to 3 weeks. Drain before serving. Makes about 8 cups.

Per ¼ cup: 18 calories (3% fat, 91% carbohydrates, 6% protein), 0.1 g total fat (0 g saturated fat), 4 g carbohydrates, 0.3 g protein, 0 mg cholesterol, 104 mg sodium

Crabby Potatoes

Preparation time: About 20 minutes
Baking time: 45 to 55 minutes
Broiling time: 3 to 5 minutes

Stuffed with a creamy combination of crab, chives, and cheese, these one-bite tidbits are irresistible. For best results, look for very small red potatoes, no more than 2 inches in diameter (in the produce department, these tiny potatoes may be singled out as "creamers").

12 small red thin-skinned potatoes (*each* 1½ to 2 inches in diameter), scrubbed

1 teaspoon olive oil

4 ounces flaked cooked crabmeat

2 tablespoons *each* plain nonfat yogurt and reduced-calorie mayonnaise

2 tablespoons minced chives or thinly sliced green onion

2 teaspoons lemon juice

1 tablespoon chopped parsley

2 tablespoons grated Parmesan cheese
   Pepper

Pierce each potato in several places with a fork. Arrange potatoes in a single layer in a shallow baking pan; add oil and turn potatoes to coat. Bake in a 375° oven until tender throughout when pierced (45 to 55 minutes). Let cool slightly. (At this point, you may cover and refrigerate for up to 1 day.)

Cut potatoes in half crosswise. Using a small melon baller, scoop out centers of potato halves, leaving about a ¼-inch shell. Reserve centers for other uses. Set potato halves, cut side up, in a shallow baking pan (if necessary, trim a sliver from rounded side of potato halves to steady them in the pan).

In a small bowl, stir together crab, yogurt, mayonnaise, chives, lemon juice, parsley, and cheese until evenly blended. Season to taste with pepper. Spoon mixture into potato shells. Broil about 4 inches below heat until golden (3 to 5 minutes). Makes 24 appetizers.

Per appetizer: 32 calories (22% fat, 57% carbohydrates, 21% protein), 0.8 g total fat (0.2 g saturated fat), 4 g carbohydrates, 2 g protein, 5 mg cholesterol, 31 mg sodium

Sweet Potatoes with Caviar

Preparation time: About 15 minutes
Baking time: About 25 minutes

Crisp-baked sweet potato slices are a delectable base for dollops of sour cream and a touch of crunchy golden caviar. Select an inexpensive caviar, such as flying fish roe (*tobiko*), crab roe (*masago*), or lumpfish, whitefish, or salmon caviar.

2 pounds sweet potatoes (*each* about 2 inches in diameter)
   Vegetable oil cooking spray

¼ cup caviar

⅓ to ½ cup reduced-fat sour cream

Scrub sweet potatoes well, but do not peel them. Cut off and discard ends of potatoes; then cut potatoes crosswise into ¼-inch-thick slices. Coat two 10- by 15-inch rimmed baking pans with cooking spray. Arrange potatoes in a single layer in pans. Coat lightly with cooking spray.

Bake in a 400° oven until slices are golden brown on bottom (about 15 minutes); turn slices over and continue to bake until browned on top (about 10 more minutes). Potatoes at edges of pans tend to brown faster, so move these to centers of pans when you turn slices.

While potatoes are baking, place caviar in a fine wire strainer and rinse under cool running water; drain well, then refrigerate until ready to use.

Lift baked potato slices onto a tray or platter in a single layer. Dot each with a small dollop of sour cream, then with a little caviar. Serve hot or warm. Makes about 60 appetizers.

Per appetizer: 22 calories (23% fat, 66% carbohydrates, 11% protein), 0.6 g total fat (0.1 g saturated fat), 4 g carbohydrates, 0.6 g protein, 7 mg cholesterol, 18 mg sodium

Prized for its sweet, delicate flavor, *Dungeness crab—named for a small community on the Strait of Juan de Fuca in Washington—is the best-known West Coast crab. It's delicious in appetizers such as the stuffed potatoes above.*

Beef Rillettes

Preparation time: About 25 minutes
Baking time: About 4 hours
Chilling time: At least 7 hours

Rillettes, an appetizer spread popular in the Loire Valley of France, is usually made from succulent pork cooked and preserved in its own fat. Our version of this treat uses naturally lean beef shanks, oven-braised until very tender; the softly jelled cooking juices moisten the mixture without adding much fat.

	About 1¼ pounds beef shanks (about 1 inch thick)
1	**clove garlic, peeled**
½	**teaspoon *each* pepper and dry thyme**
1	**dry bay leaf**
2	**cups water**
	Salt
2	**small French bread baguettes (about 8 oz. *each*), thinly sliced**
2	**heads Belgian endive (about 6 oz. *total*), separated into spears, rinsed, and crisped (optional)**
	Dijon mustard (optional)

Place beef in a 1¼- to 1½-quart casserole; add garlic, pepper, thyme, and bay leaf. Pour in water; cover tightly and bake in a 250° oven until meat is so tender it falls apart in shreds when prodded with a fork (about 4 hours).

Lift meat from casserole, reserving liquid. Let meat stand until cool enough to touch; then remove and discard all fat, bones, and connective tissue. Tear meat into fine shreds, cover, and refrigerate.

Refrigerate cooking liquid separately until surface fat has hardened (about 4 hours). Lift off and discard fat. Measure liquid (it should be softly jelled); you need 1½ cups. (If liquid is still fluid, transfer to a small pan and boil until reduced to 1½ cups; if it is rigid, add enough water to make 1½ cups.) Heat liquid until hot, then add meat and heat until warm. Season to taste with salt. Pour into a 2½- to 3-cup crock or jar. Cover and refrigerate until firm (at least 3 hours) or for up to 3 days (gelatin may weep if mixture is kept for longer than 3 days).

To serve, spread on bread slices or, if desired, spoon into endive spears. Add mustard to taste, if desired. Makes about 2¼ cups.

Per 1-tablespoon serving on bread: 48 calories (15% fat, 56% carbohydrates, 29% protein), 0.8 g total fat (0.2 g saturated fat), 7 g carbohydrates, 3 g protein, 4 mg cholesterol, 83 mg sodium

Mini-Calzones

Preparation time: About 1 hour
Rising time: About 1 hour
Cooking time: About 10 minutes
Baking time: About 15 minutes

Tiny spinach-stuffed turnovers made with whole wheat pizza dough are perfect party fare. For convenience, you can bake them a day ahead, then reheat just before serving. If you have leftovers, enjoy them with Warm-up Vegetable Soup (page 27) at lunch or supper.

	Whole Wheat Dough (recipe follows)
2	**tablespoons olive oil**
2	**tablespoons minced shallot**
2	**ounces Black Forest ham, chopped**
4	**cups coarsely chopped, lightly packed spinach**
¼	**cup part-skim ricotta cheese**
½	**teaspoon ground nutmeg**

Prepare Whole Wheat Dough.

While dough is rising, prepare filling. Heat 1 tablespoon of the oil in a wide frying pan over medium-high heat. Add shallot and ham; cook, stirring occasionally, until shallot is soft (about 5 minutes). Add spinach and cook, stirring often, until liquid has evaporated (about 5 minutes). Remove from heat. Add ricotta cheese and nutmeg; mix well. Let cool.

Punch Whole Wheat Dough down and knead briefly on a lightly floured board to release air. Shape dough into a ball, then roll out ⅛ inch thick. Cut dough into 3-inch rounds. Place about 1 teaspoon of the spinach filling on half of each round. Fold plain half of each round over filling; press edges together to seal. Transfer calzones to oiled, cornmeal-dusted baking sheets. Brush tops with remaining 1 tablespoon oil; prick tops with a fork.

Bake calzones in a 425° oven until lightly browned (about 15 minutes). Serve warm. If made ahead, let cool, then cover and refrigerate for up to 1 day. To reheat, arrange on baking sheets and heat, uncovered, in a 425° oven for about 5 minutes. Makes about 36 calzones.

Whole Wheat Dough. In a large bowl, combine 1 package **active dry yeast** and ¾ cup **warm water** (about 110°F); let stand until yeast is softened (about 5 minutes).

Add 1 teaspoon *each* **salt** and **sugar;** stir in 1 cup **all-purpose flour.** Beat with a heavy spoon or an electric mixer until smooth. Then mix in about 1 cup **whole wheat flour** or enough to make dough hold together. Turn dough out onto a lightly floured board and knead until smooth and elastic (about 5 minutes), adding more flour as needed to prevent sticking. Place dough in an oiled bowl and turn over to oil top; cover with plastic wrap and let rise in a warm place until almost doubled (about 1 hour).

Per calzone: 40 calories (28% fat, 56% carbohydrates, 16% protein), 1 g total fat (0.2 g saturated fat), 6 g carbohydrates, 2 g protein, 1 mg cholesterol, 93 mg sodium

Norwegian Meatballs
· ·

Preparation time: About 25 minutes
Baking time: About 12 minutes
Cooking time: About 10 minutes

Use ground chicken breast to create this updated version of a long-time party favorite. Seasoned with sage and fennel, the delicate meatballs are served in a creamy cheese sauce.

¼	cup low-sodium chicken broth or water
6	tablespoons all-purpose flour
2	pounds ground skinless chicken or turkey breast
2	large egg whites (about ¼ cup)
1	teaspoon *each* pepper and dry sage
½	teaspoon *each* fennel seeds and salt
	Gjetost Sauce (recipe follows)

In a bowl, smoothly mix broth and flour; then add chicken, egg whites, pepper, sage, fennel seeds, and salt. Mix well. Shape meat mixture into 1-tablespoon mounds (you will have about 48); set slightly apart in 2 nonstick or lightly oiled 10- by 15-inch rimmed baking pans.

Bake meatballs in a 500° oven for 10 minutes. Meanwhile, prepare Gjetost Sauce; keep hot. Turn meatballs over with a wide spatula and continue to bake until well browned on outside and no longer pink in center; cut to test (about 2 more minutes).

To serve, add meatballs to hot Gjetost Sauce; stir gently to mix. Keep hot on a warming tray. Spear meatballs with small skewers to eat. Makes about 24 servings.

Gjetost Sauce. In a wide frying pan, combine 1 large **onion,** chopped, and ¼ cup **low-sodium chicken broth.** Cook over medium-high heat, stirring, until liquid evaporates and onion begins to brown. To deglaze, add ¼ cup more **low-sodium chicken broth** and stir to scrape browned bits free. Then continue to cook, stirring occasionally, until onion is richly browned. Stir in 2 tablespoons **cornstarch;** smoothly mix in 2 cups **low-sodium chicken broth.** Bring to a rapid boil over high heat, stirring. Reduce heat to low and add 1 cup (about 4 oz.) shredded **gjetost cheese;** stir until cheese is melted. Pour into a serving bowl; use hot (sauce thins if reheated).

Per serving: 82 calories (23% fat, 26% carbohydrates, 51% protein), 2 g total fat (1 g saturated fat), 5 g carbohydrates, 10 g protein, 22 mg cholesterol, 110 mg sodium

__With interest in low-fat cooking__ on the rise, ground chicken and turkey have grown in popularity and availability. When you shop, look for ground skinless meat, since much of the fat in poultry lies just beneath the skin. The leanest choice of all is ground skinless breast, called for in our Norwegian Meatballs. Both chicken or turkey work well in these tender, cheese-sauced morsels.

Chili Chicken Chunks with Blender Salsa

Preparation time: About 10 minutes
Baking time: About 20 minutes

Treat company to these crisp, spicy nuggets of chicken; they're baked instead of fried to keep them lean. A super-easy salsa goes alongside for dipping.

	Blender Salsa (recipe follows)
¾	cup soft whole wheat bread crumbs
¼	cup yellow cornmeal
2	teaspoons chili powder
½	teaspoon *each* paprika, ground cumin, and dry oregano
	Vegetable oil cooking spray or salad oil
1½	pounds boneless, skinless chicken breast halves
2	large egg whites (about ¼ cup)

Prepare Blender Salsa and refrigerate.

Spread bread crumbs in a shallow baking pan and bake in a 350° oven, stirring once, until lightly browned (about 5 minutes). Add cornmeal, chili powder, paprika, cumin, and oregano; stir well. Set aside.

Lightly coat a baking sheet with cooking spray. Rinse chicken and pat dry; then cut each breast half into 8 equal pieces. Place egg whites in a small bowl and beat lightly with a fork. Dip chicken pieces into egg whites; lift out and drain briefly. Then roll in crumb mixture to coat, place on baking sheet, and bake until meat in center is no longer pink; cut to test (about 15 minutes). Serve with salsa. Makes 8 servings.

Blender Salsa. In a blender or food processor, combine 12 ounces **tomatoes,** cut into chunks; ½ small **onion,** cut into chunks; 3 tablespoons **canned diced green chiles;** 4 teaspoons **distilled white vinegar;** and 1 tablespoon chopped **cilantro.** Whirl until smooth.

Per serving: 142 calories (11% fat, 26% carbohydrates, 63% protein), 2 g total fat (0.3 g saturated fat), 9 g carbohydrates, 22 g protein, 49 mg cholesterol, 124 mg sodium

Apricot-Orange Glazed Chicken

Preparation time: About 15 minutes
Soaking time: At least 30 minutes
Broiling time: About 8 minutes

An easy apricot-jam sauce gives this broiled chicken-on-a-stick its luscious flavor.

6	boneless, skinless chicken breast halves (about 2 lbs. *total*)
1	cup apricot jam
2	tablespoons *each* prepared horseradish, minced fresh ginger, grated orange peel, and firmly packed brown sugar
¼	cup orange juice

Soak thirty-six 6- to 8-inch bamboo skewers in hot water to cover for at least 30 minutes.

Rinse chicken and pat dry. Cut each breast half lengthwise into 6 equal slices, then weave each slice onto a skewer. Place skewers on a lightly oiled rack in a broiler pan.

In a 1- to 1½-quart pan, combine jam, horseradish, ginger, orange peel, sugar, and orange juice. Stir over medium-high heat until jam is melted; keep mixture warm.

Brush chicken with some of the jam mixture. Broil 6 inches below heat, turning once and brushing 2 or 3 times with remaining jam mixture, until meat in thickest part is no longer pink; cut to test (about 8 minutes). Brush with any remaining jam mixture; serve hot. Makes 36 appetizers.

Per appetizer: 54 calories (5% fat, 51% carbohydrates, 44% protein), 0.3 g total fat (0.1 g saturated fat), 7 g carbohydrates, 6 g protein, 15 mg cholesterol, 21 mg sodium

Chicken Yakitori

• •

Preparation time: About 30 minutes
Marinating time: About 15 minutes
Grilling time: About 10 minutes

For a casual appetizer, thread chicken and green onions on skewers and marinate briefly in a soy-sherry blend; then grill over low coals.

½ cup *each* reduced-sodium soy sauce and cream sherry

3 tablespoons sugar

4 bunches green onions

2 pounds boneless, skinless chicken breasts, cut into bite-size pieces

Soak sixteen 6- to 8-inch bamboo skewers in hot water to cover for at least 30 minutes.

Meanwhile, in a small pan, combine soy sauce, sherry, and sugar. Bring to a boil over high heat; then reduce heat and simmer for 3 minutes. Pour into a 9- by 13-inch dish and set aside.

Trim roots and any wilted tops from onions; then cut onions into 1½-inch lengths. Thread onions and chicken on skewers, alternating chicken with onion pieces on each skewer. Place skewers in soy mixture, turn to coat, and let stand for 15 minutes.

Lift skewers from marinade and drain briefly (reserve marinade). Place skewers on a lightly oiled grill 4 to 6 inches above a solid bed of low coals. Cook, turning as needed to brown evenly and basting with marinade, until meat in thickest part is no longer pink; cut to test (about 10 minutes). Makes 16 appetizers.

Per appetizer: 101 calories (7% fat, 31% carbohydrates, 62% protein), 0.8 g total fat, 0.2 g saturated fat, 7 g carbohydrates, 14 g protein, 33 mg cholesterol, 559 mg sodium

Swordfish with Lemon Relish

· ·

Preparation time: About 30 minutes
Baking time: About 16 minutes
Cooking time: 20 to 25 minutes

These canape-style appetizers are perfect finger food for a stand-up cocktail party. Toasted baguette slices are topped with a sweet-tart fresh lemon relish, squares of lean, meaty swordfish, and thin tomato strips. (You'll enjoy the tangy relish served on grilled fish entrées, too.)

Lemon Peel Relish (recipe follows)

32 **French bread baguette slices (*each* about 2 inches wide and ¼ inch thick)**

1 **pound boneless, skinless swordfish steaks (about ½ inch thick)**

¼ cup dry white wine
Salt and pepper

2 small pear-shaped (Roma-type) tomatoes (about 4 oz. *total*), seeded and cut into thin strips

Prepare Lemon Peel Relish and set aside.

Arrange bread slices in a single layer on baking sheets. Bake in a 350° oven until lightly toasted (about 10 minutes). Let cool. (At this point, you may store airtight at room temperature for up to 2 days.)

Rinse fish, pat dry, and cut into 16 equal pieces, each about 1 inch square. Then cut each piece in half horizontally so that pieces are about ¼ inch thick. Arrange fish in a single layer in a foil-lined 10- by 15-inch rimmed baking pan. Drizzle with wine; season to taste with salt and pepper. Cover loosely with additional foil.

Bake in a 375° oven until fish is just opaque but still moist in center; cut to test (about 6 minutes). Let cool in pan. (At this point, you may cover and refrigerate for up to 4 hours.)

Up to 30 minutes before serving, spoon equal amounts of Lemon Peel Relish onto each bread slice. Just before serving, drain fish and pat dry; set a piece atop relish on each bread slice. Top with tomatoes. Makes 32 appetizers.

Lemon Peel Relish. With a vegetable peeler, pare yellow peel (including a little white pith) from 6 large **lemons**. Mince peel. Cut off and discard remaining pith from 2 of the lemons (reserve remaining 4 lemons for other uses). Cut the 2 lemons into chunks; remove and discard seeds. Chop fruit coarsely.

Heat 1 tablespoon **salad oil** in a medium-size frying pan over medium-high heat. Add ½ cup finely chopped **onion;** cook, stirring often, until onion is soft but not browned (about 5 minutes). Add lemon peel, chopped lemons, ½ cup **dry white wine,** ⅓ cup **sugar,** and 1 teaspoon **pepper.** Cook, stirring often, until almost all liquid has evaporated and mixture is syrupy (15 to 18 minutes). Let cool. If made ahead, cover and refrigerate for up to 2 weeks.

Per appetizer: 56 calories (20% fat, 54% carbohydrates, 26% protein), 1 g total fat (0.2 g saturated fat), 8 g carbohydrates, 4 g protein, 6 mg cholesterol, 60 mg sodium

Barbecued Shrimp

Preparation time: About 25 minutes
Marinating time: At least 4 hours
Cooking time: About 4 minutes

First marinated in a sweet-sharp tomato sauce, then threaded on bamboo skewers, these succulent shrimp can be grilled or broiled.

1	can (about 8 oz.) tomato sauce
½	cup light molasses
1	teaspoon dry mustard
	Dash of liquid hot pepper seasoning
1	clove garlic, minced or pressed
1	tablespoon salad oil
⅛	teaspoon dry thyme
	Pepper
2	pounds medium-size raw shrimp (about 36 per lb.), shelled and deveined

In a large glass bowl, mix tomato sauce, molasses, mustard, hot pepper seasoning, garlic, oil, and thyme. Season to taste with pepper. Add shrimp and stir to coat. Cover and refrigerate for at least 4 hours or until next day.

Meanwhile, soak about twenty-four 6- to 8-inch bamboo skewers in hot water to cover for at least 30 minutes.

Lift shrimp from bowl, reserving marinade; thread about 3 shrimp on each skewer. Place on a lightly oiled grill about 6 inches above a solid bed of low coals. (Or place on a rimmed baking sheet and broil about 6 inches below heat.) Cook, turning once and brushing often with marinade, until shrimp are opaque in center; cut to test (about 4 minutes). Makes about 24 appetizers.

Per appetizer: 41 calories (16% fat, 21% carbohydrates, 63% protein), 0.7 g total fat (0.1 g saturated fat), 2 g carbohydrates, 6 g protein, 47 mg cholesterol, 65 mg sodium

Tomato-Crab Quesadillas

Preparation time: About 15 minutes
Baking time: 7 to 9 minutes

Warm crab, tomatoes, and jack cheese make a great filling for quesadillas. Offer your favorite green chile salsa to heat up each serving.

2	medium-size firm-ripe tomatoes (about 12 oz. *total*), finely chopped
4	ounces flaked cooked crabmeat
¾	cup shredded jack cheese
1	cup sliced green onions
	Salt
10	flour tortillas (*each* 7 to 9 inches in diameter)
	Cilantro sprigs
	Purchased green chile salsa

Place tomatoes in a fine wire strainer and let drain well; discard juice.

In a bowl, mix crab, cheese, and onions. Gently mix in tomatoes. Season to taste with salt. Place 5 tortillas in a single layer on 2 lightly oiled large baking sheets. Top tortillas with crab mixture, covering tortillas to within ¾ inch of edges. Top each tortilla with one of the remaining tortillas.

Bake in a 450° oven until tortillas are lightly browned (7 to 9 minutes), switching positions of baking sheets halfway through baking.

Slide quesadillas onto a serving board; cut each into 6 wedges. Garnish with cilantro sprigs. Offer salsa to add to taste. Makes 8 to 10 servings.

Per serving: 188 calories (28% fat, 53% carbohydrates, 19% protein), 9 g protein, 25 g carbohydrates, 6 g total fat (2 g saturated fat), 23 mg cholesterol, 317 mg sodium

Nippy Shrimp Quesadillas

Follow directions for **Tomato-Crab Quesadillas,** but omit crabmeat and jack cheese. Instead, use 4 ounces **small cooked shrimp** and ¾ cup shredded **jalapeño jack cheese.** Makes 8 to 10 servings.

Per serving: 189 calories (28% fat, 53% carbohydrates, 19% protein), 6 g total fat (2 g saturated fat), 25 g carbohydrates, 9 g protein, 35 mg cholesterol, 323 mg sodium

FESTIVE BEVERAGES

If you like to entertain, you'll find it useful to assemble a collection of low-fat drinks. There are plenty of choices for any time of day; just keep the focus on fruits, juices, plain and flavored sparkling waters, and low-fat dairy products.

CRANBERRY MARGARITAS

Preparation time: About 15 minutes

1¼	**cups cranberry juice cocktail**
½	**cup sugar**
1½	**cups fresh or frozen cranberries**
¾	**cup *each* lime juice and tequila**
½	**cup orange-flavored liqueur**
3	**cups coarsely crushed ice or small ice cubes**

Pour ¼ cup of the cranberry juice into a shallow bowl. Spread 3 tablespoons of the sugar on a flat plate. Dip rims of 4 to 6 wide-mouth stemmed glasses (¾- to 1-cup size) into juice, then into sugar. Set glasses aside.

Reserve 12 of the cranberries. In a blender, combine remaining cranberries, remaining 1 cup cranberry juice, remaining 5 tablespoons sugar, lime juice, tequila, liqueur, and ice. Whirl until smooth and slushy. (If necessary, whirl in 2 batches, then mix.)

To serve, pour into glasses; garnish with reserved cranberries. Makes 4 to 6 servings.

Per serving: 287 calories (1% fat, 98% carbohydrates, 1% protein), 0.2 g total fat (0 g saturated fat), 43 g carbohydrates, 0.2 g protein, 0 mg cholesterol, 8 mg sodium

MOCHA AU LAIT

Preparation time: About 10 minutes
Cooking time: About 5 minutes

1½	**cups nonfat or low-fat (1% or 2%) milk**
2	**tablespoons sweetened ground chocolate**
1½	**cups hot espresso or hot strong coffee**
	Ground cinnamon or sweetened ground chocolate (optional)

In a 1½- to 2-quart pan, combine milk and the 2 tablespoons ground chocolate; stir until well blended. Place over medium heat and stir until milk mixture is steaming. Leaving pan over heat, beat milk mixture with an electric mixer on high speed until frothy (or whirl mixture in a blender).

Pour espresso equally into 2 large (at least 1½-cup) cups or mugs; then pour in foamy milk mixture and spoon on foam. Sprinkle with cinnamon or ground chocolate, if desired. Makes 2 servings.

Per serving: 122 calories (28% fat, 50% carbohydrates, 22% protein), 4 g total fat (2 g saturated fat), 16 g carbohydrates, 7 g protein, 4 mg cholesterol, 101 mg sodium

STRAWBERRY-MINT LEMONADE

Preparation time: About 20 minutes
Cooking time: About 10 minutes
Chilling time: At least 3 hours

4	**cups water**
	About 1¼ cups sugar
5	**cups lightly packed mint sprigs**
4	**cups strawberries, hulled**
1	**cup lemon juice**

In a 3- to 4-quart pan, combine 2 cups of the water, 1 cup of the sugar, and mint sprigs. Bring to a boil over high heat; reduce heat, cover, and simmer for 10 minutes. Pour through a fine strainer into a blender; press to extract liquid. Discard mint.

Thinly slice about 1 cup of the strawberries and set aside. Add half the remaining strawberries to blender and whirl until smooth; pour into a wide-mouth 2½- to 3-quart pitcher or bowl. In blender, whirl lemon juice and remaining whole strawberries until smoothly puréed; add to pitcher. Stir in sliced strawberries and remaining 2 cups water. Sweeten to taste with more sugar, if desired; stir until sugar is dissolved.

Cover and refrigerate for at least 3 hours or up to 8 hours. Before serving, stir well. Makes 8 servings.

Per serving: 159 calories (3% fat, 94% carbohydrates, 3% protein), 0.6 g total fat (0 g saturated fat), 40 g carbohydrates, 1 g protein, 0 mg cholesterol, 7 mg sodium

SOUPS

Whether you're looking for a light first course, a quick one-bowl lunch or supper, or a robust main dish for a blustery night, our nourishing soups are the right choice. From simple vegetable purée to elegant fish pot-au-feu to complex minestrone brimming with fresh produce and dried beans, the recipes in this chapter all deliver great taste as well as good nutrition. And all of them are based on ingredients containing little if any fat. Full-flavored broth is the starting point for many a superb soup. On page 41, you'll find directions for making three lean, wholesome stocks—chicken, beef, and an all-vegetable variety based on mushrooms, leeks, and tomatoes. If you prefer the convenience of canned broth or bouillon cubes or granules, look for low-sodium types.

Spirited Cherry Soup

30 MINUTES OR LESS

Preparation time: About 20 minutes
Cooking time: About 5 minutes

Light or dark sweet cherries—or a combination of the two—go into a hot, citrus-accented soup to enjoy as a first course or an unconventional dessert.

4	cups pitted light or dark sweet cherries (or use some of each)
3½	cups white grape juice
2	teaspoons grated lemon peel
2	tablespoons lemon juice
3	tablespoons orange-flavored liqueur or 1½ teaspoons grated orange peel
	Mint sprigs and thin strips of orange peel (optional)

Divide cherries among 4 bowls.

In a 2- to 3-quart pan, combine grape juice and lemon peel; bring to a boil over high heat. Stir in lemon juice and liqueur; then pour juice mixture equally over cherries. Garnish each serving with mint sprigs and orange peel, if desired. Makes 4 servings.

Per serving: 278 calories (5% fat, 93% carbohydrates, 2% protein), 1 g total fat (0.3 g saturated fat), 63 g carbohydrates, 2 g protein, 0 mg cholesterol, 19 mg sodium

Cantaloupe-Tangerine Soup

NATURALLY LOW IN FAT

Preparation time: About 10 minutes

Tangy tangerine juice blended with sweet cantaloupe makes a refreshing summertime breakfast treat—or a cool, soothing finish for a warm-weather meal.

1	large cantaloupe (about 3 lbs.), chilled
1	small can (about 6 oz.) frozen tangerine or orange juice concentrate, partially thawed
	Mint sprigs

Cut cantaloupe in half; scoop out and discard seeds. Scoop fruit from rind and place in a food processor or blender; add tangerine juice concentrate and whirl until smoothly puréed. If made ahead, cover and refrigerate for up to 1 day; whirl again to blend before serving.

To serve, pour soup into bowls and garnish with mint sprigs. Makes 4 servings.

Per serving: 146 calories (4% fat, 90% carbohydrates, 6% protein), 0.7 g total fat (0 g saturated fat), 35 g carbohydrates, 2 g protein, 0 mg cholesterol, 17 mg sodium

Golden Tomato-Papaya Gazpacho with Basil

NATURALLY LOW IN FAT

Preparation time: About 25 minutes
Chilling time: At least 1 hour

Ripe golden tomatoes combine with diced papaya and savory seasonings in this distinctive cold soup. It's a nice choice for a picnic or a patio party.

2	pounds yellow regular or cherry tomatoes
1	large ripe papaya (about 1¼ lbs.), peeled, seeded, and diced
1	cup diced cucumber
¼	cup finely chopped white onion
2	tablespoons white wine vinegar
2	cups canned or homemade (page 41) vegetable broth or low-sodium chicken broth
2	tablespoons minced fresh basil
⅛	teaspoon liquid hot pepper seasoning
	Salt
	Basil sprigs

Dice tomatoes and place in a large bowl. Stir in papaya, cucumber, onion, vinegar, broth, minced basil, and hot pepper seasoning. Season to taste with salt. Cover and refrigerate until cold (at least 1 hour) or for up to 1 day.

To serve, ladle soup into bowls and garnish with basil sprigs. Makes 10 to 12 servings.

Per serving: 38 calories (11% fat, 80% carbohydrates, 9% protein), 0.5 g total fat (0.1 g saturated fat), 9 g carbohydrates, 1 g protein, 0 mg cholesterol, 195 mg sodium

Garden Gazpacho

Preparation time: About 30 minutes
Chilling time: At least 1 hour

Chock-full of crisp, cool vegetables, gazpacho combines soup and salad in a single bowl. This version can take two forms. Made with chicken broth, it's light and mild-tasting; if you use tomato cocktail, it has more flavor and substance.

1	large cucumber
2	large tomatoes (about 1 lb. *total*), peeled, seeded, and chopped
1	large red or green bell pepper (about 8 oz.), seeded and chopped
⅓	cup sliced ripe olives
¼	cup lime juice
4	cups low-sodium chicken broth or spicy tomato cocktail
1	clove garlic, minced or pressed
½	cup thinly sliced green onions
1	tablespoon minced fresh thyme or 1 teaspoon dry thyme
	Liquid hot pepper seasoning
	Lime wedges

Peel cucumber and cut in half lengthwise; scoop out and discard seeds. Chop cucumber; place in a large bowl and add tomatoes, bell pepper, olives, lime juice, broth, garlic, onions, and thyme. Stir well; season to taste with hot pepper seasoning. Cover and refrigerate until cold (at least 1 hour) or for up to 1 day.

To serve, stir gazpacho well. Ladle into bowls and serve with lime wedges. Makes 8 servings.

Per serving: 47 calories (28% fat, 55% carbohydrates, 17% protein), 2 g total fat (0.3 g saturated fat), 7 g carbohydrates, 2 g protein, 0 mg cholesterol, 84 mg sodium

---

Not long ago, *virtually every bell pepper in the market was green. But times have changed! These sweet New World natives can now be found in hues of red, orange, yellow, and even purple. Peppers of every color are rich in vitamin C; red and yellow types are good sources of vitamin A as well.*

Golden Pepper Bisque

Preparation time: About 50 minutes
Baking time: 12 to 15 minutes
Broiling time: 15 to 20 minutes
Cooking time: 30 to 35 minutes

Cooked until very soft, then puréed, thin-skinned potatoes lend a silky texture to this distinctive golden soup. Top each serving with crisp croutons and a sprinkling of Parmesan.

	French Bread Croutons (recipe follows)
2	large yellow bell peppers (about 1 lb. *total*)
1	tablespoon olive oil or salad oil
1	large onion, chopped
2	large thin-skinned potatoes (about 1 lb. *total*), peeled and diced
2	large carrots, cut into ½-inch-thick slices
1	large stalk celery, thinly sliced
6	cups low-sodium chicken broth
	Salt and pepper
	Grated Parmesan cheese (optional)

Prepare French Bread Croutons; set aside.

Place bell peppers in a 9-inch baking pan and broil about 4 inches below heat, turning as needed, until charred all over (15 to 20 minutes). Cover with foil and let cool in pan for 30 minutes. Remove and discard stems, skins, and seeds; rinse peppers and chop coarsely. Set aside.

Heat oil in a 4- to 5-quart pan over medium-high heat. Add onion and cook, stirring often, until soft (about 5 minutes). Add bell peppers, potatoes, carrots, celery, and broth. Bring to a boil; reduce heat, cover, and boil gently until carrots are very soft to bite (20 to 25 minutes).

In a food processor or blender, whirl vegetable mixture, a portion at a time, until smoothly puréed. Return vegetable purée to pan; cook over medium heat, stirring often, until heated through. Season to taste with salt and pepper.

To serve, ladle soup into bowls. Sprinkle croutons over each serving; offer cheese to add to taste, if desired. Makes 6 to 8 servings.

French Bread Croutons. Coat a shallow rimmed baking pan with **olive oil cooking spray.** Spread

4 cups (about 4 oz.) ¾-inch cubes **French bread** in pan. Lightly coat bread cubes with **olive oil cooking spray.** Bake in a 350° oven until crisp and golden brown (12 to 15 minutes). If made ahead, let cool; then cover and store at room temperature for up to 2 days.

Per serving: 182 calories (21% fat, 66% carbohydrates, 13% protein), 4 g total fat (0.7 g saturated fat), 31 g carbohydrates, 6 g protein, 0 mg cholesterol, 168 mg sodium

Caribbean Corn Chowder

30 MINUTES OR LESS

Preparation time: About 15 minutes
Cooking time: About 15 minutes

Served hot or cool, this mellow soup is equally good as a starter or a simple entrée. Fresh chiles add a pleasantly spicy accent to the broth.

1	tablespoon salad oil
1	large onion, finely chopped
1	large red bell pepper (about 8 oz.), seeded and chopped
3	large fresh green Anaheim or other large mild chiles (about 8 oz. *total*), seeded and chopped
5½	cups low-sodium chicken broth
2	tablespoons minced fresh tarragon or 1 teaspoon dry tarragon
¼	teaspoon pepper
5	large ears corn (about 3½ lbs. *total*), husks and silk removed
	Tarragon sprigs (optional)

Heat oil in a 5- to 6-quart pan over medium-high heat. Add onion, bell pepper, and chiles. Cook, stirring often, until onion is soft (about 5 minutes). Add broth, minced tarragon, and pepper; bring to a boil. Meanwhile, cut corn kernels from cobs.

Add corn to boiling broth mixture. Reduce heat, cover, and simmer until corn is hot (about 5 minutes). If made ahead, let cool; then cover and refrigerate for up to 1 day. Serve hot or cool.

To serve, ladle soup into bowls; garnish with tarragon sprigs, if desired. Makes 6 servings.

Per serving: 165 calories (25% fat, 61% carbohydrates, 14% protein), 5 g total fat (0.8 g saturated fat), 28 g carbohydrates, 6 g protein, 0 mg cholesterol, 67 mg sodium

Leek & Green Onion Chowder

Preparation time: About 35 minutes
Cooking time: 12 to 15 minutes

Top each serving of this light, tangy soup with a few thin lemon slices and a spoonful of smooth sour cream.

3	pounds leeks
1	tablespoon butter or margarine
2	tablespoons all-purpose flour
½	teaspoon ground white pepper
6	cups low-sodium chicken broth
3	cups thinly sliced green onions
3	tablespoons lemon juice
	Salt
	Thin lemon slices
	Reduced-fat sour cream

Trim ends and all but 3 inches of green tops from leeks; remove tough outer leaves. Split leeks lengthwise; rinse well, then thinly slice crosswise.

Melt butter in a 5- to 6-quart pan over medium-high heat. Add leeks; cook, stirring often, until soft (8 to 10 minutes). Stir in flour and white pepper; then stir in broth. Bring to a boil over high heat, stirring. Add onions; cook, stirring, just until onions turn bright green (about 2 minutes). Stir in lemon juice and season to taste with salt.

To serve, ladle soup into bowls. Garnish each serving with lemon slices and a dollop of sour cream. Makes 6 servings.

Per serving: 136 calories (24% fat, 62% carbohydrates, 14% protein), 4 g total fat (2 g saturated fat), 22 g carbohydrates, 5 g protein, 5 mg cholesterol, 102 mg sodium

Squash & Yam Soup with Prosciutto

. . . .

Preparation time: About 25 minutes
Cooking time: About 40 minutes

Red pepper and fresh ginger add a spicy-hot note to the pleasantly sweet flavor of this smooth, soothing soup.

1¾	pounds butternut or other yellow-fleshed squash, peeled, seeded, and cut into 1-inch chunks
1¾	pounds yams or sweet potatoes, peeled and cut into 1-inch chunks
7	cups low-sodium chicken broth
¼	cup balsamic vinegar
2	tablespoons firmly packed brown sugar
1	tablespoon minced fresh ginger
¼	to ½ teaspoon crushed red pepper flakes
1	tablespoon butter or margarine
6	ounces thinly sliced prosciutto, cut into thin slivers

In a 5- to 6-quart pan, combine squash, yams, broth, vinegar, sugar, ginger, and red pepper flakes. Bring to a boil over high heat; then reduce heat, cover, and simmer gently until squash and yams are soft enough to mash easily (about 30 minutes).

In a food processor or blender, whirl vegetable-broth mixture, a portion at a time, until smoothly puréed. Return to pan; cook over high heat, stirring often, until steaming (about 5 minutes).

Meanwhile, melt butter in a wide frying pan over medium-high heat. Add prosciutto and cook,

stirring often, until lightly browned and crisp (6 to 8 minutes). Drain prosciutto well on paper towels.

To serve, ladle soup into bowls; top with prosciutto. Makes 6 to 8 servings.

Per serving: 276 calories (22% fat, 62% carbohydrates, 16% protein), 7 g total fat (2 g saturated fat), 44 g carbohydrates, 12 g protein, 24 mg cholesterol, 533 mg sodium

Roasted Eggplant Soup

. . . .

Preparation time: About 15 minutes
Baking time: About 1¼ hours
Cooking time: About 5 minutes

Accompanied with crisp sesame breadsticks, this mild purée makes a beautifully simple first course. If you like, you can roast the vegetables up to 8 hours in advance, then finish the soup shortly before serving.

1	large eggplant (about 1½ lbs.)
1	small onion
3	cups low-sodium chicken broth
2	tablespoons lemon juice
	Pepper
12	thin red bell pepper strips
4	teaspoons finely chopped parsley

Pierce eggplant in several places with a fork; then place eggplant and unpeeled onion in a small, shallow baking pan. Bake in a 350° oven until vegetables are very soft when squeezed (about 1¼ hours). Let stand until cool enough to handle. (At this point, you may cover and refrigerate for up to 8 hours.)

Peel eggplant and onion; then transfer to a food processor or blender and add ½ cup of the broth. Whirl until puréed. Add remaining 2½ cups broth and whirl until blended. Pour into a 2- to 3-quart pan and bring to a boil over high heat, stirring occasionally. Remove from heat; stir in lemon juice and season to taste with pepper.

To serve, ladle soup into 4 bowls; top each serving with 3 bell pepper strips and 1 teaspoon of the parsley. Makes 4 servings.

Per serving: 79 calories (14% fat, 68% carbohydrates, 18% protein), 1 g total fat (0.3 g saturated fat), 15 g carbohydrates, 4 g protein, 0 mg cholesterol, 49 mg sodium

Potato, Cauliflower & Watercress Soup

. . . .

Preparation time: About 20 minutes
Cooking time: 40 to 45 minutes

A generous measure of fresh watercress lightens this sturdy blend of two winter vegetables—and adds a peppery jolt of flavor. Topped with tart yogurt, cups of the smooth-textured soup make a satisfying opener for a cold-weather meal.

1½	cups cauliflower flowerets, cut into bite-size pieces
2½	cups nonfat milk
2	tablespoons butter or margarine
½	cup slivered shallots
⅛	teaspoon ground nutmeg
2	large russet potatoes (about 1 lb. *total*), peeled and diced
1¾	cups low-sodium chicken broth
8	cups lightly packed watercress sprigs
	Salt and ground white pepper
¼	to ⅓ cup plain low-fat yogurt or reduced-fat sour cream

In a 2- to 3-quart pan, combine cauliflower and milk. Bring to a boil over medium heat; then reduce heat to medium-low and cook until cauliflower is tender when pierced (8 to 10 minutes). Place a strainer over a large bowl and pour cauliflower mixture through it; then set cauliflower and milk aside.

Rinse pan; set over medium heat and add butter. When butter is melted, add shallots and nutmeg; cook, stirring occasionally, until shallots are soft but not browned (3 to 5 minutes). Add potatoes and broth; increase heat to medium-high and bring to a boil. Reduce heat, cover, and simmer until potatoes are very tender when pierced (15 to 20 minutes). Reserve several watercress sprigs for garnish, then stir remaining watercress into potato mixture and cook, uncovered, for 5 minutes. Add cauliflower to pan and cook until heated through (about 3 minutes).

In a food processor or blender, whirl potato mixture, a portion at a time, until smooth. Return to pan, add reserved strained milk, and heat just until steaming (do not boil). Season to taste with salt and white pepper.

To serve, ladle soup into bowls. Garnish each serving with a dollop of yogurt and a watercress sprig. Makes 4 to 6 servings.

Per serving: 195 calories (26% fat, 54% carbohydrates, 20% protein), 6 g total fat (3 g saturated fat), 27 g carbohydrates, 10 g protein, 16 mg cholesterol, 179 mg sodium

Spinach & Buttermilk Soup

. . . .

30 MINUTES OR LESS

Preparation time: About 10 minutes
Cooking time: About 10 minutes

This quick, creamy soup is a versatile treat. Try it as the first course at a formal dinner, or serve it with a sandwich for an easygoing lunch.

1	package (about 10 oz.) frozen chopped spinach
4	cups low-sodium chicken broth
2	tablespoons grated lemon peel
2	tablespoons cornstarch
2	cups low-fat buttermilk
	Salt and pepper

In a 3- to 4-quart pan, combine spinach and 2 cups of the broth. Bring to a boil over high heat, using a spoon to break spinach apart. As soon as you have broken spinach into chunks, pour broth-spinach mixture into a food processor or blender; add 1 tablespoon of the lemon peel and whirl until smoothly puréed.

In pan, mix remaining 2 cups broth with cornstarch until smooth; add spinach mixture. Bring to a boil over high heat, stirring often. Stir in buttermilk, season to taste with salt and pepper, and serve at once. (Do not heat soup after adding buttermilk; the color will change for the worse.)

To serve, pour soup into bowls or mugs; sprinkle with remaining 1 tablespoon lemon peel. Makes 4 servings.

Per serving: 114 calories (22% fat, 49% carbohydrates, 29% protein), 3 g total fat (1 g saturated fat), 14 g carbohydrates, 8 g protein, 5 mg cholesterol, 235 mg sodium

Faux-Fresh Tomato Soup

· ·

Preparation time: About 20 minutes
Baking time: About 20 minutes
Cooking time: 35 to 40 minutes

It may sound like heresy—but fresh tomatoes can't always be counted on for great tomato flavor. We've chosen to base this warming soup on canned tomato purée; basil and braised vegetables help give it a fresh, lively taste. Herbed croutons provide a crunchy contrast to the soup. Float a few in each bowl, then offer the extras alongside.

	Herbed Cheese Croutons (recipe follows)
1	teaspoon olive oil
1	medium-size onion, chopped
1	large carrot, chopped
5	cups low-sodium chicken broth
1	can (about 15 oz.) tomato purée
3	tablespoons dry basil or ⅓ cup chopped fresh basil
¾	teaspoon sugar
½	teaspoon ground white pepper

Prepare Herbed Cheese Croutons and set aside.

In a 3- to 4-quart pan, combine oil, onion, carrot, and 1 cup of the broth. Bring to a boil over high heat; then boil, uncovered, stirring occasionally, until liquid evaporates and vegetables begin to brown (about 10 minutes). To deglaze, add 3 tablespoons water and stir to scrape browned bits free. Then continue to cook, stirring occasionally, until mixture begins to brown again. Repeat deglazing and browning steps about 2 more times, using 3 tablespoons water each time; vegetable mixture should be golden brown.

Add remaining 4 cups broth. Stir to scrape browned bits free. Stir in tomato purée, basil, sugar, and white pepper. Bring to a boil over high heat; then reduce heat, cover, and simmer until vegetables are very tender to bite (about 20 minutes). Whirl mixture, a portion at a time, in a food processor or blender until smoothly puréed. Return purée to pan; bring to a simmer over medium heat.

To serve, ladle soup into bowls; top each serving with 2 croutons. Accompany with remaining croutons. Makes 4 servings.

Herbed Cheese Croutons. Slice 1 small **French bread baguette** (about 8 oz.) crosswise into ¼-inch-thick slices. Sprinkle slices with 2 tablespoons grated **Romano or Parmesan cheese;** then sprinkle lightly with about 1 teaspoon **dry basil** and about ¼ teaspoon **coarse salt.** Place bread slices in a single layer on large baking sheets. Bake in a 300° oven until toasted and golden brown (about 20 minutes), switching positions of baking sheets after 10 minutes. Serve croutons warm or at room temperature.

Per serving: 297 calories (17% fat, 68% carbohydrates, 15% protein), 6 g total fat (1 g saturated fat), 51 g carbohydrates, 12 g protein, 3 mg cholesterol, 968 mg sodium

Peas & Lettuce in Mint Broth

· ·

NATURALLY LOW IN FAT

Preparation time: About 20 minutes
Standing time: At least 15 minutes
Cooking time: About 5 minutes

Is it soup or salad? By either name, this simple pairing of tiny peas and lettuce in a lemony, mint-infused broth is a handsome first course.

4	cups low-sodium chicken broth
1¼	cups firmly packed fresh mint leaves
	Peel (colored part only) pared from 1 medium-size lemon
2	cups frozen tiny peas
1	teaspoon lemon juice
1	tablespoon slivered fresh mint
1	teaspoon shredded lemon peel
4	butter lettuce leaves, rinsed and crisped

In a 2- to 3-quart pan, combine broth, the 1¼ cups mint leaves, and peel of 1 lemon. Bring to a boil over high heat. Cover, remove from heat, and let stand for at least 15 minutes to allow mint to flavor broth (or refrigerate for up to 1 day). With a slotted spoon, remove mint from broth; discard mint and lemon peel.

Return broth to a boil over high heat. Add peas and stir until hot (1 to 2 minutes). Stir in lemon juice. Pour broth through a strainer equally into each of 4 wide, shallow bowls. Quickly mix peas with slivered mint and shredded lemon peel. Place a lettuce leaf in each bowl; spoon pea mixture into leaves, dividing equally. Eat with a knife, fork, and spoon. Makes 4 servings.

Per serving: 100 calories (18% fat, 54% carbohydrates, 28% protein), 2 g total fat (0.5 g saturated fat), 14 g carbohydrates, 7 g protein, 0 mg cholesterol, 181 mg sodium

Warm-up Vegetable Soup

Preparation time: 25 minutes
Cooking time: About 40 minutes

Start off a casual supper with bowls of comforting vegetable soup. Herb-scented chicken broth holds pasta shells and a colorful medley of mushrooms, potato chunks, squash, and tomatoes.

1	tablespoon olive oil or salad oil
1	medium-size onion, finely chopped
8	ounces mushrooms, thinly sliced
1	teaspoon *each* dry oregano, dry basil, and dry marjoram
6	cups low-sodium chicken broth
1	medium-size thin-skinned potato (about 6 oz.), peeled and cut into ½-inch cubes
1	pound banana squash, peeled and cut into ½-inch cubes
¾	cup dry small shell-shaped pasta
1	cup diced pear-shaped (Roma-type) tomatoes
	Salt and pepper

Heat oil in a 5- to 6-quart pan over medium heat. Add onion, mushrooms, oregano, basil, and marjoram. Cook, stirring often, until vegetables are tinged with brown (about 10 minutes). Stir in broth, potato, and squash. Bring to a boil; reduce heat, cover, and boil gently until potato is tender to bite (about 15 minutes).

Add pasta, cover, and continue to cook until pasta is just tender to bite (10 to 12 minutes). Stir in tomatoes; simmer until heated through (about 2 minutes). Season to taste with salt and pepper. Makes 6 servings.

Per serving: 171 calories (23% fat, 61% carbohydrates, 16% protein), 5 g total fat (0.8 g saturated fat), 27 g carbohydrates, 7 g protein, 0 mg cholesterol, 65 mg sodium

Red Onion Borscht

Preparation time: About 15 minutes
Cooking time: 40 to 45 minutes

Traditional dishes are often rich, too—but this flavorful borscht is low in both fat and calories. Slow cooking brings out the natural sweetness of red onions, while shredded beets intensify the vivid color. Try cups of the soup as a lead-in to lean braised brisket or another hearty main course.

1½	tablespoons salad oil
2½	to 3 pounds red onions, thinly sliced
½	cup red wine vinegar
2	medium-size beets (8 to 10 oz. *total*), peeled and shredded
2½	tablespoons all-purpose flour
6	cups low-sodium chicken broth
⅓	cup port
	Salt and pepper
	Reduced-fat sour cream (optional)

Heat oil in a 5- to 6-quart pan over medium-low heat. Reserve several onion slices for garnish; then add remaining onions to pan along with vinegar and beets. Cook, stirring often, until onions are very soft but not browned (25 to 30 minutes). Add flour and stir until bubbly. Remove pan from heat and gradually stir in broth. (At this point, you may cover and refrigerate for up to 2 days.)

Return soup to medium heat and bring to a boil, stirring occasionally; then reduce heat and simmer for 10 minutes. Stir in port. Season to taste with salt and pepper.

To serve, ladle soup into bowls. Garnish each serving with a dollop of sour cream, if desired, and a few of the reserved onion slices. Makes 8 servings.

Per serving: 144 calories (25% fat, 61% carbohydrates, 14% protein), 4 g total fat (0.6 g saturated fat), 21 g carbohydrates, 5 g protein, 0 mg cholesterol, 73 mg sodium

To keep vegetables such as red onions and red cabbage from taking on an unappetizing bluish-purple color as they cook, add an acid ingredient—such as lemon juice or vinegar—to the pan.

Minestrone with Chard

Preparation time: About 35 minutes
Cooking time: About 30 minutes

Whether served hot for a cool-weather lunch or at room temperature for dinner on a warm summer evening, this vegetable-rich soup is sure to be a hit. Round out the meal with crunchy-crusted whole-grain bread and fresh fruit.

1	tablespoon olive oil
1	large onion, chopped
1	clove garlic, minced or pressed
2	stalks celery, diced
2	ounces thinly sliced Canadian bacon, cut into thin shreds
3	quarts beef broth
2	large carrots, diced
1	tablespoon minced fresh rosemary or 1 teaspoon dry rosemary
⅔	cup medium-grain rice
1	pound Swiss chard
3	cans (about 15 oz. *each*) pinto beans, drained and rinsed; or 6 cups cooked pinto beans (page 149), drained and rinsed
1	large can (about 28 oz.) pear-shaped tomatoes, drained and chopped
8	ounces green beans (ends removed), cut into 1-inch lengths
1	pound zucchini, cut into ¾-inch-thick slices
	Salt and pepper
	Grated Parmesan cheese

Heat oil in an 8- to 10-quart pan over medium-high heat. Add onion, garlic, celery, and bacon; cook, stirring often, until onion is soft (6 to 8 minutes). Add broth, carrots, rosemary, and rice. Bring to a boil over high heat; then reduce heat, cover, and simmer for 10 minutes.

Meanwhile, trim and discard stem ends from chard; then rinse chard well, drain, and cut crosswise into ¼-inch-wide strips. Set aside.

Mash a third of the pinto beans. Add mashed and whole pinto beans, tomatoes, green beans, and zucchini to pan. Bring to a boil over high heat; then reduce heat, cover, and simmer for 5 minutes. Stir in chard; simmer, uncovered, until zucchini is tender to bite (about 5 more minutes). Season to taste with salt and pepper.

Serve soup hot or at room temperature; offer cheese to add to taste. Makes 10 to 12 servings.

Per serving: 201 calories (16% fat, 63% carbohydrates, 21% protein), 4 g total fat (0.4 g saturated fat), 33 g carbohydrates, 11 g protein, 3 mg cholesterol, 1,375 mg sodium

Double Pea Soup

Preparation time: About 10 minutes
Cooking time: About 55 minutes

Warm up a chilly evening with this thick pea soup. Start with lightly sautéed garlic, chicken broth, and dried split peas; at the last minute, add tiny green peas for extra color and texture.

2	pounds dried yellow or green split peas
1	tablespoon butter or margarine
4	cloves garlic, minced
10	cups low-sodium chicken broth
1	package (about 10 oz.) frozen tiny peas
	Salt and pepper

Rinse and sort split peas, discarding any debris. Drain peas; set aside.

Melt butter in a 5- to 6-quart pan over medium-high heat; add garlic and cook, stirring, until golden (about 2 minutes). Add split peas and broth; increase heat to high. Bring broth to a boil; then reduce heat, cover, and simmer until split peas are very tender to bite (about 45 minutes). Add frozen peas and continue to simmer, stirring often, until heated through (about 5 more minutes). Season to taste with salt and pepper. Makes 8 servings.

Per serving: 463 calories (9% fat, 63% carbohydrates, 28% protein), 5 g total fat (2 g saturated fat), 75 g carbohydrates, 32 g protein, 4 mg cholesterol, 146 mg sodium

Black & White Soup

Preparation time: About 25 minutes
Cooking time: About 15 minutes

Striking to look at, this first-course soup features black and white bean purées, poured side by side into each bowl for a two-tone effect.

1	large onion, chopped
1	clove garlic, peeled and sliced
½	cup water
3½	cups low-sodium chicken broth
⅓	cup drained oil-packed dried tomatoes, minced
4	green onions, thinly sliced
¼	cup dry sherry
2	cans (about 15 oz. *each*) black beans, drained and rinsed; or 4 cups cooked black beans (page 149), drained and rinsed
2	cans (about 15 oz. *each*) cannellini (white kidney beans), drained and rinsed; or 4 cups cooked cannellini (page 149), drained and rinsed
	Slivered green onions (optional)

In a 5- to 6-quart pan, combine chopped onion, garlic, and water. Cook over high heat, stirring often, until liquid evaporates and onion begins to brown. To deglaze, add 2 tablespoons of the broth; stir to scrape browned bits free. Continue to cook, stirring occasionally, until mixture begins to brown again. Add 2 more tablespoons broth; stir to scrape browned bits free. Stir in ½ cup more broth; pour mixture into a food processor or blender.

In same pan, combine tomatoes and sliced green onions. Stir over high heat until onions are wilted (about 2 minutes). Add sherry and cook, stirring, until liquid has evaporated. Remove from heat.

To onion mixture in food processor, add black beans. Whirl, gradually adding 1¼ cups of the broth, until smooth. Pour into a 3- to 4-quart pan.

Rinse processor; add cannellini and whirl until smooth, gradually adding remaining 1½ cups broth. Stir puréed cannellini into pan with tomato mixture. Place both pans of soup over medium-high heat and cook, stirring often, until steaming.

To serve, pour soup into 6 bowls as follows: from pans (or from 2 lipped containers such as 1-quart pitchers, which are easier to handle), pour soups simultaneously into opposite sides of each wide 1½- to 2-cup soup bowl so that soups flow together but do not mix. Garnish with slivered green onions, if desired. Makes 6 servings.

Per serving: 301 calories (27% fat, 52 % carbohydrates, 21% protein), 9 g total fat (1 g saturated fat), 38 g carbohydrates, 15 g protein, 0 mg cholesterol, 446 mg sodium

Winter Vegetable Lentil Chowder

Preparation time: About 35 minutes
Cooking time: About 1 hour

For a cold-weather lunch, offer this thick soup with hearty bread and your favorite cheese.

10	cups low-sodium chicken broth
1	teaspoon *each* whole white peppercorns and coriander seeds
½	teaspoon whole allspice
3	strips lemon peel (yellow part only; *each* about ½ by 3 inches)
1	cup lentils, rinsed and drained
3	medium-size leeks (about 1 lb. *total*)
1½	pounds banana squash, peeled and cut into ½-inch cubes
12	ounces Swiss chard
	Salt and pepper

In a 5- to 6-quart pan, combine broth, white peppercorns, coriander seeds, allspice, and lemon peel. Bring to a boil over high heat; then reduce heat, cover, and simmer until flavors are blended (20 to 30 minutes). Remove and discard lemon peel. Add lentils to broth; cover and simmer for 15 minutes.

Trim ends and all but 3 inches of green tops from leeks; remove tough outer leaves. Split leeks lengthwise; rinse well, then thinly slice crosswise.

Add leeks and squash to lentil mixture. Cover; simmer until squash is tender to bite (about 15 minutes). Trim and discard stem ends from chard; rinse chard well, drain, and cut crosswise into ¼-inch-wide strips. Add chard to broth; simmer, uncovered, until wilted (about 5 minutes). Season to taste with salt and pepper. Makes 6 servings.

Per serving: 221 calories (13% fat, 60% carbohydrates, 27% protein), 3 g total fat (0.8 g saturated fat), 34 g carbohydrates, 16 g protein, 0 mg cholesterol, 215 mg sodium

Albóndigas Soup

Preparation time: About 25 minutes
Baking time: About 15 minutes
Cooking time: About 35 minutes

Warm a stack of corn or flour tortillas to serve alongside this colorful Mexican-inspired soup. To keep the rice-studded meatballs low in fat, brown them in the oven instead of frying them.

	Meatballs with Rice (recipe follows)
1	tablespoon salad oil
1	large onion, cut into slivers
1½	teaspoons ground cumin
1	teaspoon dry oregano
2	cloves garlic, minced or pressed
1	can (about 14½ oz.) pear-shaped tomatoes
2	cans (about 14½ oz. *each*) beef broth
1	large can (about 46 oz.) low-sodium tomato juice
¼	cup coarsely chopped cilantro
	Salt
	Lime wedges

Prepare Meatballs with Rice.

While meatballs are baking, heat oil in a 5- to 6-quart pan over medium heat. Add onion, cumin, and oregano. Cook, stirring often, until onion is golden (6 to 8 minutes); then stir in garlic. Cut up tomatoes; add tomatoes and their liquid, broth, and tomato juice to pan. Bring to a boil over high heat; then reduce heat, cover, and simmer for 15 minutes.

Transfer meatballs to soup. Cover and simmer until meatballs are heated through (about 10 minutes). Skim and discard fat from soup, if necessary. Just before serving, stir in cilantro and season to taste with salt. Serve soup with lime wedges. Makes 6 servings.

Meatballs with Rice. In a large bowl, lightly mix 1½ pounds **extra-lean ground beef,** ½ cup **cooked white or brown rice,** ¼ cup *each* **all-purpose flour** and **water,** and 1 teaspoon *each* **chili powder** and **ground cumin.** Shape mixture into 1-inch balls and place slightly apart in a shallow nonstick baking pan. Bake in a 450° oven until well browned

(about 15 minutes). Remove pan from oven; loosen meatballs from baking pan with a wide spatula.

Per serving: 290 calories (23% fat, 35% carbohydrates, 42% protein), 7 g total fat (2 g saturated fat), 26 g carbohydrates, 31 g protein, 65 mg cholesterol, 700 mg sodium

Beef & Pumpkin Soup

Preparation time: About 25 minutes
Cooking time: About 55 minutes

Coarsely mashed Hubbard or banana squash—called "pumpkin" by the islanders of St. Lucia—adds texture to this Caribbean soup.

1	tablespoon salad oil
1	large onion, chopped
1	stalk celery, thinly sliced
8	cups low-sodium chicken broth
8	ounces boneless beef chuck, trimmed of fat and cut into ½-inch cubes
3½	pounds Hubbard or banana squash, peeled, seeded, and cut into ½-inch cubes (you should have about 10 cups)
2	large carrots, coarsely chopped
8	ounces spinach, stems removed, leaves rinsed and cut crosswise into ¼-inch-wide strips
	Salt and pepper

Heat oil in a 6- to 8-quart pan over medium-high heat. Add onion and celery; cook, stirring often, until onion is soft (about 5 minutes). Add broth and beef. Bring to a boil; then reduce heat, cover, and simmer for 30 minutes. Add squash and carrots. Bring to a boil; then reduce heat, cover, and simmer until squash and beef are very tender when pierced (about 15 more minutes).

With a slotted spoon, lift about three-fourths of the squash from pan; mash coarsely. Return mashed squash to pan, then stir in spinach. Bring to a boil over high heat; then reduce heat and simmer, uncovered, until spinach is wilted (about 3 minutes). Skim and discard fat from soup, if necessary; season soup to taste with salt and pepper. Makes 6 to 8 servings.

Per serving: 183 calories (28% fat, 44% carbohydrates, 28% protein), 6 g total fat (1 g saturated fat), 21 g carbohydrates, 14 g protein, 19 mg cholesterol, 127 mg sodium

READING FOOD LABELS

Thanks to the nutrition labels now found on virtually every packaged food, it's easier than ever to make low-fat choices. Furthermore, today's rules specify that claims such as "low fat" and "cholesterol free" can be used *only* if the food meets specific government standards.

Reading the label. The new label is shown at right. *Serving size* is listed first, followed by the number of servings per package.

A *calorie count* comes next, letting you determine how a serving of the food adds to your daily total. *Calories from fat* and *total fat* also appear prominently. To limit fat in your diet, choose foods with a big difference between total calories and the number of calories from fat.

Saturated fat is noted as well. Though part of the total fat in food, it's listed separately due to the key role it plays in raising blood cholesterol and increasing the risk of heart disease. For better health, keep the saturated fat in your meals to a minimum.

Cholesterol, listed next, can also lead to heart disease if consumed in excess. Try to keep your cholesterol consumption below 300 mg each day.

Sodium can contribute to high blood pressure. Many nutritionists recommend that healthy adults eat no more than 2,400 mg of sodium daily.

Carbohydrates are listed, too. In your meals, go easy on choices

Nutrition Facts

Serving Size 1 cup (228g)
Servings Per Container 2

Amount Per Serving

Calories 260   Calories from Fat 120

	% Daily Value*
Total Fat 13g	**20**%
Saturated Fat 5g	**25**%
Cholesterol 30mg	**10**%
Sodium 660mg	**28**%
Total Carbohydrate 31g	**10**%
Dietary Fiber 0g	**0**%
Sugars 5g	
Protein 5g	

Vitamin A 4%	•	Vitamin C 2%
Calcium 15%	•	Iron 4%

* Percent Daily Values are based on a 2,000 calorie diet. Your daily values may be higher or lower depending on your calorie needs:

	Calories:	2,000	2,500
Total Fat	Less than	65g	80g
Sat Fat	Less than	20g	25g
Cholesterol	Less than	300mg	300mg
Sodium	Less than	2,400mg	2,400mg
Total Carbohydrate		300g	375g
Dietary Fiber		25g	30g

Calories per gram:
Fat 9 • Carbohydrate 4 • Protein 4

such as soft drinks and candy (these are high in *sugars,* one form of carbohydrate). Instead, emphasize nutritious high-carbohydrate foods like breads, fruits, and vegetables. These same foods are likely to provide *dietary fiber.* Other good sources of fiber include grains (and whole-grain foods), beans, and peas. Fiber-rich foods help reduce the risk of heart disease and cancer.

Protein is important for good health, but many Americans get more than they really need. Opt for small servings of lean meats,

fish, and poultry, low-fat dairy products, and vegetable foods such as beans and grains.

Vitamins and minerals are listed as well. Don't count on any one food to provide 100% of all the vitamins and minerals you need each day; combine foods to reach the total.

Percent of daily value (listed to the right of total fat, sodium, and so on) has been calculated for a diet of 2,000 to 2,500 calories per day. If your daily calorie count differs, percentages will vary accordingly. As a general rule, though, select foods that make up a low percentage of each day's total fat, saturated fat, cholesterol, and sodium. Do try to reach 100% of the carbohydrates, fiber, vitamins, and minerals you need.

Understanding health claims. When used on product labels, the following words and phrases must now meet certain criteria.

Fat free Less than 0.5 g fat per serving

Low fat 3 g fat (or less) per serving

Lean Less than 10 g fat, 4 g saturated fat, and 95 mg cholesterol per serving

Light (lite) One-third fewer calories or no more than half the fat of the higher-calorie, higher-fat version; or no more than half the sodium of the higher-sodium version

Cholesterol free Less than 2 mg cholesterol and no more than 2 g saturated fat per serving

Pozole

Preparation time: About 20 minutes
Baking time: About 4 minutes
Cooking time: About 1¾ hours

Pozole is a pork, chicken, and hominy soup that's a favorite in Mexico. The recipe varies from place to place; as you travel across the country, you'll notice slight variations in ingredients and seasonings. Our pozole calls for canned hominy, but you can substitute the dried or partially cooked frozen product sold at Mexican markets.

1	**pound pork tenderloin, trimmed of fat and silvery membranes and cut into 1½-inch chunks**
1	**pound boneless, skinless chicken or turkey thighs, trimmed of fat and cut into 1½-inch chunks**
3	**quarts low-sodium chicken broth**
2	**large onions, cut into chunks**
1	**teaspoon dry oregano**
½	**teaspoon cumin seeds**
	Crisp Corn Tortilla Strips (recipe follows)
2	**cans (about 14 oz. *each*) yellow hominy, drained**
	Salt and pepper
	Lime slices or wedges

Place pork and chicken in a 6- to 8-quart pan. Add broth, onions, oregano, and cumin seeds. Bring to a boil over high heat; then reduce heat, cover, and simmer until meat is tender when pierced (about 1½ hours). Meanwhile, prepare Crisp Corn Tortilla Strips and set aside.

Lift meat from pan with a slotted spoon; place in a bowl to cool.

Pour cooking broth into a strainer set over another bowl and press to remove liquid; discard residue. Return broth to pan and bring to a boil over high heat. Add hominy and reduce heat; simmer, uncovered, until flavors are blended (about 10 minutes).

Tear meat into shreds; return to broth. Season soup to taste with salt and pepper. If made ahead, let cool; then cover and refrigerate for up to 1 day. Reheat before serving.

To serve, ladle soup into bowls; serve with lime slices and tortilla strips. Makes 8 to 10 servings.

Crisp Corn Tortilla Strips. Dip 3 **corn tortillas** (*each* about 6 inches in diameter), one at a time, in **hot water;** drain briefly. Season to taste with **salt.** Stack tortillas; cut stack in half, if desired. Then cut stacked tortillas into ¼-inch-wide strips.

Arrange tortilla strips in a single layer on a large baking sheet. Bake in a 500° oven for 3 minutes. With a metal spatula, turn strips over; continue to bake until crisp and browned (about 1 more minute). If made ahead, let cool; then store airtight at room temperature for up to 5 days.

Per serving: 263 calories (24% fat, 36% carbohydrates, 40% protein), 7 g total fat (2 g saturated fat), 23 g carbohydrates, 26 g protein, 75 mg cholesterol, 340 mg sodium

Italian Sausage Soup

Preparation time: About 20 minutes
Cooking time: 40 to 45 minutes

Homemade sausage based on pork tenderloin starts this hearty main course off right. Try serving the soup with a crisp salad and Rosemary & Lemon Stretch Breadsticks (page 189).

	No-fat Italian Sausage (recipe follows)
2	**large onions, chopped**
2	**cloves garlic, minced or pressed**
5	**cups beef broth**
1	**large can (about 28 oz.) pear-shaped tomatoes**
1½	**cups dry red wine**
1	**tablespoon *each* dry basil and sugar**
1	**medium-size green bell pepper (about 6 oz.), seeded and chopped**
2	**medium-size zucchini, cut into ¼-inch-thick slices**
2	**cups dry pasta bow ties (about 1½-inch size)**
	Salt and pepper
½	**cup chopped parsley**

Prepare No-fat Italian Sausage; refrigerate.

In a 5- to 6-quart pan, combine onions, garlic, and 1 cup of the broth. Bring to a boil over high heat; boil, uncovered, stirring occasionally, until liquid evaporates and onions begin to brown (about 10 minutes). To deglaze, add 3 tablespoons water and stir to scrape browned bits free. Then continue to cook, stirring occasionally, until mixture begins to brown again. Repeat deglazing and browning steps about 3 more times, using 3 tablespoons water each time; mixture should be richly browned (about 10 minutes *total*).

Stir in sausage and ½ cup more water. Cook, stirring gently, until liquid evaporates and meat begins to brown (about 8 minutes).

Add remaining 4 cups broth. Stir to scrape browned bits free. Cut up tomatoes; then add tomatoes and their liquid, wine, basil, sugar, bell pepper, zucchini, and pasta to pan. Bring to a boil over high heat. Reduce heat, cover, and simmer until pasta is just tender to bite (about 15 minutes). Season to taste with salt and pepper. If made ahead, let cool; then cover and refrigerate for up to 1 day. Reheat before serving.

To serve, ladle soup into bowls and sprinkle with parsley. Makes 6 servings.

No-fat Italian Sausage. Cut 1 pound **pork tenderloin** or boneless pork loin, trimmed of fat and silvery membranes, into 1-inch chunks. Whirl in a food processor, about half at a time, until coarsely chopped (or put through a food chopper fitted with a medium blade). In a bowl, mix pork, ¼ cup **dry white wine,** 2 tablespoons chopped **parsley,** 1½ teaspoons crushed **fennel seeds,** ½ teaspoon **crushed red pepper flakes,** and 2 cloves **garlic,** minced. If made ahead, cover airtight and refrigerate for up to 1 day.

Per serving: 332 calories (14% fat, 53% carbohydrates, 33% protein),
5 g total fat (1 g saturated fat), 39 g carbohydrates, 24 g protein,
49 mg cholesterol, 954 mg sodium

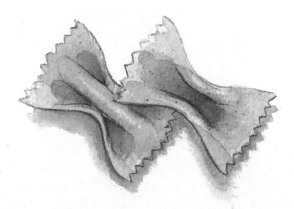

Split Pea & Lamb Soup

Preparation time: About 30 minutes
Cooking time: About 1¾ hours

Whole-grain bread is the perfect partner for this thick, warming soup. If you have time, make the soup ahead; it will taste even better when reheated after a night in the refrigerator.

12	**ounces dried green or yellow split peas**
4	**cups thinly sliced celery**
1	**large onion, chopped**
8	**ounces boneless lamb shoulder or neck, trimmed of fat and cut into ½-inch chunks**
2	**cloves garlic, minced**
1	**large dry bay leaf**
	About 7 cups low-sodium chicken broth

Rinse and sort peas, discarding any debris; then drain peas and set aside.

In a 5- to 6-quart pan, combine celery, onion, lamb, garlic, bay leaf, and ½ cup water. Cover and boil gently over medium-high heat for 10 minutes. Then uncover and continue to cook, stirring often, until liquid evaporates and vegetables and meat begin to brown. To deglaze, add ⅓ cup water and stir to scrape browned bits free. Then continue to cook, stirring occasionally, until mixture begins to brown again. Repeat deglazing and browning steps several more times, using about ⅓ cup water each time; mixture should be richly browned (about 30 minutes *total*).

To pan, add split peas and 7 cups of the broth; bring to a boil over high heat. Reduce heat, cover, and simmer until peas are very tender to bite (about 1 hour). Remove and discard bay leaf. (At this point, you may let cool, then cover and refrigerate for up to 1 day. Reheat before continuing.)

Transfer 3 cups of the soup (but no meat) to a food processor or blender. Whirl until smoothly puréed; return to pan. If desired, thin soup with a little more broth. Stir over high heat until steaming. Makes 4 to 6 servings.

Per serving: 375 calories (15% fat, 54% carbohydrates, 31% protein),
6 g total fat (2 g saturated fat), 51 g carbohydrates, 30 g protein,
30 mg cholesterol, 202 mg sodium

Lamb Meatball & Lentil Soup

. . . .

Preparation time: About 45 minutes
Cooking time: About 1½ hours

To keep this lentil-and-vegetable soup as low in fat as possible, ask your meat dealer to grind lamb loin or leg for the spiced meatballs. Or use your food processor and mince the lamb in your own kitchen.

     Olive oil cooking spray

1   **large onion, finely chopped**

2   **cups plus 2 tablespoons water**

2   **cloves garlic, minced or pressed**

1   **teaspoon *each* dry thyme and ground cumin**

¼   **teaspoon whole allspice**

1   **dry bay leaf**

1   **cinnamon stick (about 3 inches long)**

1   **cup finely chopped celery**

2   **medium-size carrots, thinly sliced**

1½ **cups lentils, rinsed and drained**

1   **can (about 15 oz.) tomato purée**

6   **cups low-sodium chicken broth**
     Lamb Meatballs (recipe follows)

4   **cups coarsely shredded spinach**
     Salt and pepper

Coat a 5- to 6-quart pan with cooking spray. Add onion and 2 tablespoons of the water. Cook over medium heat, stirring often, until onion is soft but not browned (about 5 minutes). Stir in garlic, thyme, cumin, allspice, bay leaf, cinnamon stick, celery, and carrots. Add lentils, tomato purée, broth, and remaining 2 cups water. Bring to a boil over high heat; then reduce heat, cover, and boil gently until lentils and vegetables are very tender to bite (about 1 hour).

Meanwhile, prepare Lamb Meatballs.

Add Lamb Meatballs to soup. Cover, increase heat to medium, and simmer until meatballs are cooked through; cut into one meatball to test (about 20 minutes). Stir in spinach and continue to cook, uncovered, just until spinach is wilted and bright green (2 to 3 minutes). Remove and discard bay leaf and cinnamon stick. Skim and discard fat from soup, if necessary. Season to taste with salt and pepper. Makes 6 servings.

Lamb Meatballs. In a medium-size bowl, beat 1 large **egg white** (about 2 tablespoons) slightly. Mix in ¼ cup finely chopped **onion**, 12 ounces **ground lamb loin or leg,** ¼ teaspoon *each* **pepper** and **ground cinnamon,** ½ teaspoon **salt,** and 3 tablespoons chopped **parsley.** Shape mixture into 1-inch balls. Arrange meatballs in a single layer, cover, and refrigerate until ready to use.

Per serving: 351 calories (15% fat, 50% carbohydrates, 35% protein), 6 g total fat (2 g saturated fat), 46 g carbohydrates, 31 g protein, 37 mg cholesterol, 629 mg sodium

Chicken, Shiitake & Bok Choy Soup

. . . .

Preparation time: About 25 minutes
Cooking time: About 35 minutes

Too pretty to eat? Almost, but this combination of tender-crisp vegetables, rice, and chicken in a clear broth is too tempting to resist. A bold ginger-garlic paste, passed at the table, gives each bowlful a flavor boost.

     Ginger-Garlic Paste (recipe follows)

1½ **tablespoons Oriental sesame oil or salad oil**

5   **to 6 ounces fresh shiitake or regular mushrooms, thinly sliced**

8   **green onions, sliced**

3   **cups low-sodium chicken broth**

4   **boneless, skinless chicken breast halves (about 1½ lbs. *total*)**

2	large carrots, cut into thin slanting slices
8	baby bok choy (about 12 oz. *total*), coarse outer leaves removed
2	cups hot cooked short- or medium-grain rice
3	tablespoons minced cilantro

Prepare Ginger-Garlic Paste and set aside.

Heat oil in a 4- to 5-quart pan over medium heat. Add mushrooms and half the onions; cook, stirring often, until mushrooms are lightly browned (about 10 minutes). Add broth and stir to scrape browned bits free. Cover pan and bring broth to a boil over high heat.

Rinse chicken; pat dry. Add chicken and carrots to boiling broth, making sure meat and vegetables are covered with liquid. Reduce heat to low, cover, and simmer until meat in thickest part of chicken breasts is no longer pink; cut to test (about 15 minutes).

Lift chicken to a cutting board. Add bok choy and remaining onions to pan; cover and simmer over medium heat until bok choy is bright green and just tender when pierced (about 5 minutes). Meanwhile, cut chicken across the grain into ½-inch-wide slanting slices.

Place a ½-cup scoop of rice off center in each of 4 wide, shallow soup bowls. Arrange a sliced chicken breast around each mound of rice. With a slotted spoon, distribute vegetables evenly among bowls. Stir cilantro into broth; then gently pour broth into bowls over chicken and vegetables. Offer Ginger-Garlic Paste to stir into soup to taste. Makes 4 servings.

Ginger-Garlic Paste. In a blender or food processor, combine ¾ cup coarsely chopped **fresh ginger**, 3 cloves **garlic** (peeled), and 3 tablespoons **seasoned rice vinegar** (or 3 tablespoons distilled white vinegar plus 1 tablespoon sugar). Whirl until very smooth. Spoon into a small bowl. If made ahead, cover and refrigerate for up to 4 hours. Makes about ½ cup.

Per serving of soup: 441 calories (19% fat, 38% carbohydrates, 43% protein), 9 g total fat (2 g saturated fat), 42 g carbohydrates, 47 g protein, 99 mg cholesterol, 230 mg sodium

Per teaspoon of Ginger-Garlic Paste: 4 calories (4% fat, 89% carbohydrates, 7% protein), 0 g total fat (0 g saturated fat), 0.9 g carbohydrates, 0.1 g protein, 0 mg cholesterol, 38 mg sodium

Chinese Chicken & Shrimp Soup

. . . .

30 MINUTES OR LESS

Preparation time: About 15 minutes
Cooking time: About 5 minutes

This Asian-style soup is ready to serve almost as soon as it boils. Once you've prepared the nourishing ingredients—chicken, shrimp, tofu, and vegetables—there's little left to do but combine and heat them, then savor the result.

5	cups low-sodium chicken broth
2	tablespoons finely chopped fresh ginger
2	to 3 teaspoons reduced-sodium soy sauce
12	ounces boneless, skinless chicken breasts, cut into ½-inch cubes
6	ounces mushrooms, sliced
3	cups thinly sliced bok choy
1	cup cubed firm tofu (about ½-inch cubes)
½	cup sliced green onions
8	ounces small cooked shrimp
¼	cup chopped cilantro
	Ground red pepper (cayenne) or chili oil (optional)

In a 4- to 5-quart pan, combine broth, ginger, and soy sauce; bring to a boil over high heat. Add chicken, mushrooms, bok choy, tofu, and onions. Reduce heat, cover, and simmer until chicken is no longer pink in center; cut to test (about 2 minutes). Remove pan from heat and stir in shrimp and cilantro. Season to taste with red pepper, if desired. Makes 4 to 6 servings.

Per serving: 244 calories (27% fat, 12% carbohydrates, 61% protein), 7 g total fat (1 g saturated fat), 8 g carbohydrates, 37 g protein, 128 mg cholesterol, 409 mg sodium

Bok choy, a familiar ingredient in Chinese cooking, is easily recognized by its thick white stalks and white-veined dark green leaves. The raw vegetable tastes slightly hot; cooked bok choy has a more subdued flavor, similar to that of Swiss chard. Baby bok choy is milder than the full-sized type, but both forms are rich in calcium and vitamins A and C.

Citrus Chicken Soup

Preparation time: About 25 minutes
Cooking time: About 1 hour

This vibrant Mexican-inspired chicken soup goes together in easy stages. To make it, you'll need mild fresh chiles; either the Anaheim (California) or New Mexico variety works well. Alongside, serve a basket of warm flour or corn tortillas.

4	**chicken breast halves (about 2 lbs. *total*)**
6	**cups low-sodium chicken broth**
1	**medium-size onion, finely chopped**
1	**can (about 14½ oz.) diced tomatoes**
1	**teaspoon grated lemon peel**
½	**teaspoon dry oregano**
¼	**teaspoon pepper**
2	**medium-size thin-skinned potatoes (about 12 oz. *total*), scrubbed and diced**
1	**medium-size ear corn**
⅓	**cup coarsely chopped cilantro**
2	**medium-size fresh red or green Anaheim or other large mild chiles (about 4 oz. *total*), seeded and finely chopped**
1	**small firm-ripe avocado**
2	**tablespoons lime juice**
	Lime wedges

Rinse chicken, pat dry, and place in a 5- to 6-quart pan. Add broth, onion, tomatoes, lemon peel, oregano, and pepper; bring to a boil over medium-high heat. Then reduce heat, cover, and simmer until meat in thickest part of chicken breasts is no longer pink; cut to test (about 25 minutes). Lift out chicken and set aside until cool enough to handle.

While chicken is cooling, add potatoes to pan; cover and cook over medium-low heat until tender when pierced (about 25 minutes). Meanwhile, remove and discard skin and bones from chicken; tear meat into bite-size pieces and set aside.

Remove and discard husk and silk from corn; cut corn kernels from cob.

Skim and discard fat from soup. Add chicken, corn, cilantro, and chiles. Cook just until meat and vegetables are heated through (3 to 5 minutes). Pit, peel, and dice avocado; mix gently with lime juice.

To serve, ladle soup into bowls. Offer avocado to sprinkle atop soup and lime wedges to squeeze into each serving. Makes 6 servings.

Per serving: 270 calories (23% fat, 35% carbohydrates, 42% protein), 7 g total fat (1 g saturated fat), 24 g carbohydrates, 28 g protein, 57 mg cholesterol, 241 mg sodium

Tortellini & Chicken Soup

30 MINUTES OR LESS

Preparation time: About 10 minutes
Cooking time: About 15 minutes

Here's a soup with everything—meat, rice, vegetables, even cheese-filled spinach pasta. Let diners add Parmesan cheese to taste.

3	**large cans (about 49½ oz. *each*) chicken broth; or 4½ quarts Homemade Chicken Broth (page 41)**
1	**package (about 9 oz.) fresh cheese-filled spinach tortellini**
1	**pound spinach, stems removed, leaves rinsed and coarsely chopped**
1	**pound boneless, skinless chicken breasts, cut into ½-inch chunks**
8	**ounces mushrooms, sliced**
1	**medium-size red bell pepper (about 6 oz.), seeded and diced**
1	**cup cooked rice**
2	**teaspoons dry tarragon**
	Salt and pepper
	Grated Parmesan cheese

In an 8- to 10-quart pan, bring broth to a boil over high heat. Add tortellini; reduce heat and boil gently, uncovered, until just tender to bite (about 6 minutes).

Add spinach, chicken, mushrooms, bell pepper, rice, and tarragon to broth; return to a boil over high heat. Then reduce heat, cover, and simmer until chicken is no longer pink in center; cut to test (about 2 minutes). Season soup to taste with salt and pepper; serve with cheese to add to taste. Makes 10 to 12 servings.

Per serving: 200 calories (19% fat, 41% carbohydrates, 40% protein), 4 g total fat (0.2 g saturated fat), 21 g carbohydrates, 20 g protein, 37 mg cholesterol, 1,824 mg sodium

Sausage-Barley Soup with Swiss Chard

Preparation time: About 25 minutes
Cooking time: About 1 hour

Try this soup with big, chewy pretzels and a plate of crunchy cucumber spears. For dessert, you might offer warm, spicy baked apples topped with scoops of vanilla frozen yogurt.

1	pound turkey kielbasa, cut into ¼-inch-thick slices
1	large onion, chopped
2	large carrots, thinly sliced
10	cups beef broth
1	cup pearl barley, rinsed and drained
1	tablespoon minced fresh oregano or 1 teaspoon dry oregano
8	ounces Swiss chard
	Prepared horseradish and Dijon mustard

In a 5- to 6-quart pan, combine sausage, onion, and carrots. Cook over medium heat, stirring often, until sausage and vegetables are lightly browned (about 15 minutes). Discard any fat from pan.

To pan, add broth, barley, and oregano. Bring to a boil; then reduce heat, cover, and simmer until barley is tender to bite—about 30 minutes. (At this point, you may let cool, then cover and refrigerate for up to 1 day. Reheat before continuing.)

Trim and discard stem ends from chard; rinse chard well, then coarsely chop and stir into soup. Simmer, uncovered, until chard stems are tender-crisp to bite (6 to 8 minutes). Serve soup with horseradish and mustard to add to taste. Makes 6 servings.

Per serving: 298 calories (25% fat, 48% carbohydrates, 27% protein), 8 g total fat (2 g saturated fat), 37 g carbohydrates, 21 g protein, 52 mg cholesterol, 2,134 mg sodium

Harvest Turkey Soup

Preparation time: About 20 minutes
Cooking time: About 40 minutes

Hearty and warming, this meaty soup holds pasta, fragrant herbs, and plenty of fresh vegetables. Use the leanest packaged ground turkey you can find (check the label for the fat content); or have the meat market grind turkey breast for you.

	Vegetable oil cooking spray
1	**pound ground skinless turkey**
1	**medium-size onion, chopped**
1	**teaspoon dry oregano**
1	**teaspoon Italian herb seasoning; or ¼ teaspoon *each* dry basil, dry marjoram, dry oregano, and dry thyme**
3	**large firm-ripe tomatoes (about 1¼ lbs. *total*), chopped**
3	**large carrots, thinly sliced**
1	**large potato (about 8 oz.), peeled and diced**
6	**cups beef broth**
1	**cup *each* tomato juice and dry red wine**
1	**tablespoon Worcestershire**
½	**cup dry tiny pasta bow ties (tripolini) or other small shapes**
2	**medium-size zucchini, coarsely diced**
	Liquid hot pepper seasoning

Coat a wide 4- to 5-quart pan with cooking spray. Crumble turkey into pan; add onion, oregano, and herb seasoning. Cook over medium heat, stirring often, until turkey is no longer pink and onion is soft but not browned (about 5 minutes). Stir in tomatoes, carrots, potato, broth, tomato juice, wine, and Worcestershire. Increase heat to medium-high and bring to a boil; then reduce heat, cover, and boil gently for 20 minutes.

Add pasta; cover and cook for 5 minutes. Stir in zucchini and boil gently, uncovered, until pasta and zucchini are just tender to bite (8 to 10 minutes). Season to taste with hot pepper seasoning. Makes 6 to 8 servings.

Per serving: 241 calories (25% fat, 47% carbohydrates, 28% protein), 7 g total fat (1 g saturated fat), 29 g carbohydrates, 18 g protein, 47 mg cholesterol, 949 mg sodium

Tuna Bean Soup

. . . .

Preparation time: About 15 minutes
Cooking time: About 30 minutes

Keep this chowder in mind for a busy week-night. It's quickly assembled with staples from the pantry cupboard—canned tuna, two kinds of beans, and tomatoes.

1	large onion, chopped
4	ounces mushrooms, sliced
5	cups low-sodium chicken broth
2	cans (about 15 oz. *each*) pinto beans, drained and rinsed; or 4 cups cooked pinto beans (page 149), drained and rinsed
2	cans (about 15 oz. *each*) red kidney beans, drained and rinsed; or 4 cups cooked red kidney beans (page 149), drained and rinsed
1	large can (about 28 oz.) chopped tomatoes
1	can (about 8 oz.) tomato sauce
½	teaspoon dry oregano
2	cans (about 6 oz. *each*) water-packed albacore tuna, drained
	Thinly sliced green onions (optional)

In a 5- to 6-quart pan, combine chopped onion and mushrooms. Cover and cook over medium-high heat until vegetables release their liquid (5 to 8 minutes). Uncover. Bring to a boil over high heat; then boil, stirring often, until liquid evaporates and vegetables begin to brown. To deglaze, add ¼ cup of the broth and stir to scrape browned bits free. Continue to cook, stirring occasionally, until vegetables begin to brown again.

Add pinto and kidney beans to pan; then add remaining 4¾ cups broth, tomatoes, tomato sauce, and oregano. Stir to combine. Bring to a boil over high heat; then reduce heat, cover, and simmer for 15 minutes. (At this point, you may let cool, then cover and refrigerate for up to 1 day. Reheat before continuing.)

Stir tuna into soup; heat through. Ladle soup into bowls and top with green onions, if desired. Makes 8 to 10 servings.

Per serving: 223 calories (12% fat, 51% carbohydrates, 37% protein), 3 g total fat (0.6 g saturated fat), 28 g carbohydrates, 21 g protein, 15 mg cholesterol, 738 mg sodium

Seafood & Spinach Soup-Stew

. . . .

Preparation time: About 30 minutes
Cooking time: About 30 minutes

Cut down on cleanup with this handsome one-pot meal, just right for a warm-weather supper. Halibut, shrimp, potatoes, and fresh tomatoes simmer together in lemon-scented chicken broth; slivers of deep green spinach make a pretty garnish.

4	cups low-sodium chicken broth
1	tablespoon shredded lemon peel
¼	cup minced fresh basil or 2 tablespoons dry basil
1	tablespoon minced fresh thyme or 1 teaspoon dry thyme
1	pound small red thin-skinned potatoes (*each* 1½ to 2 inches in diameter), scrubbed
12	ounces firm-textured white-fleshed fish fillets such as halibut, sea bass, or shark, cut into 1½-inch chunks
12	ounces large raw shrimp (31 to 35 per lb.), shelled and deveined
1	pound pear-shaped (Roma-type) tomatoes, coarsely chopped
8	ounces spinach, stems removed, leaves rinsed and cut lengthwise into ⅛-inch-wide slivers

In a 4- to 5-quart pan, combine broth, lemon peel, basil, thyme, and potatoes. Bring to a boil over high heat; then reduce heat, cover, and simmer until potatoes are just tender when pierced (about 20 minutes).

Return broth to a rolling boil over high heat; add fish. Reduce heat to low, cover, and simmer for 2 minutes. Stir in shrimp, tomatoes, and half the spinach. Cover and continue to simmer until fish is just opaque but still moist in thickest part; cut to test (about 3 minutes).

To serve, ladle soup into bowls. Garnish each serving with a sixth of the remaining spinach. Makes 6 servings.

Per serving: 220 calories (15% fat, 38% carbohydrates, 47% protein), 4 g total fat (0.6 g saturated fat), 21 g carbohydrates, 26 g protein, 88 mg cholesterol, 169 mg sodium

Gingered Shrimp Soup

Preparation time: About 25 minutes
Cooking time: About 10 minutes

Steeping—cooking foods in hot liquid off the heat—is an especially gentle technique that's perfect for delicate-textured foods such as shrimp. Here, the shellfish are steeped in seasoned chicken broth; green peas and translucent bean thread noodles go into the pot as well.

1	package (about 10 oz.) frozen tiny peas
6	cups low-sodium chicken broth
2	tablespoons minced fresh ginger
12	ounces extra-large raw shrimp (26 to 30 per lb.), shelled and deveined
1	package (about 2 oz.) dried bean threads (*sai fun* or cellophane noodles)
½	cup thinly sliced green onions
	Fish sauce (*nam pla* or *nuoc mam*), oyster sauce, or reduced-sodium soy sauce

Place peas in a colander; rinse with hot water and set aside.

In a 5- to 6-quart pan, combine broth and ginger. Bring to a rolling boil over high heat. Add shrimp and bean threads, cover, and immediately remove from heat. Let stand for 4 minutes (do not uncover during this time). After 4 minutes, check doneness; shrimp should be opaque in center (cut to test). If shrimp are still translucent, cover and let stand until done, checking at 2-minute intervals.

Add peas to pan, cover, and let stand until warm (about 3 minutes). Stir in onions. Serve soup with fish sauce to add to taste. Makes 4 servings.

Per serving: 221 calories (16% fat, 45% carbohydrates, 39% protein), 4 g total fat (0.9 g saturated fat), 24 g carbohydrates, 21 g protein, 105 mg cholesterol, 281 mg sodium

Fish Pot-au-Feu

MODIFIED CLASSIC

Preparation time: About 15 minutes
Cooking time: About 30 minutes

A classic pot-au-feu simmers slowly all afternoon, but this quick contemporary version delivers equally rich flavor after just half an hour. Each bowlful offers carrot and leek halves, a tiny whole potato, and mild, firm fish. For colorful, crunchy contrast, accompany the soup with a salad made with radicchio or red cabbage.

5	cups low-sodium chicken broth
1	cup dry white wine; or 1 cup low-sodium chicken broth plus 3 tablespoons white wine vinegar
½	teaspoon dry tarragon
4	small red thin-skinned potatoes (*each* 1½ to 2 inches in diameter), scrubbed
4	medium-size carrots, cut into halves
4	medium-size leeks (about 2 lbs. *total*)
1½	pounds firm-textured white-fleshed fish fillets such as lingcod or sea bass

In a 5- to 6-quart pan, combine broth, wine, and tarragon; bring to a boil over high heat. Add potatoes and carrots; return to a boil. Then reduce heat, cover, and boil gently for 10 minutes.

Meanwhile, trim ends and all but 3 inches of green tops from leeks; remove tough outer leaves. Split leeks lengthwise; rinse well. Add leeks to pan, cover, and boil gently until leeks and potatoes are tender when pierced (about 10 more minutes). Lift leeks from broth with a slotted spoon, cover, and keep warm.

Rinse fish and pat dry; then cut into 4 equal portions. Add fish to soup, cover, and simmer until carrots are tender when pierced and fish is just opaque but still moist in thickest part; cut to test (7 to 10 minutes).

With a slotted spatula, carefully lift fish from pan and arrange in 4 wide, shallow bowls. Evenly distribute vegetables alongside fish and ladle broth over all. Makes 4 servings.

Per serving: 316 calories (12% fat, 42% carbohydrates, 46% protein), 4 g total fat (0.9 g saturated fat), 32 g carbohydrates, 36 g protein, 89 mg cholesterol, 219 mg sodium

Fish & Pea Soup

Preparation time: About 15 minutes
Cooking time: About 20 minutes

Ladle chunks of lean white fish and tarragon-scented broth into wide bowls, then slice a baguette—and you have a satisfying family supper.

3   large leeks (about 1¾ lbs. *total*)
2   tablespoons salad oil
1   clove garlic, minced or pressed
1   large carrot, finely chopped
1   cup dry white wine or low-sodium chicken broth
6   cups low-sodium chicken broth
1   dry bay leaf
1   teaspoon dry tarragon
1½ to 2 pounds rockfish or lingcod fillets, cut into 1-inch chunks
1   package (about 10 oz.) frozen tiny peas
    Salt and pepper

Trim ends and and all but 3 inches of green tops from leeks; remove tough outer leaves. Split leeks lengthwise; rinse well, then thinly slice crosswise.

Heat oil in a 5- to 6-quart pan over medium heat. Add leeks, garlic, and carrot; cook, stirring occasionally, until leeks are soft but not browned (8 to 10 minutes). Add wine, broth, bay leaf, and tarragon. Bring to a boil; then reduce heat to medium-low and simmer for 5 minutes.

Add fish and peas to pan. Cover and cook until fish is just opaque but still moist in thickest part; cut to test (about 6 minutes). Season to taste with salt and pepper. Makes 6 servings.

Per serving: 298 calories (29% fat, 26% carbohydrates, 45% protein), 9 g total fat (1 g saturated fat), 18 g carbohydrates, 31 g protein, 46 mg cholesterol, 216 mg sodium

---

Leeks, *in season from October through May, are a fairly mild-tasting member of the onion family. Despite their temperate nature— some of their relatives are far more assertive— leeks are valued for the depth they bring to the overall flavor of soup stocks.*

Cool Scallop Soup

NATURALLY LOW IN FAT

Preparation time: About 20 minutes
Chilling time: At least 4 hours

Part soup and part salad, this frosty main-dish offering features tart marinated scallops atop a creamy vegetable purée. Diced tomatoes and sliced cucumbers add crunch. Round out the meal with iced tea and squares of the moist cornbread on page 178.

1   pound bay or sea scallops
⅔   cup lemon juice
    About 1¾ pounds cucumbers
⅓   cup firmly packed watercress sprigs
⅓   cup thinly sliced green onions
1   cup plain low-fat yogurt
    Salt
2   medium-size pear-shaped (Roma-type) tomatoes (about 6 oz. *total*), seeded and diced

Rinse scallops and pat dry. If using sea scallops, cut them into ½-inch pieces. Place scallops in a non-metal bowl, add lemon juice, and stir to combine.

Cover and refrigerate, stirring occasionally, for at least 4 hours or up to 1 day. With a slotted spoon, lift out scallops, reserving lemon juice. Cover scallops and return to refrigerator.

Cut off a third of one of the cucumbers; score its skin lengthwise with a fork, then thinly slice. Set cucumber slices aside. Also reserve 4 of the watercress sprigs.

Coarsely chop remaining cucumbers. Place in a food processor or blender with reserved lemon juice, remaining watercress sprigs, onions, and yogurt; whirl until smooth. Season purée to taste with salt.

Drain scallops, reserving any liquid; stir liquid into cucumber purée. To serve, pour purée into bowls; add scallops, tomatoes, and reserved cucumber slices to each serving. Garnish with reserved watercress sprigs. Makes 4 servings.

Per serving: 181 calories (11% fat, 38% carbohydrates, 51% protein), 2 g total fat (0.7 g saturated fat), 18 g carbohydrates, 24 g protein, 41 mg cholesterol, 241 mg sodium

LOW-FAT HOMEMADE BROTHS

Great-tasting soups begin with lean, flavorful broths. Here are three choices.

BEEF STOCK

Preparation time: About 20 minutes
Baking time: 20 to 25 minutes
Cooking time: About 2½ hours
Chilling time: At least 4 hours

4	pounds beef and veal shanks, cut up
2	carrots, cut into chunks
2	medium-size onions, quartered
2	stalks celery, cut into pieces (include leaves)
1	dry bay leaf
2	cloves garlic, peeled
2	whole cloves
6	whole black peppercorns
¼	teaspoon dry thyme

Place meat in a roasting pan and bake in a 450° oven until browned (20 to 25 minutes). Transfer to a 6- to 8-quart pan. Add 1 cup water to roasting pan and stir to scrape browned bits free; then pour over beef along with 11 more cups water. Add carrots, onions, celery, bay leaf, garlic, cloves, peppercorns, and thyme.

Bring to a boil over high heat; reduce heat, cover, and simmer until meat falls from bones (about 2½ hours). Let cool.

Pour stock through a fine strainer into a bowl; discard residue. Cover stock; refrigerate for at least 4 hours or up to 2 days. Lift off and discard fat. To store, freeze in 1- to 4-cup portions. Makes about 3 quarts.

Per cup: Due to variations in ingredients and cooking time, precise nutritional data is not available. The nutritional value of this broth is similar to that of canned beef broth, but the homemade version is lower in sodium.

HOMEMADE CHICKEN BROTH

Preparation time: About 20 minutes
Cooking time: About 3 hours
Chilling time: At least 4 hours

5	pounds bony chicken pieces
2	large onions, cut into chunks
2	large carrots, cut into chunks
6	to 8 parsley sprigs
½	teaspoon whole black peppercorns

Rinse chicken and place in a 6- to 8-quart pan. Add onions, carrots, parsley sprigs, peppercorns, and 3½ quarts water. Bring to a boil over high heat; then reduce heat, cover, and simmer for 3 hours. Let cool.

Pour broth through a fine strainer into a bowl; discard residue. Cover broth; refrigerate for at least 4 hours or up to 2 days. Lift off and discard fat. To store, freeze in 1- to 4-cup portions. Makes about 10 cups.

Per cup: Due to variations in ingredients and cooking time, precise nutritional data is not available. The nutritional value of this broth is similar to that of canned low-sodium chicken broth.

VEGETABLE BROTH

Preparation time: About 20 minutes
Cooking time: About 2 hours

1	pound leeks
1	large onion, chopped
3	cloves garlic, minced
2	cups chopped parsley
8	ounces mushrooms, coarsely chopped
1	large can (about 28 oz.) crushed tomatoes
1	teaspoon *each* salt and dry thyme
1	dry bay leaf
½	teaspoon whole black peppercorns
¼	teaspoon whole cloves

Cut ends and all but 3 inches of green tops from leeks. Discard tough outer leaves. Split leeks in half lengthwise; rinse well, then thinly slice crosswise.

In a 5½- to 6-quart pan, combine leeks, onion, garlic, parsley, mushrooms, tomatoes, salt, thyme, bay leaf, peppercorns, cloves, and 10 cups water. Bring to a boil; then reduce heat, cover, and simmer until broth is richly flavored (about 2 hours).

Pour broth through a fine strainer into a bowl, pressing down on solids to remove as much liquid as possible. Discard residue. If made ahead, let cool; then cover and refrigerate for up to 3 days. Makes about 10 cups.

Per cup: 30 calories (8% fat, 75% carbohydrates, 17% protein), 0.3 g total fat (0 g saturated fat), 6 g carbohydrates, 1 g protein, 0 mg cholesterol, 355 mg sodium

SALADS

*S*treamlined salads, brimming with crisp vegetables and juicy fruits, are on everyone's list of favorites. They're easy to make, too: you can't fail to please if you start with the freshest, prettiest produce from market and garden. As for salad dressings, cooks who forgo fat have found ways to enhance flavors and textures while using oil sparingly—if at all. You'll learn some of these tricks from our recipes. Leafy greens glisten with flavorful vinegars and sparkling citrus juices; hearty potato salads are creamy with yogurt; seafood combinations gain savory flavor from wine and broth. When you do use a touch of oil, be sure to make a heart-healthy selection. Good choices include distinctive-tasting olive oil as well as milder types such as corn, safflower, and sunflower.

Spinach Salad with Garlic Croutons

Preparation time: About 20 minutes
Broiling time: About 4 minutes

Iron-rich spinach teams up with onion rings, sweet red peppers, and mushrooms in this pretty luncheon salad, inspired by a warm-weather favorite from Greece. Toss the greens with a tangy feta dressing; serve garlicky toasted baguette slices alongside.

1½	**pounds spinach, stems removed, leaves rinsed and crisped**
1	**medium-size red onion, thinly sliced and separated into rings**
8	**ounces mushrooms, thinly sliced**
1	**large red bell pepper (about 8 oz.), seeded and thinly sliced**
2	**ounces feta cheese, crumbled**
½	**cup lemon juice**
4	**teaspoons olive oil**
½	**teaspoon dry oregano**
2	**cloves garlic, peeled**
1	**small French bread baguette (about 8 oz.), cut into ½-inch-thick slices**

Tear spinach leaves into bite-size pieces, if desired. Place spinach, onion, mushrooms, and bell pepper in a large bowl; set aside.

In a blender, whirl cheese, lemon juice, oil, oregano, and 1 clove of the garlic until smoothly blended; set aside.

Place baguette slices in a single layer on a baking sheet and broil about 5 inches below heat, turning once, until golden on both sides (about 4 minutes). Let toast slices cool briefly. Rub remaining garlic clove evenly over top of each toast slice; then discard garlic clove.

Pour dressing over salad and mix gently. Spoon salad onto individual plates. Arrange toasted baguette slices atop salads (or arrange toast on a plate and serve on the side). Makes 6 servings.

Per serving: 208 calories (28% fat, 56% carbohydrates, 16% protein), 7 g total fat (2 g saturated fat), 31 g carbohydrates, 9 g protein, 8 mg cholesterol, 410 mg sodium

Peking Spinach Salad

Preparation time: About 30 minutes
Baking time: About 3 minutes

Baked won ton squares add appealing crunch to this light, lively spinach-and-fruit salad. To keep the won tons crisp, add them—and the sweet-tart plum dressing—just before serving.

12	**won ton skins (*each* about 3 inches square)**
⅓	**cup plum jam**
1	**tablespoon reduced-sodium soy sauce**
3	**tablespoons lemon juice**
½	**teaspoon ground cinnamon**
6	**cups lightly packed stemmed spinach leaves, rinsed and crisped**
4	**ounces mushrooms, thinly sliced**
¾	**cup *each* shredded carrots and lightly packed cilantro sprigs**
2	**medium-size red-skinned plums, pitted and thinly sliced**

Cut each won ton skin into quarters. Arrange in a single layer on a greased baking sheet; spray or brush with water. Bake in a 500° oven until golden (about 3 minutes), watching carefully to prevent burning. Set aside.

In a small bowl, stir together jam, soy sauce, lemon juice, and cinnamon. Set aside.

Place spinach in a large bowl. Top with mushrooms, carrots, cilantro, and plums. Just before serving, add won ton skins and dressing; mix gently and serve immediately. Makes 8 servings.

Per serving: 99 calories (5% fat, 82% carbohydrates, 13% protein), 0.6 g total fat (0.1 g saturated fat), 22 g carbohydrates, 3 g protein, 1 mg cholesterol, 196 mg sodium

To save time at dinner, *you can make green salads in advance—up to a point. Rinse, crisp, and tear the greens as directed, then cover and refrigerate them. Prepare the dressing and any additional ingredients and set them aside. At the last moment before serving, stir or shake the dressing; then mix the salad and add any crisp toppings.*

Orange & Olive Patio Salad

· ·

Preparation time: About 20 minutes
Cooking time: About 1 minute
Cooling time: About 1 hour

A salad is the quintessential "light" entrée—but if you choose a traditional dressing, it's surprising how quickly the calories can add up. By using an oil-free vinaigrette, we've cut the fat in this refreshing salad to a minimum.

½	**cup water**
1	**teaspoon arrowroot**
4	**teaspoons honey**
2	**tablespoons finely chopped fresh mint**
1	**small mild red onion, thinly sliced crosswise**
¼	**cup red wine vinegar**
6	**cups lightly packed mixed bite-size pieces of butter lettuce and radicchio (or all butter lettuce), rinsed and crisped**
6	**cups lightly packed watercress sprigs, rinsed and crisped**
2	**medium-size oranges (about 1 lb. *total*), peeled and thinly sliced crosswise**
¼	**cup small pitted ripe or Niçoise olives**
¼	**cup lime juice**
	About ¼ cup mixed fresh basil and fresh mint leaves (optional)
	Salt and pepper

In a small pan, combine water, arrowroot, honey, and chopped mint. Bring to a boil over high heat, stirring constantly. Remove from heat and let stand until cold (about 1 hour).

Meanwhile, in a large salad bowl, combine onion and vinegar. Let stand for at least 15 minutes or up to 3 hours. Drain, discarding vinegar; separate onion slices into rings.

In same salad bowl, combine onion rings, lettuce, radicchio, and watercress; mix lightly. Top with orange slices and olives.

Stir lime juice into honey-mint mixture, then pour through a fine wire strainer over salad; discard residue. Garnish with basil and mint leaves,

if desired; season to taste with salt and pepper. Makes 8 to 10 servings.

Per serving: 49 calories (10% fat, 77% carbohydrates, 13% protein), 0.6 g total fat (0.1 g saturated fat), 11 g carbohydrates, 2 g protein, 0 mg cholesterol, 49 mg sodium

Caesar Salad

· ·

Preparation time: About 15 minutes
Baking time: 12 to 15 minutes

How do you lighten up Caesar salad? Our solution: omit the rich oil-and-egg dressing; instead, use a tangy blend of nonfat sour cream, anchovies, and other seasonings.

	Garlic Croutons (recipe follows)
⅔	**cup nonfat or reduced-fat sour cream**
1	**or 2 cloves garlic, minced or pressed**
2	**tablespoons lemon juice**
1	**teaspoon Worcestershire (optional)**
6	**to 8 canned anchovy fillets, rinsed, drained, patted dry, and finely chopped**
8	**cups lightly packed bite-size pieces of romaine lettuce, rinsed and crisped**
	Grated Parmesan cheese

Prepare Garlic Croutons; set aside.

In a large bowl, beat sour cream, garlic, lemon juice, and Worcestershire (if used) until blended. Stir in anchovies.

Add lettuce to bowl with dressing; mix gently but thoroughly. Spoon salad onto individual plates and add cheese and croutons to taste. Makes 4 to 6 servings.

Garlic Croutons. In a small bowl, combine 1 tablespoon **olive oil,** 1 tablespoon **water,** and 1 clove **garlic** (minced or pressed). Spread 3 cups (about 3 oz.) ¾-inch cubes **French bread** in a shallow baking pan. Brush oil mixture evenly over bread cubes. Bake in a 350° oven until croutons are crisp and golden brown (12 to 15 minutes). If made ahead, let cool; then cover and store at room temperature for up to 2 days.

Per serving: 125 calories (29% fat, 47% carbohydrates, 24% protein), 4 g total fat (0.6 g saturated fat), 14 g carbohydrates, 7 g protein, 3 mg cholesterol, 341 mg sodium

Golden Pepper Salad

30 MINUTES OR LESS

Preparation time: About 25 minutes

One sweet yellow bell pepper goes into this mixed green salad; another is puréed for the dressing that's spooned on top. If you like, substitute other favorite mild and sharp greens for those suggested below.

Golden Dressing (recipe follows)
1   **head red leaf lettuce (about 8 oz.)**
1   **small head red oak leaf lettuce (about 4 oz.)**
1   **small head chicory (about 12 oz.)**
1   **large bunch watercress (about 8 oz.)**
1   **head Belgian endive (about 3 oz.)**
1   *each* **medium-size yellow and red bell pepper (about 12 oz.** *total***)**
1   **can (about 15 oz.) garbanzo beans, drained and rinsed; or 2 cups cooked garbanzo beans (page 149), drained and rinsed**

Prepare Golden Dressing; set aside.

Separate lettuces into leaves (tear larger leaf lettuce leaves in half). Discard outer leaves from chicory. Discard tough stems from watercress. Rinse and crisp lettuces, chicory, and watercress; then place all greens in a 3- to 4-quart bowl.

Cut endive in half lengthwise, then cut each half crosswise into thin strips. Cut bell peppers in half lengthwise; remove seeds, then cut each pepper half crosswise into thin strips. Add endive, bell peppers, and beans to bowl of greens.

Stir Golden Dressing to blend, pour over salad, and mix gently. Makes 8 servings.

Golden Dressing. In a blender or food processor, combine 1 tablespoon **olive oil,** ½ cup diced **yellow bell pepper,** 1 tablespoon minced **shallot,** and ⅛ teaspoon *each* **salt** and **ground red pepper** (cayenne). Whirl until mixture is smoothly puréed. (At this point, you may cover dressing and refrigerate for up to 1 day.) Just before using, add 2 tablespoons **white wine vinegar** and stir until thoroughly blended.

Per serving: 84 calories (28% fat, 54% carbohydrates, 18% protein), 3 g total fat (0.3 g saturated fat), 12 g carbohydrates, 4 g protein, 0 mg cholesterol, 125 mg sodium

Watercress, Butter Lettuce & Shrimp Salad

Preparation time: About 10 minutes
Standing time: At least 10 minutes
Baking time: 12 to 15 minutes

To make this pert first-course salad, toss watercress, butter lettuce, and tiny shrimp with a dressing of balsamic vinegar and Dijon mustard; then sprinkle crunchy baked croutons over all.

1   **tablespoon mustard seeds**
¼   **cup boiling water**
   Olive oil cooking spray
2   **cups (about 2 oz.) ½-inch cubes French bread**
¼   **cup balsamic or red wine vinegar**
2   **teaspoons Dijon mustard**
1   **tablespoon olive oil or salad oil**
8   **cups bite-size pieces of butter lettuce, rinsed and crisped**
3   **cups lightly packed watercress sprigs, rinsed and crisped**
8   **ounces small cooked shrimp**

Place mustard seeds in a small bowl; pour boiling water over them. Let stand for at least 10 minutes or up to 8 hours; drain well.

Coat a shallow baking pan with cooking spray. Spread bread cubes in pan; coat with cooking spray. Bake in a 350° oven until crisp and golden brown (12 to 15 minutes). Let cool.

In a small bowl, stir together mustard seeds, vinegar, mustard, and oil. In a large bowl, combine lettuce, watercress, and shrimp. Add dressing and mix gently; top with croutons. Makes 6 servings.

Per serving: 123 calories (29% fat, 35% carbohydrates, 36% protein), 4 g total fat (1 g saturated fat), 11 g carbohydrates, 11 g protein, 74 mg cholesterol, 228 mg sodium

---

To crisp greens for salads, *first rinse them thoroughly, using plenty of cold water. Drain or shake excess moisture from the leaves, or spin them in a salad spinner. Dry the greens well; then wrap them loosely in paper towels, place in a plastic bag, and store in the refrigerator.*

Salad of Leaves & Fruit

Preparation time: About 15 minutes

A simple berry vinegar–citrus dressing splashes over this colorful combination of greens, oranges, and juicy ripe raspberries.

> **Citrus Dressing (recipe follows)**
> 1 **large orange (about 10 oz.)**
> 1 **medium-size head butter lettuce (about 8 oz.), separated into leaves, rinsed, and crisped**
> 1 **head radicchio or Belgian endive (about 3 oz.), separated into leaves, rinsed, and crisped**
> 1 **cup raspberries or seedless red grapes**

Prepare Citrus Dressing; set aside. Cut peel and all white membrane from orange. Cut between membranes to release orange segments; set aside.

Tear lettuce and radicchio leaves into bite-size pieces. Place leaves in a bowl and toss to mix. Then mound leaves equally on 4 individual plates; top with oranges and raspberries. Spoon Citrus Dressing over salads. Makes 4 servings.

Citrus Dressing. In a small bowl, stir together ¼ cup **orange juice,** 2 tablespoons **raspberry vinegar** or red wine vinegar, and ½ teaspoon **honey.** Season to taste with **salt.**

Per serving: 61 calories (6% fat, 84% carbohydrates, 10% protein), 0.5 g total fat (0 g saturated fat), 14 g carbohydrates, 2 g protein, 0 mg cholesterol, 5 mg sodium

Ginger Pear & Hazelnut Salad

Preparation time: About 20 minutes
Baking time: About 10 minutes

Top fresh pear halves with toasted nuts and a tingling honey-ginger dressing to make this fruit salad. For best flavor, use only fully ripe, fork-tender pears; you may need to let them stand for a day or two at room temperature before using.

> ⅓ **cup hazelnuts**
> ½ **cup balsamic or red wine vinegar**
> 3 **tablespoons *each* honey and minced crystallized ginger**
> 8 **small or 4 large firm-ripe Bartlett pears (about 2 lbs. *total*)**
> 2 **tablespoons lemon juice**
> **Leaf lettuce leaves, rinsed and crisped**

Spread hazelnuts in a shallow baking pan and toast in a 350° oven until pale golden beneath skins (about 10 minutes). Let cool slightly; then rub off as much of skins as possible with your fingers. Chop nuts coarsely and set aside.

In a small bowl, stir together vinegar, honey, and ginger; set aside. Halve and core pears; brush cut sides with lemon juice. Line a platter with lettuce leaves; arrange pear halves, cut side up, on lettuce. Spoon dressing over pears, then sprinkle with hazelnuts. Makes 8 servings.

Per serving: 138 calories (20% fat, 77% carbohydrates, 3% protein), 3 g total fat (0.2 g saturated fat), 29 g carbohydrates, 1 g protein, 0 mg cholesterol, 4 mg sodium

Cherry Salad with Orange Dressing

Preparation time: About 30 minutes

Fresh cherries aren't just for eating plain or baking in pies—try them in soups (page 21) and salads, too. Here, a yogurt dressing tops dark, glossy cherries and pineapple chunks.

> **Orange Dressing (recipe follows)**
> 1 **medium-size head iceberg lettuce**
> 1 **small pineapple (about 2½ lbs.), peeled, cored, and cut into 1-inch chunks**
> 2½ **cups dark sweet cherries, stemmed and pitted**

Prepare Orange Dressing; set aside.

Remove 4 of the largest lettuce leaves; set aside. Break remaining lettuce into bite-size pieces and place in a large bowl. Add pineapple and cherries. Pour dressing over salad and mix to coat evenly.

Line a salad bowl with reserved lettuce leaves; spoon in salad. Makes 6 servings.

Orange Dressing. Toast 2 tablespoons **sesame seeds** in a wide frying pan over medium-high heat until golden (2 to 4 minutes), stirring often. Pour out of pan and set aside. In a bowl, stir together 1 cup **plain nonfat yogurt,** 3 tablespoons *each* **frozen orange juice concentrate** (thawed) and **lime juice,** and ¼ teaspoon **salt.** Add sesame seeds; stir until well blended.

Per serving: 162 calories (14% fat, 74% carbohydrates, 12% protein), 3 g total fat (0.4 g saturated fat), 33 g carbohydrates, 5 g protein, 0.8 mg cholesterol, 130 mg sodium

Pineapple, Strawberry & Apple Salad

. . . .

3 0 M I N U T E S O R L E S S

Preparation time: About 25 minutes

A trio of fresh fruits, dressed with yogurt and served with cottage cheese, makes a handsome salad to enjoy with bran muffins for a light warm-weather lunch or supper.

1   **medium-size pineapple (about 3 lbs.)**
1   **small tart green-skinned apple (about 4 oz.)**
1   **cup coarsely chopped strawberries**
⅓   **cup plain low-fat yogurt**
8   **to 16 butter lettuce leaves, rinsed and crisped**
8   **whole strawberries**
1   **cup small-curd cottage cheese**

Cut peel and eyes from pineapple. Slice off top third of pineapple; cut out and discard core, then chop fruit. Place chopped pineapple in a medium-size bowl and set aside. Cut remaining pineapple lengthwise into 8 wedges; cut off and discard core from each wedge. Core apple and cut into ½-inch chunks. Add apple, chopped strawberries, and yogurt to chopped pineapple; mix lightly.

On each of 8 individual plates, arrange 1 or 2 lettuce leaves, a pineapple wedge, a whole strawberry, an eighth of the cottage cheese, and an eighth of the fruit mixture. Makes 8 servings.

Per serving: 92 calories (17% fat, 65% carbohydrates, 18% protein), 2 g total fat (0.9 g saturated fat), 16 g carbohydrates, 4 g protein, 4 mg cholesterol, 115 mg sodium

Summer Fruit & Almond Salad

. . . .

Preparation time: About 45 minutes
Cooking time: About 5 minutes

C elebrate summer's bounty with color, flavor, and style: serve a rainbow of melons, grapes, and berries in a slightly sweet, almond-flavored citrus dressing.

½   **cup sliced almonds**
8   **ounces jicama, peeled and cut into matchstick pieces**
¼   **cup orange juice**
2   **tablespoons lemon juice**
1   **teaspoon *each* poppy seeds and sugar**
¼   **teaspoon almond extract**
2   **cups cubed, seeded watermelon**
2   **cups cubed cantaloupe**
1   **cup seedless grapes, halved**
1   **cup strawberries, hulled and sliced**
12   **to 16 large lettuce leaves, rinsed and crisped**
1   **large kiwi fruit (about 4 oz.), peeled and thinly sliced**

Toast almonds in a wide frying pan over medium-high heat until golden (about 3 minutes), stirring often. Pour out of pan and set aside.

In a large bowl, mix jicama, orange juice, lemon juice, poppy seeds, sugar, and almond extract. Add watermelon, cantaloupe, grapes, and strawberries; mix gently.

Arrange lettuce leaves on 6 to 8 individual plates; evenly mound fruit mixture on lettuce. Garnish salad with kiwi fruit and almonds. Makes 6 to 8 servings.

Per serving: 128 calories (29% fat, 62% carbohydrates, 9% protein), 4 g total fat (0.4 g saturated fat), 21 g carbohydrates, 3 g protein, 0 mg cholesterol, 12 mg sodium

Green & White
Sesame Salad

30 MINUTES OR LESS

Preparation time: About 20 minutes
Cooking time: 4 to 7 minutes

Serve this green-and-white springtime salad with roast chicken or a plain grilled steak. Choose the slimmest, most tender asparagus and green beans you can find; cook them for just a minute or two, then toss with a piquant hoisin dressing.

⅓ **cup seasoned rice vinegar (or ⅓ cup distilled white vinegar plus 1 tablespoon sugar)**

1 **tablespoon *each* sugar, hoisin sauce, and Dijon mustard**

3 **tablespoons sesame seeds**

1 **pound slender asparagus, tough ends removed**

10 **to 12 ounces slender green beans, ends removed**

12 **ounces jicama, peeled and cut into long matchstick strips**

In a small bowl, stir together vinegar, sugar, hoisin sauce, and mustard. Set aside.

Toast sesame seeds in a wide frying pan over medium-high heat until golden (2 to 4 minutes), stirring often. Add to dressing and stir to mix.

Pour water into frying pan to a depth of ½ inch and bring to a boil over high heat. Add asparagus and beans. Cover and cook just until vegetables are tender-crisp to bite (2 to 3 minutes). Drain, immerse in cold water until cool, and drain again.

Arrange asparagus, beans, and jicama on a platter. Stir dressing well; drizzle over vegetables. Makes 6 servings.

Per serving: 100 calories (22% fat, 62% carbohydrates, 16% protein), 3 g total fat (0.4 g saturated fat), 17 g carbohydrates, 4 g protein, 0 mg cholesterol, 429 mg sodium

Mildly acidic rice vinegar, *popular in the cooking of Japan and other Asian countries, is available both seasoned and unseasoned. The seasoned type contains added sugar and salt.*

Cucumber &
Green Onion Salad

NATURALLY LOW IN FAT

Preparation time: About 20 minutes
Standing time: About 30 minutes

Crisp sliced cucumbers in a plain vinaigrette are excellent alongside Asian-seasoned dishes. You might try them with grilled soy-marinated chicken or with lean beef or lamb.

3 **large English cucumbers (about 3 lbs. *total*), thinly sliced**

1 **tablespoon salt**

½ **cup thinly sliced green onions**

1 **tablespoon sugar**

⅓ **cup seasoned rice vinegar (or ⅓ cup unseasoned rice vinegar plus 1 tablespoon sugar)**

In a large bowl, mix cucumbers and salt. With your hands, lightly crush cucumbers. Let stand for about 30 minutes; then transfer cucumbers to a colander and squeeze gently. Let drain briefly; rinse with cold water, squeeze gently, and drain again. (At this point, you may cover and refrigerate for up to 1 day.)

In another large bowl, combine cucumbers, onions, sugar, and vinegar; mix well. If desired, transfer to a rimmed platter with a slotted spoon before serving. Makes 8 to 10 servings.

Per serving: 34 calories (5% fat, 85% carbohydrates, 10% protein), 0.2 g total fat (0 g saturated fat), 8 g carbohydrates, 0.9 g protein, 0 mg cholesterol, 300 mg sodium

Red & Yellow Pepper
Salad-Salsa

30 MINUTES OR LESS

Preparation time: About 15 minutes

Show off the season's best sweet bell peppers in this nutritious salad. You use the peppers as edible individual bowls—so for the prettiest salad, choose bright, glossy peppers that are firm and well-shaped.

5   large yellow bell peppers (about 2½ lbs. *total*)
1   large red bell pepper (about 8 oz.), seeded and diced
⅔   cup minced jicama
2   tablespoons minced cilantro
1½ tablespoons distilled white vinegar
1   teaspoon honey
     Ground red pepper (cayenne)

Set 4 of the yellow bell peppers upright, then cut off the top quarter of each. Remove and discard seeds from pepper shells; set shells aside. Cut out and discard stems from top pieces of peppers; then dice these pieces and transfer to a large bowl.

Seed and dice remaining yellow bell pepper and add to bowl. Add red bell pepper, jicama, cilantro, vinegar, and honey. Mix gently; season to taste with ground red pepper. Spoon mixture into pepper shells. Makes 4 servings.

Per serving: 90 calories (5% fat, 84% carbohydrates, 11% protein), 0.6 g total fat (0.1 g saturated fat), 21 g carbohydrates, 3 g protein, 0 mg cholesterol, 7 mg sodium

Carrot Slaw

. . . .

NATURALLY LOW IN FAT

Preparation time: About 20 minutes
Chilling time: At least 1 hour

This piquant slaw is delightful as a crunchy side dish with grilled fish steaks, and just as good as a relish-like topping for turkey sandwiches.

1½ pounds carrots, shredded
1   teaspoon grated lime peel
⅓   cup lime juice
2   tablespoons *each* distilled white vinegar and honey
1   tablespoon Dijon mustard
1   teaspoon caraway seeds
¼   teaspoon crushed red pepper flakes
     Salt

In a medium-size bowl, combine carrots, lime peel, lime juice, vinegar, honey, mustard, caraway seeds, and red pepper flakes. Mix gently; then season to taste with salt. Cover and refrigerate until

cold (at least 1 hour) or for up to 2 days. To serve, lift to individual plates with a slotted spoon. Makes 4 to 6 servings.

Per serving: 94 calories (5% fat, 89% carbohydrates, 6% protein), 0.5 g total fat (0 g saturated fat), 23 g carbohydrates, 2 g protein, 0 mg cholesterol, 141 mg sodium

Thai Coleslaw

. . . .

Preparation time: About 40 minutes

The cabbage in this unconventional slaw is the curly Savoy variety. Combine it with crisp bok choy and rosy radicchio, then toss the greens with a complex, spicy-hot dressing.

⅓   cup *each* unseasoned rice vinegar and lime juice
¼   cup slivered red pickled ginger
2   small fresh serrano or jalapeño chiles, seeded and finely chopped
1   tablespoon *each* sugar and Oriental sesame oil
1   tablespoon fish sauce (*nam pla* or *nuoc mam*)
½   teaspoon wasabi (green horseradish) powder
2   teaspoons sesame seeds
     About 1 pound bok choy (coarse outer leaves removed), rinsed and crisped
1   small red onion, cut into thin slivers
2   medium-size carrots, thinly sliced
8   cups finely slivered Savoy or green cabbage
1   small head radicchio (about 3 oz.), cut into thin slivers

In a small bowl, stir together vinegar, lime juice, ginger, chiles, sugar, oil, fish sauce, and wasabi powder; set aside.

Toast sesame seeds in small frying pan over medium-high heat until golden (2 to 4 minutes), stirring often. Pour out of pan and set aside.

Thinly slice bok choy and place in a large bowl. Add onion, carrots, cabbage, radicchio, and dressing; mix gently. Sprinkle with sesame seeds. Makes 8 to 12 servings.

Per serving: 62 calories (26% fat, 59% carbohydrates, 15% protein), 2 g total fat (0.3 g saturated fat), 10 g carbohydrates, 3 g protein, 0 mg cholesterol, 64 mg sodium

Green Pea Salad

Preparation time: 15 minutes
Chilling time: At least 3 hours

Assemble this easy-to-make salad ahead of time to let the flavors blend; then serve it as a colorful accompaniment to cold roast turkey or poached salmon.

⅓   cup plain low-fat yogurt
1½ tablespoons Dijon mustard
⅛   teaspoon pepper
1   package (about 10 oz.) frozen tiny peas, thawed
1   hard-cooked large egg, chopped
½   cup finely chopped red or green bell pepper
⅓   cup thinly sliced green onions
¼   cup thinly sliced celery
    Butter lettuce leaves, rinsed and crisped

In a large bowl, stir together yogurt, mustard, and pepper. Add peas, egg, bell pepper, onions, and celery. Mix gently. Cover and refrigerate for at least 3 hours or up to 1 day.

To serve, line a platter or individual plates with lettuce; spoon salad onto lettuce. Makes 6 servings.

Per serving: 61 calories (22% fat, 51% carbohydrates, 27% protein), 2 g total fat (0.4 g saturated fat), 8 g carbohydrates, 4 g protein, 36 mg cholesterol, 201 mg sodium

Tomatillo & Tomato Salad

30 MINUTES OR LESS

Preparation time: About 15 minutes

Sliced tomatillos and a potpourri of tiny tomatoes—red, green, and gold—combine in this refreshing salad. When buying tomatoes, purchase only those that have not been refrigerated. Keep unripe fruit at room temperature. Once it's fully ripe, refrigerate it (to slow spoilage) and use it within a day or two.

3   pounds (8 to 10 cups) ripe cherry tomatoes (red, yellow, yellow-green, orange); include some that are ½ inch or less in diameter

10 medium-size tomatillos (about 10 oz. *total*), husked, rinsed, and thinly sliced
1   fresh jalapeño chile, seeded and minced
½   cup lightly packed cilantro leaves
¼   cup lime juice
    Salt and pepper
    Lime wedges

If any tomatoes are over ¾ inch in diameter, cut them into halves. Place tomatoes in a large bowl and add tomatillos, chile, cilantro, and lime juice. Mix gently. Season to taste with salt and pepper; serve with lime wedges. Makes 8 to 10 servings.

Per serving: 42 calories (12% fat, 74% carbohydrates, 14% protein), 0.6 g total fat (0.1 g saturated fat), 9 g carbohydrates, 2 g protein, 0 mg cholesterol, 15 mg sodium

Golden Potato Salad

Preparation time: About 20 minutes
Cooking time: About 30 minutes
Cooling time: About 30 minutes

Tender-crisp green beans and golden bell pepper accent this turmeric-tinted potato salad. It's great for barbecue meals; you might serve it with Turkey & Mushroom Burgers (page 118).

3½ pounds small red thin-skinned potatoes (*each* 1½ to 2 inches in diameter), scrubbed
8   ounces slender green beans, ends removed
¾   cup chopped yellow bell pepper
    About ⅓ cup low-sodium chicken broth
3   tablespoons red wine vinegar
1   tablespoon *each* balsamic vinegar and olive oil
1   teaspoon *each* ground turmeric, crushed anise seeds, and dry tarragon
    Salt and pepper

Place unpeeled potatoes in a 5- to 6-quart pan and add enough water to cover. Bring to a boil; reduce heat, partially cover, and boil gently until potatoes are tender when pierced (about 25 minutes). Lift out with a slotted spoon and let stand until cool (about 30 minutes). Meanwhile, return water in pan to a boil over high heat. Add beans and cook, uncovered, just until tender-crisp to bite (2 to 3 minutes). Drain, immerse in cold water until cool, and drain again. Cut potatoes into ½-inch-thick slices; cut beans into 1-inch lengths.

In a large bowl, combine bell pepper, ⅓ cup of the broth, red wine vinegar, balsamic vinegar, oil, turmeric, anise seeds, and tarragon. Add potatoes and beans; mix gently. For a moister salad, add a little more broth. Season to taste with salt and pepper. Makes 8 servings.

Per serving: 190 calories (10% fat, 80% carbohydrates, 10% protein), 2 g total fat (0.2 g saturated fat), 39 g carbohydrates, 5 g protein, 0 mg cholesterol, 19 mg sodium

Chili Potato Salad

· ·

Preparation time: About 15 minutes
Cooking time: 25 to 30 minutes
Cooling time: About 30 minutes

Tired of the same old potato salad? Try this chili-flavored version at your next picnic. It's good cold or at room temperature.

1½	pounds large thin-skinned potatoes, scrubbed
1	can (about 17 oz.) corn kernels, drained
½	cup *each* sliced celery and chopped red onion
⅔	cup chopped red bell pepper
2	tablespoons salad oil
¼	cup cider vinegar
2	teaspoons chili powder
1	clove garlic, minced or pressed
½	teaspoon liquid hot pepper seasoning
	Salt and pepper

Place unpeeled potatoes in a 5- to 6-quart pan and add enough water to cover. Bring to a boil over high heat; then reduce heat, partially cover, and boil gently until potatoes are tender when pierced (25 to 30 minutes). Drain, immerse in cold water

until cool, and drain again. Cut into ¾-inch cubes.

In a large bowl, combine potatoes, corn, celery, onion, and bell pepper. Add oil, vinegar, chili powder, garlic, and hot pepper seasoning; mix gently, then season to taste with salt and pepper. If made ahead, cover and refrigerate for up to 1 day. Serve cold or at room temperature. Makes 6 servings.

Per serving: 210 calories (21% fat, 71% carbohydrates, 8% protein), 5 g total fat (0.6 g saturated fat), 39 g carbohydrates, 5 g protein, 0 mg cholesterol, 257 mg sodium

Pesto-Orange Potato Salad

· ·
30 MINUTES OR LESS

Preparation time: About 25 minutes

Here's a distinctive green-and-gold potato salad to serve with grilled pork tenderloin or turkey breast.

2	medium-size oranges (about 1 lb. *total*)
½	cup *each* lightly packed parsley sprigs and cilantro leaves
¼	cup grated Parmesan cheese
¾	cup plain low-fat yogurt
1	teaspoon sugar
2	pounds russet potatoes, cooked, peeled, and cut into ½-inch cubes
	Salt and pepper
½	cup walnut halves

Grate 2 teaspoons peel (colored part only) from oranges; set peel aside. Cut remaining peel and all white membrane from oranges. Holding fruit over a bowl to catch juice, cut between membranes to release orange segments; set segments aside.

Pour juice in bowl into a blender or food processor; add the 2 teaspoons grated orange peel, parsley, cilantro, cheese, yogurt, and sugar. Whirl until smooth.

Place potatoes in a large bowl; pour yogurt mixture over potatoes and mix gently. Season to taste with salt and pepper. Garnish with orange segments and walnuts. Makes 6 to 8 servings.

Per serving: 196 calories (27% fat, 61% carbohydrates, 12% protein), 6 g total fat (1 g saturated fat), 31 g carbohydrates, 6 g protein, 4 mg cholesterol, 82 mg sodium

Potato Salad with Seed Vinaigrette

Preparation time: About 15 minutes
Cooking time: 30 to 35 minutes

A light vinaigrette, fragrant with herb seeds, seasons this potato salad. It's a good choice for picnics, since you can safely serve it at room temperature.

Seed Vinaigrette (recipe follows)
5   **large red thin-skinned potatoes (2 to 2½ lbs. *total*), scrubbed**
1   **cup thinly sliced celery**
½   **cup thinly sliced green onions**
1   **small red bell pepper (about 5 oz.), seeded and finely chopped**
    Salt

Prepare Seed Vinaigrette and set aside.

Place unpeeled potatoes in a 5- to 6-quart pan and add enough water to cover. Bring to a boil over high heat; then reduce heat, partially cover, and boil gently until potatoes are tender when pierced (25 to 30 minutes). Drain, immerse in cold water until cool, and drain again. Cut into ¾-inch cubes.

In a large bowl, gently mix potatoes, celery, onions, bell pepper, and Seed Vinaigrette. Season to taste with salt. If made ahead, cover and refrigerate for up to 1 day. Serve cold or at room temperature. Makes 6 to 8 servings.

Seed Vinaigrette. In a wide frying pan, combine 1 teaspoon *each* **mustard seeds, cumin seeds,** and **fennel seeds.** Cook over medium heat until fragrant (3 to 5 minutes), stirring often. Using the back of a heavy spoon, coarsely crush seeds. Remove from heat and mix in 2 tablespoons **salad oil,** ⅓ cup

---

Thin-skinned potatoes are usually preferred for salads: their firm, waxy texture makes them ideal for boiling or steaming. The paper-thin, red or creamy white skin is so tender that you needn't peel it away before or after cooking. Leaving the skin on helps retain the potato's vitamin C, as well.

---

cider vinegar, ½ teaspoon coarsely ground **pepper,** and 1 clove **garlic** (minced or pressed).

Per serving: 169 calories (23% fat, 69% carbohydrates, 8% protein), 4 g total fat (0.5 g saturated fat), 30 g carbohydrates, 3 g protein, 0 mg cholesterol, 29 mg sodium

Sweet Potato & Apple Salad

Preparation time: About 30 minutes
Cooking time: About 30 minutes
Cooling time: About 30 minutes

This colorful combination will remind you of a Waldorf salad—with the addition of sweet potatoes. Try it with cold roast turkey or chicken.

2   **pounds small sweet potatoes or yams**
½   **cup walnuts**
2   **tablespoons honey**
1   **teaspoon grated lemon peel**
1   **tablespoon lemon juice**
¾   **teaspoon ground ginger**
½   **teaspoon ground cinnamon**
1   **cup plain nonfat yogurt**
2   **large red-skinned apples (about 1 lb. *total*), cored and cut into ¾-inch cubes**
¾   **cup thinly sliced celery**
    Salt

Place unpeeled potatoes in a 5- to 6-quart pan and add enough water to cover. Bring to a boil over high heat; then reduce heat, partially cover, and boil gently until potatoes are tender when pierced (25 to 30 minutes). Drain and let stand until cool (about 30 minutes). Meanwhile, toast walnuts in a wide frying pan over medium-high heat until lightly browned and fragrant (about 3 minutes), stirring often. Pour out of pan and let cool.

In a large bowl, stir together honey, lemon peel, lemon juice, ginger, cinnamon, and yogurt. Peel potatoes and cut into ¾-inch cubes; then add potatoes, apples, celery, and ⅓ cup of the walnuts to dressing in bowl. Mix gently. Season to taste with salt. Transfer to a serving bowl and garnish with remaining walnuts. Makes 8 to 10 servings.

Per serving: 207 calories (19% fat, 73% carbohydrates, 8% protein), 5 g total fat (0.5 g saturated fat), 39 g carbohydrates, 4 g protein, 0.5 mg cholesterol, 42 mg sodium

Viennese Potato Salad

Preparation time: About 30 minutes
Cooking time: About 30 minutes

Our poppy seed–speckled potato salad boasts red-skinned apples, toasted pecans, sweet raisins, and a simple dressing of fruity late-harvest wine and tart cider vinegar. It's a delicious partner for broiled chicken breasts.

2½	**pounds small red thin-skinned potatoes** (*each 1½ to 2 inches in diameter*), **scrubbed**
½	**cup pecan or walnut pieces**
3	**large red-skinned apples (about 1½ lbs.** *total***)**
½	**cup sliced green onions**
⅓	**cup raisins**
⅓	**cup late-harvest gewürztraminer or Johannisberg Riesling**
⅓	**cup cider vinegar**
2	**tablespoons salad oil**
1	**tablespoon grated lemon peel**
2	**teaspoons poppy seeds**

Place unpeeled potatoes in a 5- to 6-quart pan and add enough water to cover. Bring to a boil over high heat; then reduce heat, partially cover, and boil gently until potatoes are tender when pierced (about 25 minutes). Drain, immerse in cold water until cool, and drain again. Cut into 1-inch cubes and set aside.

Toast pecans in a wide frying pan over medium-high heat until lightly browned and fragrant (about 3 minutes), stirring often. Pour out of pan and let cool; chop coarsely and set aside.

Core 2 of the apples and cut fruit into 1-inch chunks (set remaining apple aside to use for garnish). In a large bowl, combine apple chunks, potatoes, pecans, onions, raisins, wine, vinegar, oil, lemon peel, and poppy seeds; mix gently. If made ahead, cover and refrigerate for up to 6 hours.

To serve, mound salad on a large rimmed platter. Core remaining apple and cut into slices; fan slices out next to salad along one side of platter. Makes 6 to 8 servings.

Per serving: 307 calories (29% fat, 65% carbohydrates, 6% protein), 10 g total fat (1 g saturated fat), 51 g carbohydrates, 4 g protein, 0 mg cholesterol, 15 mg sodium

Black Bean, Corn & Pepper Salad

Preparation time: About 15 minutes
Chilling time: At least 1 hour

This substantial salad nicely complements favorite outdoor fare. Try it with grilled marinated top round, or alongside a turkey breast rubbed with lime and chiles and cooked in a covered barbecue.

2	**cans (about 15 oz.** *each***) black beans or cannellini (white kidney beans), drained and rinsed; or 4 cups cooked black beans or cannellini (page 149), drained and rinsed**
1½	**cups cooked fresh yellow or white corn kernels (from 2 medium-size ears corn); or 1 package (about 10 oz.) frozen corn kernels, thawed**
1	**large red bell pepper (about 8 oz.), seeded and finely chopped**
2	**small fresh jalapeño chiles, seeded and finely chopped**
½	**cup firmly packed chopped cilantro**
¼	**cup lime juice**
2	**tablespoons salad oil**
	Salt and pepper
	Lettuce leaves, rinsed and crisped

In a large bowl, combine beans, corn, bell pepper, chiles, cilantro, lime juice, and oil; mix lightly. Season to taste with salt and pepper. Cover and refrigerate for at least 1 hour or for up to 1 day.

To serve, line a serving bowl with lettuce leaves; spoon in bean mixture. Makes 6 servings.

Per serving: 197 calories (26% fat, 56% carbohydrates, 18% protein), 6 g total fat (0.7 g saturated fat), 29 g carbohydrates, 9 g protein, 0 mg cholesterol, 186 mg sodium

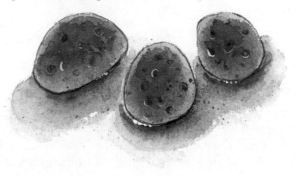

White Bean & Cherry Tomato Salad

· ·

Preparation time: About 15 minutes
Soaking time: 1 hour
Cooking time: About 1 hour
Chilling time: At least 6 hours

A cool, colorful salad of beans and tomatoes in a mustard vinaigrette is a perfect make-ahead choice for a potluck or picnic.

1	**pound dried small white beans**
1	**teaspoon salt**
2	**tablespoons white wine vinegar**
1	**tablespoon Dijon mustard**
4	**drops liquid hot pepper seasoning**
2	**tablespoons salad oil**
2	**tablespoons chopped fresh basil or 2 teaspoons dry basil**
1½	**teaspoons chopped fresh mint or ½ teaspoon dry mint**
3	**tablespoons *each* chopped parsley and thinly sliced green onions**
1	**small clove garlic, minced or pressed**
2	**cups (about 12 oz.) cherry tomatoes, cut into halves**
1	**large red bell pepper (about 8 oz.), seeded and chopped**
	Mint sprigs

Rinse and sort beans, removing any debris. Drain beans. In a 4- to 5-quart pan, bring 8 cups water to a boil over high heat. Add beans and cook, uncovered, for 2 minutes. Remove from heat, cover, and let stand for 1 hour. Drain beans, discarding water.

In same pan, combine salt and 6 cups water; bring to a boil over high heat. Add beans. Reduce heat, partially cover, and simmer until beans are tender to bite (about 1 hour). Drain beans well; then set aside.

In a medium-size bowl, stir together vinegar, mustard, and hot pepper seasoning. Beating constantly with a whisk, slowly add oil; then set dressing aside.

In a large bowl, combine beans, basil, chopped mint, parsley, onions, and garlic. Mix in dressing. Cover and refrigerate for at least 6 hours or up to 1 day. Just before serving, lightly mix tomatoes and

bell pepper into salad; garnish with mint sprigs. Makes 8 to 10 servings.

Per serving: 214 calories (16% fat, 64% carbohydrates, 20% protein), 4 g total fat (0.5 g saturated fat), 35 g carbohydrates, 11 g protein, 0 mg cholesterol, 183 mg sodium

Grapefruit-Bulgur Salad

· ·

Preparation time: About 30 minutes
Cooking time: 5 to 10 minutes
Standing & cooling time: About 45 minutes

Hearty enough to serve as a main course, this unusual salad pairs chewy cracked wheat with winter's sweet, juicy grapefruit. The seeds you'll need are sold in bulk at spice shops and health food stores. (Cardamom is typically sold as whole pods. To remove the seeds, crack the pods or crush them with the flat side of a heavy knife.)

4	**cups low-sodium chicken broth**
¼	**cup mustard seeds**
1	**teaspoon *each* cumin seeds, coriander seeds, crushed red pepper flakes, and dry thyme**
½	**teaspoon hulled cardamom seeds**
2	**tablespoons minced fresh ginger**
2	**cups bulgur**
4	**large grapefruit (about 4 lbs. *total*)**
⅓	**cup unseasoned rice vinegar**
¼	**cup fish sauce (*nam pla* or *nuoc mam*) or reduced-sodium soy sauce**
1	**tablespoon sugar**
½	**cup minced fresh basil or mint**

In a 3- to 4-quart pan, combine broth, mustard seeds, cumin seeds, coriander seeds, red pepper flakes, thyme, cardamom seeds, and ginger. Bring to a boil over high heat; then reduce heat, cover, and simmer for 5 minutes. Stir in bulgur; then remove from heat, cover, and let stand for 10 minutes. Drain off and reserve cooking liquid; let bulgur and liquid stand, uncovered, until cool (about 35 minutes).

Cut peel and all white membrane from grapefruit. Holding fruit over a bowl to catch juice, cut between membranes to release grapefruit segments. Place segments in bowl; squeeze juice from membranes into bowl.

Drain grapefruit juice from bowl into another, smaller bowl; stir in vinegar, fish sauce, and sugar. Pour juice mixture into bulgur; stir in basil. For a moister texture, stir in some of the reserved cooking liquid. Spoon bulgur mixture into a shallow serving bowl; top with grapefruit segments. Makes 6 servings.

Per serving: 308 calories (14% fat, 71% carbohydrates, 15% protein), 5 g total fat (0.7 g saturated fat), 58 g carbohydrates, 12 g protein, 0 mg cholesterol, 48 mg sodium

Golden Couscous Salad
. . . .

Preparation time: About 30 minutes
Cooking time: About 3 minutes
Standing time: About 5 minutes

Orange slices encircle a mound of spiced couscous studded with raisins, crisp cucumber, and green onions.

1¼	cups low-sodium chicken broth
1	cup couscous
½	cup golden raisins
2	tablespoons finely chopped crystallized ginger
1	teaspoon grated orange peel
½	teaspoon ground cumin
3	tablespoons seasoned rice vinegar (or 3 tablespoons unseasoned rice vinegar plus 2 teaspoons sugar)
3	tablespoons orange juice
½	cup *each* finely chopped cucumber and thinly sliced green onions
4	large oranges (about 2½ lbs. *total*)
1	to 2 tablespoons chopped salted roasted almonds

In a 3- to 4-quart pan, bring broth to a boil over high heat. Stir in couscous, raisins, ginger, orange peel, and cumin; cover pan and remove from heat. Let stand until all liquid has been absorbed (about 5 minutes). Fluff couscous lightly with a fork; then stir in vinegar, orange juice, cucumber, and onions. (At this point, you may cover and let stand for up to 4 hours. Stir before using.)

Cut peel and all white membrane from oranges; thinly slice oranges crosswise. Arrange orange slices in a ring around edge of a rimmed platter;

mound couscous in center. Sprinkle salad with almonds. Makes 4 to 6 servings.

Per serving: 324 calories (8% fat, 83% carbohydrates, 9% protein), 3 g total fat (0.4 g saturated fat), 70 g carbohydrates, 8 g protein, 0 mg cholesterol, 226 mg sodium

Indonesian Rice Salad
. . . .
NATURALLY LOW IN FAT

Preparation time: About 20 minutes
Cooking time: About 45 minutes
Cooling time: About 30 minutes

Dressed with a light sesame vinaigrette, this vegetable-rice salad is a super accompaniment for simply prepared meat, fish, or poultry.

2	cups long-grain brown rice
4½	cups water
	Lime Dressing (recipe follows)
5	to 6 ounces Chinese pea pods (also called snow or sugar peas), ends and strings removed
1	medium-size red or green bell pepper (about 6 oz.), seeded and chopped
5	green onions, thinly sliced
1	can (about 8 oz.) water chestnuts, drained and chopped
¼	cup chopped cilantro
¼	cup raisins (optional)

In a 3- to 4-quart pan, combine rice and water. Bring to a boil over high heat; then reduce heat, cover, and simmer until rice is tender to bite (about 45 minutes). Let stand, uncovered, until cool (about 30 minutes). Meanwhile, prepare Lime Dressing.

Thinly slice pea pods. Place in a large bowl; add bell pepper, onions, water chestnuts, cilantro, raisins (if used), rice, and Lime Dressing. Mix well. Spoon salad into a serving bowl. Makes 8 servings.

Lime Dressing. In a small bowl, stir together ⅔ cup **unseasoned rice vinegar,** 2 tablespoons *each* **lime juice** and **reduced-sodium soy sauce,** 1 tablespoon minced **fresh ginger,** 2 teaspoons minced **garlic,** and 1 teaspoon **Oriental sesame oil.**

Per serving: 214 calories (8% fat, 82% carbohydrates, 10% protein), 2 g total fat (0.3 g saturated fat), 44 g carbohydrates, 5 g protein, 0 mg cholesterol, 162 mg sodium

Warm Wild Rice & Asparagus Salad

. . . .

Preparation time: About 25 minutes
Cooking time: About 50 minutes

This elegant salad, meant to be served warm, is a nice choice for a cool spring night.

1   **cup wild rice, rinsed and drained**
4   **cups water**
1   **pound mushrooms, thinly sliced**
1   **large onion, finely chopped**
    About 2½ cups canned or homemade (page 41) vegetable broth or low-sodium chicken broth
1   **pound asparagus, tough ends removed**
3   **tablespoons balsamic vinegar**
1   **tablespoon olive oil**

In a 3- to 3½-quart pan, combine rice and water. Bring to a boil over high heat; then reduce heat, cover, and simmer until rice is tender to bite (about 50 minutes). Meanwhile, combine mushrooms, onion, and ¾ cup of the broth in a wide frying pan. Bring to a boil; then boil, stirring often, until liquid evaporates and vegetables begin to brown (about 12 minutes). To deglaze, add ⅓ cup more broth and stir to scrape browned bits free. Then continue to cook, stirring occasionally, until mixture begins to brown again. Repeat deglazing and browning steps 3 or 4 more times, using ⅓ cup broth each time; vegetables should be well browned. Meanwhile, thinly slice asparagus.

Stir ⅓ cup more broth into vegetables. Add asparagus and cook, stirring often, until asparagus is tender-crisp to bite (about 2 minutes).

Drain rice well; transfer to a serving bowl. Stir in asparagus-mushroom mixture, vinegar, and oil. Makes 8 servings.

Per serving: 126 calories (17% fat, 67% carbohydrates, 16% protein), 3 g total fat (0.3 g saturated fat), 22 g carbohydrates, 5 g protein, 0 mg cholesterol, 322 mg sodium

Wild Rice Salad with Raspberry Vinaigrette

. . . .

Preparation time: About 20 minutes
Cooking time: About 50 minutes
Cooling time: About 30 minutes

A fruity vinaigrette enhances this wholesome, satisfying combination of white and wild rices, crunchy jicama strips, and sweet mandarin oranges. Serve it with grilled or roast chicken, turkey, or lean pork.

1   **cup wild rice, rinsed and drained**
5   **cups water**
1   **cup long-grain white rice**
    Raspberry Vinaigrette (recipe follows)
¾   **cup chopped cilantro**
2   **cups julienne strips jicama**
½   **cup thinly sliced green onions**
2   **cans (about 11 oz. *each*) mandarin oranges**
    Salt and pepper

In a 3- to 4-quart pan, combine wild rice and water. Bring to a boil over high heat; then reduce heat, cover, and simmer for 30 minutes. Stir in white rice. Cover and simmer until both wild and white rices are tender to bite (15 to 20 more minutes). Drain off and discard any cooking liquid from rice; then let rice stand, uncovered, until cool (about 30 minutes). Meanwhile, prepare Raspberry Vinaigrette.

Pour rice into a serving bowl and mix in cilantro, jicama, and onions. Drain mandarin oranges; reserve ½ cup of the juice and stir into Raspberry Vinaigrette. Then stir Raspberry Vinaigrette into salad. Season salad to taste with salt and pepper; scatter drained mandarin oranges over top. If made ahead, cover and refrigerate for up to 6 hours. Makes 10 servings.

Raspberry Vinaigrette. In a small bowl, stir together 3 tablespoons **plain nonfat yogurt** or reduced-fat sour cream, ¼ cup **raspberry vinegar,** ½ teaspoon grated **orange peel,** and 2 tablespoons **salad oil.**

Per serving: 202 calories (14% fat, 77% carbohydrates, 9% protein), 3 g total fat (0.4 g saturated fat), 40 g carbohydrates, 5 g protein, 0.1 mg cholesterol, 12 mg sodium

Pasta & Grapefruit Salad

Preparation time: About 40 minutes
Cooking time: About 5 minutes

Juicy grapefruit segments add sweet-tart flavor to a salad of tiny pasta bow ties and green peas.

8	ounces dry tiny pasta bow ties (tripolini) or other small shapes
1	package (about 1 lb.) frozen tiny peas, thawed
1	cup chopped celery
½	cup thinly sliced green onions
⅓	cup chopped fresh mint
3	large red grapefruit (3 to 3½ lbs. *total*)
½	teaspoon grated lemon peel
2	tablespoons lemon juice
½	to 1 teaspoon minced fresh hot chile
	Fish sauce (*nam pla* or *nuoc mam*) or salt
8	to 12 large butter lettuce leaves, rinsed and crisped
8	ounces thinly sliced cooked ham
	Mint sprigs

In a 5- to 6-quart pan, cook pasta in about 3 quarts boiling water until just tender to bite (about 5 minutes); or cook according to package directions. Drain, rinse with cold water until cool, and drain again.

In a large bowl, combine pasta, peas, celery, onions, and chopped mint.

Cut peel and all white membrane from grapefruit. Holding fruit over a bowl to catch juice, cut between membranes to release grapefruit segments; add segments to pasta mixture. Squeeze membranes over bowl of juice, then measure collected juice; you need about ½ cup. Add lemon peel and lemon juice to the ½ cup grapefruit juice. Add juice mixture and chile to pasta mixture; mix gently. Season to taste with fish sauce.

To serve, arrange lettuce leaves on 4 to 6 individual plates. Spoon pasta salad over lettuce. Roll ham slices and set on plates. Garnish with mint sprigs. Makes 4 to 6 servings.

Per serving: 366 calories (13% fat, 63% carbohydrates, 24% protein), 5 g total fat (2 g saturated fat), 58 g carbohydrates, 22 g protein, 27 mg cholesterol, 831 mg sodium

Orzo with Spinach & Pine Nuts

Preparation time: About 20 minutes
Cooking time: About 15 minutes

You can make this salad with orzo, riso, tiny pasta shells, or any other favorite small shape.

8	ounces dry orzo or tiny shell-shaped pasta
2	tablespoons pine nuts
1	tablespoon olive oil
½	cup minced red onion
4	ounces stemmed spinach leaves, rinsed and chopped
2	medium-size pear-shaped (Roma-type) tomatoes (about 6 oz. *total*), seeded and diced
3	ounces feta cheese, crumbled
¼	cup chopped parsley
	Pepper

In a 5- to 6-quart pan, cook orzo in about 3 quarts boiling water until just tender to bite (about 5 minutes); or cook according to package directions. Drain, rinse with cold water until cool, and drain again.

Toast pine nuts in a medium-size frying pan over medium heat until golden (3 to 5 minutes), stirring often. Pour out of pan and set aside.

Heat oil in pan. Add onion; cook, stirring often, until soft (about 5 minutes). Add spinach and cook, stirring, just until wilted (about 2 more minutes).

In a large bowl, gently mix pasta, pine nuts, and spinach mixture. Add tomatoes, cheese, and parsley. Mix again; season to taste with pepper. If made ahead, cover and refrigerate for up to 4 hours. Serve at room temperature. Makes 6 servings.

Per serving: 229 calories (29% fat, 56% carbohydrates, 15% protein), 8 g total fat (3 g saturated fat), 32 g carbohydrates, 9 g protein, 13 mg cholesterol, 181 mg sodium

Wild rice, native to the northern Great Lakes region, is now grown in the Sacramento and San Joaquin valleys of California. This cultivated variety has the rich, nutty flavor and firm texture of truly "wild" wild rice, but its grains are larger.

Spiced Pork & Orange Salad

Preparation time: About 45 minutes
Cooking time: About 5 minutes

Bright green spinach leaves frame this warm main-dish salad of quick-cooked pork tenderloin in a cilantro-lime dressing.

Cilantro Dressing (recipe follows)
5 **large oranges (about 3 lbs. *total*)**
About 36 large spinach leaves, rinsed and crisped
1 **teaspoon salad oil**
1 **pound pork tenderloin or boneless pork loin, trimmed of fat and silvery membranes and cut into ½-inch-wide strips**
1 **tablespoon minced garlic**
1 **teaspoon *each* chili powder and dry oregano**
1 **teaspoon reduced-sodium soy sauce**
Cilantro sprigs

Prepare Cilantro Dressing; set aside. Cut peel and all white membrane from oranges; then cut oranges crosswise into thin slices. Arrange a fourth each of the spinach leaves and orange slices on each of 4 individual plates.

Heat oil in a wide frying pan over high heat. Add pork, garlic, chili powder, and oregano. Cook, stirring, until pork is no longer pink in center; cut to test (about 5 minutes).

Pour Cilantro Dressing and soy sauce into pan; stir to scrape browned bits free. Spoon hot pork mixture equally over oranges. Garnish with cilantro sprigs. Makes 4 servings.

Cilantro Dressing. In a small bowl, stir together ½ cup **lime juice**, 2 tablespoons **sugar**, and ¼ cup chopped **cilantro**.

Per serving: 307 calories (14% fat, 51% carbohydrates, 35% protein), 5 g total fat (1 g saturated fat), 41 g carbohydrates, 28 g protein, 74 mg cholesterol, 174 mg sodium

Cool Curry Turkey Salad

Preparation time: About 30 minutes
Chilling time: At least 1 hour

Accompanied by slender wedges of honeydew melon, this piquant turkey-rice salad makes a tempting main dish for a warm evening.

1 **tablespoon salad oil**
1 **tablespoon *each* minced fresh ginger and curry powder**
2 **cups diced cooked turkey or chicken**
2½ **cups cold cooked rice**
1 **cup plain nonfat yogurt**
¾ **cup thinly sliced green onions**
½ **cup thinly sliced water chestnuts**
¼ **teaspoon salt**
1 **small honeydew melon (about 2½ lbs.), seeded, cut into slender wedges, and peeled**
Romaine lettuce leaves, rinsed and crisped
Lime wedges

Heat oil in a medium-size frying pan over medium heat. Add ginger and curry powder. Cook, stirring, just until seasonings are lightly browned (about 1 minute). Remove from heat and let cool slightly.

In a 2-quart bowl, combine ginger–curry powder mixture, turkey, rice, yogurt, ½ cup of the onions, water chestnuts, and salt; mix lightly to blend. Cover and refrigerate for at least 1 hour or up to 3 hours.

Just before serving, arrange melon wedges on one side of a platter. Line other side of platter with lettuce leaves; mound turkey salad atop lettuce. Garnish with lime wedges and remaining ¼ cup onions. Makes 6 servings.

Per serving: 247 calories (18% fat, 52% carbohydrates, 30% protein), 5 g total fat (1 g saturated fat), 32 g carbohydrates, 18 g protein, 37 mg cholesterol, 167 mg sodium

Chicken Salad with Kumquats

Preparation time: About 30 minutes
Cooking time: About 5 minutes
Standing time: About 20 minutes

Inspired of the cuisine of Vietnam, this light main dish is a refreshingly different version of the popular chicken-and-fruit salad.

1½   pounds chicken breast halves, skinned
      Ginger-Mint Dressing (recipe follows)
¾   cup kumquats, thinly sliced, seeds and ends discarded
1   small cucumber, cut in half lengthwise, then thinly sliced crosswise
16   Belgian endive spears or 8 large radicchio leaves, rinsed and crisped
      Mint sprigs (optional)

In a 5- to 6-quart pan, bring about 3 quarts water to a boil over high heat. Rinse chicken and add to water; return to a boil. Then cover pan tightly, remove from heat, and let stand until meat in thickest part is no longer pink; cut to test (about 20 minutes). If chicken is not done after 20 minutes, return it to water, cover pan, and let stand longer, checking at 2- to 3-minute intervals. Remove chicken from water and let cool; then tear meat into shreds and discard bones. (At this point, you may cover and refrigerate until next day.)

Prepare Ginger-Mint Dressing. Add kumquats to bowl with dressing; mix gently. Mix in cucumber and chicken. On each of 4 individual plates, place 4 endive spears or 2 radicchio leaves; top equally with chicken mixture. Garnish with mint sprigs, if desired. Makes 4 servings.

Ginger-Mint Dressing. In a large bowl, combine ½ cup **lemon juice,** ¼ cup finely shredded **fresh mint** or 2 tablespoons dry mint, 2 tablespoons *each* **water** and minced **crystallized ginger,** 2½ teaspoons **sugar,** and 1 tablespoon **fish sauce** (*nam pla* or *nuoc mam*) or reduced-sodium soy sauce.

Per serving: 211 calories (9% fat, 39% carbohydrates, 52% protein), 2 g total fat (0.5 g saturated fat), 21 g carbohydrates, 28 g protein, 65 mg cholesterol, 90 mg sodium

Chicken Salad in Cantaloupe Halves

Preparation time: About 25 minutes

These individual salads are just right for a warm-weather brunch or lunch. You might complete the meal with warm bran muffins.

1   medium-size yellow bell pepper (about 6 oz.), seeded and finely chopped
1   medium-size firm-ripe papaya (about 1 lb.), peeled, seeded, and cut into ⅜-inch cubes
3   cups shredded cooked chicken
¼   cup minced cilantro
2   tablespoons drained capers
2   teaspoons grated lime peel
¼   cup *each* lime juice and orange juice
      Salt and pepper
2   small cantaloupes (about 2¼ lbs. *each*)
      Lime wedges

In a large bowl, combine bell pepper, papaya, chicken, cilantro, and capers. (At this point, you may cover and refrigerate for up to 4 hours.)

In a small bowl, stir together lime peel, lime juice, and orange juice. Pour juice mixture over chicken mixture; stir to combine. Season to taste with salt and pepper.

To serve, cut each melon in half; scoop out and discard seeds. If necessary, trim a thin slice from the base of each melon half so it sits steadily. Spoon chicken salad into melon halves; garnish with lime wedges. Makes 4 servings.

Per serving: 339 calories (22% fat, 39% carbohydrates, 39% protein), 9 g total fat (2 g saturated fat), 34 g carbohydrates, 34 g protein, 93 mg cholesterol, 229 mg sodium

Hollowed-out fruits and vegetables make attractive—and generally edible—containers for many types of salads. Mound pasta salad in a scooped-out tomato half; offer rice salad in a slender cucumber shell. Present a fresh fruit medley in a pineapple boat. Or spoon tuna salad into a seeded red bell pepper half.

Chinese Noodle Salad with Five-spice Chicken

30 MINUTES OR LESS

Preparation time: About 15 minutes
Cooking time: 8 to 11 minutes

Asian flavors star in this handsome entrée: both the cool pasta and the hot grilled chicken are seasoned with soy sauce, sesame oil, and fragrant five-spice.

	Five-spice Dressing (recipe follows)
10	**ounces (about 3 cups; part of a 14-oz. package) fresh Chinese-style noodles**
½	**cup coarsely chopped cilantro**
1	**tablespoon grated fresh ginger**
½	**teaspoon grated lemon peel**
4	**boneless, skinless chicken breast halves (about 1½ lbs. *total*)**
4	**to 6 cups lightly packed stemmed spinach leaves, rinsed and crisped**
¼	**cup thinly sliced green onions**

Prepare Five-spice Dressing and set aside.

In a 5- to 6-quart pan, cook noodles in about 3 quarts boiling water until just tender to bite (2 to 3 minutes); or cook according to package directions. Drain, rinse with cold water until cool, and drain again. Transfer to a large bowl. Add ¼ cup of the Five-spice Dressing; then add cilantro, ginger, and lemon peel. Mix gently and set aside.

Rinse chicken, pat dry, and place on a lightly oiled grill 4 to 6 inches above a solid bed of medium-hot coals. Cook, turning once and basting lightly with some of the remaining dressing, until meat in thickest part is no longer pink; cut to test (6 to 8 minutes). Place chicken on a carving board and cut into ½-inch-wide slices.

Line 4 individual plates with spinach. Top with noodles and chicken; drizzle with any remaining dressing, then sprinkle with onions. Makes 4 servings.

Five-spice Dressing. In a bowl, stir together 2 tablespoons **seasoned rice vinegar** (or 2 tablespoons unseasoned rice vinegar plus 1 teaspoon sugar), 1 tablespoon *each* **reduced-sodium soy sauce** and **lemon juice**, 1 clove **garlic** (minced or pressed), ½ teaspoon **Chinese five-spice powder** (or ⅛ teaspoon *each* ground cloves, crushed anise seeds, ground cinnamon, and ground ginger), 1 tablespoon **Oriental sesame oil,** and 2 tablespoons **salad oil.**

Per serving: 525 calories (25% fat, 35% carbohydrates, 40% protein), 14 g total fat (2 g saturated fat), 47 g carbohydrates, 52 g protein, 182 mg cholesterol, 528 mg sodium

Spinach & Shrimp Salad with Warm Mustard Dressing

NATURALLY LOW IN FAT

Preparation time: About 20 minutes
Cooking time: About 3 minutes

The ever-popular wilted spinach and bacon salad provided the inspiration for this recipe. But our salad is considerably leaner than the traditional dish: shrimp replace the bacon, and the tangy dressing is made without fat.

12	**cups firmly packed stemmed spinach leaves, rinsed and crisped**
12	**ounces small cooked shrimp**
1	**teaspoon cornstarch**
1	**tablespoon sugar**
1	**tablespoon unseasoned rice vinegar**
¼	**cup low-sodium chicken broth or water**
⅓	**cup Dijon mustard**
2	**tablespoons minced fresh dill or 1½ teaspoons dry dill weed**

Cut spinach leaves into ⅜-inch-wide strips, then place in a wide, shallow bowl and top with shrimp. (At this point, you may cover and refrigerate for up to 4 hours.)

In a 1- to 1½-quart pan, blend cornstarch and sugar. Stir in vinegar, broth, and mustard. Bring to a boil over high heat, stirring; then stir in dill. Pour hot dressing over salad; mix gently and serve immediately. Makes 6 to 8 servings.

Per serving: 109 calories (15% fat, 33% carbohydrates, 52% protein), 2 g total fat (0.3 g saturated fat), 10 g carbohydrates, 15 g protein, 95 mg cholesterol, 584 mg sodium

LIGHT DRESSINGS

It's a cinch to whip up a salad dressing that's sophisticated in flavor but innocent of fat. Go light on oil and mayonnaise; focus instead on flavor-filled ingredients such as citrus juices, fruity vinegars, and low-fat yogurt and other dairy products. Experiment with sprightly seasonings, too—spices, fresh and dried herbs, and piquant mustard.

GARLIC BUTTERMILK DRESSING

Preparation time: About 5 minutes

½ **cup low-fat buttermilk**

1 **tablespoon seasoned rice vinegar (or 1 tablespoon white wine vinegar plus ½ teaspoon sugar)**

2 **teaspoons Dijon mustard**

¼ **teaspoon *each* salt and pepper**

3 **green onions, thinly sliced**

1 **clove garlic, minced or pressed**

In a small bowl, stir together buttermilk, vinegar, mustard, salt, pepper, onions, and garlic. If made ahead, cover and refrigerate for up to 1 day. Before using dressing, stir to blend well. Makes about ⅔ cup.

Per tablespoon: 9 calories (16% fat, 63% carbohydrates, 21% protein), 0.2 g total fat (0.1 g saturated fat), 1 g carbohydrates, 0.5 g protein, 0.5 mg cholesterol, 127 mg sodium

CREAMY HERB DRESSING

Preparation time: About 5 minutes

1 **cup plain nonfat yogurt**

3 **tablespoons balsamic vinegar**

1 **teaspoon chopped fresh oregano or ¼ teaspoon dry oregano**

1 **teaspoon Dijon mustard**

2 **to 3 teaspoons sugar**

In a small bowl, stir together yogurt, vinegar, oregano, mustard, and sugar. If made ahead, cover and refrigerate for up to 3 days. Before using dressing, stir to blend well. Makes about 1¼ cups.

Per tablespoon: 9 calories (3% fat, 68% carbohydrates, 29% protein), 0 g total fat (0 g saturated fat), 2 g carbohydrates, 0.6 g protein, 0.2 mg cholesterol, 16 mg sodium

PIMENTO DRESSING

Preparation time: About 5 minutes

¼ **cup dry white wine**

1 **teaspoon Dijon mustard**

2 **tablespoons thinly sliced green onion**

1 **tablespoon white wine vinegar**

1 **clove garlic, minced or pressed**

1 **jar (about 2 oz.) diced pimentos, drained**
   Salt and pepper

In a small bowl, stir together wine and mustard. Then stir in onion, vinegar, garlic, and pimentos. Season to taste with salt and pepper. If made ahead, cover and refrigerate for up to 1 day. Before using dressing , stir to blend well. Makes about ⅔ cup.

Per tablespoon: 7 calories (11% fat, 77% carbohydrates, 12% protein), 0 g total fat (0 g saturated fat), 0.6 g carbohydrates, 0.1 g protein, 0 mg cholesterol, 16 mg sodium

CITRUS DRESSING

Preparation time: About 15 minutes

2 **teaspoons grated orange peel**

½ **cup orange juice**

2 **tablespoons white wine vinegar**

2 **tablespoons minced fresh basil or 2 teaspoons dry basil**

1 **jalapeño chile, seeded and minced**

1 **tablespoon honey**

2 **teaspoons Dijon mustard**

1 **teaspoon ground cumin**

2 **cloves garlic, minced or pressed**
   Salt

In a small bowl, stir together orange peel, orange juice, vinegar, basil, chile, honey, mustard, cumin, and garlic. Season to taste with salt. If made ahead, cover and refrigerate for up to 4 hours. Before using dressing, stir to blend well. Makes about ¾ cup.

Per tablespoon: 14 calories (5% fat, 90% carbohydrates, 5% protein), 0.1 g total fat (0 g saturated fat), 3 g carbohydrates, 0.2 g protein, 0 mg cholesterol, 26 mg sodium

Thai Noodle Salad Buffet

Preparation time: About 1 hour
Cooking time: About 10 minutes
Standing time: About 35 minutes

Guests assemble their own servings of this zesty main dish from an array of fresh and spicy ingredients: crisp vegetables, thin angel hair or Asian rice noodles, shredded chicken, and a gingery sesame dressing. Follow the meal with a dessert of cooling fresh pineapple.

4	chicken breast halves (about 2 lbs. *total*), skinned
1	pound dry angel hair pasta (capellini) or thin rice noodles (*mai fun*)
2	teaspoons Oriental sesame oil or salad oil
	Spicy Sesame Dressing (recipe follows)
1	large English cucumber (about 1 lb.), cut into thin slivers
8	to 12 ounces bean sprouts
¾	cup thinly sliced green onions
½	cup chopped fresh basil
½	cup finely chopped salted dry-roasted peanuts
¾	cup chopped cilantro
	Lemon wedges (optional)

In a 5- to 6-quart pan, bring about 3 quarts water to a boil over high heat. Rinse chicken and add to water; return to a boil. Then cover pan tightly, remove from heat, and let stand until meat in thickest part is no longer pink; cut to test (about 20 minutes). If chicken is not done after 20 minutes, return it to water, cover pan, and let stand longer, checking at 2- to 3-minute intervals. Remove chicken from water and let cool; then tear meat into shreds and discard bones.

While chicken is cooling, return water to a boil over high heat. Add pasta and cook until just tender to bite (about 3 minutes); or cook according to package directions. Drain, then immerse in a bowl of cold water. Add oil to water. Let pasta stand until cool (about 15 minutes); then lift from water in small handfuls, draining briefly. Loosely coil each handful of pasta; set coils on a wide platter, stacking if necessary.

Prepare Spicy Sesame Dressing. Arrange chicken, cucumber, bean sprouts, onions, and basil in separate groups around pasta on platter. Arrange peanuts, cilantro, and lemon wedges (if used) in small bowls. To assemble each salad, place a few pasta coils on an individual plate. Add other ingredients to taste; spoon on Spicy Sesame Dressing to taste. Makes 6 servings.

Spicy Sesame Dressing. In a small bowl, combine ¾ cup **unseasoned rice vinegar** or white wine vinegar; ½ cup **reduced-sodium soy sauce;** 3 tablespoons **sugar;** 2 tablespoons *each* **Oriental sesame oil** and minced **fresh ginger;** 1 to 2 teaspoons **crushed red pepper flakes;** and 2 cloves **garlic** (minced or pressed). Stir until sugar is dissolved.

Per serving: 591 calories (23% fat, 51% carbohydrates, 26% protein), 15 g total fat (2 g saturated fat), 76 g carbohydrates, 39 g protein, 57 mg cholesterol, 981 mg sodium

Shrimp & Jicama with Chile Vinegar

NATURALLY LOW IN FAT

Preparation time: About 35 minutes

Enjoy a taste of Mexico with this main-dish combination of shrimp, tomatillos, and crisp, fruity jicama. The oil-free dressing is hot and full of flavor.

	Chile Vinegar (recipe follows)
2	cups shredded jicama
1	pound small cooked shrimp
4	large ripe tomatoes (about 2 lbs. *total*), sliced

4   large tomatillos (about 12 oz. *total*),
     husked, rinsed, and sliced
     Cilantro sprigs

Prepare Chile Vinegar. Place jicama and shrimp in separate bowls. Add ¼ cup of the Chile Vinegar to each bowl; mix gently. Reserve remaining vinegar.

On each of 4 individual plates, arrange tomatoes and tomatillos, overlapping slices slightly. Mound jicama over or beside tomato slices. Spoon shrimp over jicama; spoon remaining Chile Vinegar over all. Garnish with cilantro sprigs. Makes 4 servings.

Chile Vinegar. In a small bowl, stir together ⅔ cup **white wine vinegar,** ¼ cup **sugar,** 2 to 3 tablespoons seeded, minced **fresh hot green chiles,** and 3 to 4 tablespoons chopped **cilantro.**

Per serving: 261 calories (8% fat, 50% carbohydrates, 42% protein), 2 g total fat (0.4 g saturated fat), 34 g carbohydrates, 28 g protein, 221 mg cholesterol, 279 mg sodium

'90s Niçoise Salad
. . . .

Preparation time: About 45 minutes
Cooking time: 30 to 35 minutes
Cooling time: About 30 minutes

In the south of France, greengrocers sell *mesclun,* a mixture of small salad greens with distinctive flavors. Many American markets now offer similar blends. Here, the mixed greens make a convenient foundation for a lightened-up version of popular *salade Niçoise.*

1¼   pounds medium-size red thin-skinned
     potatoes (*each* about 2½ inches in
     diameter), scrubbed
8   ounces slender green beans, ends
     removed
     Caper Dressing (recipe follows)
     Aïoli Crusts (recipe follows)
8   ounces mesclun or bite-size pieces of
     mixed salad greens, rinsed and crisped
3   hard-cooked large eggs, sliced
1   jar (about 7 oz.) roasted red peppers,
     drained and cut into thin strips
1   large can (about 12½ oz.) water-packed
     albacore tuna, drained and broken into
     chunks
½   cup Niçoise olives

Place unpeeled potatoes in a 4- to 5-quart pan and add enough water to cover. Bring to a boil over high heat; then reduce heat, partially cover, and boil gently until potatoes are tender when pierced (25 to 30 minutes). Lift from pan with a slotted spoon and let stand until cool (about 30 minutes). Meanwhile, return water in pan to a boil over high heat. Add beans and cook, uncovered, until tender-crisp to bite (2 to 3 minutes). Drain, immerse in cold water until cool, and drain again.

Prepare Caper Dressing and Aïoli Crusts.

Cut cooled potatoes into 1½-inch chunks. To assemble salads, divide greens evenly among 4 individual plates; top greens equally with potatoes, beans, eggs, peppers, tuna, and olives. Accompany each salad with 3 Aïoli Crusts; offer Caper Dressing to add to taste. Makes 4 servings.

Caper Dressing. In a small bowl, stir together 6 tablespoons **cider vinegar,** 1 tablespoon **extra-virgin olive oil** or salad oil, 1 tablespoon drained **capers,** 1½ teaspoons **Dijon mustard,** 1 teaspoon minced **fresh thyme** or ½ teaspoon dry thyme, and ¼ teaspoon **sugar.**

Aïoli Crusts. In a small bowl, stir together ⅓ cup **reduced-calorie mayonnaise,** 2 cloves **garlic** (minced or pressed), and 1 tablespoon grated **Parmesan cheese.** Spread mixture equally over twelve ½-inch-thick **French bread baguette slices.** Place slices, topping side up, in a shallow baking pan; sprinkle with 1 tablespoon grated **Parmesan cheese.** Broil slices 4 to 6 inches below heat until topping is browned (about 4 minutes).

Per serving: 651 calories (28% fat, 48% carbohydrates, 24% protein), 20 g total fat (5 g saturated fat), 78 g carbohydrates, 40 g protein, 202 mg cholesterol, 1,265 mg sodium

---

***Jicama** is a popular Mexican root vegetable that looks like a giant brown turnip. Its thick, rough skin conceals crisp, white, slightly sweet flesh that's reminiscent of water chestnuts in both flavor and texture. Serve it raw as an appetizer or snack (with lime and salt or other dips), or cut it into matchstick pieces or thin slices to include in salads of all types. Jicama is low in fat and rich in potassium; it contains some vitamin C.*

Party Paella Salad

Preparation time: About 1¼ hours
Cooking time: 45 minutes to 1 hour
Cooling & chilling time: At least 2½ hours

Generously proportioned, this main-dish seafood salad makes a great centerpiece for a summer party—and you can prepare it up to a day in advance. Serve the salad with chewy sourdough bread and a dry white wine; offer juicy melon wedges for dessert.

3	cups *each* low-sodium chicken broth and water
1½	cups dry white wine
1	dry bay leaf
2	pounds large raw shrimp (31 to 35 per lb.), shelled and deveined
1	pound bay scallops
24	to 36 small hard-shell clams in shell, scrubbed
	Caper & Garlic Dressing (recipe follows)
2	tablespoons olive oil
2	large onions, chopped
2	cloves garlic, minced or pressed
4	cups long-grain white rice
⅛	teaspoon powdered saffron or saffron threads (if using saffron threads, grind with a mortar and pestle before measuring)
2	packages (about 9 oz. *each*) frozen artichoke hearts, thawed
1	jar (about 5 oz.) or ½ cup pimento-stuffed green olives
2	large red bell peppers (about 1 lb. *total*), seeded and chopped
1	pound (about 3 cups) cherry tomatoes, cut into halves
1	package (about 1 lb.) frozen tiny peas, thawed

In a 5- to 6-quart pan, combine broth, water, wine, and bay leaf. Bring to a boil over high heat; then stir in shrimp. Cover pan tightly, remove from heat, and let stand until shrimp are just opaque in center; cut to test (about 3 minutes). With a slotted spoon, transfer shrimp to a large bowl.

Rinse and drain scallops. Return broth in pan to a boil; add scallops. Cover pan tightly, remove from heat, and let stand until scallops are just opaque in center; cut to test (about 3 minutes). With a slotted spoon, transfer scallops to bowl with shrimp.

Return broth to a boil. Add clams; reduce heat, cover, and boil gently until shells pop open (5 to 10 minutes). With a slotted spoon, transfer clams to bowl with shrimp and scallops; discard any unopened clams. Set seafood aside.

Pour broth into a 2-quart measure, leaving gritty sediment behind in pan; then rinse pan thoroughly, discarding grit. Measure broth; you need 7½ cups. If necessary, add water to make 7½ cups, or boil broth to reduce to 7½ cups. Prepare Caper & Garlic Dressing, using 1 cup of the broth; set remaining 6½ cups broth aside.

Mix 1 cup of the Caper & Garlic Dressing with seafood. Cover and refrigerate until cold (at least 2 hours) or for up to 1 day, stirring occasionally.

To rinsed pan, add oil, onions, and garlic. Cook over medium heat, stirring often, until onions are soft (6 to 8 minutes). Add rice; cook, stirring, until grains look opaque (about 5 minutes). Add saffron and remaining 6½ cups broth. Bring to a boil; then boil gently, uncovered, until almost all broth has been absorbed (8 to 10 minutes). Then reduce heat to very low, cover, and cook until rice is tender to bite (about 15 minutes). Let rice stand, uncovered, until cool (about 30 minutes), stirring several times. Then stir in artichokes, olives, bell peppers, and remaining Caper & Garlic Dressing. Mix gently. (At this point, you may cover and refrigerate for up to 1 day.)

Up to 6 hours before serving, gently stir tomatoes and peas into rice. Mound rice mixture on a large platter. With a slotted spoon, transfer seafood onto rice; spoon dressing left in bowl over all. Cover and refrigerate until ready to serve. Makes 10 to 12 servings.

Caper & Garlic Dressing. In a bowl, stir together 1 cup *each* **white wine vinegar** and **reserved broth from seafood**; ⅓ cup **olive oil**; 3 tablespoons drained **capers**; 1 tablespoon minced **fresh oregano** or 1 teaspoon dry oregano; ¾ to 1 teaspoon **crushed red pepper flakes**; and 2 cloves **garlic**, minced or pressed.

Per serving: 570 calories (22% fat, 53% carbohydrates, 25% protein), 14 g total fat (2 g saturated fat), 74 g carbohydrates, 36 g protein, 129 mg cholesterol, 660 mg sodium

Smoked Trout & Onion Salad

Preparation time: About 15 minutes
Standing time: About 15 minutes

Cool greens, crisp red onion, and smoked seafood combine in an appetizing no-cook entrée. Stir up a smooth dill-horseradish dressing to spoon over individual servings. To complete the meal, slice a crusty loaf and pour glasses of white wine or iced tea.

1   medium-size red onion, thinly sliced
¼   cup distilled white vinegar
2   cups *each* water and ice cubes
     Dill Dressing (recipe follows)
1   large head romaine lettuce (about 1¼ lbs.), separated into leaves, rinsed, and crisped
12   ounces boneless, skinless smoked trout fillets, torn into ½-inch pieces
     Dill sprigs (optional)

Place onion slices in a deep bowl and cover with water. With your hands, squeeze slices until they are almost limp. Drain, rinse, and drain again.

In same bowl, combine onion slices, vinegar, and the 2 cups *each* water and ice cubes; let stand until onion is crisp (about 15 minutes). Drain onion well, then lift to a large bowl.

Prepare Dill Dressing; set aside.

Line each of 4 individual plates with 2 or 3 large lettuce leaves. Cut remaining lettuce crosswise into ¼-inch-wide strips.

Add lettuce strips and trout to bowl with onion; mix gently. Mound equal portions of salad on each plate; spoon Dill Dressing evenly over salads. Garnish salads with dill sprigs, if desired. Makes 4 servings.

Dill Dressing. In a small bowl, stir together ½ cup **reduced-fat sour cream,** 1 tablespoon **lemon juice,** 2 teaspoons **prepared horseradish,** and 1 teaspoon chopped **fresh dill** or ½ teaspoon dry dill weed.

Per serving: 193 calories (24% fat, 22% carbohydrates, 54% protein), 5 g total fat (2 g saturated fat), 11 g carbohydrates, 26 g protein, 75 mg cholesterol, 668 mg sodium

Veracruz Fish Salad

Preparation time: About 20 minutes
Baking time: About 12 minutes
Chilling time: At least 2 hours

Keep this chilled salad in mind for a summer lunch or dinner. Tomatoes, olives, and capers are tossed with lime juice and chunks of mahi mahi for a refreshing Latin-influenced meal.

2   pounds mahi mahi or rockfish fillets
4   large tomatoes (about 2 lbs. *total*), coarsely diced
⅔   cup lime juice
3   cloves garlic, minced or pressed
1   cup sliced pimento-stuffed green olives
⅓   cup drained capers
½   cup thinly sliced green onions
     Salt and pepper
     About 12 large iceberg lettuce leaves
     Lime wedges

Rinse fish and pat dry. Place in a 9- by 13-inch baking dish, overlapping fillets slightly. Cover and bake in a 400° oven until just opaque but still moist in thickest part; cut to test (about 12 minutes). Let cool; then cover and refrigerate for at least 2 hours or up to 1 day.

Lift fish from pan; discard pan juices. Pull out and discard any bones. Break fish into bite-size chunks. In a large bowl, combine fish, tomatoes, lime juice, garlic, olives, capers, and onions; mix gently. Season to taste with salt and pepper.

To serve, line a serving bowl with lettuce leaves; spoon in salad. Garnish with lime wedges. Makes 8 servings.

Per serving: 152 calories (20% fat, 22% carbohydrates, 58% protein), 3 g total fat (0.5 g saturated fat), 8 g carbohydrates, 23 g protein, 83 mg cholesterol, 670 mg sodium

MEATS

*B*eef, lamb, pork, veal—can you still serve these favorites after you've switched to a low-fat eating scheme? Will you ever again experience the joy of cutting into a juicy roast or spooning up a succulent stew? Indeed you will—and here's how. First, shop wisely. Choose the leanest cuts the meat counter has to offer, then trim away any remaining fat before you start to cook. Second, learn the low-fat cooking methods presented in our recipes: techniques such as grilling, broiling, braising, oven-stewing, and the curiously named but wonderfully effective process called "sweating." Third, keep servings of meat to a 3-ounce cooked portion—and complement the main course with one of the wholesome vegetable or grain dishes you'll find on pages 156 to 171.

Grilled Orange-Coriander Steak

Preparation time: About 10 minutes
Marinating time: At least 4 hours
Grilling time: About 8 minutes

Top round is at its juicy, full-flavored best when it's soaked in a tart orange marinade, then grilled just until rare. Thinly sliced and sauced with some of the marinade, it's a main dish that's sure to please the beef-eaters in your family. Potato Salad with Seed Vinaigrette (page 52) makes a delightful accompaniment.

1   teaspoon grated orange peel
¼   cup orange juice
1   medium-size onion, minced
3   cloves garlic, minced or pressed
¼   cup white wine vinegar
1½ tablespoons ground coriander
1   teaspoon *each* cracked pepper and dry basil
1½ pounds boneless beef top round (cut about 1 inch thick), trimmed of fat
    Finely shredded orange peel

In a bowl, stir together grated orange peel, orange juice, onion, garlic, vinegar, coriander, pepper, and basil. Measure out ½ cup of this marinade; cover and refrigerate until serving time.

Pour remaining marinade into a shallow bowl; add beef and turn to coat. Cover and refrigerate for at least 4 hours or up to 1 day, turning beef over occasionally.

Lift beef from marinade and drain briefly; reserve marinade. Place beef on a lightly oiled grill 4 to 6 inches above a solid bed of medium coals. Cook, turning once and basting often with marinade, until done to your liking; cut to test (about 8 minutes for rare). Meanwhile, pour reserved ½ cup marinade into a small pan. Place over low heat; heat until steaming.

To serve, thinly slice beef across the grain. Garnish with shredded orange peel; accompany with heated marinade. Makes 6 servings.

Per serving: 175 calories (22% fat, 12% carbohydrates, 66% protein), 4 g total fat (1 g saturated fat), 5 g carbohydrates, 28 g protein, 71 mg cholesterol, 54 mg sodium

Hungarian Beef Stew

MODIFIED CLASSIC

Preparation time: About 20 minutes
Cooking time: About 2 hours

Red bell pepper and a spoonful of paprika give this sturdy entrée its Hungarian character. When the stew is almost done, cook a package of eggless noodles to serve alongside.

1½ pounds boneless beef top round, trimmed of fat and cut into 1-inch cubes
1   can (about 14½ oz.) beef broth
1   clove garlic, minced or pressed
1   tablespoon sweet Hungarian paprika
3   medium-size leeks (1 to 1½ lbs. *total*)
1   large red bell pepper (about 8 oz.), seeded and cut into 1-inch squares
8   ounces small mushrooms
½   teaspoon salt
¼   teaspoon pepper
2   tablespoons port or Madeira
½   cup plain low-fat yogurt blended with 1 tablespoon cornstarch

In a wide 3½- to 4-quart pan, combine beef and ½ cup of the broth. Cover and cook over medium heat for 30 minutes. Uncover, add garlic and paprika, and continue to cook, stirring occasionally, until almost all liquid has evaporated and drippings are browned (about 30 minutes).

Meanwhile, trim and discard ends and all but 1½ inches of green tops from leeks; remove tough outer leaves. Split leeks lengthwise; rinse well, then cut crosswise into 1-inch lengths. Set aside.

Blend remaining 1¼ cups broth into stew, stirring to scrape browned bits free. Mix in leeks, bell pepper, mushrooms, salt, and pepper. Bring to a boil; reduce heat, cover, and simmer until beef is very tender when pierced (about 1 hour).

When beef is done, stir port and yogurt mixture into stew. Increase heat to medium-high and bring to a boil; then boil, stirring, until sauce is bubbly and thickened. Makes 6 servings.

Per serving: 223 calories (20% fat, 26% carbohydrates, 54% protein), 5 g total fat (2 g saturated fat), 14 g carbohydrates, 30 g protein, 66 mg cholesterol, 507 mg sodium

Citrus-seasoned Steak & Brown Rice

Preparation time: About 10 minutes
Marinating time: At least 3 hours
Cooking time: 45 to 50 minutes
Broiling time: 20 to 25 minutes

Orange juice and aromatic orange peel add a tangy accent to this pairing of rare beef and herbed brown rice. Look for top round cut in a thick slice; it may be labeled "London broil."

1	teaspoon grated orange peel
½	teaspoon dry thyme
¼	cup white wine vinegar
1	tablespoon salad oil
⅓	cup orange juice
2½	pounds boneless beef top round (cut 1½ to 2 inches thick), trimmed of fat
	Brown Rice à l'Orange (recipe follows)
	Salt
	Orange slices
	Sage sprigs

In a wide, shallow bowl, stir together orange peel, thyme, vinegar, oil, and 3 tablespoons of the orange juice. Add beef and turn to coat. Cover and refrigerate for at least 3 hours or up to 1 day, turning occasionally.

About 30 minutes before broiling beef, prepare Brown Rice à l'Orange. Lift beef from marinade and drain briefly; reserve marinade. Place beef on a rack in a broiler pan. Broil about 6 inches below heat, turning once and basting occasionally with marinade, until beef is well browned and a meat thermometer inserted in thickest part registers 120° to 125°F for rare (20 to 25 minutes).

Transfer beef to a carving board and keep warm. Skim and discard fat from pan drippings, if necessary. Pour remaining orange juice into broiler pan and stir over medium heat until blended. Season pan juices to taste with salt.

To serve, cut beef across the grain into thin slanting slices. Garnish with orange slices and sage sprigs. Serve with Brown Rice à l'Orange; offer pan juices to spoon over beef and rice. Makes 8 to 10 servings.

Brown Rice à l'Orange. In a 3- to 3½-quart pan, combine 2 cups **orange juice,** 1 cup *each* **water** and **dry white wine,** 5 **sage sprigs** (or ½ teaspoon dry sage), and 3 thin strips **orange peel** (*each* about 2 inches long).

Bring juice mixture to a boil over high heat; stir in 2 cups **long-grain brown rice.** Reduce heat, cover, and simmer until rice is tender to bite (45 to 50 minutes). Remove from heat; let stand, uncovered, for 5 minutes. Discard orange peel and sage sprigs; fluff rice with a fork.

Per serving: 348 calories (16% fat, 46% carbohydrates, 38% protein), 6 g total fat (2 g saturated fat), 39 g carbohydrates, 32 g protein, 72 mg cholesterol, 70 mg sodium

Sichuan Beef

Preparation time: About 15 minutes
Soaking time: 30 minutes
Cooking time: About 10 minutes

Carrot strips, cauliflowerets, and bamboo shoots bring color and crispness to this chile-accented beef stir-fry. Serve it over hot rice; offer fresh fruit and fortune cookies for dessert.

	Cooking Sauce (recipe follows)
8	medium-size dried shiitake mushrooms (*each* about 2 inches in diameter)
1	pound boneless beef top round, trimmed of fat
1	tablespoon salad oil
16	small dried hot red chiles
3	large carrots, cut into thin 3-inch-long strips
4	cups bite-size pieces cauliflower
2	cans (about 8 oz. *each*) sliced bamboo shoots, drained

2   cans (about 8 oz. *each*) sliced water chestnuts, drained
    Cilantro leaves

Prepare Cooking Sauce and set aside.

Soak mushrooms in warm water to cover for 30 minutes; then drain. Cut off and discard stems; squeeze caps dry, thinly slice, and set aside.

Cut beef with the grain into 1½-inch-wide strips; then cut each strip across the grain into ⅛-inch-thick slanting slices. Set aside.

Heat oil in a wok or wide frying pan over medium-high heat. Add chiles and cook, stirring, until chiles just begin to char. Remove chiles from pan; set aside.

Add beef to pan and cook, stirring, until browned (1½ to 2 minutes); remove with a slotted spoon and set aside. Add carrots, cauliflower, and mushrooms. Cook, stirring, for 1 minute; then cover and cook until carrots and cauliflower are tender-crisp to bite (about 3 minutes). Add bamboo shoots and water chestnuts; cook, stirring, for 1 more minute.

Return beef and chiles to pan. Stir Cooking Sauce, then pour into pan; cook, stirring, until sauce is bubbly and thickened. Garnish with cilantro. Makes 6 servings.

Cooking Sauce. In a small bowl, stir together 3 tablespoons **reduced-sodium soy sauce,** 1½ tablespoons **dry sherry,** 1 tablespoon **sugar,** and ¾ teaspoon **cornstarch.**

Per serving: 290 calories (24% fat, 46% carbohydrates, 30% protein), 8 g total fat (2 g saturated fat), 37 g carbohydrates, 24 g protein, 43 mg cholesterol, 383 mg sodium

Steak & Spaghetti

. . . .

Preparation time: About 15 minutes
Baking time: About 3 hours
Cooking time: 8 to 10 minutes

Here's a good busy-day dinner. Beef chunks and vegetables simmer together in the oven, demanding next to no attention from the cook. Serve the stew over hot spaghetti; round out the meal with warm bread and a salad of shredded zucchini in a low-fat dressing (see page 61).

1   pound boneless beef top round, trimmed of fat and cut into 1-inch cubes
2   to 3 tablespoons all-purpose flour
1½ cups beef broth
½   cup dry white wine
1   large onion, chopped
2   teaspoons minced or pressed garlic
1   large carrot, sliced
8   ounces mushrooms, sliced
¼   cup tomato paste
2   tablespoons chopped parsley
2   teaspoons dry oregano
1   can (about 14½ oz.) stewed tomatoes
1   pound dry spaghetti

Coat beef cubes with flour and arrange slightly apart in an ungreased shallow 3- to 3½-quart baking dish. Bake in a 500° oven for 20 minutes, then remove from oven and let cool in baking dish for about 5 minutes.

Reduce oven temperature to 350°. Gradually add broth and wine to beef in baking dish; stir to scrape browned bits free. Stir in onion, garlic, carrot, mushrooms, tomato paste, parsley, oregano, and tomatoes. Cover tightly and bake until beef is very tender when pierced (about 2½ hours), stirring once or twice.

When beef is almost done, cook spaghetti in a 6- to 8-quart pan in about 4 quarts boiling water until just tender to bite (8 to 10 minutes); or cook according to package directions. Drain well, pour onto a deep platter, and keep warm.

To serve, spoon meat and sauce over pasta. Makes 6 servings.

Per serving: 456 calories (9% fat, 65% carbohydrates, 26% protein), 4 g total fat (1 g saturated fat), 73 g carbohydrates, 30 g protein, 43 mg cholesterol, 522 mg sodium

For cooking pasta, choose a deep, capacious pan that will hold at least 4 quarts of water for each pound of pasta. Common practice notwithstanding, there's no need to add oil to the pan—vigorous boiling in plenty of water is the best way to keep spaghetti, noodles, or pieces of macaroni from clinging together or sticking to the pan.

Flemish Beef Stew

MODIFIED CLASSIC

Preparation time: About 15 minutes
Cooking time: About 2 hours

Based on the classic Belgian *carbonnade*, this robust stew features dark beer, herbs, and plenty of onions. The dish is traditionally served with mashed potatoes, but it's good with toasted sourdough bread and Brussels sprouts, too.

- 2 **pounds boneless beef round tip, trimmed of fat and cut into 1½-inch cubes**
- 2 **bottles or cans (about 12 oz. *each*) dark beer, ale, or stout**
- 3 **large onions, thinly sliced**
- ½ **teaspoon pepper**
- 2 **tablespoons all-purpose flour**
- 1 **large clove garlic, minced or pressed**
- 1 **dry bay leaf**
- 1 **teaspoon dry thyme**
- ⅓ **cup finely chopped parsley**
- 1½ **tablespoons red wine vinegar**
   Salt

In a wide 3½- to 4-quart pan, combine beef and ½ cup of the beer. Cover and cook over medium heat for 30 minutes. Uncover, add onions and pepper, and continue to cook, stirring occasionally, until almost all liquid has evaporated and onions are browned (30 to 35 minutes).

Add flour and stir gently for 30 seconds. Gradually blend in remaining beer, stirring to scrape browned bits free. Stir in garlic, bay leaf, thyme, and all but 1 tablespoon of the parsley. Reduce heat, cover, and simmer until beef is very tender when pierced (about 1 hour). Stir in vinegar and season to taste with salt. Sprinkle with reserved 1 tablespoon parsley. Makes 8 servings.

Per serving: 198 calories (21% fat, 26% carbohydrates, 53% protein), 4 g total fat (1 g saturated fat), 13 g carbohydrates, 26 g protein, 68 mg cholesterol, 79 mg sodium

Use a potato masher or an electric mixer to mash potatoes. A food processor breaks up the potatoes' starch buds, and that makes for gluey potatoes.

Rich Brown Braised Beef

Preparation time: About 10 minutes
Cooking time: 1½ to 1¾ hours

The sauce for this savory-sweet stew owes its appetizingly rich color to an unusual combination of seasonings, including soy sauce, red wine vinegar, paprika, and grape jelly.

- 2 **pounds boneless beef round tip, trimmed of fat and cut into 1-inch cubes**
- 2 **cloves garlic, minced or pressed**
- 1 **tablespoon salad oil**
- 2 **cups water**
- 2 **tablespoons *each* low-sodium soy sauce, red wine vinegar, and grape jelly**
- ¼ **teaspoon *each* pepper, paprika, and dry oregano**
- 4 **drops liquid hot pepper seasoning**
- 1 **pound dry medium-wide eggless noodles**
- 1½ **teaspoons cornstarch blended with 1 tablespoon cold water**
   Salt
   Chopped parsley

In a 3- to 3½-quart pan, combine beef, garlic, oil, and ½ cup of the water. Cover and cook over medium heat for 30 minutes. Uncover and continue to cook, stirring occasionally, until almost all liquid has evaporated and drippings are browned (15 to 20 minutes). Stir in soy sauce, vinegar, jelly, pepper, paprika, oregano, hot pepper seasoning, and remaining 1½ cups water. Bring to a boil; then reduce heat, cover, and simmer until beef is very tender when pierced (about 45 minutes).

When beef is almost done, cook noodles in a 6- to 8-quart pan in about 4 quarts boiling water until just tender to bite (7 to 9 minutes); or cook according to package directions. Drain well, pour onto a deep platter, and keep warm.

Gradually stir cornstarch mixture into stew. Increase heat to medium and cook, stirring occasionally, just until sauce is bubbly and thickened. Season to taste with salt. Spoon stew over noodles; sprinkle with parsley. Makes 8 servings.

Per serving: 373 calories (18% fat, 48% carbohydrates, 34% protein), 7 g total fat (2 g saturated fat), 44 g carbohydrates, 32 g protein, 68 mg cholesterol, 236 mg sodium

Cranberry-Port Pot Roast

Preparation time: About 15 minutes
Baking time: About 3¾ hours

Perfect for a winter evening, this chunky beef roast bakes to tenderness in a savory port wine sauce. For color and sweet-tart flavor, cook tiny onions and bright cranberries along with the meat.

1	beef eye of round roast or rump roast (3½ to 4 lbs.), trimmed of fat
1	tablespoon salad oil
1	can (about 14½ oz.) beef broth
1¾	cups port
⅓	cup firmly packed brown sugar
2	packages (about 10 oz. *each*) frozen tiny onions
2	cups fresh or frozen cranberries
6	cups hot cooked eggless noodles
2	tablespoons cornstarch blended with 3 tablespoons cold water
	Salt and pepper

Rub beef all over with oil, place in a 10- by 14-inch roasting pan, and bake in a 450° oven until well browned (about 45 minutes), turning often. Then reduce oven temperature to 400°. Add broth and port to pan, cover tightly, and bake for 1½ hours.

Mix sugar and onions into pan juices; cover tightly and bake for 1 more hour. Stir in cranberries; cover tightly and bake until beef is tender when pierced (about 30 more minutes).

Transfer beef to a platter; spoon noodles alongside. With a slotted spoon, ladle onions and cranberries onto noodles; keep warm. Skim and discard fat from pan juices; then bring juices to a boil over high heat. Stir in cornstarch mixture; cook, stirring, until sauce is bubbly and thickened. Season to taste with salt and pepper, then pour into a small bowl.

To serve, thinly slice beef across the grain. Accompany beef and noodles with sauce. Makes 10 to 12 servings.

Per serving: 368 calories (21% fat, 37% carbohydrates, 42% protein), 9 g total fat (3 g saturated fat), 34 g carbohydrates, 37 g protein, 84 mg cholesterol, 234 mg sodium

Roast Beef with Couscous

Preparation time: About 10 minutes
Cooking time: About 45 minutes

For a company-pleasing main dish, coat a lean beef roast with red wine, hoisin sauce, garlic, and coriander; then use the basting sauce and meat juices to flavor the accompanying couscous.

1	boneless beef triangle tip (tri-tip) or top round roast (about 1¾ lbs.), trimmed of fat
½	cup dry red wine
2	tablespoons hoisin sauce
2	cloves garlic, minced or pressed
½	teaspoon ground coriander
	About 2¼ cups beef broth
1½	cups couscous
1	package (about 10 oz.) frozen tiny peas, thawed
¼	cup sliced green onions
	Parsley sprigs

Place beef in an 8- by 12-inch roasting pan. In a small bowl, stir together wine, hoisin sauce, garlic, and coriander; brush evenly over beef. Roast in a 425° oven until a meat thermometer inserted in thickest part registers 135°F for rare (about 35 minutes; after 25 minutes, check temperature every 5 minutes). During roasting, brush beef 4 times with wine mixture. If pan juices begin to burn, add 4 to 6 tablespoons water to pan and stir to scrape browned bits free.

Transfer beef to a carving board; keep warm. Combine any remaining wine mixture and all the pan juices, then measure; add enough broth to make 2¼ cups total. Pour broth mixture into roasting pan; bring to a boil over medium-high heat, stirring to scrape browned bits free. Add couscous; return to a boil, stirring. Remove pan from heat, cover tightly with foil, and let stand until liquid has been absorbed (about 5 minutes). Stir in peas, onions, and any juices that have accumulated around beef. To serve, thinly slice beef across the grain. Arrange beef and couscous mixture on a platter; garnish with parsley sprigs. Makes 4 to 6 servings.

Per serving: 466 calories (14% fat, 47% carbohydrates, 39% protein), 7 g total fat (2 g saturated fat), 53 g carbohydrates, 45 g protein, 95 mg cholesterol, 758 mg sodium

Marinated Daube of Beef

MODIFIED CLASSIC

Preparation time: About 30 minutes
Marinating time: At least 8 hours
Cooking time: 2¾ to 3 hours

Here's a low-fat version of a classic wine-marinated French beef stew. Olives and orange peel lend unusual flavor to the vegetable-enriched mushroom sauce. Serve the dish with steamed or baked new potatoes.

2	pounds beef eye of round, trimmed of fat and cut into 1-inch cubes
1	cup dry red wine
2	teaspoons olive oil
¼	cup chopped parsley
1	dry bay leaf
½	teaspoon dry thyme
¼	teaspoon ground white pepper
2	strips orange peel (*each* about ½ by 3 inches)
2	medium-size onions, thinly sliced
1½	cups water
1	clove garlic, minced or pressed
4	medium-size carrots, cut into ¼-inch-thick slanting slices
3	medium-size tomatoes (1 to 1¼ lbs. *total*), peeled and cut into thin wedges
8	ounces mushrooms, cut into quarters
⅓	cup Niçoise or pitted ripe olives
1	tablespoon cornstarch blended with 2 tablespoons cold water
	Salt
12	small thin-skinned potatoes (*each* 1½ to 2 inches in diameter), steamed or baked

In a 2- to 3-quart bowl, combine beef, wine, oil, parsley, bay leaf, thyme, white pepper, and orange peel. Cover and refrigerate for at least 8 hours, turning occasionally.

Lift beef from marinade and drain briefly; reserve marinade. Place beef in a heavy 3½- to 4-quart pan and add onions, ½ cup of the water, and garlic. Cover and cook over low heat, stirring occasionally, for 30 minutes. Uncover, increase heat to medium, and continue to cook, stirring occasionally, until almost all liquid has evaporated and drippings are browned (about 25 minutes). Stir in reserved marinade and remaining 1 cup water. Bring to a boil; then reduce heat, cover, and simmer for 45 minutes.

Stir in carrots and tomatoes; cover and cook for 30 minutes. Add mushrooms and olives; cover and continue to cook until beef is very tender when pierced (30 to 45 minutes). Blend in cornstarch mixture; increase heat to medium-high and cook, stirring, until sauce is bubbly and thickened. Season to taste with salt. Serve stew with potatoes. Makes 8 servings.

Per serving: 294 calories (22% fat, 39% carbohydrates, 39% protein), 7 g total fat (2 g saturated fat), 29 g carbohydrates, 28 g protein, 61 mg cholesterol, 138 mg sodium

Lean Sirloin Stroganoff

MODIFIED CLASSIC

Preparation time: About 15 minutes
Cooking time: About 10 minutes

To keep this elegant dish low in fat, substitute cornstarch-thickened yogurt for the traditional sour cream.

2	to 3 teaspoons salad oil
1	pound boneless top sirloin steak, trimmed of fat and cut into ⅛-inch-thick, bite-size strips
⅓	cup thinly sliced shallots or sweet red onion
8	ounces mushrooms, thinly sliced
1	package (about 9 oz.) fresh fettuccine or 8 ounces dry fettuccine
2	teaspoons Worcestershire
¼	teaspoon sweet Hungarian paprika

⅛ teaspoon ground white pepper
¼ cup dry vermouth
¾ cup plain low-fat yogurt blended with 1 tablespoon cornstarch
¼ teaspoon sugar
  Salt
  Chopped parsley

Heat 1 teaspoon of the oil in a wide nonstick frying pan over medium-high heat. Add half the beef. Cook, stirring, just until meat is browned on all sides; remove from pan. Repeat with 1 more teaspoon oil and remaining beef. Set all beef aside.

Add shallots and mushrooms to pan; add 1 more teaspoon oil, if necessary. Cook, stirring, until almost all liquid has evaporated and mushrooms are browned.

Meanwhile, cook fettuccine in a 5- to 6-quart pan in about 3 quarts boiling water until just tender to bite (3 to 4 minutes for fresh pasta, 8 to 10 minutes for dry); or cook according to package directions. Drain pasta, pour onto a deep platter, and keep warm.

To mushroom mixture, add Worcestershire, paprika, white pepper, and vermouth. Blend in yogurt mixture and sugar. Cook, stirring, until sauce is bubbly and thickened. Return beef to pan and stir to coat; then cook, stirring, just until heated through. Season to taste with salt. Spoon beef mixture over pasta and sprinkle with parsley. Makes 4 servings.

Per serving: 435 calories (22% fat, 44% carbohydrates, 34% protein), 10 g total fat (3 g saturated fat), 46 g carbohydrates, 36 g protein, 147 mg cholesterol, 145 mg sodium

Grilled Beef Pocket Sandwiches

· ·

Preparation time: About 15 minutes
Marinating time: At least 30 minutes
Grilling time: About 4 minutes

Easy to assemble and easy to eat, these sandwiches will be walk-away winners at your next barbecue. Guests fill pita bread halves with cilantro sprigs, grilled bell peppers, and beef strips basted with a lively soy marinade.

1½ pounds lean tender beef steak such as top sirloin (cut about 1 inch thick), trimmed of fat
1 large clove garlic, peeled
½ small onion, cut into chunks
2 tablespoons *each* sugar, water, salad oil, and lemon juice
⅓ cup reduced-sodium soy sauce
2 large red bell peppers (about 1 lb. *total*), seeded and cut into 1½-inch squares
6 pita breads (*each* about 6 inches in diameter), cut into halves
2 cups lightly packed cilantro sprigs, rinsed and crisped

Cut beef into long slices about ¼ inch thick. In a blender or food processor, combine garlic, onion, sugar, water, oil, lemon juice, and soy sauce; whirl until puréed. Pour into a bowl. Add beef and bell peppers; stir to coat with marinade. Then cover and refrigerate for at least 30 minutes or up to 1 day, stirring occasionally.

Drain marinade from beef and peppers; reserve marinade. Thread beef strips alternately with peppers on thin metal skewers. (To thread each beef strip, pierce one end of strip with skewer; then fold strip back and forth several times, piercing each time. Threaded meat will have a "rippled" look.) Place skewers on a grill 4 to 6 inches above a solid bed of medium-hot coals. Cook, turning often and basting with marinade, until beef is done to your liking; cut to test (about 4 minutes for medium-rare).

To eat, fill pita bread halves with beef, bell peppers, and cilantro sprigs. Makes 6 servings.

Per serving: 420 calories (25% fat, 43% carbohydrates, 32% protein), 12 g total fat (3 g saturated fat), 44 g carbohydrates, 33 g protein, 76 mg cholesterol, 911 mg sodium

You can keep bunches of cilantro fresh in the refrigerator for several days. First, rinse cilantro and shake or drain off any moisture. Next, clip off the stem ends and stand bunched herbs upright in 2 to 3 inches of cold water in a straight-sided container. Cover lightly with a plastic bag or plastic wrap; then chill. This tactic works for watercress, basil, and other fresh herbs, too.

Low-fat Spaghetti & Meatballs

MODIFIED CLASSIC

Preparation time: About 20 minutes
Standing time: About 15 minutes
Baking time: 25 to 30 minutes
Cooking time: 35 to 40 minutes

An all-time family favorite, spaghetti-and-meatballs is one dish that's easily streamlined. We trimmed down the recipe by using a fat-free tomato-mushroom sauce and making the meatballs from very lean beef mixed with soaked bulgur; oven-browning the meatballs is another fat-sparing step. Because these meatballs soak up liquid readily, heat them only briefly in the sauce before serving.

¾	**cup bulgur**
1½	**cups boiling water**
12	**ounces boneless beef top round, trimmed of fat (or use ground beef with 15 percent or less fat)**
1	**large onion, chopped**
4	**cloves garlic, minced or pressed**
1	**teaspoon dry oregano**
¼	**teaspoon black pepper**
	About ½ teaspoon salt
4	**ounces mushrooms, sliced**
1	**tablespoon dry basil**
¼	**teaspoon crushed red pepper flakes**
1	**to 1¼ cups beef broth**
1	**large can (about 28 oz.) crushed tomatoes**
1	**pound dry spaghetti**
	Chopped parsley
	Grated Parmesan cheese

In a bowl, mix bulgur and boiling water. Let stand until bulgur is tender to bite (about 15 minutes).

Cut beef into ½-inch cubes and whirl in a food processor until coarsely ground (or put through a food chopper). In a bowl, mix beef, onion, 2 cloves of the garlic, oregano, black pepper, and ½ teaspoon of the salt. Shape into ¼-cup-size balls; place meatballs slightly apart in a lightly oiled shallow baking pan and bake in a 425° oven until well browned (25 to 30 minutes).

Meanwhile, in 5- to 6-quart pan, combine mushrooms, remaining 2 cloves garlic, basil, red pepper flakes, and ¼ cup water. Cook over high heat, stirring often, until liquid evaporates and vegetables begin to brown (about 10 minutes). To deglaze, add ¼ cup broth and stir to scrape browned bits free. Then continue to cook, stirring occasionally, until mixture begins to brown again. Repeat deglazing and browning steps 1 or 2 more times, using ¼ cup broth each time; mushrooms should be browned. Stir in tomatoes; reduce heat, cover, and simmer for 10 minutes. Add meatballs; cover and simmer for about 5 minutes. (Meatballs absorb liquid quickly; if sauce sticks, stir in a little broth.) Season to taste with salt.

While sauce is simmering, cook spaghetti in a 6- to 8-quart pan in about 4 quarts boiling water until just tender to bite (8 to 10 minutes); or cook according to package directions. Drain well. In pan, bring ⅓ cup of the broth to a boil; return pasta to pan, stir to mix, and pour into a wide bowl.

To serve, top pasta with meatballs and sprinkle with parsley. Offer cheese to add to taste. Makes 4 to 6 servings.

Per serving: 562 calories (8% fat, 69% carbohydrates, 23% protein), 5 g total fat (1 g saturated fat), 97 g carbohydrates, 33 g protein, 39 mg cholesterol, 732 mg sodium

Spinach Meat Loaf

MODIFIED CLASSIC

Preparation time: About 40 minutes
Baking time: About 1½ hours

Combining lean beef with ground turkey breast and grated potato helps cut the fat in this spinach-swirled, tomato-glazed meat loaf.

1	**large egg white (about 2 tablespoons)**
¼	**cup evaporated skim milk**
1	**can (about 8 oz.) tomato sauce**
1½	**cups soft French bread crumbs**
1	**small onion, finely chopped**
1	**large potato (about 8 oz.), scrubbed and grated**
1	**clove garlic, minced or pressed**
2	**teaspoons Dijon mustard**
¾	**teaspoon dry oregano**

¼ teaspoon pepper

1 pound *each* extra-lean ground beef and ground skinless turkey breast

1 package (about 10 oz.) frozen chopped spinach, thawed and squeezed dry

¼ cup grated Romano or Parmesan cheese

1 tablespoon *each* firmly packed brown sugar and red wine vinegar

1¼ teaspoons Worcestershire

In a large bowl, combine egg white, milk, and ½ cup of the tomato sauce; beat until well combined. Stir in bread crumbs, onion, potato, garlic, mustard, oregano, and pepper. Add beef and turkey; mix lightly. On a large sheet of plastic wrap, pat meat mixture into a 12-inch square. Distribute spinach over meat to within ½ inch of edges; sprinkle evenly with cheese.

Using plastic wrap to lift meat, roll up meat jelly roll style. Pinch seam and ends closed to seal in filling. Carefully place meat loaf, seam side down, in a shallow baking pan.

Bake meat loaf in a 350° oven for 1¼ hours. Meanwhile, in a small bowl, stir together sugar, vinegar, Worcestershire, and remaining tomato sauce until well blended. Set aside.

Remove pan from oven; spoon out and discard any drippings. Spoon tomato sauce mixture over meat loaf. Return to oven and continue to bake until meat is well browned (15 to 20 more minutes). With wide spatulas, carefully transfer meat loaf to a platter. Let stand for about 5 minutes before slicing. Makes 8 servings.

Per serving: 259 calories (25% fat, 28% carbohydrates, 47% protein), 7 g total fat (2 g saturated fat), 18 g carbohydrates, 30 g protein, 73 mg cholesterol, 418 mg sodium

Chili Verde

· ·

MODIFIED CLASSIC

Preparation time: About 15 minutes
Cooking time: About 1½ hours

To streamline this classic Mexican stew, we used lean pork shoulder that's sweated in tomato juice until richly browned. Serve the spicy dish over hot, fluffy white rice or, if you prefer, with warm corn or flour tortillas.

1 pound boneless pork shoulder, trimmed of fat and cut into ¾-inch cubes

1 large can (about 28 oz.) tomatoes

2 medium-size onions, chopped

1½ cups thinly sliced celery

1 teaspoon dry oregano

½ teaspoon rubbed sage

2 dry bay leaves

1 large green bell pepper (about 8 oz.), seeded and chopped

2 medium-size fresh green Anaheim, poblano, or other large mild chiles (3 to 4 oz. *total*), seeded and chopped

About 4 cups hot cooked rice

Cilantro sprigs

Place pork in a wide nonstick frying pan. Drain about ½ cup liquid from tomatoes into pan. Bring to a boil over high heat; then reduce heat, cover, and simmer for 30 minutes.

Uncover pan; add onions, celery, oregano, and sage. Cook over high heat, stirring often, until liquid has evaporated and drippings are browned (8 to 10 minutes). Add bay leaves. Cut up tomatoes; then add tomatoes and their remaining liquid and stir to scrape browned bits free. Reduce heat, cover, and simmer for 30 more minutes. Stir in bell pepper and chiles; cover and continue to cook, stirring occasionally, until pork is very tender when pierced (about 15 more minutes). If chili is too thin, uncover and simmer until it's as thick as you like. Skim and discard fat, if necessary.

To serve, spoon chili over rice and garnish with cilantro sprigs. Makes 4 servings.

Per serving: 541 calories (17% fat, 60% carbohydrates, 23% protein), 10 g total fat (3 g saturated fat), 80 g carbohydrates, 31 g protein, 76 mg cholesterol, 458 mg sodium

Grilled Pork with Couscous Salad

· ·

Preparation time: About 30 minutes
Marinating time: At least 30 minutes
Cooking time: About 30 minutes

If you think that all cuts of pork are high in fat, you may be surprised to learn that well-trimmed tenderloin has little more internal fat than skinned chicken breast. For a tempting meal from the barbecue, serve the soy-marinated, grilled meat with crisp snow peas and a tangy-sweet couscous salad.

2	**pork tenderloins (1½ to 2 lbs. *total*), trimmed of fat and silvery membranes**
¼	**cup reduced-sodium soy sauce**
2	**tablespoons sake or dry sherry**
1½	**tablespoons honey**
1	**tablespoon grated fresh ginger**
1	**clove garlic, minced or pressed**
1	**pound Chinese pea pods (also called snow or sugar peas), ends and strings removed**
	Couscous Salad (recipe follows)

Fold thin end of each tenderloin under to make meat evenly thick; tie to secure. Set a large heavy-duty plastic bag in a shallow pan. In bag, combine soy sauce, sake, honey, ginger, and garlic. Add pork. Seal bag and turn to coat pork with marinade; then refrigerate for at least 30 minutes or up to 1 day, turning occasionally.

In a 5- to 6-quart pan, cook pea pods in about 3 quarts boiling water just until they turn a brighter green (about 2 minutes). Drain, immerse in cold water until cool, and drain again. Set aside.

Lift pork from bag and drain briefly; reserve marinade. Place pork on a lightly oiled grill 4 to 6 inches above a solid bed of medium coals. Cook, turning as needed and basting often with marinade, just until meat in thickest part is no longer pink; cut to test (20 to 25 minutes). When pork is almost done, prepare Couscous Salad.

To serve, spoon Couscous Salad around edge of a platter. Thinly slice pork across the grain and arrange in center of platter; arrange pea pods around pork. Makes 6 to 8 servings.

Couscous Salad. In a 3- to 4-quart pan, bring 3½ cups **low-sodium chicken broth** to a boil over high heat. Add 3 tablespoons **unseasoned rice vinegar;** 1 tablespoon *each* **honey** and minced **fresh ginger;** and ½ teaspoon **dry mustard.** Stir in 2 cups **couscous.** Cover and remove from heat; let stand for 5 minutes. Fluff couscous with a fork.

Per serving: 410 calories (13% fat, 54% carbohydrates, 33% protein), 6 g total fat (2 g saturated fat), 54 g carbohydrates, 33 g protein, 69 mg cholesterol, 427 mg sodium

Jerk Pork with Papaya

· ·

Preparation time: About 30 minutes
Marinating time: At least 20 minutes
Grilling time: About 20 minutes

To flavor grilled meats and fish, Jamaicans favor an aromatic seasoning mix called jerk. Though the mixture does deliver a real kick, the name "jerk" doesn't refer to the pungency of the spices—it's simply a reference to the original use of these seasonings as preservatives for smoked meats (jerky). To temper the bite of this jerk-style pork tenderloin, serve the meat with pasta, ripe papaya, and a sweet-tart banana chutney.

	Jerk Seasoning Paste (recipe follows)
2	**pork tenderloins (about 1⅓ lbs. *total*), trimmed of fat and silvery membranes**
1	**large firm-ripe banana, coarsely chopped**
¾	**cup Major Grey's or other mango chutney**
¼	**cup lime juice**
3	**tablespoons sweetened flaked coconut**
1	**pound dry angel hair pasta (capellini)**
¾	**cup low-sodium chicken broth**
¼	**cup seasoned rice vinegar (or ¼ cup unseasoned rice vinegar plus 1 tablespoon sugar)**

¼ cup minced cilantro

2 teaspoons sugar

2 medium-size firm-ripe papayas (1¾ to 2 lbs. *total*), peeled, seeded, and cut into ½-inch-thick slices

Cilantro sprigs

Prepare Jerk Seasoning Paste. Coat pork with seasoning paste, wrap airtight, and refrigerate for at least 20 minutes or up to 1 day.

In a bowl, combine banana, chutney, 1 tablespoon of the lime juice, and coconut. Set aside.

At least 30 minutes before grilling, ignite 60 charcoal briquets on fire grate in a barbecue with a lid. When coals are coated with ash (after about 30 minutes), push half of them to each side of grate. Set a drip pan between coals; set grill 4 to 6 inches above coals. When coals are medium-hot, oil grill.

Place pork in center of grill above drip pan. Cover barbecue, open vents, and cook until a meat thermometer inserted in thickest part of pork registers 155°F (about 20 minutes).

When pork is done, transfer it to a platter and keep warm. Then cook pasta in a 5- to 6-quart pan in about 3 quarts boiling water until just tender to bite (about 3 minutes); or cook according to package directions. Drain pasta well; return to pan. Add broth and stir over medium heat until pasta has absorbed almost all broth; then mix in vinegar, minced cilantro, remaining 3 tablespoons lime juice, and sugar.

To serve, cut pork across the grain into ½-inch-thick slices; serve with pasta and papayas. Garnish with cilantro sprigs; offer banana-chutney mixture to add to taste. Makes 6 servings.

Jerk Seasoning Paste. In a blender or food processor, combine ¼ cup firmly packed **cilantro leaves,** 3 tablespoons *each* **water** and minced **fresh ginger,** 2 tablespoons **whole black peppercorns,** 1 tablespoon *each* **ground allspice** and firmly packed **brown sugar,** 2 cloves **garlic** (peeled), ½ teaspoon **crushed red pepper flakes,** and ¼ teaspoon *each* **ground coriander** and **ground nutmeg.** Whirl to make a smooth paste. If made ahead, cover and refrigerate for up to 5 days.

Per serving: 622 calories (10% fat, 68% carbohydrates, 22% protein), 7 g total fat (2 g saturated fat), 105 g carbohydrates, 34 g protein, 71 mg cholesterol, 622 mg sodium

Pork in Escabeche Sauce

Preparation time: About 15 minutes
Roasting time: 20 to 30 minutes

The tenderloin is one of the leanest cuts of pork, ideal for oven-roasting. Here, it's marinated before cooking in *escabeche*, a potent blend of spices and garlic.

Escabeche Paste (recipe follows)

2 **pork tenderloins (about 1½ lbs. *total*), trimmed of fat and silvery membranes**

4 **large oranges (about 2½ lbs. *total*), peeled (if desired) and sliced crosswise**

Prepare Escabeche Paste; spread evenly over pork. (At this point, you may cover and refrigerate for up to 1 day.)

Place pork tenderloins, side by side, on a rack in a 9- by 13-inch baking pan. Roast in a 450° oven until a meat thermometer inserted in thickest part of pork registers 155°F (20 to 30 minutes). After 15 minutes, check temperature every 5 to 10 minutes.

When pork is done, let it stand for about 5 minutes. Then thinly slice pork across the grain and transfer to a platter. Garnish with orange slices. Makes 6 servings.

Escabeche Paste. In a small bowl, stir together 4 cloves **garlic,** minced or pressed; 1 tablespoon *each* **orange juice** and **white wine vinegar;** 1 teaspoon **dry oregano;** ¾ teaspoon **ground cinnamon;** ½ teaspoon *each* **ground allspice, ground cloves, ground cumin,** and **ground coriander;** ¼ teaspoon **black pepper;** and ⅛ teaspoon **ground red pepper** (cayenne). If made ahead, cover and refrigerate for up to 3 days.

Per serving: 209 calories (19% fat, 34% carbohydrates, 47% protein), 4 g total fat (1 g saturated fat), 18 g carbohydrates, 25 g protein, 66 mg cholesterol, 48 mg sodium

__The escabeche paste__ above, superb with pork, is a good flavoring for other roast meats, roast poultry, and baked fish as well. Try it spread over boneless lamb, turkey breast, or lean firm fish such as lingcod, rockfish, or orange roughy.

CROCK-POT MEATS

When you prepare stews and pot roasts in a Crock-Pot* or other electric slow cooker, you may be pleasantly surprised to learn how little fat is needed. Meats seldom require browning in oil or butter before they go into the cooker; only one of the following four recipes calls for this step, and that one uses just 2 teaspoons of oil. If meat or poultry does release fat during slow-simmering, be sure to skim the cooking liquid before completing and serving the dish.

STOUT-HEARTED BEEF WITH GARLIC MASHED POTATOES

Preparation time: About 30 minutes
Cooking time: 8 to 9 hours
Baking time: 25 to 30 minutes

- 1   **large onion, thinly sliced**
- 2   **cloves garlic, minced or pressed**
- 4   **medium-size carrots, cut into ¼-inch-thick slanting slices**
- ½   **cup finely chopped parsley**
- 1   **dry bay leaf**
- ½   **cup pitted prunes**
- 2   **to 2½ pounds boneless beef chuck, trimmed of fat and cut into 1-inch cubes**
- ¼   **cup all-purpose flour**
- ¼   **teaspoon pepper**
- ¾   **cup stout or dark ale**
        Garlic Mashed Potatoes (recipe follows)
        Salt

In a 3-quart or larger electric slow cooker, combine onion, garlic, carrots, parsley, bay leaf, and prunes.

Coat beef cubes with flour, then add to cooker and sprinkle with pepper. Pour in stout. Cover and cook at low setting until beef is very tender when pierced (8 to 9 hours).

About 30 minutes before beef is done, prepare Garlic Mashed Potatoes. Skim and discard fat from stew, if necessary; season to taste with salt. Serve over potatoes. Makes 6 to 8 servings.

Garlic Mashed Potatoes. Pour 1 tablespoon **olive oil** into an 8-inch baking pan. Cut 2 large heads **garlic** (about 6 oz. *total*) in half crosswise through cloves; place halves, cut side down, in pan. Bake in a 375° oven until garlic is golden brown on bottom (25 to 30 minutes).

Meanwhile, peel and quarter 3 pounds **russet potatoes;** then place potatoes in a 5- to 6-quart pan and add **water** to cover. Bring to a boil over high heat; reduce heat, cover, and boil gently until potatoes are tender when pierced (20 to 25 minutes). Drain well.

While potatoes are cooking, loosen garlic from baking pan with a wide spatula. Squeeze soft garlic from cloves into a large bowl. Beat garlic with an electric mixer to mash it; then add hot potatoes, ½ cup warm

evaporated skim milk, and 1 tablespoon **butter** or margarine. Beat until smooth. Season to taste with **salt** and **pepper.** Makes 6 to 8 servings.

Per serving of stew: 277 calories (22% fat, 29% carbohydrates, 49% protein), 7 g total fat (2 g saturated fat), 19 g carbohydrates, 33 g protein, 88 mg cholesterol, 116 mg sodium

Per serving of Garlic Mashed Potatoes: 219 calories (16% fat, 73% carbohydrates, 11% protein), 4 g total fat (1 g saturated fat), 41 g carbohydrates, 6 g protein, 5 mg cholesterol, 55 mg sodium

SWEET-SPICED POT ROAST WITH CHILES

Preparation time: About 15 minutes
Cooking time: 8¼ to 10¼ hours

- 2   **teaspoons olive oil**
- 1   **boneless beef rump roast (3 to 3½ lbs.), trimmed of fat**
- ½   **cup dried currants**
- 6   **cloves garlic, minced or pressed**
- 1   **large can (about 7 oz.) diced green chiles**
- 1   **small dried hot red chile, crushed**
- 1   **teaspoon ground cinnamon**
- ½   **teaspoon *each* dry oregano and dry marjoram**
- ¼   **teaspoon ground allspice**
- ¾   **cup beef broth**
- ¼   **cup red wine vinegar**
- 2   **tablespoons cornstarch blended with 2 tablespoons cold water**
        Salt

Heat oil in a wide nonstick frying pan over medium-high heat. Add beef and cook, turning as needed, until well browned on all sides.

Meanwhile, in a 3-quart or larger electric slow cooker, combine currants, garlic, green chiles, and red chile. Place browned beef on top of currant mixture; sprinkle with cinnamon, oregano, marjoram, and allspice. Pour in broth and vinegar. Cover and cook at low setting until beef is very tender when pierced (8 to 10 hours).

Lift beef to a platter and keep warm. Skim and discard fat from cooking liquid, if necessary; then blend in cornstarch mixture. Increase cooker heat setting to high; cover and cook, stirring 2 or 3 times, until sauce is thickened (10 to 15 more minutes). Season to taste with salt.

To serve, slice beef across the grain. Serve with sauce. Makes 8 to 10 servings.

Per serving: 250 calories (25% fat, 17% carbohydrates, 58% protein), 7 g total fat (2 g saturated fat), 10 g carbohydrates, 35 g protein, 98 mg cholesterol, 306 mg sodium

BRAISED LAMB & VEGETABLES WITH MINT

Preparation time: About 20 minutes
Cooking time: 7¼ to 8¼ hours

1   **medium-size onion, finely chopped**

2   **cloves garlic, minced or pressed**

2   **medium-size carrots, cut into ¼-inch-thick slanting slices**

1   **teaspoon ground cinnamon**

⅓   **cup chopped fresh mint or 1½ teaspoons dry mint**

4   **lamb shoulder blade or arm chops, cut about 1 inch thick (2¼ to 2½ lbs. *total*), trimmed of fat**
    Pepper

2   **tablespoons all-purpose flour**

½   **cup beef broth**

2   **medium-size zucchini, cut into ⅛-inch-thick slanting slices**

1   **cup frozen peas, thawed**

In a 4-quart or larger electric slow cooker, combine onion, garlic, and carrots; sprinkle with cinnamon and mint. Sprinkle lamb chops with pepper, dust with flour, and arrange over onion mixture, overlapping slightly. Pour in broth. Cover and cook at low setting until lamb is very tender when pierced (7 to 8 hours).

Lift lamb to a platter and keep warm. Skim and discard fat from cooking liquid, then add zucchini and peas. Increase cooker heat setting to high; cover and cook until zucchini is just tender to bite (12 to 15 more minutes). Spoon vegetables and liquid over and around lamb. Makes 4 to 6 servings.

Per serving: 232 calories (25% fat, 26% carbohydrates, 49% protein), 6 g total fat (2 g saturated fat), 15 g carbohydrates, 28 g protein, 82 mg cholesterol, 135 mg sodium

TURKEY RAGOUT

Preparation time: About 20 minutes
Cooking time: 7½ to 8½ hours

1   **large onion, thinly sliced**

2   **cloves garlic, minced or pressed**

8   **ounces mushrooms, cut into quarters**

½   **teaspoon dry thyme**

⅛   **teaspoon ground white pepper**

2   **pounds boneless, skinless turkey breast**

3   **tablespoons all-purpose flour**

⅓   **cup dry white wine or low-sodium chicken broth**

1   **tablespoon tomato paste**
    Salt

In a 3-quart or larger electric slow cooker, combine onion, garlic, mushrooms, thyme, and white pepper.

Rinse turkey, pat dry, and cut into 1½-inch cubes. Coat turkey cubes with flour; arrange on top of onion mixture. Mix wine and tomato paste; pour evenly over turkey.

Cover and cook at low setting until turkey is very tender when pierced (7½ to 8½ hours). Stir gently to coat turkey with sauce, then season to taste with salt. Makes 6 servings.

Per serving: 211 calories (5% fat, 18% carbohydrates, 77% protein), 1 g total fat (0.3 g saturated fat), 9 g carbohydrates, 39 g protein, 94 mg cholesterol, 99 mg sodium

Japanese Country-style Pork & Potatoes

Preparation time: About 15 minutes
Cooking time: About 1¼ hours

Japanese flavors make this stew different: pork cubes and sliced potatoes are seasoned with soy, mirin, and sake. For easy dining, you might serve the dish in big soup bowls.

8	green onions
1	tablespoon salad oil
1½	pounds boneless pork shoulder, trimmed of fat and cut into ½-inch cubes
1	large onion, sliced
¼	cup reduced-sodium soy sauce
⅔	cup sake or dry vermouth
½	cup water
½	cup mirin (sweet rice wine) or cream sherry
1½	pounds red thin-skinned potatoes, scrubbed and cut into ¼-inch-thick slices
¼	teaspoon pepper
2	teaspoons sugar

Cut green onions into 1-inch lengths, keeping green and white parts separate; set aside.

Heat oil in a 5- to 6-quart pan over medium-high heat. Add half the pork; cook, stirring, until well browned (about 10 minutes). Remove from pan and set aside. Repeat to brown remaining pork; remove from pan.

Discard all but 1 tablespoon of the drippings from pan. Add sliced onion to pan and cook, stirring occasionally, until soft (about 5 minutes). Return pork to pan and add soy sauce, sake, water, and mirin. Bring to a boil; then reduce heat, cover, and simmer for 25 minutes. Add potatoes, white part of green onions, pepper, and sugar. Return to a boil; then reduce heat, cover, and simmer until pork and potatoes are tender when pierced (about 25 minutes). Skim and discard fat from stew, if necessary. Garnish with tops of green onions. Makes 6 servings.

Per serving: 385 calories (29% fat, 42% carbohydrates, 29% protein), 12 g total fat (3 g saturated fat), 38 g carbohydrates, 26 g protein, 76 mg cholesterol, 502 mg sodium

Lentil Cassoulet

MODIFIED CLASSIC

Preparation time: About 40 minutes
Marinating time: At least 6 hours
Baking time: About 1½ hours
Cooking time: 50 minutes to 1 hour

Traditional *cassoulet* is made with white beans, but we've substituted lentils to cut down on cooking time. Thick with sausage and meaty pork ribs, the hearty dish is an excellent choice for entertaining: it serves a crowd, and it can be assembled—all ready to slip into the oven—up to a day ahead.

3	to 4 pounds country-style pork ribs, trimmed of fat
2	tablespoons *each* salt and sugar
1	teaspoon pepper
1	pound turkey kielbasa
	About 10 cups low-sodium chicken broth
2	large onions, chopped
3	cloves garlic, minced or pressed
2	teaspoons *each* dry thyme and coriander seeds
1	dry bay leaf
2	pounds lentils, rinsed and drained
3	large carrots, coarsely chopped
1	cup coarse soft bread crumbs
2	teaspoons olive oil
2	tablespoons chopped parsley

Cut pork ribs apart between bones. Mix salt, sugar, and pepper; rub all over pork. Place pork in a large heavy-duty plastic bag; seal bag and refrigerate for at least 6 hours or up to 1 day, turning occasionally. Rinse pork well and pat dry.

Place pork and whole sausage in a single layer in a 10- by 15-inch rimmed baking pan; bake in a 450° oven until browned (about 30 minutes). Discard fat from pan; set ribs and sausage aside.

In a 6- to 8-quart pan, combine 1 cup of the broth, onions, garlic, thyme, coriander seeds, and bay leaf. Cook over high heat, stirring often, until liquid evaporates and onions begin to brown (about 10 minutes). To deglaze, add ⅓ cup more broth and stir to scrape browned bits free. Then continue to cook, stirring occasionally, until mixture begins to brown again. Repeat deglazing and browning steps 1 or 2 more times, using ⅓ cup broth each time; onions should be well browned.

Add lentils, pork ribs, 8 cups of the broth, and carrots to pan. Bring to a boil; then reduce heat, cover, and simmer until lentils are tender to bite (30 to 40 minutes). Meanwhile, cut sausage into ¼-inch-thick slanting slices.

With a slotted spoon, lift pork ribs from lentil mixture and set aside; then pour lentil mixture into a shallow 5- to 6-quart casserole (about 12 by 16 inches). Nestle sausage slices and ribs into lentils. Cover casserole tightly. (At this point, you may let cool, then refrigerate for up to 1 day.)

Bake, covered, in a 350° oven until hot in center (about 35 minutes; about 1½ hours if refrigerated). Mix bread crumbs and oil; uncover casserole and sprinkle with crumbs. Continue to bake, uncovered, until crumbs are golden (20 to 25 more minutes). Sprinkle with parsley. Makes 8 to 10 servings.

Per serving: 627 calories (20% fat, 45% carbohydrates, 35% protein), 14 g total fat (4 g saturated fat), 72 g carbohydrates, 55 g protein, 83 mg cholesterol, 848 mg sodium

Italian Pork Stew with Polenta

. . . .

Preparation time: About 15 minutes
Cooking time: About 2 hours

Perfect fare for cool autumn nights, this earthy stew will warm you up without weighing you down. Look for polenta (coarsely ground cornmeal) in Italian delicatessens and well-stocked supermarkets.

1½	pounds boneless pork leg or shoulder, trimmed of fat and cut into 1½-inch cubes
3½	cups water
12	ounces small mushrooms, cut into halves
1	large onion, chopped
2	cloves garlic, minced or pressed
1	large can (about 28 oz.) pear-shaped tomatoes
1	cup dry red wine
½	teaspoon *each* dry rosemary, dry marjoram, dry oregano, and dry thyme
2	cups polenta
4	cups low-sodium chicken broth
½	cup chopped Italian parsley

In a 5- to 6-quart pan, combine pork and ½ cup of the water. Cover and cook over medium-high heat for 10 minutes. Uncover and continue to cook, stirring occasionally, until liquid has evaporated and pork is browned (about 5 more minutes). Add mushrooms, onion, and garlic; reduce heat to medium and cook, stirring often, until onion is soft (about 5 minutes).

Cut up tomatoes; add tomatoes and their liquid to pan. Then add wine, rosemary, marjoram, oregano, and thyme, stirring to scrape browned bits free from pan. Bring to a boil; then reduce heat, partially cover, and simmer until pork is tender when pierced (about 1½ hours). Skim and discard fat from stew, if necessary.

About 30 minutes before stew is done, place polenta in a heavy 3- to 4-quart pan; stir in broth and remaining 3 cups water. Bring to a boil over high heat, stirring often with a long-handled wooden spoon (mixture will spatter). Reduce heat and simmer gently, uncovered, stirring often, until polenta tastes creamy (about 20 minutes).

Spoon polenta onto a platter and top with stew; sprinkle parsley over all. Makes 6 servings.

Per serving: 405 calories (19% fat, 49% carbohydrates, 32% protein), 9 g total fat (3 g saturated fat), 50 g carbohydrates, 32 g protein, 77 mg cholesterol, 323 mg sodium

▬▬▬▬

Fresh leg of pork *(our first choice for the stew above) is sometimes labeled "fresh ham." It's most widely available around the year-end holidays. Ideal for stewing, this cut is also good roasted or grilled.*

▬▬▬▬

Garlic Pork Chops with Balsamic Vinegar

Preparation time: 15 to 20 minutes
Cooking time: About 20 minutes

Dark, rich-tasting balsamic vinegar is a specialty from the area around Modena, Italy. Combined with mustard and vermouth, it makes a tempting sauce for juicy pork chops sautéed with plenty of garlic.

1	small head garlic (about 1½ oz.), separated into cloves
6	center-cut loin pork chops (about 2 lbs. *total*), trimmed of fat
	Pepper
	Vegetable oil cooking spray
12	ounces dry medium-wide eggless noodles
¼	cup sweet vermouth
1	tablespoon Dijon mustard
⅓	cup balsamic vinegar
	Salt
	Chopped parsley

In a medium-size pan, bring about 4 cups water to a boil. Add unpeeled garlic cloves and boil for 1 minute; drain. Let garlic cool slightly, then peel cloves and set aside.

Sprinkle pork chops generously with pepper. Coat a wide frying pan with cooking spray and place over medium-high heat. Add chops and cook until well browned on bottom (4 to 5 minutes); turn chops over, arrange garlic cloves around them, and continue to cook until chops are browned on other side (4 to 5 more minutes).

Meanwhile, in a 5- to 6-quart pan, cook noodles in about 3 quarts boiling water until just tender to

---

Looks aren't everything. *Pork shoulder appears to be too fatty to include in a lean diet—but careful trimming can streamline this flavorful cut considerably. Use a sharp knife to remove most of the fat from the surface and between the muscles.*

---

bite (7 to 9 minutes); or cook according to package directions. Drain well, pour onto a deep platter, and keep warm.

While noodles are cooking, mix vermouth and mustard; pour over browned chops. Reduce heat to low, cover, and cook until chops are done but still moist and slightly pink in center; cut to test (about 5 minutes). Arrange chops over noodles and keep warm.

Add vinegar to sauce in pan. Increase heat to medium-high and stir to scrape browned bits free. Bring to a boil; then boil, uncovered, until sauce is reduced to about ½ cup (2 to 3 minutes). Season to taste with salt. Spoon sauce over chops; sprinkle chops and noodles with parsley. Makes 6 servings.

Per serving: 366 calories (17% fat, 49% carbohydrates, 34% protein), 7 g total fat (2 g saturated fat), 44 g carbohydrates, 30 g protein, 62 mg cholesterol, 155 mg sodium

Smoked Pork Chops with Polenta

30 MINUTES OR LESS

Preparation time: About 5 minutes
Baking time: 25 to 30 minutes

Thanks to quick-cooking instant polenta, this warming one-pan dinner can be ready to serve in about half an hour.

3½	cups low-sodium chicken broth
1	cup instant polenta
1	small can (about 8 oz.) cream-style corn
4	smoked pork chops (about 1¼ lbs. *total*)
2	tablespoons *each* grated Parmesan cheese and chopped parsley

In a small pan, bring broth to a boil over high heat; then pour broth into a shallow 2½- to 3-quart baking dish. Gradually add polenta, stirring constantly. Stir in corn. Arrange pork chops on top of polenta mixture.

Bake in a 350° oven until pork chops are heated through; cut to test (25 to 30 minutes). Sprinkle chops with cheese and parsley. Makes 4 servings.

Per serving: 346 calories (21% fat, 47% carbohydrates, 32% protein), 8 g total fat (3 g saturated fat), 40 g carbohydrates, 28 g protein, 52 mg cholesterol, 1,781 mg sodium

Hearty Baked Pork & Apple Stew

Preparation time: About 45 minutes
Cooking time: About 20 minutes
Baking time: About 1½ hours

Thickened with tart apples and spicy apple butter, this pork stew tastes good with sweet potatoes. (You can bake them in their jackets, right alongside the stew.)

2	**pounds boneless pork shoulder, trimmed of fat and cut into 2-inch cubes**
2	**medium-size onions, chopped**
½	**cup water**
1¾	**cups beef broth**
¾	**cup apple butter**
1	**large bell pepper (about 8 oz.), seeded and cut into thin strips**
1¾	**cups sliced carrots**
½	**cup sliced celery**
3	**large Granny Smith apples (about 1½ lbs. *total*), peeled, cored, and sliced**

In an ovenproof 5- to 6-quart pan, combine pork, onions, and water. Bring to a boil over high heat; cover and boil for 10 minutes. Uncover; continue to boil, stirring often, until liquid has evaporated and drippings are browned (about 5 minutes).

Add broth and apple butter; stir to scrape browned bits free. Cover tightly and bake in a 350° oven for 30 minutes. Stir in bell pepper, carrots, celery, and apples. Cover tightly and continue to bake until pork is very tender when pierced (about 1 more hour). Skim and discard fat from stew, if necessary. Makes 6 servings.

Per serving: 405 calories (28% fat, 41% carbohydrates, 31% protein), 13 g total fat (4 g saturated fat), 42 g carbohydrates, 31 g protein, 101 mg cholesterol, 378 mg sodium

Hickory Baked Pork Chops

MODIFIED CLASSIC

Preparation time: About 10 minutes
Baking time: About 1 hour
Cooking time: 3 to 4 minutes

These succulent pork chops are oven-baked in a smoky tomato-based sauce. Serve them over fresh fettuccine or another fresh or dry pasta of your choice. Alongside, offer a salad of assorted tender greens in a light vinaigrette dressing.

1	**small can (about 8 oz.) stewed tomatoes**
1	**small onion, thinly sliced**
1	**clove garlic, minced or pressed**
1	**teaspoon *each* sugar and dry oregano**
1	**can (about 8 oz.) tomato sauce**
2	**tablespoons hickory smoke–flavored barbecue sauce**
4	**center-cut loin pork chops (about 1¼ lbs. *total*), trimmed of fat**
1	**package (about 9 oz.) fresh fettuccine or 8 ounces dry fettuccine; or 8 ounces dry wide eggless noodles** **Chopped parsley**

In a shallow 2-quart casserole, stir together tomatoes, onion, garlic, sugar, oregano, tomato sauce, and barbecue sauce. Add pork chops and spoon about half the tomato mixture over them. Cover and bake in a 350° oven until chops are done but still moist and slightly pink in center; cut to test (about 1 hour).

When chops are almost done, cook fettuccine in a 5- to 6-quart pan in about 3 quarts boiling water until just tender to bite (3 to 4 minutes for fresh pasta, 8 to 10 minutes for dry); or cook according to package directions. Drain well, pour onto a deep platter, and keep warm.

To serve, lift chops from sauce and arrange atop pasta; spoon a little of the sauce over chops and sprinkle with parsley. Accompany with remaining sauce. Makes 4 servings.

Per serving: 399 calories (17% fat, 48% carbohydrates, 35% protein), 8 g total fat (2 g saturated fat), 48 g carbohydrates, 35 g protein, 146 mg cholesterol, 644 mg sodium

Roast Pork with Date & Fig Sauce

Preparation time: About 15 minutes
Roasting time: About 1½ hours
Cooking time: About 10 minutes

Turn a weekend supper into something special with this creative meat-and-fruit combination. Pork roast is seasoned with garlic, pepper, and savory, then served with a sweet sauce of figs, dates, and fresh apple.

1	boneless pork loin roast (3 to 4 lbs.), trimmed of fat
1	clove garlic, peeled and halved
½	teaspoon dry summer savory
1	teaspoon pepper
1	cup finely chopped unpeeled tart apple
¼	cup water
½	cup dry white wine
½	cup firmly packed brown sugar
1	cup pitted dates, cut into pieces
6	dried figs, coarsely chopped

Rub pork all over with garlic; discard garlic. Place pork in a 9- by 13-inch baking pan and sprinkle evenly with savory and pepper. Roast in a 375° oven until a meat thermometer inserted in thickest part registers 155°F (about 1½ hours). Transfer pork to a platter; keep warm.

While pork is roasting, combine apple and water in a 2- to 3-quart pan. Cover and cook over medium heat, stirring occasionally, until apple is tender to bite (about 5 minutes). Remove from heat; set aside.

Skim and discard fat from juices in roasting pan; add wine to pan. Place pan over medium heat and stir to scrape browned bits free. Add apple mixture, sugar, dates, and figs; cook, stirring, until mixture is hot and sugar is dissolved (about 3 minutes). Pour into a small bowl.

To serve, thinly slice pork across the grain. Accompany with fruit sauce to spoon over meat to taste. Makes 8 to 10 servings.

Per serving: 402 calories (23% fat, 38% carbohydrates, 39% protein), 10 g total fat (3 g saturated fat), 37 g carbohydrates, 39 g protein, 104 mg cholesterol, 99 mg sodium

Cuban-style Mini-Roast with Black Beans & Rice

Preparation time: About 15 minutes
Marinating time: At least 4 hours
Roasting time: 35 to 55 minutes
Cooking time: About 10 minutes

A compact roast of leg of pork—sometimes called fresh ham—is marinated Caribbean style and served with rice and savory black beans.

1½	to 1¾ pounds boneless fresh leg of pork, trimmed of fat
2	cloves garlic, minced or pressed
½	teaspoon dry oregano
¼	teaspoon *each* cumin seeds (coarsely crushed) and crushed red pepper flakes
¼	cup lime juice
	Cuban Black Beans (recipe follows)
3	cups hot cooked long-grain white rice
¼	cup thinly sliced green onions
	Lime wedges

Roll pork compactly; then tie securely with cotton string at 1½-inch intervals. Set a large heavy-duty plastic bag in a shallow pan. In bag, combine garlic, oregano, cumin seeds, red pepper flakes, and lime juice; add pork. Seal bag and turn to coat pork with marinade; then refrigerate for at least 4 hours or up to 1 day, turning occasionally.

Lift pork from bag and drain briefly; reserve marinade. Place pork on a rack in a roasting pan and roast in a 350° oven, drizzling once or twice with marinade, until a meat thermometer inserted in thickest part registers 155°F (35 to 55 minutes). After 25 minutes, check temperature every 5 to 10 minutes. Meanwhile, prepare Cuban Black Beans.

When pork is done, let it stand for about 5 minutes. Then thinly slice pork across the grain and transfer to a platter. Spoon rice alongside pork. Garnish pork and rice with green onions and lime wedges; serve with Cuban Black Beans. Makes 6 servings.

Cuban Black Beans. Heat 2 teaspoons **olive oil** in a wide nonstick frying pan over medium heat. Add 1 medium-size **onion,** thinly sliced, and ½ cup finely chopped **green bell pepper;** cook, stir ring often, until onion is soft but not browned (about 5 minutes). Stir in 1 clove **garlic,** minced or pressed, ½ teaspoon **ground cumin,** and 1 can (about 15 oz.) **black beans** and their liquid (or use 2 cups drained cooked black beans, page 149, plus ⅓ cup low-sodium chicken broth). Cook, stirring, until heated through (about 3 minutes). Just before serving, stir in 2 teaspoons **cider vinegar.**

Per serving: 435 calories (26% fat, 42% carbohydrates, 32% protein), 12 g total fat (4 g saturated fat), 45 g carbohydrates, 34 g protein, 87 mg cholesterol, 338 mg sodium

Penne all'Arrabbiata

Preparation time: About 20 minutes
Cooking time: 45 to 50 minutes

Arrabbiata means "angry"—and as the name suggests, this Italian favorite is fiery in flavor. Serve the spicy tomato sauce over quill-shaped pasta such as penne or ziti.

1	tablespoon olive oil
6	ounces cooked ham, chopped
1	large onion, finely chopped
½	cup *each* finely chopped carrot and finely chopped celery
½	teaspoon crushed red pepper flakes
1	large can (about 28 oz.) diced pear-shaped tomatoes
1	pound dry bite-size tube-shaped pasta such as penne or ziti
¼	cup grated Parmesan cheese
	Salt and black pepper

Heat oil in a 3- to 4-quart pan. Add ham and cook over medium-high heat, stirring often, until lightly browned (6 to 8 minutes). Add onion, carrot, celery, and red pepper flakes; reduce heat to medium and cook, stirring often, until vegetables are soft (about 15 minutes). Stir in tomatoes and bring to a boil; then reduce heat and simmer, uncovered, stirring often, until sauce is reduced to about 3½ cups (25 to 30 minutes).

When sauce is almost done, cook pasta in a 6- to 8-quart pan in about 4 quarts boiling water until just tender to bite (10 to 12 minutes); or cook according to package directions. Drain well, pour into a large bowl, and keep warm.

To serve, mix sauce and cheese with pasta; season to taste with salt and black pepper. Makes 4 to 6 servings.

Per serving: 496 calories (16% fat, 65% carbohydrates, 19% protein), 9 g total fat (2 g saturated fat), 80 g carbohydrates, 23 g protein, 23 mg cholesterol, 866 mg sodium

Crusted Lamb &Potatoes

Preparation time: About 25 minutes
Roasting time: About 1¼ hours

A savory crust of garlic, lemon, and stuffing mix makes this half-leg of lamb special. Roasted atop a bed of sliced potatoes, it's perfect for a small dinner party.

3	pounds russet potatoes, peeled and cut into ¾-inch-thick slices
1½	cups low-sodium chicken broth
	Upper thigh half (3 to 3½ lbs.) of 1 leg of lamb, trimmed of fat
	Seasoning Paste (recipe follows)
	Salt and pepper

Arrange potatoes over bottom of a 12- by 15-inch roasting pan; pour broth into pan, then set lamb on potatoes. Roast in a 400° oven for 45 minutes. Meanwhile, prepare Seasoning Paste.

Spread paste evenly over lamb and potatoes. Continue to roast until crust on meat is well browned and a meat thermometer inserted in thickest part of lamb at bone registers 140° to 145°F for medium-rare (about 25 more minutes). Transfer lamb and potatoes to a platter; pour any pan juices over all.

To serve, slice lamb across the grain; season lamb and potatoes to taste with salt and pepper. Makes 6 servings.

Seasoning Paste. In a small bowl, mash together 3 cloves **garlic,** minced or pressed; 1 small **onion,** minced; 3 tablespoons minced **parsley;** 1 cup **seasoned stuffing mix;** 3 tablespoons **butter** or margarine, at room temperature; 1 tablespoon grated **lemon peel;** and 2 tablespoons **lemon juice.**

Per serving: 482 calories (27% fat, 41% carbohydrates, 32% protein), 14 g total fat (6 g saturated fat), 49 g carbohydrates, 39 g protein, 116 mg cholesterol, 357 mg sodium

Gingered Butterflied Lamb with Yams

Preparation time: About 25 minutes
Marinating time: At least 4 hours
Roasting time: About 1 hour

A tart and spicy marinade flavors every part of this entrée—oven-roasted yam wedges, tender onion halves, and thinly sliced boned leg of lamb.

⅓	cup chopped fresh ginger
8	cloves garlic, peeled
¼	teaspoon pepper
1½	tablespoons reduced-sodium soy sauce
¾	cup red wine vinegar
2	to 2½ pounds boneless butterflied leg of lamb, trimmed of fat
2	teaspoons sugar
¼	cup raisins
	Vegetable oil cooking spray
8	to 10 small yams or sweet potatoes (3½ to 4 lbs. *total*), scrubbed
8	to 10 small onions (*each* about 2 inches in diameter), unpeeled, cut lengthwise into halves
1	cup beef broth

In a blender or food processor, combine ginger, garlic, pepper, soy sauce, and 2 tablespoons of the vinegar. Whirl until mixture forms a paste; set aside.

Lay lamb flat in 9- by 13-inch baking dish; spoon ginger mixture around lamb. Mix sugar, raisins, and remaining 10 tablespoons vinegar; pour over lamb. Cover and refrigerate for at least 4 hours or up to 1 day.

Coat a 12- by 17-inch or larger roasting pan with cooking spray. Cut unpeeled yams lengthwise into

---

Baked Lemon Pilaf (see facing page) is a versatile side dish. Try it with skewered lamb, as we suggest—or serve it alongside a baked whole salmon or with a marinated turkey breast or leg of lamb cooked in a covered barbecue.

¾-inch-thick wedges. Arrange yams and onion halves (cut side down) in pan. Coat all vegetables with cooking spray. Roast on lower rack of a 425° oven for 15 minutes. Meanwhile, lift lamb from marinade and drain briefly; reserve marinade. Place lamb, boned side down, on a rack in a shallow baking pan.

After vegetables have roasted for 15 minutes, place lamb in oven on middle rack. Continue to roast both lamb and vegetables, basting lamb occasionally with marinade, for 30 minutes. Lift raisins from marinade and sprinkle over lamb. Drizzle vegetables with all but 3 tablespoons of the remaining marinade. Continue to roast until vegetables are tender when pierced and a meat thermometer inserted in thickest part of lamb registers 140° to 145°F for medium-rare (10 to 15 more minutes).

Transfer lamb, onions, and yams to a platter; keep warm. To lamb cooking pan, add broth and reserved 3 tablespoons marinade; cook over medium heat, stirring to scrape browned bits free, until sauce is reduced to about ¾ cup. Pour into a small bowl.

To serve, thinly slice lamb across the grain. Serve lamb with yams, onions, and sauce. Makes 8 to 10 servings.

Per serving: 328 calories (17% fat, 51% carbohydrates, 32% protein), 6 g total fat (2 g saturated fat), 41 g carbohydrates, 27 g protein, 73 mg cholesterol, 282 mg sodium

Spicy Lamb Skewers with Baked Lemon Pilaf

MODIFIED CLASSIC

Preparation time: About 20 minutes
Marinating time: At least 3 hours
Baking time: 45 to 50 minutes
Grilling time: 8 to 10 minutes

A marinade of curry- and chili-seasoned apricot nectar gives grilled lamb a wonderful fruity, spicy flavor. While the meat is marinating, bake a lemon-scented pilaf to serve alongside.

1	large onion, finely chopped
1	teaspoon salad oil
3	tablespoons cider vinegar
1	tablespoon curry powder

1   dry bay leaf
2   teaspoons chili powder
½   teaspoon salt
1   clove garlic, minced or pressed
¾   cup apricot nectar
2   pounds boneless lamb loin, trimmed
    of fat and cut into 1-inch cubes
    Baked Lemon Pilaf (recipe follows)

In a medium-size pan, combine onion, oil, and vinegar. Cook over medium-low heat, stirring, until almost all liquid has evaporated and onion is soft (6 to 8 minutes). Stir in curry powder, bay leaf, chili powder, salt, garlic, and apricot nectar. Bring to a boil over high heat; then reduce heat to low and simmer for 5 minutes.

Place lamb in a bowl, pour in apricot marinade, and stir to combine. Cover and refrigerate for at least 3 hours or up to 8 hours, stirring occasionally. About 1 hour before cooking lamb, prepare Baked Lemon Pilaf.

Lift lamb from marinade and drain briefly; reserve marinade. Thread lamb on 8 metal skewers. Place skewers on an oiled grill 4 to 6 inches above a solid bed of hot coals. Cook, brushing with remaining marinade and turning as needed, until lamb is well browned on outside but still pink in center; cut to test (8 to 10 minutes). Serve with pilaf. Makes 8 servings.

Baked Lemon Pilaf. Coat a deep 2-quart baking dish with **vegetable oil cooking spray.** Add 3 cups **low-sodium chicken broth,** 1½ cups **long-grain white rice,** 1 tablespoon grated **lemon peel,** 3 tablespoons **lemon juice,** ⅓ cup thinly sliced **green onions,** and 2 teaspoons **butter** or margarine. Stir to blend well. Cover baking dish tightly and bake in a 350° oven until rice is tender to bite (45 to 50 minutes). Fluff with a fork before serving.

Per serving: 347 calories (27% fat, 40% carbohydrates, 33% protein), 10 g total fat (4 saturated fat), 34 g carbohydrates, 28 g protein, 79 mg cholesterol, 194 mg sodium

Broiled Lamb Chops with Papaya Chutney

Preparation time: About 15 minutes
Cooking time: About 10 minutes

Broiled lamb chops are always a hit at dinnertime, especially when they're served juicy and still pink inside. For an appealing blend of flavors and textures, serve the meat with homemade papaya chutney, cumin-seasoned yogurt, and crisp raw cucumber.

        Seasoned Yogurt (recipe follows)
8   lamb rib chops, cut about ¾ inch thick
    (about 1½ lbs. *total*), trimmed of fat
¼   cup *each* sugar and cider vinegar
1   small onion, minced
½   cup raisins
1   teaspoon *each* ground cinnamon and
    ground ginger
1   large papaya (about 1¼ lbs.), peeled,
    seeded, and cut into ¼-inch-thick slices
1   large cucumber, seeded and cut into strips

Prepare Seasoned Yogurt; set aside.

Place lamb chops on a lightly oiled rack in a broiler pan. Broil about 4 inches below heat, turning once, until well browned on both sides but still pink in center; cut to test (8 to 10 minutes).

Meanwhile, in a wide frying pan, combine sugar, vinegar, onion, raisins, cinnamon, and ginger. Cook over medium-high heat, stirring occasionally, until onion is soft (about 5 minutes). Add papaya and stir gently until heated through (about 3 minutes).

Transfer chops to a platter; spoon papaya mixture over chops. Serve Seasoned Yogurt and cucumber strips alongside. Makes 4 servings.

Seasoned Yogurt. In a small bowl, stir together 1 cup **plain nonfat yogurt,** 1 tablespoon **mustard seeds,** 1 teaspoon **sugar,** ¼ teaspoon **ground cumin,** and ⅛ teaspoon **chili powder.**

Per serving: 343 calories (21% fat, 55% carbohydrates, 24% protein), 8 g total fat (3 g saturated fat), 49 g carbohydrates, 21 g protein, 51 mg cholesterol, 98 mg sodium

Minted Lamb Chops & Mushrooms with Pilaf Salad

. . . .

Preparation time: About 15 minutes
Marinating time: At least 30 minutes
Cooking time: 50 to 55 minutes

Here's the perfect choice for a patio party. Juicy grilled lamb chops and skewered mushrooms accompany an unusual salad that combines wild and brown rices with a yogurt dressing.

	Pilaf Salad (recipe follows)
4	**lamb loin chops, cut about 1 inch thick (about 1½ lbs.** *total***), trimmed of fat**
1	**teaspoon olive oil**
2	**tablespoons dry vermouth**
½	**teaspoon pepper**
¼	**cup coarsely chopped fresh mint**
16	**medium-large mushrooms (about 1 lb.** *total***)**

Prepare and refrigerate Pilaf Salad. While salad is chilling, set a large heavy-duty plastic bag in a shallow pan. Place lamb chops in bag; add oil, vermouth, pepper, and mint. Seal bag and turn to coat chops with marinade. Refrigerate for at least 30 minutes or up to 1 day, turning occasionally.

Thread mushrooms onto 4 slender metal skewers. Lift lamb chops from bag and drain briefly; reserve marinade. Brush mushrooms with marinade. Place chops on a lightly oiled grill 4 to 6 inches above a solid bed of hot coals; place skewered mushrooms around edge of grill, where heat is less intense. Cook, turning chops once and mushrooms several times, until mushrooms are lightly browned and chops are browned on outside but still pink in center; cut to test (about 10 minutes).

Spoon Pilaf Salad onto a large platter; arrange chops and skewered mushrooms over salad. Makes 4 servings.

Pilaf Salad. Rinse and drain ½ cup **wild rice;** place in a 2- to 3-quart pan and add 1 can (about 14½ oz.) **low-sodium chicken broth** and 1 cup **water.** Bring to a boil over high heat; reduce heat, cover, and simmer for 20 minutes. To partially cooked wild rice, add ¾ cup **long-grain brown rice.** Continue to cook, covered, until all rice is tender to bite (20 to 25 more minutes). Remove from heat. With a fork, stir in 3 tablespoons **lemon juice** and ¼ cup **sliced ripe olives.** Cover and refrigerate until cool (about 30 minutes) or for up to 1 day. Before serving, stir in ⅓ cup **plain low-fat yogurt** and 1 cup halved **cherry tomatoes;** season to taste with **salt.**

Per serving: 425 calories (23% fat, 49% carbohydrates, 28% protein), 11 g total fat (3 g saturated fat), 53 g carbohydrates, 30 g protein, 63 mg cholesterol, 178 mg sodium

Dilled Lamb Stew with Peas

. . . .

Preparation time: About 20 minutes
Cooking time: About 1½ hours

This stew gets its appealingly tart flavor from yogurt and fresh dill. When you shop for ingredients, look for boneless lamb cut from the leg; it's leaner and cooks more quickly than a shoulder cut.

1½	**pounds boneless leg of lamb, trimmed of fat and cut into 1-inch chunks**
2	**cups dry red wine**
½	**cup chopped fresh dill or 1 tablespoon dry dill weed**
4	**small onions, cut lengthwise into eighths**
2	**pounds carrots, cut into ½-inch lengths**
2	**cups fresh or frozen peas**
½	**cup plain low-fat yogurt blended with 1 tablespoon cornstarch**

In a 5- to 6-quart pan, combine lamb and ½ cup of the wine. Bring to a boil over high heat; then reduce heat, cover, and simmer for 30 minutes. Uncover and cook over medium-high heat until liquid has evaporated; then continue to cook, turning lamb chunks once, until meat is browned (about 5 more minutes). Remove lamb from pan and set aside. Discard any fat from pan.

Add remaining 1½ cups wine and dill to pan, stirring to scrape browned bits free. Return lamb to pan and add onions and carrots. Bring to a boil; then reduce heat, cover, and simmer, stirring occasionally, until lamb is very tender when pierced (about 45 minutes). Skim and discard fat from stew, if necessary.

Stir in peas and cook until tender to bite (about 5 more minutes). Stir in yogurt mixture; cook, stirring, until sauce is bubbly and thickened. Makes 6 servings.

Per serving: 305 calories (18% fat, 43% carbohydrates, 39% protein), 6 g total fat (2 g saturated fat), 34 g carbohydrates, 30 g protein, 74 mg cholesterol, 147 mg sodium

Cider-baked Lamb Stew with Turnips

MODIFIED CLASSIC

Preparation time: About 25 minutes
Baking time: 1¾ to 2¼ hours

In this easy version of a French country favorite, floured lamb cubes are browned in a hot oven, then simmered in cider until tender. Complement the stew with baked sweet potatoes and steamed fresh spinach, if you like.

3	tablespoons all-purpose flour
½	teaspoon ground cloves
¼	teaspoon ground white pepper
2	pounds boneless leg of lamb, trimmed of fat and cut into 1-inch cubes
1½	cups apple cider
4	medium-size turnips (about 1¼ lbs. *total*), peeled and cut lengthwise into wedges
2	medium-size onions, sliced
1	clove garlic, minced or pressed
⅓	cup chopped parsley
	Salt

Combine flour, cloves, and white pepper. Coat lamb cubes with flour mixture and arrange slightly apart in an ungreased shallow 3- to 3½-quart baking dish. Bake in a 500° oven for 20 minutes, then remove from oven and let cool in baking dish for about 5 minutes.

Reduce oven temperature to 375°. Gradually add cider to lamb in baking dish, stirring to scrape browned bits free. Add turnips, onions, garlic, and all but 1 tablespoon of the parsley.

Cover tightly and bake until lamb and turnips

are very tender when pierced (1½ to 2 hours), stirring occasionally. Skim and discard fat from stew, if necessary. Season to taste with salt. Sprinkle with reserved 1 tablespoon parsley. Makes 8 servings.

Per serving: 211 calories (23% fat, 29% carbohydrates, 48% protein), 5 g total fat (2 g saturated fat), 15 g carbohydrates, 25 g protein, 73 mg cholesterol, 113 mg sodium

Veal Stew with Caraway

Preparation time: About 15 minutes
Cooking time: About 1¾ hours

This delicate veal stew is at its best served over helpings of hot, tender noodles.

1	to 1½ pounds boneless veal shoulder, trimmed of fat and cut into 1-inch cubes
1	tablespoon salad oil
¼	teaspoon salt
⅛	teaspoon ground white pepper
1	large onion, finely chopped
½	cup dry white wine
2	teaspoons caraway seeds
1	can (about 14½ oz.) low-sodium chicken broth
2	medium-size carrots, chopped
3	to 4 cups hot cooked eggless noodles
	Chopped parsley

In a wide 3½- to 4-quart pan, combine veal, oil, salt, white pepper, onion, and wine. Cover and cook over medium-low heat for 30 minutes. Uncover pan and stir in caraway seeds. Increase heat to medium and continue to cook, stirring occasionally, until almost all liquid has evaporated and onion is browned (15 to 20 minutes). Add broth and carrots to pan, stirring to scrape browned bits free.

Reduce heat to low, cover, and simmer until veal is tender when pierced (35 to 45 minutes). Increase heat to medium and cook, uncovered, stirring often, until sauce is slightly thickened (12 to 15 minutes). To serve, spoon stew over noodles; sprinkle with parsley. Makes 4 to 6 servings.

Per serving: 288 calories (24% fat, 37% carbohydrates, 39% protein), 8 g total fat (2 g saturated fat), 27 g carbohydrates, 28 g protein, 98 mg cholesterol, 251 mg sodium

Neoclassical Blanquette de Veau

Preparation time: About 30 minutes
Cooking time: 1½ to 2 hours

Classic French *blanquette de veau* relies on butter, cream, and egg yolks for its velvety, rich-tasting sauce. Our version of the dish also features a smooth and savory sauce—but it's based on a lean purée of leeks, potatoes, and other vegetables.

1   tablespoon butter or margarine
2   medium-size onions, finely chopped
¼   cup chopped shallots
1   medium-size carrot, finely chopped
2   pounds boneless veal shoulder, trimmed of fat and cut into 1¼-inch cubes
2   sprigs *each* parsley and tarragon, tied together with string
2   leeks (white parts only), thinly sliced
1   large thin-skinned potato (about 8 oz.), peeled and quartered
3   tablespoons lemon juice
    About ½ teaspoon salt
⅛   teaspoon ground white pepper
½   cup *each* dry white wine and low-sodium chicken broth
½   cup evaporated skim milk
⅛   teaspoon ground nutmeg
1   package (about 9 oz.) frozen artichoke hearts, thawed and cut into bite-size pieces
½   cup frozen peas, thawed
    Tarragon sprigs (optional)

Melt butter in a wide 3½- to 4-quart pan over medium heat. Add onions, shallots, and carrot; cook, stirring often, until onions are soft but not browned (about 5 minutes). Stir in veal, parsley-tarragon bundle, leeks, potato, lemon juice, ½ teaspoon of the salt, white pepper, wine, and broth. Bring to a boil; then reduce heat, cover, and simmer until veal is very tender when pierced (1 to 1½ hours).

Using a slotted spoon, lift veal and most of the vegetables from cooking liquid and transfer to a bowl. Remove and discard parsley-tarragon bundle. Bring cooking liquid to a boil over high heat. Boil, uncovered, stirring occasionally, until reduced to about 1¼ cups.

Separate vegetables from veal. Place vegetables in a food processor or blender with about ¼ cup of the reduced cooking liquid; whirl until puréed. Add purée to remaining reduced cooking liquid; blend in milk and nutmeg. Bring to a gentle boil over medium heat, stirring often. Stir in veal, artichokes, and peas. Cook, stirring, just until meat and vegetables are heated through (2 to 3 minutes). Season to taste with salt and garnish with tarragon sprigs, if desired. Makes 6 to 8 servings.

Per serving: 261 calories (21% fat, 32% carbohydrates, 47% protein), 6 g total fat (2 g saturated fat), 21 g carbohydrates, 30 g protein, 117 mg cholesterol, 359 mg sodium

Baked Polenta with Veal Sauce

Preparation time: About 15 minutes
Baking time: 40 to 45 minutes
Cooking time: About 25 minutes

Soft, creamy baked polenta is delicious on its own as a side dish, but even better when topped with a lean ground veal and tomato sauce, richly flavored with garlic and herbs.

    Baked Polenta (recipe follows)
1   teaspoon olive oil
1   small onion, finely chopped
1   small carrot, shredded
4   ounces mushrooms, cut into quarters
1   clove garlic, minced or pressed
2   teaspoons Italian herb seasoning; or ½ teaspoon *each* dry basil, dry marjoram, dry oregano, and dry thyme
1   pound lean ground veal
1   large can (about 28 oz.) pear-shaped tomatoes
¼   cup tomato paste
½   cup dry white wine
    Salt and pepper
    Grated Parmesan cheese (optional)

Prepare Baked Polenta. While polenta is baking, combine oil, onion, carrot, mushrooms, garlic, and herb seasoning in a wide nonstick frying pan. Cook over medium-high heat, stirring often, until onion is soft (about 5 minutes). Crumble veal into pan and cook, stirring often, until it begins to brown. Cut up tomatoes; then add tomatoes and their liquid, tomato paste, and wine to pan. Bring to a boil. Adjust heat so mixture boils gently; cook, uncovered, stirring occasionally, until thickened (about 20 minutes). Season to taste with salt and pepper.

Spoon Baked Polenta into wide, shallow bowls and top with veal sauce. Offer cheese to add to taste, if desired. Makes 4 to 6 servings.

Baked Polenta. In an oiled shallow 2-quart baking dish, stir together 4 cups **low-sodium chicken broth,** 1¼ cups **polenta,** ¼ cup finely chopped **onion,** and 1 tablespoon **olive oil.** Bake in a 350° oven until liquid has been absorbed (40 to 45 minutes).

Per serving: 397 calories (29% fat, 45% carbohydrates, 26% protein), 12 g total fat (3 g saturated fat), 43 g carbohydrates, 25 g protein, 74 mg cholesterol, 494 mg sodium

Grilled Veal Shanks with Apricot Glaze

Preparation time: About 40 minutes
Baking time: About 1½ hours
Cooking time: About 15 minutes
Grilling time: About 20 minutes

In hot weather, people look for quick-cooking meals—and that usually rules out moist, fork-tender braised veal shanks, which require long baking or simmering. But if you cook the meat early in the morning or the night before, you can keep your house cool at suppertime: when you're ready to eat, reheat and brown the meat on the barbecue grill.

4	slender veal shanks, *each* about 6 inches long (about 4 lbs. *total*)
3	cups low-sodium chicken broth
1	cup dried apricots
2	tablespoons lemon juice
1	tablespoon minced fresh rosemary or 1 teaspoon dry rosemary
1	tablespoon grated orange peel
	Rosemary sprigs (optional)
4	cups hot cooked couscous

Arrange veal shanks in a single layer in a 9- by 13-inch baking pan. Add broth, apricots, lemon juice, minced rosemary, and orange peel; be sure apricots are covered with broth. Cover tightly and bake in a 400° oven for 45 minutes. Turn veal shanks over, cover tightly, and continue to bake until meat is tender when pierced but not falling off the bone—45 to 50 more minutes. (At this point, you may let cool, then cover and refrigerate for up to 1 day.)

At least 30 minutes before grilling, prepare a covered barbecue for indirect grilling as directed for Jerk Pork with Papaya (page 76).

Transfer veal shanks to a platter. Skim and discard any fat from pan juices. Pour juices and apricots into a food processor or blender; whirl until smoothly puréed. Return mixture to baking pan, bring to a boil over high heat, and boil, stirring often, until reduced to 2 cups (about 12 minutes). Pour 1 cup of the sauce into a small bowl; keep warm. Use remaining sauce as a baste.

Brush veal with about half the basting sauce. Place veal in center of prepared grill above drip pan. Cover barbecue, open vents, and cook until meat is lightly browned on bottom (about 10 minutes). With a wide spatula, gently loosen veal from grill and, using tongs, turn each shank over; meat is inclined to fall off bones. Brush with remaining basting sauce. Cover barbecue; cook until meat is evenly browned all over (10 to 12 more minutes).

Transfer veal to a platter; garnish with rosemary sprigs, if desired. Serve with couscous and reserved sauce. Makes 4 servings.

Per serving: 491 calories (12% fat, 53% carbohydrates, 35% protein), 7 g total fat (2 g saturated fat), 64 g carbohydrates, 43 g protein, 124 mg cholesterol, 154 mg sodium

SAUCES, SALSAS & MORE

Lighter meat dishes call for slimmer sauces—and salsa may well be the most popular such sauce today. In many homes, this fresh-tasting Mexican-inspired condiment is almost a staple; some even call it "the catsup of the '90s." Whether based on ripe tomatoes, crisp cucumber and jicama (see page 108), or juicy tropical fruits, salsa brings spirit to almost any simply cooked meat.

Other, less well-known sauces also enhance your favorite meats. Piquant Pickled Maui Onions add excitement to barbecued top round or soy-marinated broiled chicken. Roasted Eggplant Marmalade seems made for grilled or roasted lamb. And our Cherry Meat Sauce is delightful over lamb, beef, pork, or poultry.

When you make these sauces and salsas, keep in mind that they'll make seafood sparkle, too. You'll enjoy them on such fish as trout, swordfish, and fresh tuna.

SCORCHED CORN & CHILE SALSA

Preparation time: About 20 minutes
Grilling time: About 8 minutes

2 **medium-size ears corn**
1 **small tomato (about 4 oz.), seeded and finely chopped**
1 **medium-size fresh green Anaheim or other mild green chile, seeded and finely chopped**

2 **cloves garlic, minced or pressed**
2 **tablespoons lime juice**
1 **tablespoon ground dried California or New Mexico chiles**
   Salt

Remove and discard husks and silk from corn. Place corn on a lightly oiled grill 4 to 6 inches above a solid bed of medium-hot coals. Cook, turning as needed, until kernels are browned (about 8 minutes). Meanwhile, in a medium-size bowl, combine tomato, chopped chile, garlic, lime juice, and ground chiles; set aside.

Cut corn kernels from cobs and stir into tomato mixture; season to taste with salt. If made ahead, let cool; then cover and refrigerate for up to 4 hours. Serve at room temperature. Makes about 3 cups.

Per ¼ cup: 14 calories (11% fat, 76% carbohydrates, 13% protein), 0.2 g total fat (0 g saturated fat), 3 g carbohydrates, 0.5 g protein, 0 mg cholesterol, 3 mg sodium

SALSA FRESCA

Preparation time: About 20 minutes

2 **medium-size ripe tomatoes (about 12 oz. *total*), coarsely chopped**
2 **large tomatillos (about 6 oz. *total*), husked, rinsed, and chopped; or 1 medium-size ripe tomato (about 6 oz.), coarsely chopped**
¼ **cup chopped cilantro**

⅓ **cup chopped onion or thinly sliced green onions**
2 **tablespoons lime juice**
2 **to 6 tablespoons minced fresh or canned hot chiles**
   Salt

In a medium-size bowl, combine tomatoes, tomatillos, cilantro, onion, lime juice, and chiles. Stir to mix well; then season to taste with salt. If made ahead, cover and refrigerate for up to 4 hours. Makes 2½ to 3 cups.

Per ¼ cup: 14 calories (9% fat, 76% carbohydrates, 15% protein), 0.2 g total fat (0 g saturated fat), 3 g carbohydrates, 0.6 g protein, 0 mg cholesterol, 4 mg sodium

PINEAPPLE SALSA

Preparation time: About 15 minutes

1 **cup diced fresh or canned pineapple**
½ **cup chopped peeled, seeded cucumber**
1 **fresh jalapeño chile, seeded and minced**
1 **teaspoon grated lime peel**
3 **tablespoons lime juice**
2 **tablespoons minced cilantro**

In a medium-size bowl, mix pineapple, cucumber, chile, lime peel, lime juice, and cilantro. If made ahead, cover and refrigerate for up to 4 hours. Makes about 1¾ cups.

Per ¼ cup: 15 calories (6% fat, 90% carbohydrates, 4% protein), 0.1 g total fat (0 g saturated fat), 4 g carbohydrates, 0.2 g protein, 0 mg cholesterol, 2 mg sodium

PAPAYA SALSA

Preparation time: About 10 minutes

1	medium-size firm-ripe papaya (about 1 lb.), peeled, seeded, and cut into ¼-inch cubes
¼	cup chopped cilantro
3	green onions, thinly sliced
1	fresh jalapeño chile, seeded and minced
2	tablespoons lime juice

In a medium-size bowl, gently mix papaya, cilantro, onions, chile, and lime juice. If made ahead, cover and refrigerate for up to 4 hours. Makes about 2 cups.

Per ¼ cup: 18 calories (3% fat, 90% carbohydrates, 7% protein), 0.1 g total fat (0 g saturated fat), 5 g carbohydrates, 0.4 g protein, 0 mg cholesterol, 3 mg sodium

PICKLED MAUI ONIONS

Preparation time: About 10 minutes
Cooking time: About 5 minutes
Chilling time: At least 3 days

1	large Maui onion or other mild white onion
¾	cup water
6	tablespoons distilled white vinegar
3	tablespoons sugar
2	cloves garlic, peeled and crushed
1	small dried hot red chile
1½	teaspoons salt

Cut onion lengthwise into 1-inch-wide wedges. Place in a 3-to 4-cup heatproof wide-mouth jar. In a 1- to 1½-quart pan, combine water, vinegar, sugar, garlic, chile, and salt. Bring to a boil over high heat, stirring until sugar is dissolved. Pour hot liquid over onion; cover tightly. Let cool; then refrigerate for at least 3 days or up to 1 month. Makes about 2 cups.

Per ¼ cup: 33 calories (2% fat, 92% carbohydrates, 6% protein), 0.1 g total fat (0 g saturated fat), 8 g carbohydrates, 0.5 g protein, 0 mg cholesterol, 415 mg sodium

ROASTED EGGPLANT MARMALADE

Preparation time: About 30 minutes
Baking time: About 2 hours

4	medium-size eggplants (about 4 lbs. *total*), unpeeled, cut into ½-inch cubes
¼	cup *each* minced garlic and minced fresh ginger
⅓	cup firmly packed brown sugar
¼	cup red wine vinegar
2	tablespoons Oriental sesame oil
2	tablespoons chopped fresh tarragon or 2 teaspoons dry tarragon
2	teaspoons fennel seeds
1	cup low-sodium chicken broth

In a 10- by 15- by 2-inch baking pan, mix eggplant, garlic, ginger, sugar, vinegar, oil, tarragon, and fennel seeds. Bake in a 400° oven, stirring occasionally, until liquid evaporates and eggplant browns and begins to stick to pan (about 1½ hours). To deglaze, add ½ cup of the broth and stir to scrape browned bits free. Then continue to bake until eggplant begins to brown again (about 20 minutes). Repeat deglazing and browning steps, using remaining ½ cup broth. Serve marmalade warm or cool. If made ahead, let cool; then cover and refrigerate for up to 10 days (freeze for longer storage). Makes about 4 cups.

Per ¼ cup: 70 calories (23% fat, 68% carbohydrates, 9% protein), 2 g total fat (0.3 g saturated fat), 13 g carbohydrates, 2 g protein, 0 mg cholesterol, 11 mg sodium

CHERRY MEAT SAUCE

Preparation time: About 10 minutes
Cooking time: 3 to 5 minutes

⅓	cup red currant jelly
¼	cup raspberry vinegar
2	tablespoons orange juice
½	teaspoon dry tarragon
¾	cup pitted dark sweet cherries

In a 1½- to 2-quart pan, combine jelly, vinegar, orange juice, and tarragon. Place over high heat and cook, stirring, until steaming. Gently stir in cherries, then remove from heat. Makes about ¾ cup (4 servings).

Per serving: 94 calories (3% fat, 95% carbohydrates, 2% protein), 0.3 g total fat (0.1 g saturated fat), 24 g carbohydrates, 0.5 g protein, 0 mg cholesterol, 9 mg sodium

POULTRY

*G*reat-tasting and naturally low in fat, economical chicken and turkey are perennial favorites for healthful eating. Both adapt to nearly every style of cooking and accept either simple or sophisticated seasonings. And because they're so agreeable to so many different treatments, these birds suit almost any kind of meal, whether you're putting together a quick family supper or a holiday feast. Both chicken and turkey are sold as whole birds and as individual parts. As you'll learn from the recipes in this chapter, any cut you choose—from boneless, skinless chicken breasts to meaty turkey thighs—takes well to low-fat cooking methods. Try baking, grilling, braising, and stir-frying in very little fat (for more on lean cooking techniques, see page 119).

Arroz con Pollo

MODIFIED CLASSIC

Preparation time: About 15 minutes
Cooking time: About 1¼ hours

This classic chicken-and-rice dish is perfect for a casual Mexican-style dinner. You might complete the meal with refreshing Orange & Olive Patio Salad (page 44) and warm corn tortillas.

1	can (about 14½ oz.) tomatoes
	About 1½ cups low-sodium chicken broth
1	chicken (3 to 3½ lbs.), cut up and skinned
1	teaspoon salad oil
1	large onion, chopped
1	small green pepper (about 5 oz.), seeded and chopped
2	cloves garlic, minced or pressed
1	cup long-grain white rice
1	teaspoon dry oregano
¼	teaspoon *each* ground cumin and pepper
1	dry bay leaf
1	package (about 10 oz.) frozen tiny peas, thawed
	Salt
¼	cup thinly sliced green onions

Drain liquid from tomatoes into a glass measure. Add enough of the broth to make 2 cups liquid. Set drained tomatoes and broth mixture aside.

Rinse chicken and pat dry. Heat oil in a wide nonstick frying pan or 4- to 5-quart pan over medium-high heat. Add several pieces of chicken (do not crowd pan) and 2 tablespoons water; cook, turning as needed, until chicken is browned on all sides (about 10 minutes). Add more water, 1 tablespoon at a time, if pan appears dry. Repeat to brown remaining chicken, setting pieces aside as they are browned. Discard all but 1 teaspoon of the drippings.

Add chopped onion, bell pepper, and garlic to pan; cook, stirring often, until onion is soft (about 5 minutes). Cut up tomatoes; then add tomatoes, broth mixture, rice, oregano, cumin, pepper, and bay leaf to pan. Bring to a boil.

Return chicken to pan. Reduce heat, cover, and simmer, adding more broth as needed to prevent sticking, until rice is tender to bite and meat near thighbone is no longer pink; cut to test (about 45 minutes). Add peas and stir until heated through. Season to taste with salt. Just before serving, garnish with green onions. Makes 4 to 6 servings.

Per serving: 402 calories (15% fat, 47% carbohydrates, 38% protein), 7 g total fat (1 g saturated fat), 46 g carbohydrates, 38 g protein, 99 mg cholesterol, 340 mg sodium

Devilishly Spicy Chicken

Preparation time: About 15 minutes
Cooking time: About 1 hour

Simmered in beer and chili sauce and seasoned with plenty of dry mustard, these chicken pieces taste decidedly piquant.

1	chicken (about 4 lbs.), cut up and skinned
2	tablespoons butter or margarine
2	medium-size onions, chopped
1	tablespoon dry mustard
1	can or bottle (about 12 oz.) beer
⅓	cup tomato-based chili sauce
3	tablespoons Worcestershire
4	cups hot cooked eggless noodles
1	package (about 10 oz.) frozen tiny peas, thawed

Rinse chicken, pat dry, and set aside.

Melt butter in a wide frying pan over medium-high heat. Add onions; cook, stirring often, until golden brown (12 to 15 minutes). Stir in mustard, beer, chili sauce, and Worcestershire. Add all chicken pieces except breasts; turn to coat. Reduce heat, cover, and simmer for 20 minutes. Turn chicken over. Add breasts to pan, cover, and continue to simmer until meat near thighbone is no longer pink; cut to test (about 20 more minutes).

Spoon noodles onto a deep platter. Lift chicken from pan and arrange over noodles; keep warm. Bring cooking liquid to a boil; boil, uncovered, stirring often, until reduced to 2 cups (6 to 8 minutes). Add peas and stir until heated through. Spoon sauce over chicken. Makes 4 to 6 servings.

Per serving: 461 calories (22% fat, 37% carbohydrates, 41% protein), 11 g total fat (4 g saturated fat), 43 g carbohydrates, 46 g protein, 134 mg cholesterol, 610 mg sodium

Baked Chicken with Pears

Preparation time: About 10 minutes
Baking time: 15 to 20 minutes
Cooking time: 5 to 10 minutes

Enhance simple baked chicken with fresh pears poached in brandy or apple juice.

	Vegetable oil cooking spray or salad oil
6	**boneless, skinless chicken breast halves (about 2¼ lbs. *total*)**
3	**tablespoons lemon juice**
4	**teaspoons cornstarch**
1	**cup pear-flavored brandy or apple juice**
2	**large red Bartlett or other firm-ripe pears (about 1 lb. *total*)**

Lightly coat a 9- by 13-inch baking pan with cooking spray. Rinse chicken and pat dry; then rub with lemon juice and arrange, skinned side up, in pan. Bake in a 425° oven until meat in thickest part is no longer pink; cut to test (15 to 20 minutes).

Meanwhile, in a medium-size pan, smoothly blend cornstarch and brandy. Halve and core pears; cut lengthwise into ½-inch-thick slices. Add to brandy mixture and stir gently. Bring to a boil over medium-high heat; then reduce heat, cover, and simmer until pears are tender when pierced (about 5 minutes).

When chicken is done, pour pear mixture into baking pan; shake pan to mix gently. Transfer chicken and pears to individual plates; drizzle with sauce. Makes 6 servings.

Per serving: 348 calories (8% fat, 35% carbohydrates, 57% protein), 3 g total fat (0.6 g saturated fat), 25 g carbohydrates, 40 g protein, 99 mg cholesterol, 112 mg sodium

Fresh fruits *such as pears (and apricots, avocados, peaches, and plums) are often picked underripe so they'll come to market undamaged. If the fruit you buy is too firm to peel and slice easily, ripen it at home by placing it in a loosely closed paper bag or vented plastic bag for a day or two.*

Jamaican Jerk Chicken with Spiced Fettuccine

Preparation time: About 25 minutes
Marinating time: At least 20 minutes
Cooking time: About 20 minutes
Grilling time: About 10 minutes

Pasta and a splash of fresh lime juice temper the spicy heat of these grilled chicken breasts. The seasoning paste we use here is delicious with pork, too; see page 76.

	Jerk Seasoning Paste (page 77)
4	**boneless, skinless chicken breast halves (about 1½ lbs. *total*)**
2	**cups low-sodium chicken broth**
¼	**cup whipping cream**
12	**ounces dry fettuccine**
	Salt
	Cilantro sprigs
	Lime wedges

Prepare Jerk Seasoning Paste. Reserve and refrigerate 1 tablespoon of the seasoning paste. Rinse chicken and pat dry; then coat evenly with remaining seasoning paste. Cover and refrigerate for at least 20 minutes or up to 1 day.

In a wide frying pan, combine the reserved 1 tablespoon Jerk Seasoning Paste, broth, and cream. Bring mixture to a boil over high heat; then boil, uncovered, until reduced to 1½ cups (about 10 minutes). Remove from heat.

Place chicken on an oiled grill 4 to 6 inches above a solid bed of medium-hot coals. Cook, turning as needed, until meat in thickest part is no longer pink; cut to test (about 10 minutes).

When chicken is done, transfer it to a platter and keep warm. Cook fettuccine in a 5- to 6-quart pan in about 3 quarts boiling water until just tender to bite (8 to 10 minutes); or cook according to package directions. Drain pasta well and return to cooking pan; then add broth-cream mixture. Using 2 forks, mix pasta with broth-cream mixture over medium heat until almost all broth has been absorbed. Stir in any juices that have accumulated around chicken. Season to taste with salt.

To serve, spoon pasta equally onto 4 individual

plates. Top each serving of pasta with a piece of chicken. Garnish with cilantro sprigs; serve with lime wedges. Makes 4 servings.

Per serving: 602 calories (17% fat, 47% carbohydrates, 36% protein), 11 g total fat (4 g saturated fat), 70 g carbohydrates, 53 g protein, 196 mg cholesterol, 166 mg sodium

Chicken Breasts with Blueberries

Preparation time: About 5 minutes
Cooking time: About 30 minutes

Here's a chicken dish with a difference—blueberries! The fruit is mixed with apricot jam and mustard for a tangy sauce. Because the recipe uses frozen berries, you can make this entrée all year round.

4	boneless, skinless chicken breast halves (about 1½ lbs. *total*)
1	tablespoon salad oil
½	cup apricot jam
3	tablespoons Dijon mustard
½	cup frozen unsweetened blueberries
⅓	cup white wine vinegar
	Watercress sprigs

Rinse chicken and pat dry. Heat oil in a wide frying pan over medium-high heat. Add chicken; cook, turning as needed, until browned on both sides (about 6 minutes).

Meanwhile, in a small bowl, stir together jam and mustard. Spread jam mixture over tops of chicken pieces; sprinkle with blueberries. Reduce heat to medium-low, cover, and cook until meat in thickest part is no longer pink; cut to test (about 15 minutes). With a slotted spoon, lift chicken and blueberries to a platter. Keep warm.

Add vinegar to pan, increase heat to high, and bring sauce to a boil. Then boil, uncovered, stirring occasionally, until sauce is reduced by about a third (about 5 minutes). Pour sauce evenly over chicken; garnish with watercress sprigs. Makes 4 servings.

Per serving: 340 calories (17% fat, 36% carbohydrates, 47% protein), 6 g total fat (1 g saturated fat), 30 g carbohydrates, 40 g protein, 99 mg cholesterol, 464 mg sodium

Sake-steamed Chicken

Preparation time: About 20 minutes
Marinating time: At least 30 minutes
Cooking time: About 12 minutes

Serve these sake-marinated, steamed chicken breasts with hot rice, crisp iceberg lettuce, and a pungent horseradish-soy dipping sauce.

½	cup sake or unseasoned rice vinegar
½	teaspoon salt
6	boneless, skinless chicken breast halves (about 2¼ lbs. *total*)
1	small head iceberg lettuce
	About ⅓ cup reduced-sodium soy sauce
1	tablespoon prepared horseradish
	Lemon wedges
3	cups hot cooked rice
½	cup thinly sliced green onions

In a medium-size bowl, stir together sake and salt until salt is dissolved. Rinse chicken and pat dry; add to marinade and turn to coat. Cover and refrigerate for at least 30 minutes or up to 2 hours.

Lift chicken from bowl and drain briefly; discard marinade. Arrange chicken, with thickest parts toward outside, in a single layer in a 10- to 11-inch-round heatproof nonmetal dish. Cover with wax paper or foil and set on a rack in a large pan above 1 inch of boiling water. Cover and steam, keeping water at a steady boil, until meat in thickest part is no longer pink; cut to test (about 12 minutes).

Meanwhile, place 1 or 2 large lettuce leaves on each of 6 individual plates. Finely shred remaining lettuce; mound atop leaves. Divide soy sauce among 6 tiny dipping bowls; add ½ teaspoon of the horseradish to each, then place bowls on plates. Place a few lemon wedges on each plate.

Cut chicken crosswise into ½-inch-wide strips. Spoon rice and chicken over lettuce; sprinkle with onions. To eat, squeeze lemon into soy mixture. Dip chicken into sauce. Or tear lettuce leaves into pieces and fill with chicken, rice, and shredded lettuce; season with sauce and eat out of hand. Makes 6 servings.

Per serving: 360 calories (7% fat, 41% carbohydrates, 52% protein), 3 g total fat (0.7 g saturated fat), 35 g carbohydrates, 44 g protein, 99 mg cholesterol, 742 mg sodium

Broccoli-stuffed Chicken Breasts

Preparation time: About 45 minutes
Baking time: About 15 minutes
Broiling time: About 2 minutes

Stuffed with bright green broccoli and topped with Jarlsberg cheese, these chicken breasts slice beautifully for a party plate. Shallots, mushrooms, and a splash of Madeira add a French flavor to the filling.

1	tablespoon salad oil
½	cup minced shallots
1	pound mushrooms, minced
2	cups broccoli flowerets
2	tablespoons Madeira
2	tablespoons grated Parmesan cheese
½	cup shredded reduced-fat Jarlsberg or Swiss cheese
6	boneless, skinless chicken breast halves (about 2¼ lbs. *total*)

Heat oil in a wide frying pan over medium heat. Add shallots and mushrooms; cook, stirring occasionally, until shallots are soft (about 5 minutes). Add broccoli and Madeira; cover and cook, stirring occasionally, until broccoli is tender-crisp to bite (about 5 minutes). Remove from heat and stir in Parmesan cheese and ¼ cup of the Jarlsberg cheese. Let cool.

Rinse chicken and pat dry. Place each breast half between 2 sheets of plastic wrap and pound with a flat-surfaced mallet to a thickness of about ¼ inch. In center of each pounded chicken piece, mound a sixth of the broccoli-mushroom mixture. Roll chicken around filling to enclose. Set chicken rolls, seam side down, in a greased 9- by 13-inch baking pan. Sprinkle evenly with remaining ¼ cup Jarlsberg cheese.

Bake in a 450° oven until meat is no longer pink and filling is hot in center; cut to test (about 15 minutes). Then broil 4 to 6 inches below heat until cheese is browned (about 2 minutes). Makes 6 servings.

Per serving: 291 calories (21% fat, 13% carbohydrates, 66% protein), 7 g total fat (2 g saturated fat), 9 g carbohydrates, 46 g protein, 105 mg cholesterol, 190 mg sodium

Plum Chicken

Preparation time: About 10 minutes
Baking time: About 25 minutes

To make the richly flavored glaze for these moist chicken breasts, start with a jar of Oriental plum sauce; then enhance it with minced onion, lemon peel, and spices. Serve chicken and sauce with rice or fresh Chinese noodles, if you like.

4	boneless, skinless chicken breast halves (about 1½ lbs. *total*)
1	cup Oriental plum sauce
¼	cup minced onion
1	teaspoon grated lemon peel
2	tablespoons lemon juice
1	tablespoon reduced-sodium soy sauce
½	teaspoon *each* dry mustard and ground ginger
¼	teaspoon *each* pepper and liquid hot pepper seasoning
¼	teaspoon anise seeds, crushed

Rinse chicken and pat dry; then place, skinned side up, in a 9- by 13-inch baking pan. In a small bowl, stir together plum sauce, onion, lemon peel, lemon juice, soy sauce, mustard, ginger, pepper, hot pepper seasoning, and anise seeds.

Pour sauce evenly over chicken. Bake in a 400° oven, basting halfway through baking, until meat in thickest part is no longer pink; cut to test (about 25 minutes).

To serve, transfer chicken to a platter and spoon sauce over top. Makes 4 servings.

Per serving: 278 calories (7% fat, 33% carbohydrates, 60% protein), 2 g total fat (0.6 g saturated fat), 23 g carbohydrates, 41 g protein, 99 mg cholesterol, 581 mg sodium

Chicken Capocollo

Preparation time: About 15 minutes
Cooking time: 10 to 12 minutes

Thin slices of spicy capocollo sausage enliven this quick sauté of pounded chicken breasts in a light mustard sauce. Serve the dish with thin fresh noodles or orzo (or another tiny pasta shape) and a steamed green vegetable such as broccoli or asparagus.

4	small boneless, skinless chicken breast halves (about 1 lb. *total*)
4	thin slices capocollo (or coppa) sausage or prosciutto (about 1 oz. *total*)
2	teaspoons olive oil
4	green onions, thinly sliced
2	cloves garlic, minced or pressed
¼	cup low-sodium chicken broth or dry white wine
2	tablespoons Dijon mustard
1	tablespoon lemon juice
½	teaspoon dry basil

Rinse chicken and pat dry. Place each breast half between 2 sheets of plastic wrap and pound with a flat-surfaced mallet to a thickness of ⅓ to ½ inch. Lay a slice of capocollo on each pounded chicken piece, pressing lightly so that chicken and sausage stick together. Set aside.

Heat oil in a wide frying pan over medium heat. Add onions and garlic; cook, stirring often, until vegetables are lightly browned (about 3 minutes). Then push vegetables to one side and place chicken in pan. Cook just until edges of chicken pieces begin to brown on bottom (about 4 minutes). Turn pieces over and continue to cook until meat in thickest part is no longer pink; cut to test (3 to 4 more minutes). Transfer chicken, sausage side up, to a platter; keep warm.

To pan, add broth, mustard, lemon juice, and basil. Bring to a boil over high heat, stirring constantly; then pour broth mixture over chicken. Makes 4 servings.

Per serving: 180 calories (27% fat, 7% carbohydrates, 66% protein), 5 g total fat (0.9 g saturated fat), 3 g carbohydrates, 29 g protein, 72 mg cholesterol, 437 mg sodium

Oven-fried Chicken

Preparation time: About 15 minutes
Marinating time: 20 minutes
Baking time: 15 to 20 minutes

Low-fat fried chicken? Yes—if you follow our recipe. Baked in an herb-seasoned crust of cornmeal and whole wheat bread crumbs, these chicken breasts are juicy inside, crisp and crunchy outside.

2	tablespoons dry sherry
2	cloves garlic, minced or pressed
4	boneless, skinless chicken breast halves (about 1½ lbs. *total*)
½	cup soft whole wheat bread crumbs
2	tablespoons cornmeal
1	teaspoon paprika
½	teaspoon *each* salt, pepper, dry sage, dry thyme, and dry basil
	Vegetable oil cooking spray

In a shallow bowl, stir together sherry and garlic. Rinse chicken and pat dry; add to sherry mixture, turn to coat, and let stand for 20 minutes.

In another shallow bowl, mix bread crumbs, cornmeal, paprika, salt, pepper, sage, thyme, and basil. Lift chicken from marinade and drain briefly; discard marinade. Turn each chicken piece in crumb mixture to coat.

Lightly coat a shallow baking pan with cooking spray; arrange chicken pieces in pan. Bake in a 450° oven until meat in thickest part is no longer pink; cut to test (15 to 20 minutes). Serve hot or cold. Makes 4 servings.

Per serving: 231 calories (12% fat, 14% carbohydrates, 74% protein), 3 g total fat (0.6 g saturated fat), 8 g carbohydrates, 40 g protein, 99 mg cholesterol, 418 mg sodium

---

Having trouble peeling garlic? *You can easily loosen the thin, papery skin by placing the garlic clove on a hard surface, then pressing down on it firmly with the flat side of a knife blade.*

Mediterranean Baked Chicken & Vegetables

Preparation time: About 15 minutes
Baking time: 20 to 25 minutes

A fresh-tasting dinner can be on the table quickly when you choose this recipe. Bake chicken breasts with zucchini, tomatoes, mushrooms, and seasonings of fennel and basil; serve over your favorite pasta.

4   **chicken breast halves (about 1¾ lbs. *total*), skinned and trimmed of fat**
8   **ounces mushrooms, sliced**
1   **pound zucchini, cut into ¼-inch-thick slices**
1   **tablespoon olive oil**
1   **teaspoon *each* pepper and dry oregano**
1   **teaspoon fennel seeds, crushed**
1   **tablespoon dry basil**
1   **can (about 14½ oz.) pear-shaped tomatoes**
     Parsley sprigs
     Grated Parmesan cheese

Rinse chicken, pat dry, and place in a 12- by 15-inch broiler pan. Arrange mushrooms and zucchini around chicken. Drizzle with oil. Sprinkle with pepper, oregano, fennel seeds, and basil; mix to coat chicken and vegetables with seasonings.

Cover pan tightly and bake in a 425° oven for 15 minutes. Cut up tomatoes, then stir tomatoes and their liquid into pan. Cover and continue to bake until meat near bone is no longer pink; cut to test (5 to 10 more minutes). Garnish with parsley sprigs; offer cheese to add to taste. Makes 4 servings.

Per serving: 230 calories (22% fat, 20% carbohydrates, 58% protein), 6 g total fat (1 g saturated fat), 12 g carbohydrates, 34 g protein, 75 mg cholesterol, 258 mg sodium

---

Long considered an exotic food *used primarily in North African cuisine, couscous is now found in most supermarkets. Quick-cooking and delicious, it's simply semolina—the durum wheat from which pasta is made—in granular form. You'll enjoy it with many of the same sauces you serve over spaghetti or noodles.*

Chicken with Pumpkin Seeds

30 MINUTES OR LESS

Preparation time: About 10 minutes
Baking time: 20 to 25 minutes

Crusted with a blend of pumpkin seeds, mild chiles, and cheese, this juicy baked chicken goes together in just 10 minutes. At the table, add a squeeze of lime to balance the zesty seasonings.

4   **chicken breast halves (about 1¾ lbs. *total*), skinned and trimmed of fat**
⅓   **cup roasted pumpkin seeds**
1   **can (about 4 oz.) diced green chiles**
½   **cup shredded jack cheese**
     Lime wedges

Rinse chicken and pat dry; then place, skinned side up, in a 9- by 13-inch baking pan. In a small bowl, mix pumpkin seeds, chiles, and cheese; pat evenly onto chicken.

Bake chicken in a 450° oven until meat near bone is no longer pink; cut to test (20 to 25 minutes). Serve with lime wedges. Makes 4 servings.

Per serving: 226 calories (28% fat, 9% carbohydrates, 63% protein), 7 g total fat (3 g saturated fat), 5 g carbohydrates, 35 g protein, 90 mg cholesterol, 334 mg sodium

Chicken-on-a-Stick with Couscous

Preparation time: About 30 minutes
Marinating time: At least 30 minutes
Grilling time: 8 to 10 minutes

Serve these lemony kebabs on fluffy couscous; offer a garlicky cumin-yogurt sauce alongside.

⅓   **cup *each* lemon juice and olive oil**
¼   **cup dry white wine**
6   **cloves garlic, minced or pressed**
2   **dry bay leaves, crumbled**
1½ **pounds boneless, skinless chicken breasts, cut into ¾-inch chunks**
     Cumin-Garlic Yogurt Sauce (recipe follows)

2½ cups low-sodium chicken broth
1¾ cups couscous
½ cup sliced green onions

In a medium-size bowl, stir together lemon juice, oil, wine, garlic, and bay leaves. Add chicken and stir to coat. Cover and refrigerate for at least 30 minutes or up to 4 hours. Meanwhile, prepare Cumin-Garlic Yogurt Sauce. Also, if using bamboo skewers, soak eight 8-inch skewers in hot water to cover for at least 30 minutes.

Lift chicken from marinade and drain briefly; reserve marinade. Thread chicken on bamboo or metal skewers; set aside.

In a 2- to 3-quart pan, bring broth to a boil over high heat. Stir in couscous. Cover, remove from heat, and let stand while you cook chicken.

Place chicken on a lightly oiled grill 4 to 6 inches above a solid bed of medium-hot coals. Cook, turning as needed and basting with reserved marinade, until meat is no longer pink in center; cut to test (8 to 10 minutes).

With a fork, stir onions into couscous; then fluff couscous and spoon onto a platter. Top with chicken skewers. Serve with Cumin-Garlic Yogurt Sauce. Makes 4 servings.

Cumin-Garlic Yogurt Sauce. In a small bowl, stir together 1½ cups **plain low-fat yogurt,** 2 tablespoons minced **cilantro,** 1 teaspoon **cumin seeds,** and 1 clove **garlic,** minced or pressed. Cover and refrigerate for at least 15 minutes or up to 1 day.

Per serving: 662 calories (20% fat, 45% carbohydrates, 35% protein), 14 g total fat (3 g saturated fat), 72 g carbohydrates, 56 g protein, 104 mg cholesterol, 218 mg sodium

Chicken Vermicelli Carbonara

. . . .

MODIFIED CLASSIC

Preparation time: About 25 minutes
Cooking time: About 30 minutes

Here's a creative low-fat version of an Italian classic. Chicken stands in for the usual pork; chopped onion braised in fennel-seasoned broth adds richness to the flavor.

1 large onion, finely chopped
½ teaspoon fennel seeds
1 can (about 14½ oz.) low-sodium chicken broth
12 to 14 ounces boneless, skinless chicken thighs, trimmed of fat and cut into ½-inch cubes
1 cup finely chopped parsley
3 large egg whites (about 6 tablespoons)
1 large egg
12 ounces to 1 pound dry vermicelli
1½ cups (about 6 oz.) finely shredded Parmesan cheese
Salt and pepper

In a wide nonstick frying pan, combine onion, fennel seeds, and 1 cup of the broth. Bring to a boil over high heat; boil, stirring occasionally, until liquid evaporates and onion begins to brown (8 to 10 minutes). To deglaze, add 2 tablespoons water, stirring to scrape browned bits free. Then continue to cook, stirring occasionally, until onion begins to brown again. Repeat deglazing and browning steps, using 2 tablespoons water each time, until onions are a uniformly light golden brown color.

To pan, add chicken and 2 tablespoons water. Cook, stirring often, until drippings begin to brown; then deglaze pan with 2 tablespoons water. When liquid has evaporated, add remaining ¾ cup broth and bring to a boil. Stir in parsley; reduce heat to very low and keep mixture warm. In a small bowl, beat egg whites and whole egg to blend well; set aside.

In a 6- to 8-quart pan, cook vermicelli in about 4 quarts boiling water until just tender to bite (8 to 10 minutes); or cook according to package directions. Drain well.

Add hot pasta to pan with chicken. Pour egg mixture over pasta and at once begin lifting with 2 forks to mix well (eggs cook if you delay mixing); add 1 cup of the cheese as you mix. Pour mixture onto a deep platter and continue to mix until almost all broth has been absorbed. Season to taste with salt and pepper. Offer remaining ½ cup cheese to add to taste. Makes 6 to 8 servings.

Per serving: 425 calories (25% fat, 45% carbohydrates, 30% protein), 11 g total fat (6 g saturated fat), 47 g carbohydrates, 31 g protein, 93 mg cholesterol, 552 mg sodium

Garlicky Broiled Chicken

Preparation time: About 10 minutes
Marinating time: At least 2 hours
Broiling time: About 20 minutes

Mushroom halves and chunks of red bell pepper broil right alongside this garlicky marinated chicken.

⅓	cup lemon juice
2	tablespoons olive oil
⅓	cup dry white wine
6	cloves garlic, minced or pressed
2	dry bay leaves, crumbled
4	small boneless, skinless chicken breast halves (1 to 1¼ lbs. *total*)
2	large red bell peppers (about 1 lb. *total*), seeded and cut into 1½-inch squares
12	ounces medium-size mushrooms, cut into halves

In a shallow bowl, stir together lemon juice, oil, wine, garlic, and bay leaves. Rinse chicken and pat dry; then add to marinade and turn to coat. Cover and refrigerate for at least 2 hours or up to 1 day, turning occasionally.

Lift chicken from marinade and drain briefly; reserve marinade. Place chicken on a rack in a broiler pan. Broil 4 inches below heat for 15 minutes, turning as needed and basting with marinade.

Arrange bell peppers and mushrooms alongside chicken, baste with pan juices, and continue to broil until meat in thickest part is no longer pink; cut to test (about 5 more minutes). Makes 4 servings.

Per serving: 252 calories (27% fat, 20% carbohydrates, 53% protein), 7 g total fat (1 g saturated fat), 12 g carbohydrates, 33 g protein, 74 mg cholesterol, 93 mg sodium

Light Chicken Stroganoff

Preparation time: About 45 minutes
Soaking time: About 30 minutes
Cooking time: About 25 minutes

To make this tempting dish, we revised a *Sunset* favorite containing a generous measure of butter and sour cream. The new version is far lower in fat than the original, but every bit as rich in flavor.

½	cup (about 1⅛ oz.) dried tomatoes
1	pound boneless, skinless chicken breasts, cut crosswise into ½-inch-wide strips
	Ground white pepper
1½	to 2 tablespoons all-purpose flour
1½	tablespoons salad oil
1	medium-size onion, thinly sliced
8	ounces mushrooms, sliced
½	teaspoon *each* grated fresh ginger and dry thyme
4	teaspoons cornstarch blended with 2 tablespoons cold water
½	teaspoon sugar
1	cup plain low-fat yogurt
8	ounces dry eggless noodles
2	cloves garlic, minced or pressed
¼	cup low-sodium chicken broth
¾	cup dry white wine
2	tablespoons dry sherry
	Chopped parsley

In a small bowl, soak tomatoes in boiling water to cover until very soft (about 30 minutes). Drain well, cut into strips, and set aside.

Sprinkle chicken with white pepper; dust with flour and shake off excess. Heat 1 tablespoon of the oil in a wide nonstick frying pan over medium-high heat. Add chicken, about half at a time, and cook, lifting and turning often, until lightly browned (4 to 5 minutes). Remove from pan with a slotted spoon and set aside.

When all chicken has been cooked, heat remaining 1½ teaspoons oil in pan. Add onion, mushrooms, ginger, and thyme; cook, stirring often, until onion is soft and mushrooms are lightly browned (10 to 12 minutes).

Meanwhile, stir cornstarch mixture and sugar into yogurt and set aside. Also, in a 5- to 6-quart pan, cook noodles in about 3 quarts boiling water until just tender to bite (7 to 9 minutes); or cook according to package directions. Drain, then arrange around edge of a deep platter; keep warm.

Stir garlic into mushroom mixture and cook for 1 minute. Then stir in broth, wine, and sherry; bring to a boil, stirring. Add tomatoes, chicken, and yogurt mixture; bring to a boil. Boil, uncovered, stirring often, until sauce is thickened. Spoon chicken mixture into center of platter and sprinkle with parsley. Makes 4 servings.

Per serving: 531 calories (17% fat, 51% carbohydrates, 32% protein), 9 g total fat (2 g saturated fat), 63 g carbohydrates, 41 g protein, 69 mg cholesterol, 148 mg sodium

Strawberry Chicken

. . . .

Preparation time: About 10 minutes
Baking time: About 45 minutes

Baked in a spicy sweet-sour sauce, these tender baked chicken thighs taste splendid atop a bed of steaming short-grain rice.

1	can (about 8 oz.) tomato sauce
1	cup strawberry jam
2	tablespoons red wine vinegar
1	tablespoon chili powder
½	teaspoon *each* dry thyme and ground ginger
12	skinless chicken thighs (2 to 2¼ lbs. *total*), trimmed of fat
	Salt
3	cups hot cooked short-grain rice
½	cup thinly sliced green onions

In a shallow 3-quart casserole, mix tomato sauce, jam, vinegar, chili powder, thyme, and ginger.

Rinse chicken and pat dry; then add to sauce and turn to coat. Bake in a 400° oven, basting occasionally, until meat near bone is no longer pink; cut to test (about 45 minutes). Season to taste with salt.

Spoon rice onto a platter. Top with chicken, sauce, and onions. Makes 4 to 6 servings.

Per serving: 505 calories (11% fat, 63% carbohydrates, 26% protein), 6 g total fat (2 g saturated fat), 81 g carbohydrates, 33 g protein, 118 mg cholesterol, 441 mg sodium

Apple Country Chicken

. . . .

Preparation time: About 15 minutes
Cooking time: About 40 minutes

Pungent curry powder accents the sweetness of apples in this cider-simmered chicken. Top the dish with tart yogurt, if you like; serve over fluffy white rice or a brown rice pilaf. Alongside, offer green beans or crunchy sugar snap peas.

1	teaspoon curry powder
1	large Golden Delicious apple (about 8 oz.), cored and chopped
1	large yellow onion, finely chopped
1	tablespoon lemon juice
4	ounces mushrooms, sliced
1	teaspoon chicken-flavored instant bouillon
2	cups apple juice or cider
3¼	to 3½ pounds chicken thighs, skinned and trimmed of fat
1	tablespoon all-purpose flour
2	tablespoons sliced green onion
	Plain low-fat yogurt or reduced-fat sour cream (optional)

Place curry powder in a wide frying pan and stir over medium heat until slightly darker in color (3 to 4 minutes). Add apple, yellow onion, lemon juice, mushrooms, bouillon, and 1½ cups of the apple juice. Increase heat to high and bring juice mixture to a boil.

Rinse chicken, pat dry, and add to pan. Then reduce heat, cover, and simmer until meat near bone is no longer pink; cut to test (about 30 minutes). Transfer chicken to a platter and keep warm.

In a small bowl, smoothly blend flour and remaining ½ cup apple juice. Gradually add to sauce in pan, stirring constantly; increase heat to high and cook, stirring, until sauce is thickened. Pour over chicken. Garnish with green onion; offer yogurt to add to taste, if desired. Makes 4 to 6 servings.

Per serving: 314 calories (22% fat, 32% carbohydrates, 46% protein), 7 g total fat (2 g saturated fat), 25 g carbohydrates, 36 g protein, 146 mg cholesterol, 380 mg sodium

Saffron & Honey Chicken

Preparation time: About 10 minutes
Cooking time: About 20 minutes
Baking time: About 35 minutes

It's no wonder this richly glazed chicken has a complex flavor—it's seasoned with lime, honey, soy, and a half-dozen herbs and spices. The sauce is lightly thickened with rice flour; look for it in well-stocked supermarkets and health-food stores.

⅔	cup low-sodium chicken broth
2	tablespoons *each* lime juice and honey
¼	teaspoon saffron threads
1	teaspoon white Worcestershire
2	teaspoons curry powder
½	teaspoon dry oregano
¼	teaspoon paprika
⅛	teaspoon pepper
2	teaspoons reduced-sodium soy sauce
2	tablespoons white rice flour blended with ¼ cup cold water
6	*each* chicken drumsticks and thighs (about 3 lbs. *total*), skinned and trimmed of fat
	Chopped parsley

In a 1½- to 2-quart pan, stir together broth, lime juice, honey, saffron, Worcestershire, curry powder, oregano, paprika, pepper, and soy sauce. Bring to a boil over high heat; then reduce heat and simmer, uncovered, stirring occasionally, until reduced to ½ cup (about 15 minutes). Stir in rice flour mixture; bring to a boil over high heat, stirring. Remove from heat.

Rinse chicken, pat dry, and arrange, skinned side up, in a 9- by 13-inch baking pan. Spoon sauce evenly over chicken. Cover and bake in a 375° oven until meat near bone is no longer pink; cut to test (about 35 minutes).

Transfer chicken to a platter; stir sauce to blend, then spoon over chicken. Sprinkle with parsley. Makes 6 servings.

Per serving: 198 calories (24% fat, 20% carbohydrates, 56% protein), 5 g total fat (1 g saturated fat), 10 g carbohydrates, 27 g protein, 104 mg cholesterol, 193 mg sodium

Oriental Chicken with Pea Pods & Rice

Preparation time: About 35 minutes
Baking time: 25 to 30 minutes
Cooking time: About 30 minutes

Pound boneless, skinless chicken thighs out thin; then roll them around a mushroom stuffing, bake, and serve with fluffy seasoned rice and crisp snow peas.

2	teaspoons sesame seeds
12	ounces Chinese pea pods (also called snow or sugar peas), ends and strings removed
	About 3 cups beef broth
⅓	cup sake or dry sherry
3	tablespoons sugar
2	tablespoons reduced-sodium soy sauce
2	cloves garlic, minced or pressed
1	cup thinly sliced mushrooms
½	cup thinly sliced green onions
8	small boneless, skinless chicken thighs (about 1 lb. *total*)
1⅓	cups long-grain white rice

Toast sesame seeds in a 3- to 4-quart pan over medium-high heat until golden (2 to 4 minutes), stirring often. Pour out of pan and set aside.

Pour water into pan to a depth of 3 inches; bring to a boil over high heat. Add pea pods and cook, uncovered, just until they turn a brighter green (about 2 minutes). Drain, immerse in cold water until cool, and drain again. Set aside.

In a small bowl, stir together ⅓ cup of the broth, sake, sugar, soy sauce, and garlic. Measure out ¼ cup of the mixture; set aside. Then measure 1 tablespoon of the remaining broth mixture into a bowl; stir in mushrooms and ¼ cup of the onions. Set aside.

Rinse chicken and pat dry. Place pieces between sheets of plastic wrap and pound with a flat-surfaced mallet to a thickness of about ⅛ inch. In center of each pounded chicken piece, mound an eighth of the mushroom mixture. Fold meat over mushroom mixture to enclose. Set chicken rolls, seam side down, about 1 inch apart in a 9- by 13-inch baking pan.

Brush some of the remaining broth mixture over chicken. Bake in a 450° oven until meat is no longer pink in center; cut to test (25 to 30 minutes). Brush chicken occasionally with remaining broth mixture, using all. If pan drippings begin to burn, add 4 to 6 tablespoons water to pan, stirring to scrape browned bits free.

In pan used to cook pea pods, combine 2¾ cups of the broth and the reserved ¼ cup broth mixture. Bring to a boil over high heat; add rice. Then reduce heat, cover, and simmer until rice is tender to bite (about 20 minutes). Keep warm.

To serve, arrange chicken rolls and pea pods on a platter. Pour any pan juices into rice; then add remaining ¼ cup onions and stir to combine. Spoon rice onto platter. Sprinkle with sesame seeds. Makes 4 servings.

Per serving: 502 calories (13% fat, 60% carbohydrates, 27% protein), 7 g total fat (1 g saturated fat), 71 g carbohydrates, 32 g protein, 94 mg cholesterol, 1,028 mg sodium

Braised Chicken with Green Chile Sauce

· ·

Preparation time: About 15 minutes
Cooking time: About 40 minutes

Cool weather calls for robust dinner dishes like this one: chicken thighs simmered with bell peppers, cilantro, and mild green chiles in an herb-onion base. Serve over rice or wrapped in warm flour tortillas, with toppings of yogurt, tomato, and lime.

1	**large onion, chopped**
2	**cloves garlic, minced or pressed**
1	**cup low-sodium chicken broth**
1	**teaspoon dry oregano**
½	**teaspoon ground cumin**
1	**tablespoon red wine vinegar**
3	**pounds boneless, skinless chicken or turkey thighs, trimmed of fat and cut into 1-inch chunks**
2	**large green bell peppers (about 1 lb. *total*), seeded and chopped**
½	**cup chopped cilantro**
1	**large can (about 7 oz.) diced green chiles**
	Salt and pepper
	Hot cooked rice or warm flour tortillas
	Tomato wedges, plain nonfat yogurt or reduced-fat sour cream, and lime wedges

In a 5- to 6-quart pan, combine onion, garlic, broth, oregano, and cumin. Bring to a boil over high heat; boil, stirring occasionally, until liquid evaporates and onion begins to brown (about 10 minutes). To deglaze, add 2 tablespoons water and stir to scrape browned bits free. Then continue to cook, stirring occasionally, until onion begins to brown again. Repeat deglazing and browning steps, using 2 tablespoons water each time, until onion is richly browned. Then deglaze one last time with vinegar and 1 tablespoon water.

Stir in chicken, bell peppers, cilantro, chiles, and 1 tablespoon water. Cover and cook over low heat, stirring often, until chicken chunks are no longer pink in center; cut to test (about 15 minutes). Skim and discard fat from sauce; season to taste with salt and pepper.

Spoon chicken mixture into a bowl. Serve over rice; offer tomato wedges, yogurt, and lime wedges to season each serving. Makes 6 to 8 servings.

Per serving: 273 calories (27% fat, 13% carbohydrates, 60% protein), 8 g total fat (2 g saturated fat), 9 g carbohydrates, 40 g protein, 161 mg cholesterol, 351 mg sodium

***The canned green chiles** called for in the recipe above are of the Anaheim or California variety. Popular and widely available, they're mild to medium-hot in flavor.*

Chicken & Mushrooms with Couscous

....

Preparation time: About 20 minutes
Cooking time: About 20 minutes

Mild, creamy, quick-cooking couscous is the perfect foil for tender stir-fried chicken in a cayenne-sparked sauce. Offer fresh asparagus spears alongside.

1	**pound boneless, skinless chicken thighs, trimmed of fat**
1	**tablespoon butter or margarine**
1	**large onion, finely chopped**
12	**ounces mushrooms, sliced**
2	**teaspoons cornstarch**
1	**cup low-sodium chicken broth**
3	**tablespoons dry sherry**
2	**tablespoons reduced-sodium soy sauce**
1⁄8	**teaspoon ground red pepper (cayenne)**
2	**cups low-fat milk**
1½	**cups couscous**
	Vegetable oil cooking spray
	Cilantro sprigs

Rinse chicken and pat dry. Place pieces between sheets of plastic wrap and pound with a flat-surfaced mallet to a thickness of about ¼ inch; then cut chicken into ½-inch-wide strips. Set aside.

Melt butter in a wide nonstick frying pan over medium-high heat. Add onion and mushrooms; cook, stirring often, until liquid has evaporated and onion is golden and sweet-tasting (10 to 12 minutes).

Meanwhile, in a small bowl, smoothly blend cornstarch and ¼ cup of the broth; stir in sherry, soy sauce, and red pepper. Set aside.

In a 2-quart pan, combine milk and remaining ¾ cup broth; bring to a boil over high heat. Stir in couscous; cover, remove from heat, and let stand while you cook chicken.

Remove onion mixture from frying pan and set aside. Coat pan with cooking spray and place over high heat. Add chicken and cook, lifting and stirring, until meat is tinged with brown and is no longer pink in center; cut to test (4 to 5 minutes).

Return onion mixture to pan; add cornstarch mixture and cook, stirring constantly, until sauce is bubbly and slightly thickened.

Fluff couscous with a fork, then mound on a platter. Spoon chicken alongside couscous and garnish with cilantro sprigs. Makes 4 to 6 servings.

Per serving: 440 calories (17% fat, 54% carbohydrates, 29% protein), 8 g total fat (3 g saturated fat), 57 g carbohydrates, 31 g protein, 85 mg cholesterol, 411 mg sodium

Chicken & Black Bean Bake

....

Preparation time: About 15 minutes
Baking time: About 20 minutes

By taking advantage of quick-cooking refried black bean mix, you can have this baked chicken on the table in very short order.

1	**package (about 7 oz.) or 1⅔ cups instant refried black bean mix**
2	**cups boiling water**
1⁄3	**to ½ cup dry sherry or water**
4	**boneless, skinless chicken breast halves (about 1½ lbs. *total*)**
8	**cups shredded iceberg lettuce**
½	**cup shredded jack cheese**
1	**fresh red or green jalapeño chile, thinly sliced crosswise (optional)**
	Cherry tomatoes
	Reduced-fat sour cream

In a shallow 2- to 2½-quart baking dish, combine refried bean mix, boiling water, and sherry (use the ½-cup amount if you prefer a saucelike consistency). Rinse chicken and pat dry; then arrange, skinned side up, atop beans. Bake in a 400° oven until meat in thickest part is no longer pink; cut to test (about 20 minutes). Stir any liquid that accumulates around chicken into beans.

Mound lettuce equally on 4 individual plates; top with beans and chicken. Sprinkle with cheese and chile (if used); garnish with cherry tomatoes. Offer sour cream to add to taste. Makes 4 servings.

Per serving: 469 calories (17% fat, 33% carbohydrates, 50% protein), 8 g total fat (3 g saturated fat), 36 g carbohydrates, 54 g protein, 114 mg cholesterol, 597 mg sodium

MARINADES & BASTES

Sizzling, smoky-tasting grilled poultry is especially enticing when enhanced with a savory marinade or baste. On this page, we offer four choices. The two glazes are intended for a whole 12- to 24-pound turkey cooked in a covered barbecue. Tomato-Wine Baste brings traditional barbecue-sauce flavor to poultry parts; Miso-Maple Marinade adds an Asian accent to chicken pieces or turkey tenderloins.

BROWN SUGAR CRACKLE GLAZE

Preparation time: About 5 minutes

2 **cups firmly packed brown sugar**

5 **tablespoons Dijon mustard**

2 **teaspoons coarsely ground pepper**

In a small bowl, mix sugar, mustard, and pepper.

About 45 minutes before turkey is done (temperature in breast will be about 135°F at bone for birds up to 18 lbs., 145°F for birds over 18 lbs.), spread turkey with half the glaze. Cook for 20 more minutes; brush with remaining glaze.

Continue to cook until a meat thermometer inserted in thickest part of breast registers 160°F at bone. If glaze becomes too dark, drape dark areas with foil. Makes about 2 cups.

Per tablespoon: 55 calories (2% fat, 97% carbohydrates, 1% protein), 0.2 g total fat (0 g saturated fat), 14 g carbohydrates, 0 g protein, 0 mg cholesterol, 76 mg sodium

CHILE-ORANGE GLAZE

Preparation time: About 10 minutes

3 **tablespoons ground dried California or New Mexico chiles (or use regular chili powder)**

1 **large can (about 12 oz.) frozen orange juice concentrate, thawed**

2 **tablespoons grated orange peel**

1 **teaspoon ground cumin**

In a small bowl, mix ground chiles, orange juice concentrate, orange peel, and cumin.

About 20 minutes before turkey is done (temperature in breast will be about 150°F at bone for birds up to 18 lbs., 155°F for birds over 18 lbs.), spread turkey with orange mixture. Continue to cook until a meat thermometer inserted in thickest part of breast registers 160°F at bone. If glaze becomes too dark, drape dark areas with foil. Makes about 1⅔ cups.

Per tablespoon: 30 calories (5% fat, 88% carbohydrates, 7% protein), 0.2 g total fat (0 g saturated fat), 7 g carbohydrates, 0.5 g protein, 0 mg cholesterol, 9 mg sodium

TOMATO-WINE BASTE

Preparation time: About 5 minutes

1 **can (about 8 oz.) tomato sauce**

¼ **cup dry red wine**

2 **tablespoons Worcestershire**

2 **large cloves garlic, minced or pressed**

In a small pan, mix tomato sauce, wine, Worcestershire, and garlic. Place pan of baste at edge of grill to warm while you cook chicken or turkey pieces.

As poultry cooks, brush it often with baste. Makes about 1⅓ cups (enough for 2 cut-up 3-lb. chickens, 8 chicken breast halves, or 3 lbs. turkey tenderloins).

Per tablespoon: 7 calories (1% fat, 83% carbohydrates, 16% protein), 0 g total fat (0 g saturated fat), 1 g carbohydrates, 0.2 g protein, 0 mg cholesterol, 81 mg sodium

MISO-MAPLE MARINADE

Preparation time: About 10 minutes

⅓ **cup *each* aka miso (red fermented soybean paste) and maple syrup**

¼ **cup sake, dry white wine, or water**

2 **tablespoons minced fresh ginger**

In a large, shallow bowl, mix miso, syrup, sake, and ginger.

Add chicken or turkey pieces to marinade. Cover and refrigerate for at least 1 hour or up to 1 day.

Lift poultry from bowl and drain briefly before grilling; baste poultry with marinade as it cooks. Makes about 1 cup (enough for 1 cut-up 3-lb. chicken, 4 chicken breast halves, or 1½ lbs. turkey tenderloins).

Per tablespoon: 32 calories (10% fat, 81% carbohydrates, 9% protein), 0.4 g total fat (0 g saturated fat), 6 g carbohydrates, 0.7 g protein, 0 mg cholesterol, 208 mg sodium

Greek Chicken Pockets

30 MINUTES OR LESS

Preparation time: About 30 minutes

Next time you roast a chicken, set aside some of the meat to make these simple pocket sandwiches. Halved pita breads are filled with tomato, bell pepper, shredded chicken, and spoonfuls of herb-seasoned yogurt.

Herb Dressing (recipe follows)

4 **to 6 pita breads (*each* about 6 inches in diameter)**

3 **small firm-ripe tomatoes (about 12 oz. *total*), thinly sliced**

2 **small green bell peppers (about 10 oz. *total*), seeded and thinly sliced**

3 **cups shredded cooked chicken**

¼ **cup crumbled feta cheese**

Prepare Herb Dressing. Cut each pita bread in half; gently open halves and fill equally with tomatoes, bell peppers, chicken, and cheese. Then spoon dressing into each sandwich. Makes 4 to 6 servings.

Herb Dressing. In a small bowl, stir together 1 cup **plain nonfat yogurt,** ½ cup minced peeled **cucumber,** and 1 tablespoon *each* minced **fresh dill** and minced **fresh mint** (or 1 teaspoon *each* dry dill weed and dry mint).

Per serving: 397 calories (20% fat, 45% carbohydrates, 35% protein), 9 g total fat (3 g saturated fat), 44 g carbohydrates, 34 g protein, 82 mg cholesterol, 512 mg sodium

Chicken Chimichangas

MODIFIED CLASSIC

Preparation time: About 30 minutes
Soaking time: About 30 minutes
Cooking time: About 40 minutes
Baking time: 8 to 10 minutes

Easy to assemble and eat, these oven-baked chimichangas offer all the authentic flavor of their traditional deep-fried counterparts, but they're lower in fat.

Cucumber & Jicama Salsa (recipe follows)
Shredded Chicken Filling (recipe follows)

5 **cups shredded lettuce**

1½ **cups shredded carrots**

8 **flour tortillas (*each* 7 to 9 inches in diameter)**

About ⅓ cup nonfat milk

½ **cup shredded sharp Cheddar cheese**

Plain nonfat yogurt

Prepare Cucumber & Jicama Salsa; refrigerate. Prepare Shredded Chicken Filling; set aside.

In a bowl, mix lettuce and carrots; set aside.

To assemble each chimichanga, brush both sides of a tortilla with milk. Spoon an eighth of the filling down center of tortilla; top with 1 tablespoon of the cheese. To enclose, lap ends of tortilla over filling; then fold sides to center to make a packet. Place chimichanga, seam side down, on a lightly oiled 12-by 15-inch nonstick baking sheet and brush with milk. Repeat to make 7 more chimichangas.

Bake in a 500° oven, brushing with milk after 5 minutes, until golden brown (8 to 10 minutes). To serve, divide lettuce mixture among 8 individual plates; place one chimichanga on each plate. Offer Cucumber & Jicama Salsa and yogurt to add to taste. Makes 8 servings.

Cucumber & Jicama Salsa. In a bowl, combine ⅔ cup peeled, seeded, diced **cucumber;** 4 ounces **jicama,** peeled and diced; 2 tablespoons *each* chopped **fresh basil** and sliced **green onion;** 1 tablespoon *each* **lemon juice** and **plain nonfat yogurt;** and 1 small **fresh jalapeño chile,** seeded and minced. Season to taste with **salt.** If made ahead, cover and refrigerate for up to 6 hours.

Shredded Chicken Filling. Place 6 **dried ancho or pasilla chiles** (about 1½ oz. *total*) on a baking sheet and toast in a 300° oven until fragrant (3 to 4 minutes). Remove from oven and let cool. Discard stems, seeds, and veins; then place chiles in a bowl, cover with 1½ cups **boiling water,** and let stand until pliable (about 30 minutes).

While chiles are soaking, combine 1 teaspoon **salad oil,** 2 large **onions** (chopped), 2 cloves **garlic** (minced or pressed), and 1 tablespoon **water** in a wide nonstick frying pan. Cook over medium heat, stirring often, until mixture is deep golden (20 to 30 minutes); if onions stick to pan, add more **water,** 1 tablespoon at a time. Remove from heat.

Drain chiles; discard liquid. In a food processor or blender, whirl chiles, 1 can (about 14½ oz.) **tomatoes** and their liquid, 2 teaspoons **sugar,** 1 teaspoon **dry oregano,** and ½ teaspoon **ground cumin** until smoothly puréed. Then stir chile-tomato mixture and 2 cups finely shredded **cooked chicken or turkey breast** into onion mixture. Bring to a boil; then reduce heat and simmer, uncovered, stirring occasionally, until mixture is thick and flavors are blended (about 10 minutes). Season to taste with **salt** and **pepper.**

Per serving: 314 calories (28% fat, 49% carbohydrates, 23% protein), 10 g total fat (3 g saturated fat), 40 g carbohydrates, 19 g protein, 39 mg cholesterol, 350 mg sodium

Roast Turkey Breast & Four Drumsticks

Preparation time: About 35 minutes
Roasting time: About 2¼ hours
Cooking time: About 10 minutes

For a grand holiday meal, serve savory glazed turkey pieces with fluffy, tomato-dotted couscous. Mound the couscous on a deep platter and lean the drumsticks around it; or, if you prefer, present it in a bowl alongside the sliced meat.

1   **boneless turkey breast half (3 to 3½ lbs.)**
4   **turkey drumsticks (about 1 lb. *each*)**
⅔   **cup apple, quince, or red currant jelly**
2   **tablespoons raspberry vinegar or red wine vinegar**
½   **teaspoon ground sage**
     Dried Tomato Couscous (recipe follows)
2   **tablespoons cornstarch**
     About 2 cups low-sodium chicken broth
     Salt and pepper

Trim and discard fat from turkey breast. Rinse breast and drumsticks; pat dry. Set breast skin side up and fold narrow end under to make an evenly thick piece; pull skin to cover as much of meat as possible. Using cotton string, tie breast snugly at 1-inch intervals lengthwise and crosswise. Set all turkey aside.

In a small pan, combine jelly, vinegar, and sage. Stir over medium heat until jelly is melted.

Arrange drumsticks slightly apart in an 11- by 17-inch roasting pan; brush with some of the jelly mixture. Roast in a 375° oven for 15 minutes. Set breast in pan and brush with jelly mixture.

Continue to roast until a meat thermometer inserted in thickest part of breast registers 165°F and until thermometer inserted in thickest part of drumsticks registers 185°F (about 2 hours). If some pieces are done before others, remove them from oven and keep warm. As turkey roasts, baste it with pan drippings and jelly mixture, using all. If drippings begin to scorch, add ⅓ cup water and stir to scrape browned bits free.

About 30 minutes before turkey is done, prepare Dried Tomato Couscous.

When turkey is done, transfer it to a carving board, cover lightly, and let stand for about 10 minutes. As juices accumulate on board, drain them into roasting pan.

To make gravy, skim and discard fat from pan drippings. Pour drippings into a 1-quart or larger glass measure; smoothly blend in cornstarch. Then add enough broth to make 2½ cups. Return mixture to roasting pan; bring to a boil over high heat, stirring. Season to taste with salt and pepper. Pour into a bowl or gravy boat.

To serve, remove strings from turkey breast, then thinly slice meat across the grain. Slice drumsticks or serve whole. Arrange turkey on platter around couscous; accompany with gravy. Makes 12 to 16 servings.

Dried Tomato Couscous. Soak ½ cup (about 1⅛ oz.) **dried tomatoes** in 5 cups **boiling water** until very soft (about 30 minutes). Drain tomatoes, pressing out excess liquid and reserving all soaking water. Chop tomatoes coarsely and set aside.

In a 3½- to 4-quart pan, combine water from tomatoes and 1 can (about 14½ oz.) **low-sodium chicken broth.** Bring to a boil over high heat. Stir in tomatoes, ½ teaspoon **dry oregano,** ¼ teaspoon **dry sage,** and 3 cups **couscous.** Cover pan, remove from heat, and let stand for about 5 minutes. Fluff couscous with a fork; mound on a large platter, allowing room for turkey.

Per serving: 465 calories (17% fat, 39% carbohydrates, 44% protein), 8 g total fat (3 g saturated fat), 44 g carbohydrates, 50 g protein, 127 mg cholesterol, 124 mg sodium

Grilled Turkey with Peaches

Preparation time: About 30 minutes
Grilling time: About 1 hour

A shiny glaze of puréed chutney seals moisture into this grilled turkey breast. Accompany the juicy meat with peaches and green onions, heated on the barbecue just until hot.

1	teaspoon minced fresh ginger
⅔	cup peach chutney or Major Grey's chutney
1	turkey breast half (about 3 lbs.), boned and skinned
3	large firm-ripe peaches (about 1¼ lbs. *total*); or 6 canned peach halves, drained
2	tablespoons lemon juice (if using fresh peaches)
6	green onions

At least 30 minutes before cooking, prepare a barbecue for indirect grilling as directed for Jerk Pork with Papaya (page 76).

In a blender or food processor, combine ginger and ⅓ cup of the chutney. Whirl until puréed. Coarsely chop remaining ⅓ cup chutney and set aside. Rinse turkey, pat dry, and brush all over with some of the chutney-ginger mixture.

Place turkey on grill directly above drip pan. Cover barbecue and open vents. Cook turkey, brushing occasionally with chutney mixture, until a meat thermometer inserted in thickest part registers 165°F (about 1 hour).

Meanwhile, immerse fresh peaches in boiling water for 30 seconds; lift out and let cool for 1 minute. Peel, halve, and pit; coat with lemon juice.

Peel off outer layer of onions; trim tops, leaving about 4 inches of green leaves.

About 10 minutes before turkey is done, lay peach halves (cut side down) and onions on grill directly above coals. Cook, turning once and brushing several times with chutney mixture, until peaches are hot and onion tops are wilted (about 10 minutes).

To serve, thinly slice turkey across the grain. Arrange on a platter and surround with peaches and onions. Offer reserved chopped chutney to add to taste. Makes 6 servings.

Per serving: 324 calories (4% fat, 39% carbohydrates, 57% protein), 1 g total fat (0.4 g saturated fat), 31 g carbohydrates, 45 g protein, 111 mg cholesterol, 406 mg sodium

Apricot-stuffed Turkey Roast

Preparationt time: About 15 minutes
Roasting time: About 1¼ hours

The combination of poultry and fruit has always been popular. Here, a rosemary-seasoned boned turkey breast is stuffed with dried apricots.

1	turkey breast half (about 3½ lbs.), boned and skinned
3	tablespoons Dijon mustard
1	teaspoon dry rosemary
10	to 12 dried apricots
1	tablespoon olive oil
1	teaspoon minced or pressed garlic Pepper

Rinse turkey and pat dry; then place, skinned side down, on a board. Make a lengthwise cut down center of thickest part of turkey, being careful not to cut all the way through. Push cut open and press meat to make it lie as flat as possible.

Spread turkey with mustard and sprinkle with ½ teaspoon of the rosemary; then top evenly with apricots. Starting at a long edge, roll up turkey firmly jelly roll style, enclosing filling. Tie roll snugly with cotton string at 2- to 3-inch intervals. Rub turkey with oil, then garlic; pat remaining ½ teaspoon rosemary over turkey and sprinkle generously with pepper.

Place turkey on a rack in a 9- by 13-inch baking pan. Roast in a 375° oven until a meat thermometer inserted in thickest part registers 165°F and meat in center is no longer pink; cut to test (1 hour and 15 to 20 minutes). Let stand for about 10 minutes; then remove strings and cut roll crosswise into thick slices. Makes 6 to 8 servings.

Per serving: 238 calories (14% fat, 8% carbohydrates, 78% protein), 4 g total fat (0.6 g saturated fat), 4 g carbohydrates, 44 g protein, 111 mg cholesterol, 282 mg sodium

Raspberry-glazed Turkey Tenderloins

NATURALLY LOW IN FAT

Preparation time: About 15 minutes
Broiling time: 8 to 10 minutes

A fruit glaze keeps lean turkey tenderloins moist during broiling. To balance the berry sweetness, you might serve a vinaigrette-dressed green salad alongside.

4	turkey breast tenderloins (about 2¼ lbs. *total*)
½	cup seedless raspberry jam
6	tablespoons raspberry vinegar
¼	cup Dijon mustard
1	teaspoon grated orange peel
½	teaspoon dry thyme

Rinse turkey, pat dry, and set aside. In a small pan, stir together jam, vinegar, mustard, orange peel, and thyme. Bring to a boil over high heat, stirring; then boil, uncovered, stirring often, until reduced by about a fourth (2 to 3 minutes). Reserve about ½ cup of the glaze; brush turkey with some of the remaining glaze.

Place turkey on a rack in a broiler pan. Broil about 4 inches below heat, turning and brushing once with remaining glaze, until meat in thickest part is no longer pink; cut to test (8 to 10 minutes).

To serve, cut turkey across the grain into thick slices. Offer reserved glaze to add to taste. Makes 6 to 8 servings.

Per serving: 230 calories (6% fat, 29% carbohydrates, 65% protein), 2 g total fat (0.3 g saturated fat), 16 g carbohydrates, 36 g protein, 90 mg cholesterol, 338 mg sodium

Summer Turkey Stir-fry

30 MINUTES OR LESS

Preparation time: About 15 minutes
Cooking time: About 15 minutes

The secret to this vibrant stir-fry lies in its crisp fresh vegetables and subtle sauce. Have all the ingredients prepared before you begin cooking.

	Cooking Sauce (recipe follows)
1¾	cups water
1	cup bulgur
1	tablespoon salad oil
3	cloves garlic, minced or pressed
1	pound boneless, skinless turkey breast, cut into ¾-inch chunks
3	cups thinly sliced carrots
2	small zucchini, sliced
2	tablespoons minced fresh ginger
½	cup thinly sliced green onions

Prepare Cooking Sauce and set aside.

In a 2- to 3-quart pan, bring 1½ cups of the water to a boil over high heat; stir in bulgur. Reduce heat, cover, and simmer until bulgur is tender to bite and water has been absorbed (about 15 minutes).

Meanwhile, heat oil in a wide frying pan or wok over high heat. Add garlic and turkey and cook, stirring, until meat is no longer pink in center; cut to test (about 5 minutes). Add carrots, zucchini, ginger, and remaining ¼ cup water. Cover and continue to cook, stirring occasionally, until vegetables are tender-crisp to bite (about 5 more minutes). Uncover, bring to a boil, and boil until almost all liquid has evaporated. Stir in Cooking Sauce; boil, stirring, until sauce is bubbly and thickened.

To serve, spoon bulgur onto individual plates and top with turkey mixture. Sprinkle with onions. Makes 4 servings.

Cooking Sauce. In a small bowl, mix ½ cup **low-sodium chicken broth,** 2 tablespoons **reduced-sodium soy sauce,** and 1 tablespoon **cornstarch.**

Per serving: 345 calories (13% fat, 47% carbohydrates, 40% protein), 5 g total fat (0.8 g saturated fat), 41 g carbohydrates, 35 g protein, 70 mg cholesterol, 402 mg sodium

Turkey Curry with Soba

Preparation time: About 10 minutes
Cooking time: About 40 minutes

To make this dish, you mix your own curry powder by blending a variety of spices. If you can't find soba in the Asian foods section of your supermarket, substitute spaghettini.

1	tablespoon salad oil
1	pound boneless, skinless turkey breast, cut into 1½-inch chunks
1	large onion, thinly sliced
1	clove garlic, minced or pressed
1	tablespoon grated fresh ginger
1	teaspoon *each* crushed red pepper flakes, ground coriander, ground cumin, and ground turmeric
½	teaspoon fennel seeds
1	cup low-sodium chicken broth
1	package (about 7 oz.) dry soba noodles
1	cup plain nonfat yogurt
¼	cup unsalted dry-roasted cashews

Heat oil in a wide frying pan over medium heat. Add turkey and cook, stirring often, until browned on all sides (about 6 minutes). Using a slotted spoon, remove turkey from pan.

Add onion and garlic to pan; cook, stirring occasionally, until onion is soft (about 10 minutes). Add ginger, red pepper flakes, coriander, cumin, turmeric, and fennel seeds; cook, stirring, for 1 minute.

Return turkey to pan. Add broth and bring to a boil. Then reduce heat, cover, and simmer until meat is no longer pink in center; cut to test (about 20 minutes). Remove from heat.

While turkey is simmering, cook noodles in boiling water according to package directions until just tender to bite; drain well and pour into a large, shallow serving bowl.

Stir yogurt into turkey mixture, then pour mixture over noodles. Sprinkle with cashews. Makes 6 servings.

Per serving: 294 calories (18% fat, 45% carbohydrates, 37% protein), 6 g total fat (1 g saturated fat), 34 g carbohydrates, 27 g protein, 48 mg cholesterol, 340 mg sodium

Picadillo Stew

Preparation time: About 15 minutes
Cooking time: About 20 minutes

Its name comes from the word *picar* ("to mince"), so it's no surprise that *picadillo* is made with chopped ingredients. This version is a hearty turkey stew, rich with raisins, spices, and almonds.

2	tablespoons slivered almonds
¼	cup dry red wine
2	tablespoons reduced-sodium soy sauce
1	tablespoon lemon juice
2	teaspoons sugar
1	teaspoon *each* ground cumin, ground coriander, and chili powder
⅛	teaspoon ground cinnamon
4	teaspoons cornstarch
1	teaspoon salad oil
1	pound boneless, skinless turkey breast, cut into 1-inch chunks
1	large onion, chopped
2	cloves garlic, minced or pressed
1	can (about 14½ oz.) tomatoes
⅔	cup raisins
	Pepper

Toast almonds in a small frying pan over medium heat until golden (about 5 minutes), stirring often. Pour out of pan and set aside.

In a small bowl, stir together wine, soy sauce, lemon juice, sugar, cumin, coriander, chili powder, cinnamon, and cornstarch. Set aside.

Heat oil in a wide nonstick frying pan or 6-quart pan over high heat. Add turkey, onion, and garlic. Cook, stirring, until onion is soft and meat is no longer pink in center; cut to test (10 to 15 minutes). If pan appears dry, add water, 1 tablespoon at a time. Cut up tomatoes; then add tomatoes and their liquid, wine mixture, and raisins to pan. Bring to a boil; then boil, stirring, just until thickened. Season to taste with pepper.

To serve, ladle stew into bowls and sprinkle with almonds. Makes 4 servings.

Per serving: 317 calories (13% fat, 46% carbohydrates, 41% protein), 5 g total fat (0.7 g saturated fat), 36 g carbohydrates, 32 g protein, 70 mg cholesterol, 538 mg sodium

Oven-baked Turkey Fajitas

Preparation time: About 20 minutes
Marinating time: At least 20 minutes
Baking time: About 30 minutes

For a new twist on familiar fajitas, oven-bake turkey breast with bell pepper and red onion, then serve the mixture in warm tortillas.

1	**pound turkey breast tenderloins** **Lime-Vinegar Marinade (recipe follows)**
1	**large green bell pepper (about 8 oz.),** **seeded and cut into eighths**
1	**large red onion, thinly sliced** **About 1 tablespoon salad oil**
4	**warm flour tortillas (*each* 7 to 9 inches** **in diameter)**

Rinse turkey and pat dry. Prepare Lime-Vinegar Marinade and pour into a large heavy-duty plastic bag; add turkey. Seal bag and turn to coat turkey. Refrigerate for at least 20 minutes or up to 1 day, turning occasionally.

Place bell pepper and onion in a 10- by 15-inch nonstick rimmed baking pan; brush lightly with oil. Bake in a 400° oven for 10 minutes. Remove from oven. Lift turkey from bag and drain briefly; reserve marinade. Arrange turkey alongside pepper and onion, overlapping meat and vegetables as little as possible.

Return pan to oven. Bake, basting with marinade and turning often, until onion is tinged with brown and meat in thickest part is no longer pink; cut to test (about 20 minutes).

To serve, thinly slice turkey across the grain; then divide turkey, pepper, and onion evenly among tortillas. Roll up tortillas to enclose filling; eat out of hand. Makes 4 servings.

Lime-Vinegar Marinade. In a small bowl, stir together ¼ cup **lime juice,** 1 tablespoon **balsamic vinegar** or red wine vinegar, 1 clove **garlic** (minced or pressed), ½ teaspoon **honey,** and ¼ teaspoon *each* **ground coriander** and **ground cumin.**

Per serving: 305 calories (20% fat, 37% carbohydrates, 43% protein), 7 g total fat (1 g saturated fat), 28 g carbohydrates, 32 g protein, 70 mg cholesterol, 230 mg sodium

Onion-Cilantro Turkey

Preparation time: About 15 minutes
Marinating time (optional): 2 to 3 hours
Grilling time: 7 to 9 minutes

A pungent seasoning rub of garlic, cilantro, ginger, and lime makes these grilled turkey tenderloins especially flavorful. To increase the meat's succulence, "cure" it for a few hours with a mixture of sugar and salt.

1½	**pounds turkey breast tenderloins** **Salt Cure (optional; recipe follows)** **Onion Mixture (recipe follows)** **Cilantro sprigs** **Green onions** **Lime wedges**

Rinse turkey and pat dry. If desired, prepare Salt Cure and rub over turkey; place in a bowl, cover, and refrigerate for 2 to 3 hours. Then rinse turkey well with cool water and pat dry.

If turkey pieces are large, cut them into serving-size portions. Place each piece of turkey between 2 sheets of plastic wrap and pound with a flat-surfaced mallet to a thickness of about ½ inch. (At this point, you may cover and refrigerate for up to 1 day.)

Prepare Onion Mixture and rub over turkey pieces. Place turkey on a lightly oiled grill 4 to 6 inches above a solid bed of hot coals. Cook, turning as needed, until meat in thickest part is no longer pink; cut to test (7 to 9 minutes).

To serve, garnish turkey with cilantro sprigs and onions. Serve with lime wedges. Makes 6 servings.

Salt Cure. Mix 1 tablespoon **salt** and 1½ teaspoons **sugar.**

Onion Mixture. In a small bowl, mix ¼ cup thinly sliced **green onions;** 2 tablespoons minced **cilantro;** 3 cloves **garlic,** minced or pressed; 1 tablespoon minced **fresh ginger;** and 1 teaspoon *each* coarsely ground **pepper** and grated **lime peel.**

Per serving: 131 calories (5% fat, 4% carbohydrates, 91% protein), 0.7 g total fat (0.2 g saturated fat), 1 g carbohydrates, 28 g protein, 70 mg cholesterol, 57 mg sodium

Turkey & Lima Stew

. . . .

Preparation time: About 20 minutes
Cooking time: About 1 hour

Repeated deglazing gives this stew its rich color and flavor. Serve over noodles—and don't forget the cranberry sauce! For dessert, choose something simple, such as fresh fruit in season or a frosty sorbet.

1	large onion, chopped
2	cups sliced mushrooms
1	cup thinly sliced carrots
1	teaspoon dry thyme
	About 3 cups low-sodium chicken broth
2	tablespoons lemon juice
2	pounds boneless, skinless turkey or chicken thighs, trimmed of fat and cut into 1-inch chunks
1	tablespoon cornstarch
1	package (about 10 oz.) frozen baby lima beans, thawed

In a 5- to 6-quart pan, combine onion, mushrooms, carrots, thyme, and 1 cup of the broth. Bring to a boil over high heat; then boil, stirring occasionally, until liquid evaporates and vegetables begin to brown (about 10 minutes). To deglaze, add ¼ cup more broth and stir to scrape browned bits free. Then continue to cook, stirring occasionally, until vegetables begin to brown again. Repeat deglazing and browning steps, using ¼ cup more broth each time, until vegetable mixture is richly browned. Then deglaze one last time with lemon juice.

Stir turkey and ½ cup more broth into vegetable mixture. Bring to a boil over high heat. Then reduce heat to low, cover, and simmer until turkey chunks are no longer pink in center; cut to test (about 40 minutes; about 25 minutes for chicken). Skim and discard fat from sauce.

Smoothly blend cornstarch with ¾ cup of the broth. Add cornstarch mixture and beans to pan; bring to a boil over medium-high heat, stirring. Continue to boil, stirring, until beans are tender to bite. Makes 6 servings.

Per serving: 299 calories (23% fat, 28% carbohydrates, 49% protein), 7 g total fat (2 g saturated fat), 20 g carbohydrates, 36 g protein, 114 mg cholesterol, 182 mg sodium

Turkey Tamale Pie with Nacho Crust

. . . .

Preparation time: About 35 minutes
Cooking time: 1 to 1¼ hours
Baking time: About 40 minutes

While you wait for this make-ahead casserole to bake, relax with an easy appetizer such as Jicama & Fresh Fruit Platter (page 11).

2	pounds turkey or chicken thighs, skinned and trimmed of fat
4	cups low-sodium chicken broth
3	tablespoons ground dried California or New Mexico chiles (or use regular chili powder)
1½	teaspoons dry oregano
2	large onions, cut lengthwise into eighths
1	can (about 14½ oz.) stewed tomatoes
18	corn tortillas (*each* about 6 inches in diameter)
1	cup pimento-stuffed green olives
1	tablespoon cornstarch blended with 1 tablespoon cold water
1	package (about 10 oz.) frozen corn kernels, thawed
½	cup *each* raisins and chopped cilantro
1	cup (about 4 oz.) shredded sharp Cheddar cheese
	Cilantro sprigs

Rinse turkey, pat dry, and place in a 4- to 5-quart pan. Add broth, ground chiles, and oregano. Bring to a boil over high heat; then reduce heat, cover, and simmer for 10 minutes. Turn turkey pieces over and add onions. Return to a simmer, cover, and cook until meat is tender when pierced (30 to

45 minutes; about 20 minutes for chicken). With a slotted spoon, lift out turkey and onions. Set onions aside. Let turkey stand until cool enough to handle; then tear meat into ½-inch-wide strips, discarding bones.

While turkey is cooling, add tomatoes to broth. Bring to a boil over high heat; then boil, uncovered, until reduced to 3¾ cups (about 15 minutes). Dunk 12 of the tortillas, one at a time, into hot broth until softened (about 10 seconds). Line a well-oiled shallow 3- to 3½-quart casserole with softened tortillas, overlapping to cover bottom and sides; make tortillas flush with casserole rim.

Arrange onions, turkey, and ⅔ cup of the olives on tortillas. Stir cornstarch mixture into broth mixture along with corn, raisins, and chopped cilantro. Pour broth mixture over ingredients in casserole; cover casserole tightly. (At this point, you may let cool, then refrigerate for up to 1 day.)

Bake, covered, in a 425° oven for 30 minutes (40 minutes if refrigerated). Meanwhile, stack remaining 6 tortillas; cut stack into 8 wedges.

Uncover casserole and scatter tortilla wedges and cheese over top. Increase oven temperature to 475° and continue to bake, uncovered, until cheese is melted and tortillas are crisp (10 to 12 more minutes).

Slice remaining ⅓ cup olives; distribute olives and cilantro sprigs evenly over casserole. Makes 6 to 8 servings.

Per serving: 461 calories (27% fat, 50% carbohydrates, 23% protein), 14 g total fat (5 g saturated fat), 60 g carbohydrates, 27 g protein, 72 mg cholesterol, 946 mg sodium

Ground Turkey Chili Mole

. . . .

MODIFIED CLASSIC

Preparation time: About 15 minutes
Cooking time: About 50 minutes

Serve this streamlined version of an intricate Mexican dish as you would chili—ladle it into big bowls to eat with a spoon. Offer Water-crisped Tortilla Chips (page 12) alongside; they complement the chili without compromising its low fat content.

1	medium-size onion, chopped
1	pound ground skinless turkey
2	cloves garlic, minced or pressed
1	can (about 8 oz.) tomato sauce
1	can (about 14½ oz.) stewed tomatoes
1	can (about 15 oz.) red kidney beans, drained and rinsed; or 2 cups cooked red kidney beans (page 149), drained and rinsed
1	tablespoon molasses
¼	teaspoon liquid hot pepper seasoning
1	tablespoon unsweetened cocoa
1	teaspoon *each* paprika and ground cumin
½	teaspoon *each* dry oregano and dry basil

In a 4- to 5-quart pan, combine onion and ¼ cup water. Bring to a boil over medium-high heat; then boil, stirring occasionally, until liquid evaporates and onion begins to brown (about 5 minutes). To deglaze, add ¼ cup more water and stir to scrape browned bits free. Then continue to cook, stirring occasionally, until onion begins to brown again. Repeat deglazing and browning steps, using ¼ cup more water.

Crumble turkey into pan; add garlic. Cook, stirring, until meat is no longer pink and liquid has evaporated. Stir in tomato sauce, tomatoes, beans, molasses, hot pepper seasoning, cocoa, paprika, cumin, oregano, and basil. Bring to a boil; reduce heat, cover, and simmer until flavors are well blended (about 30 minutes). Makes 4 to 6 servings.

Per serving: 256 calories (27% fat, 39% carbohydrates, 34% protein), 8 g total fat (2 g saturated fat), 25 g carbohydrates, 22 g protein, 66 mg cholesterol, 685 mg sodium

Mexican foods and flavors *have been prominent in the West for hundreds of years, since the days of the Spanish settlers who came north from Mexico. One favorite dish is mole poblano, the best-known of Mexico's chocolate-tinged sauces. A traditional mole poblano may contain nearly two dozen ingredients, including at least four kinds of chiles and a dazzling array of herbs and spices. Today's recipes, though, are inclined to whittle down lengthy ingredient lists and simplify preparation methods.*

Bean & Turkey Burritos

Preparation time: About 40 minutes
Standing time: At least 1 hour
Cooking time: About 2 hours

Chili-seasoned red beans mixed with leftover roast turkey make a super filling for warm flour tortillas. Acccompany the meal with a crisp, tart red cabbage salsa; it's good spooned into the burritos or simply enjoyed alongside.

1	**pound dried red beans**
2	**medium-size onions, chopped**
5	**cups low-sodium chicken broth**
½	**cup** *each* **chili powder and firmly packed brown sugar**
2	**whole star anise or 1 teaspoon anise seeds**
	Red Cabbage Salsa (recipe follows)
4	**cups bite-size pieces of cooked turkey**
	Salt
12	**warm large flour tortillas (***each* **9 to 10 inches in diameter)**
	Plain nonfat yogurt

Rinse and sort beans, discarding any debris. Drain beans and place in a 6- to 8-quart pan; add 8 cups water. Bring to a boil over high heat; boil for 2 minutes. Then cover, remove from heat, and let stand for at least 1 hour. Drain beans, discarding water.

To pan, add onions, 5 cups water, broth, chili powder, sugar, and star anise; bring to a boil over high heat. Add beans to pan. Reduce heat, cover, and simmer gently until beans are very tender to bite (about 1½ hours). Drain beans, reserving cooking liquid. Discard star anise. (At this point, you may let beans and liquid cool, then cover separately and refrigerate for up to 2 days.)

Prepare Red Cabbage Salsa.

Return cooking liquid to pan. Bring to a boil over high heat; then boil, uncovered, until reduced to about 3 cups. Add beans and mash to make the mixture as thick as you like. Add turkey and stir gently until mixture is hot. Season to taste with salt.

To eat, spoon turkey mixture onto tortillas; add Red Cabbage Salsa and yogurt to taste. Roll to enclose filling; eat out of hand. Makes 12 servings.

Red Cabbage Salsa. In a large bowl, combine 4 cups finely shredded **red cabbage,** 1 cup sliced **green onions,** ⅓ cup minced **cilantro,** ¼ cup **lime juice,** and ½ teaspoon **pepper.**

Per serving: 469 calories (15% fat, 60% carbohydrates, 25% protein), 8 g total fat (2 g saturated fat), 71 g carbohydrates, 29 g protein, 36 mg cholesterol, 384 mg sodium

Farfalle with Italian Turkey Sausage

Preparation time: About 30 minutes
Cooking time: 1 to 1¼ hours

Crumble savory Italian turkey sausage—either sweet or hot, depending on your taste—into this ruddy sauce for pasta bow ties.

2	**medium-size onions, thinly sliced**
6	**ounces mushrooms, sliced**
2	**cloves garlic, minced or pressed**
1	**medium-size carrot, shredded**
1	**can (about 14½ oz.) low-sodium chicken broth**
1	**pound Italian turkey sausages, casings removed**
1	**can (about 14½ oz.) diced tomatoes**
1	**can (about 15 oz.) tomato sauce**
½	**cup dry white wine**
1	**tablespoon dry basil**
1	**teaspoon sugar**
1	**pound dry pasta bow ties or other bite-size shapes**
¼	**cup chopped parsley**
	Salt and pepper
	Grated Romano cheese

In a 3- to 4-quart pan, combine onions, mushrooms, garlic, carrot, and 1 cup of the broth. Bring to a boil over high heat; then boil, stirring occasionally, until liquid evaporates and vegetables begin to brown (about 10 minutes). To deglaze, add about ¼ cup water and stir to scrape browned bits free. Then continue to cook, stirring occasionally, until mixture begins to brown again. Repeat deglazing and browning steps about 2 more times, using ¼ cup water each time; mixture should be richly browned.

Crumble sausages into pan, then add remaining ¾ cup broth. Cook, stirring occasionally, until liquid evaporates and meat begins to brown (about 10 minutes). Stir in tomatoes, tomato sauce, wine, basil, and sugar. Bring to a boil; then reduce heat, cover, and simmer for 30 minutes. (At this point, you may let cool, then cover and refrigerate for up to 1 day; reheat before continuing.)

Uncover pan. Increase heat to medium and cook, stirring ocasionally, until sauce is slightly thickened. Meanwhile, in a 6- to 8-quart pan, cook pasta in about 4 quarts boiling water until just tender to bite (about 10 minutes); or cook pasta according to package directions. Drain well and pour into a large bowl.

Stir parsley into sauce, then season to taste with salt and pepper. Pour sauce over pasta and mix gently. Offer cheese to add to taste. Makes 6 servings.

Per serving: 492 calories (18% fat, 60% carbohydrates, 22% protein), 10 g total fat (3 g saturated fat), 74 g carbohydrates, 27 g protein, 57 mg cholesterol, 1,036 mg sodium

Creamy Baked Turkey & Rotelle

· ·

Preparation time: About 30 minutes
Baking time: About 1½ hours

You can cater to a crowd and still enjoy the evening if you prepare this pasta dish a day ahead of time. Multicolored rotelle, ground turkey, and zucchini shreds bake in a thyme-accented sauce made with sweet red onions and a little wine vinegar. For dessert, offer dark roast coffee and Orange-topped Walnut Biscotti (page 195).

3½	pounds red onions, thinly sliced
3	ounces Canadian bacon, diced
3	tablespoons red wine vinegar
1	pound ground skinless turkey
1	pound zucchini, shredded
3	tablespoons minced fresh thyme or 1 tablespoon dry thyme
2	cups low-sodium chicken broth
1½	cups nonfat milk
3	tablespoons cornstarch blended with ¼ cup cold water
1	cup (about 4 oz.) shredded Parmesan cheese
10	ounces dry multicolored or plain rotelle

In an 11- by 17-inch roasting pan, combine onions, Canadian bacon, and vinegar. Bake in a 400° oven, stirring occasionally, until onions and bacon are well browned (about 55 minutes).

Sprinkle turkey, zucchini, and 1 tablespoon of the fresh thyme (or 1 teaspoon of the dry thyme) over onion mixture; continue to bake until turkey just turns white (about 8 more minutes). Transfer turkey mixture to a large bowl.

Add broth, milk, and remaining 2 tablespoons fresh (or 2 teaspoons dry) thyme to roasting pan. Bring to a boil over high heat, stirring to scrape browned bits free. Stir in cornstarch mixture; return to a boil, stirring. Remove from heat. Add sauce and ½ cup of the cheese to turkey mixture; stir to mix well.

In a 5- to 6-quart pan, cook rotelle in about 3 quarts boiling water until slightly underdone (about 5 minutes; or cook for two-thirds of the cooking time indicated on package). Drain.

Add pasta to turkey mixture, mix well, and spread evenly in an oiled 2- to 2½-quart casserole. Sprinkle with remaining ½ cup cheese. (At this point, you may cover and refrigerate for up to 1 day.)

Bake, uncovered, in a 400° oven until casserole is browned on top and bubbly in center (about 20 minutes; about 30 minutes if refrigerated). Makes 8 to 10 servings.

Per serving: 371 calories (22% fat, 51% carbohydrates, 27% protein), 9 g total fat (4 g saturated fat), 47 g carbohydrates, 25 g protein, 52 mg cholesterol, 483 mg sodium

Apple Turkey Loaf

Preparation time: About 25 minutes
Baking time: About 1 hour

Lightly blend spices and tart green apples with ground turkey breast for a lean, moist meat loaf. It's delicious hot, and just as good served cold in sandwiches.

1	**tablespoon butter or margarine**
2	**medium-size tart green-skinned apples (about 12 oz. *total*), cored and chopped**
1	**medium-size onion, chopped**
1½	**pounds ground skinless turkey breast**
1½	**teaspoons dry marjoram**
1	**teaspoon *each* dry thyme, dry sage, and pepper**
½	**cup chopped parsley**
2	**large egg whites (about ¼ cup)**
½	**cup *each* fine dry bread crumbs and nonfat milk**

Melt butter in a wide frying pan over medium heat. Add apples and onion. Cook, stirring occasionally, until onion is soft (about 7 minutes). Remove from heat and let cool; then spoon into a large bowl. Add turkey, marjoram, thyme, sage, pepper, parsley, egg whites, bread crumbs, and milk; mix lightly.

Pat turkey mixture into a 5- by 9-inch loaf pan. Bake in a 350° oven until browned on top and no longer pink in center; cut to test (about 1 hour). Drain and discard fat from pan, then invert pan and turn loaf out onto a platter. Serve loaf hot; or let cool, then cover and refrigerate for up to 1 day. Makes 6 servings.

Per serving: 237 calories (13% fat, 33% carbohydrates, 54% protein), 3 g total fat (2 g saturated fat), 19 g carbohydrates, 32 g protein, 76 mg cholesterol, 185 mg sodium

Turkey & Mushroom Burgers

30 MINUTES OR LESS

Preparation time: About 15 minutes
Cooking time: 8 to 10 minutes

Feel free to lavish these turkey-breast burgers with such favorite trimmings as tomato and onion slices, mustard, lettuce, and dill pickles—none will add a significant amount of fat. Or add a dollop of lean relish or chutney; we like Red Onion Horseradish Marmalade (page 171). In place of the traditional French fries or chips, offer Spicy Baked Potato Sticks (page 158) as a side dish.

1	**large egg white (about 2 tablespoons)**
¼	**cup dry white wine**
⅓	**cup soft French bread crumbs**
¼	**teaspoon salt**
⅛	**teaspoon pepper**
¼	**cup finely chopped shallots**
1	**pound ground skinless turkey breast**
4	**ounces mushrooms, finely chopped**
	Olive oil cooking spray
6	**onion hamburger rolls or kaiser rolls, split and warmed**
	Dijon mustard, sliced tomatoes, thinly sliced mild or red white onions, rinsed and crisped lettuce leaves, and/or sliced dill pickles (optional)

In a medium-size bowl, beat egg white and wine until blended. Stir in bread crumbs, salt, pepper, and shallots; then lightly mix in turkey and mushrooms. Shape mixture into six ½-inch-thick patties.

Coat a wide nonstick frying pan with cooking spray. Place pan over medium-high heat; then add turkey patties. Cook, turning once, until patties are lightly browned on both sides and juices run clear when a knife is inserted in center (8 to 10 minutes). Serve patties on rolls; add mustard, tomatoes, onions, lettuce, and pickles to taste, if desired. Makes 6 servings.

Per serving: 235 calories (12% fat, 45% carbohydrates, 43% protein), 3 g total fat (0.7 g saturated fat), 25 g carbohydrates, 24 g protein, 47 mg cholesterol, 394 mg sodium

REDUCING FAT IN COOKING

Learning a few basic techniques for minimizing the butter, margarine, or oil used in cooking can help you prepare leaner versions of your favorite dishes. To get you started, we've described a handful of fat-cutting methods on this page.

Braise-deglaze. Recipes for soups, stews, and sauces often begin with chopped vegetables (such as onions, garlic, carrots, celery and bell peppers) cooked in butter or oil to develop a flavor base. You can also achieve rich, satisfying flavor using fat-free liquid and little or no actual fat. For example, if a recipe calls for 3 to 4 tablespoons fat, omit it altogether. Instead, put the vegetables in the specified cooking pan, then almost cover them with a liquid that will complement the flavor of the finished dish—broth, dry wine, or just plain water. If you are not using a nonstick pan, coat the pan with vegetable oil cooking spray before adding the vegetables; or stir ½ to 1 teaspoon vegetable oil into the vegetables before pouring in the liquid.

Boil over high or medium-high heat, uncovered, stirring occasionally, until the liquid evaporates and the vegetables begin to brown and stick to the pan. Then add more liquid, about 2 tablespoons at a time, stirring to scrape the browned bits free from the pan (the vegetables will absorb the brown color). Repeat these browning and deglazing steps until the color is rich and

appealing, watching closely to prevent scorching. Then proceed as the recipe directs.

Many of the dishes in this book use the braising-deglazing technique. Examples include Italian Sausage Soup (page 32), Low-fat Spaghetti & Meatballs (page 74), and Chicken Vermicelli Carbonara (page 101).

Oven braise-deglaze. You can braise and deglaze in the oven as well as on top of the range. Follow the directions above, but use a shallow baking pan in a 450° oven; start with about ¼ cup liquid, then pour in additional liquid in ¼-cup portions. The initial reduction will take about 15 minutes.

Oven-fry. Small pieces of food (such as meatballs, cut-up chicken or meat, or sliced vegetables), arranged in a single layer and lightly coated with vegetable oil (or olive oil) cooking spray, brown well in a hot oven—400° to 500°, depending on the food. Be sure to leave enough space between the pieces to let moisture evaporate quickly. Norwegian Meatballs (page 15) use this technique. Or try Spicy Baked Potato Sticks (page 158) when you crave French fries.

Use more egg whites and fewer whole eggs or egg yolks. Egg whites serve much the same function as whole eggs in many recipes, and omitting all or most of the yolks reduces fat, calories, and cholesterol. Summer Hazel-

nut Torte with Berries (page 201) uses this technique.

Choose reduced-fat, low-fat, or nonfat dairy products. Lower-fat milk, yogurt, cheese, and sour cream are all widely sold. In cream sauces and in mashed potatoes or other puréed vegetables, try rich-tasting evaporated skim milk. Or use it in this frothy dessert topping.

Low-fat Whipped Topping. Pour ½ cup **evaporated skim milk** into a small, deep bowl. Cover bowl; then refrigerate bowl of milk and beaters of an electric mixer for 1 hour. Beat chilled milk on high speed until fluffy (30 seconds to 1 minute). Add 1 tablespoon **powdered sugar** and ¼ teaspoon **vanilla;** beat until mixture holds soft peaks. Serve immediately. Makes 6 to 8 servings.

Per serving: 19 calories (0% fat, 70% carbohydrates, 30% protein), 0 g total fat (0 g saturated fat), 3 g carbohydrates, 1 g protein, 1 mg cholesterol, 21 mg sodium

Fill in with water. You can give sauces a velvety quality without using much fat; just replace some or all of the butter, margarine, or oil with slightly thickened water or other liquid (as appropriate to the dish). For each cup of liquid, use 1 tablespoon flour for a thin sauce, 2 tablespoons for a medium sauce, and 3 to 4 tablespoons for a thick sauce. If you use cornstarch, arrowroot, or potato starch, you'll need just half these amounts of starch for the same thickening effect after cooking.

SEAFOOD

*T*he search for low-fat food inevitably leads to sea-food. Both fish and shellfish are naturally lean, with mild to more assertive flavors that are enhanced by all sorts of seasonings. What's more, many popular fish have a unique polyunsaturated fatty acid called omega-3, believed to be helpful in preventing cardiac disease. When you cook seafood, don't undo its benefits by adding unnecessary butter or oil. Stick to our low-fat cooking techniques: baking, poaching, broiling, steaming, and grilling (for more about light ways to cook fish, see page 143). To serve seafood at its best, start by choosing the freshest fish and shellfish you can find at the market. Then cook your seafood as soon as possible after purchase, preferably on the very day you buy it.

Cool Salmon with Radish Tartar

. . . .

Preparation time: About 15 minutes
Cooking time: About 40 minutes

The phrase "one-pot meal" usually describes a hearty stew or sturdy casserole, but this refreshing combination is more like a main-dish salad. The ingredients—salmon, beans, and tiny potatoes—are cooked in sequence in the same pan, then cooled and served with a nippy yogurt sauce.

1	pound slender green beans, ends removed
4	salmon steaks (6 to 8 oz. *each*)
12	small red thin-skinned potatoes (*each* 1½ to 2 inches in diameter), scrubbed
	Butter lettuce leaves, rinsed and crisped
1	pound (about 3 cups) cherry tomatoes
	Radish Tartar Sauce (page 131)
	Lemon wedges (optional)

In a 5- to 6-quart pan, cook beans, uncovered, in about 3 quarts boiling water just until tender-crisp to bite (2 to 3 minutes). Lift out with a slotted spoon, immerse in cold water until cool, and drain. Set aside.

Return water in pan to a boil. Rinse fish and add to boiling water. Then cover pan tightly, remove from heat, and let stand until fish is just opaque but still moist in thickest part; cut to test (about 12 minutes). Lift out, immerse in cold water until cool, and drain. Pat dry, then set aside.

Return water in pan to a boil. Add unpeeled potatoes; reduce heat, partially cover pan, and boil gently until potatoes are tender when pierced (about 25 minutes). Drain, immerse in cold water until cool, and drain again. Set aside.

Line a platter with lettuce leaves; arrange fish atop lettuce. Arrange beans, potatoes, and tomatoes around fish. If made ahead, cover and refrigerate for up to 1 day.

To serve, prepare Radish Tartar Sauce. Garnish platter with lemon wedges, if desired; offer sauce with fish and vegetables. Makes 4 servings.

Per serving without Radish Tartar Sauce: 475 calories (25% fat, 36% carbohydrates, 39% protein), 13 g total fat (2 g saturated fat), 43 g carbohydrates, 45 g protein, 109 mg cholesterol, 117 mg sodium

Salmon with Vegetable Crest

. . . .

Preparation time: About 10 minutes
Baking time: About 35 minutes

A creamy crown of vegetable-dotted Neufchâtel cheese tops popular salmon steaks in this one-dish dinner for two.

	Vegetable oil cooking spray
2	medium-size thin-skinned potatoes (about 12 oz. *total*), scrubbed and cut into ¼-inch-wide wedges
1	ounce Neufchâtel cheese, at room temperature
⅛	teaspoon *each* salt and pepper
3	tablespoons lemon juice
¼	cup *each* grated carrot and chopped tomato
2	tablespoons thinly sliced green onion
1	tablespoon finely chopped parsley
2	salmon steaks, cut about 1 inch thick (about 6 oz. *each*)

Coat a 9- by 13-inch baking pan with cooking spray. Arrange potatoes in pan, leaving enough room for fish. Bake potatoes in a 400° oven for 20 minutes. Meanwhile, in a small bowl, mix cheese, salt, pepper, and 1 tablespoon of the lemon juice until smooth and fluffy. Stir in carrot, tomato, onion, and parsley.

Rinse fish, pat dry, and place in pan alongside potatoes; drizzle fish with remaining 2 tablespoons lemon juice. Mound cream cheese mixture over fish, spreading nearly to edges. Continue to bake until potatoes are tender when pierced and fish is just opaque but still moist in thickest part; cut to test (about 12 more minutes). Makes 2 servings.

Per serving: 409 calories (30% fat, 35% carbohydrates, 35% protein), 14 g total fat (4 g saturated fat), 36 g carbohydrates, 35 g protein, 93 mg cholesterol, 287 mg sodium

__American Neufchâtel cheese__ is lower in fat and somewhat moister than cream cheese. Don't confuse it with imported Neufchâtel from the Normandy region of France, which may be much richer than the American kind.

Baby Salmon & Squash with Brown Sugar & Lime

. . . .

Preparation time: About 10 minutes
Baking time: About 1¼ hours

In this easy oven meal, the sweet-tart flavors of citrus and brown sugar enhance salmon fillets and winter squash.

2   **pounds banana or Hubbard squash, seeded and cut into 4 equal pieces**

1½   **cups low-sodium chicken broth**

4   **baby salmon fillets (about 5 oz. *each*)**

½   **teaspoon salad oil**

¼   **cup *each* firmly packed brown sugar and lime juice**
     Lime wedges
     Salt and pepper

Place squash, skin side up, in a large, shallow baking pan; pour in broth. Bake in a 350° oven until squash is tender when pierced (about 1 hour). Remove from oven; then increase oven temperature to 450°.

Rinse fish and pat dry. Turn squash over and push to one end of pan. Lift opposite end of pan so that any liquid runs down to mix with squash; then spread oil over exposed pan bottom.

Place fish fillets side by side (they can overlap slightly) in oiled part of pan. In a small bowl, mix sugar and lime juice; spoon about half the mixture over fish and squash.

Return pan to oven and bake until fish is just opaque but still moist in thickest part; cut to test (about 8 minutes). After fish has baked for 5 minutes, spoon remaining lime mixture over fish and squash.

To serve, transfer fish and squash to 4 individual plates; garnish with lime wedges. Stir pan juices to blend; season to taste with salt and pepper, then pour into a small bowl. Serve pan juices with fish and squash. Makes 4 servings.

Per serving: 331 calories (29% fat, 33% carbohydrates, 38% protein), 11 g total fat (2 g saturated fat), 28 g carbohydrates, 32 g protein, 78 mg cholesterol, 100 mg sodium

Steamed Trout with Lettuce & Peas

. . . .

30 MINUTES OR LESS

Preparation time: About 10 minutes
Cooking time: About 15 minutes

Steaming is a great cooking method: the results are fresh-tasting and flavorful, and you needn't add a bit of fat. Here, delicate trout steams with mint, lemon, peas, and lettuce for a palate-pleasing entrée. To round out a wonderful light meal, offer crunchy breadsticks and a fluffy rice or bulgur pilaf. For dessert, you might choose Summer Hazelnut Torte with Berries (page 201).

3   **tablespoons chopped fresh mint**

1   **tablespoon finely shredded lemon peel**

1   **clove garlic, minced or pressed**

2   **cups frozen tiny peas, thawed**

3   **cups shredded romaine lettuce**

4   **cleaned whole trout (about 8 oz. *each*)**

8   **to 12 lemon wedges**
     Mint sprigs

In a bowl, mix chopped mint, lemon peel, garlic, peas, and lettuce. Pat mixture gently into a neat mound in a heatproof, 1-inch-deep nonmetal dish that is at least ½ inch smaller in diameter than the pan you will use for steaming.

Rinse trout inside and out and pat dry; then arrange trout over lettuce mixture, cavity sides down and heads pointing in same direction (lean fish against each other). Arrange lemon wedges over top of fish.

Set dish on a rack in a pan above about 1 inch of boiling water. Cover and steam, keeping water at a steady boil, until fish is just opaque but still moist in thickest part; cut to test (about 15 min

utes). If necessary, add more boiling water to pan to keep water level constant.

Using thick potholders, carefully lift dish from pan. Transfer trout to individual plates and spoon lettuce mixture alongside. Garnish with mint sprigs. Serve with lemon wedges. Makes 4 servings.

Per serving: 275 calories (30% fat, 22% carbohydrates, 48% protein), 9 g total fat (2 g saturated fat), 15 g carbohydrates, 33 g protein, 78 mg cholesterol, 201 mg sodium

Grilled Tuna Steaks

MODIFIED CLASSIC

Preparation time: About 15 minutes
Marinating time: At least 1 hour
Grilling time: 6 to 7 minutes

Tuna steaks (known as *ahi* in Hawaii) take well to grilling after a quick soak in an Asian-style marinade of lime, soy, ginger, and garlic. Tropical fruits taste great alongside—try papaya, mango, and juicy fresh pineapple.

4   tuna (ahi) steaks, cut about 1 inch thick (about 7 oz. *each*)
3   tablespoons lime juice
2   tablespoons reduced-sodium soy sauce
1   tablespoon *each* minced fresh ginger and minced garlic
     Lime wedges
     Oriental sesame oil (optional)

Rinse fish steaks, pat dry, and place in a 9- by 13-inch dish. In a small bowl, stir together lime juice, soy sauce, ginger, and garlic; pour over fish. Turn fish to coat with marinade; then cover and refrigerate for at least 1 hour or up to 1 day, turning occasionally.

Lift fish from marinade and drain briefly; discard marinade. Place fish on a lightly oiled grill 4 to 6 inches above a solid bed of hot coals. Cook, turning once, until fish is browned on outside but still pale pink in thickest part; cut to test (6 to 7 minutes). Serve with lime wedges and sesame oil, if desired. Makes 4 servings.

Per serving: 206 calories (8% fat, 5% carbohydrates, 87% protein), 2 g total fat (0.4 g saturated fat), 3 g carbohydrates, 43 g protein, 81 mg cholesterol, 369 mg sodium

Baked Sole & Ratatouille

Preparation time: About 15 minutes
Baking time: About 50 minutes

Colorful, herb-seasoned ratatouille is the perfect foil for mild white sole fillets. Melt a little jack cheese over the fish and vegetables for a finishing touch.

     Vegetable oil cooking spray
8   ounces medium-size zucchini, sliced
1   small eggplant (about 12 oz.), unpeeled, cut into ½-inch cubes
1   *each* large green and red bell pepper (about 1 lb. *total*), seeded and cut into thin strips
1   tablespoon *each* dry basil and olive oil
1   teaspoon dry oregano
4   sole fillets (about 5 oz. *each*)
¼   cup shredded reduced-fat jack cheese

Lightly coat a 9- by 13-inch baking pan with cooking spray. Add zucchini, eggplant, bell peppers, basil, oil, and oregano; stir gently. Cover and bake in a 425° oven until eggplant is tender to bite (about 40 minutes).

Stir vegetables, then push to sides of pan. Rinse fish, pat dry, and place in center of pan, overlapping fillets slightly if necessary. Cover and continue to bake until fish is just opaque but still moist in thickest part; cut to test (about 8 more minutes). Uncover, sprinkle with cheese, and continue to bake, uncovered, until cheese is melted (1 to 2 more minutes). Makes 4 servings.

Per serving: 240 calories (26% fat, 23% carbohydrates, 51% protein), 7 g total fat (2 g saturated fat), 14 g carbohydrates, 31 g protein, 73 mg cholesterol, 167 mg sodium

If you do some advance preparation, you can enjoy moist, flavorful rare tuna without worrying about potentially harmful organisms that might withstand cooking to the less-than-well-done stage. First, freeze the tuna steaks at 0°F for at least 7 days; then thaw the fish in the refrigerator before getting it ready for the grill.

Sole Florentine

Preparation time: About 25 minutes
Baking time: About 17 minutes

Filled with a lemony spinach stuffing, these delicate rolled sole fillets cook quickly in broth and white wine. If you like, you can serve them directly from the baking dish.

6　thin sole fillets (about 3 oz. *each*)

2　pounds spinach, stems removed, leaves rinsed and coarsely chopped

¼　teaspoon ground nutmeg

2　tablespoons *each* grated lemon peel and chopped parsley

¼　cup *each* low-sodium chicken broth and dry white wine

1　small dry bay leaf

4　whole black peppercorns

Rinse fish and pat dry. Trim each fillet to make a 3- by 8-inch rectangle (reserve trimmings); set aside. Finely chop trimmings; place in a bowl and add 1½ cups of the spinach, nutmeg, lemon peel, and parsley. Mix well.

Spread spinach mixture evenly over fillets. Gently roll up fillets and secure with wooden picks.

Place fish rolls, seam side down, in a 9-inch baking dish. Pour broth and wine around fish; add bay leaf and peppercorns. Cover and bake in a 400° oven for 10 minutes.

Place remaining spinach in another 9-inch baking dish. With a slotted spoon, lift fish rolls from first baking dish; arrange atop spinach (discard

---

When you see the word "Florentine" *in the name of a dish, chances are good that spinach is one of the recipe's ingredients. Choose fresh spinach if possible; it's available all year round in most markets. Buy bunches with crisp, tender deep green leaves; avoid those with yellowing or blemished leaves. If some spinach remains after you've completed your dish, add it to a green salad.*

---

poaching liquid). Cover and bake until fish is just opaque but still moist in thickest part; cut to test (about 7 minutes). Remove and discard picks from fish. Makes 6 servings.

Per serving: 108 calories (12% fat, 16% carbohydrates, 72% protein), 1 g total fat (0.3 g saturated fat), 4 g carbohydrates, 19 g protein, 41 mg cholesterol, 157 mg sodium

Fish with Herbs

Preparation time: About 15 minutes
Baking time: About 15 minutes
Cooking time: 6 to 8 minutes

Choose fresh tarragon, thyme, or sage to accent fish fillets baked in broth and white wine. In spring, choose Pasta Risotto with Asparagus (page 165) to serve alongside.

2　pounds boneless, skinless striped bass or sole fillets

½　cup *each* dry white wine and low-sodium chicken broth

⅓　cup minced shallots

1　tablespoon chopped fresh tarragon, thyme, or sage

6　to 8 thin lemon slices

6　to 8 tarragon, thyme, or sage sprigs

2　teaspoons cornstarch blended with 1 tablespoon cold water
　　Salt and pepper

Rinse fish and pat dry. Then arrange fillets, overlapping slightly, in a 9- by 13-inch baking dish. Pour wine and broth over fish; sprinkle with shallots and chopped tarragon. Lay lemon slices and tarragon sprigs on fish. Bake in a 375° oven until fish is just opaque but still moist in thickest part; cut to test (about 15 minutes).

Keeping fish in dish, carefully spoon off pan juices into a small pan. Cover fish and keep warm. Bring pan juices to a boil over high heat; then boil, uncovered, until reduced to ¾ cup (about 5 minutes). Stir in cornstarch mixture; bring to a boil, stirring. Season sauce to taste with salt and pepper, then pour over fish. Makes 6 servings.

Per serving: 178 calories (21% fat, 11% carbohydrates, 68% protein), 4 g total fat (0.8 g saturated fat), 4 g carbohydrates, 27 g protein, 121 mg cholesterol, 112 mg sodium

Baked Fish & Chips

Preparation time: About 20 minutes
Baking time: About 40 minutes

You'll have time to mix a green salad while these cornmeal-crusted fish fillets, potatoes, and zucchini strips bake to crisp, golden tenderness in the oven. Serve fresh pears for dessert.

1½	**cups yellow cornmeal**
2	**teaspoons sugar**
1	**teaspoon pepper**
½	**teaspoon salt**
3	**large egg whites (about 6 tablespoons)**
3	**large potatoes (about 1½ lbs. *total*), scrubbed**
2	**large zucchini**
3	**tablespoons salad oil**
1	**to 1½ pounds firm-textured white-fleshed fish fillets such as rockfish or orange roughy, cut into 4 equal pieces**
	Malt or cider vinegar
	Tartar sauce (optional)

In a shallow dish, mix cornmeal, sugar, pepper, and salt. In another shallow dish, lightly beat egg whites until slightly frothy.

Cut each potato lengthwise into 8 wedges; cut each zucchini lengthwise into 6 slices. Dip potato wedges and zucchini slices, one piece at a time, in egg whites; then roll in cornmeal mixture. Set vegetables aside, keeping potatoes and zucchini separate and arranging them in a single layer.

Rub 1 tablespoon of the oil over bottom of each of two 10- by 15-inch rimmed baking pans. Place pans in a 450° oven for 3 minutes. Lay potato and zucchini pieces in a single layer in separate pans, placing pieces slightly apart. Bake vegetables, turning them with a wide spatula after 15 minutes, until crust on zucchini is crisp (about 25 minutes) and potatoes are tender when pierced (about 40 minutes).

Meanwhile, rinse fish and pat dry. Dip fish in egg whites, then turn in cornmeal mixture to coat.

When zucchini is done, transfer it to a platter and keep warm. Then add remaining 1 tablespoon oil to pan; place fish pieces slightly apart in pan. Bake until crusty and golden on bottom (about 4 minutes). Turn fish over and continue to bake until golden on other side and opaque but still moist in thickest part; cut to test (4 to 6 more minutes). If fish is done before potatoes, transfer to platter with zucchini and keep warm.

Serve fish and vegetables with vinegar and tartar sauce (if desired) to add to taste. Makes 4 servings.

Per serving: 576 calories (21% fat, 52% carbohydrates, 27% protein), 14 g total fat (2 g saturated fat), 74 g carbohydrates, 39 g protein, 50 mg cholesterol, 417 mg sodium

Seed-crusted Fish, Indian Style

Preparation time: About 10 minutes
Broiling time: 5 to 7 minutes

Curry-lovers will enjoy this assertively seasoned fish, broiled with a crunchy topping of pepper and spicy seeds. Choose a colorful accompaniment, such as Brussels Sprouts with Mustard Glaze (page 164).

1	**teaspoon *each* coriander seeds and mustard seeds**
½	**teaspoon *each* coarsely ground pepper, cumin seeds, and fennel seeds**
1	**pound lingcod, rockfish, or orange roughy fillets (½ to 1 inch thick)**
2	**teaspoons salad oil**
	Cilantro sprigs

Mix coriander seeds, mustard seeds, pepper, cumin seeds, and fennel seeds; set aside.

Rinse fish, pat dry, and cut into 4 equal pieces. Brush with oil and place on a rack in a 12- by 14-inch broiler pan. Broil about 3 inches below heat for 3 minutes. Turn fish over, sprinkle with seed mixture, and continue to broil until just opaque but still moist in thickest part; cut to test (2 to 4 more minutes). Garnish with cilantro sprigs. Makes 4 servings.

Per serving: 125 calories (29% fat, 3% carbohydrates, 68% protein), 4 g total fat (0.5 g saturated fat), 0.9 g carbohydrates, 20 g protein, 59 mg cholesterol, 68 mg sodium

Snapper Veracruz

Preparation time: About 10 minutes
Cooking time: About 10 minutes
Baking time: 10 to 15 minutes

Named after the Mexican seacoast town where the recipe originated, snapper Veracruz features tender fillets topped with a cinnamon-spiced sauce of bell peppers, tomatoes, olives, and capers.

1	teaspoon salad oil or olive oil
1	small green or red bell pepper (about 5 oz.), seeded and chopped
1	large onion, chopped
3	cloves garlic, minced or pressed (optional)
2	tablespoons water
1	can (about 4 oz.) diced green chiles
¼	cup sliced pimento-stuffed green olives
3	tablespoons lime juice
1	teaspoon ground cinnamon
¼	teaspoon ground white pepper
1	can (about 14½ oz.) stewed tomatoes
4	snapper or rockfish fillets (about 8 oz. *each*)
1	tablespoon drained capers

Heat oil in a wide nonstick frying pan over medium-high heat. Add bell pepper, onion, garlic, and water; cook, stirring often, until vegetables are tender-crisp to bite (3 to 5 minutes). Add chiles, olives, lime juice, cinnamon, and white pepper; cook for 1 more minute. Add tomatoes to pan and bring mixture to a boil. Boil, uncovered, stirring often, until sauce is slightly thickened (about 5 minutes).

Rinse fish, pat dry, and arrange in a lightly oiled 9- by 13-inch baking dish. Pour sauce over fish. Bake in a 350° oven until fish is just opaque but still moist in thickest part; cut to test (10 to 15 minutes).

With a slotted spoon, transfer fish and sauce to individual plates. Sprinkle with capers. Makes 4 servings.

Per serving: 318 calories (16% fat, 22% carbohydrates, 62% protein), 6 g total fat (0.9 g saturated fat), 17 g carbohydrates, 49 g protein, 84 mg cholesterol, 843 mg sodium

Oven-poached Lingcod

Preparation time: About 10 minutes
Cooking time: About 30 minutes
Baking time: About 6 minutes

Poaching is a wonderful way to prepare mild-flavored lingcod. Here, thick fillets simmer in white wine seasoned with onions, bay leaves, and allspice. Once the fish is done, you combine the cooking liquid with lightly sautéed leeks to make a memorable sauce.

2	medium-size onions, sliced
12	whole black peppercorns
4	whole allspice
⅓	cup lemon juice
2	dry bay leaves
1	cup dry white wine
8	cups water
3	large leeks (about 1¾ lbs. *total*)
1	tablespoon olive oil
2	pounds lingcod fillets (about 1 inch thick)
	Salt and pepper (optional)

In a 4- to 5-quart pan, combine onions, peppercorns, allspice, lemon juice, bay leaves, wine, and water. Bring to a boil over high heat; then reduce heat, cover, and simmer for 20 minutes. Pour liquid through a fine strainer; discard residue and return liquid to pan.

While poaching liquid is simmering, trim ends and all but 3 inches of green tops from leeks; remove tough outer leaves. Split leeks lengthwise; rinse well, then thinly slice crosswise. Heat oil in a wide frying pan over medium heat; add leeks and cook, stirring occasionally, until soft (about 10 minutes). Remove from heat.

Rinse fish, pat dry, and place in a single layer in an oiled 9- by 13-inch baking dish. Bring strained poaching liquid to a boil and pour over fish (liquid should just cover fish; if necessary, add equal parts of hot water and wine to cover fish). Cover and bake in a 425° oven until fish is just opaque but still moist in thickest part; cut to test (about 6 minutes).

Lift fish from baking dish, drain well, place in a serving dish, and keep warm. Measure ½ cup of the poaching liquid and add to leeks. Bring to a boil, stirring; season to taste with salt and pepper, if desired. Pour sauce over fish. Makes 6 servings.

Per serving: 236 calories (18% fat, 28% carbohydrates, 54% protein), 4 g total fat (0.6 g saturated fat), 15 g carbohydrates, 28 g protein, 79 mg cholesterol, 108 mg sodium

Citrus Lingcod with Orange Almond Rice

Preparation time: About 30 minutes
Cooking time: About 30 minutes

A quartet of citrus fruits goes into the sauce for broiled lingcod and fragrant rice in this glamorous treatment of a notably lean fish. You might complete the menu with a green vegetable such as slender steamed asparagus spears or tender-crisp snow peas.

4	**medium-size oranges (about 2 lbs. *total*)**
1	**medium-size red grapefruit (about 12 oz.)**
1	**medium-size lemon**
1	**medium-size lime**
¼	**cup slivered almonds**
2	**tablespoons olive oil**
6	**tablespoons chopped shallots**
2¼	**cups water**
¼	**teaspoon almond extract**
1½	**cups long-grain white rice**
2	**pounds lingcod fillets (about 1 inch thick)**
	Olive oil cooking spray
¼	**cup unseasoned rice vinegar or white wine vinegar**
	Salt and pepper

Finely shred 1½ tablespoons *each* orange and grapefruit peel (colored part only); finely shred 1 teaspoon *each* lemon and lime peel (colored part only). Mix citrus peels and set aside.

Cut remaining peel and all white membrane from grapefruit, lemon, lime, and 2 of the oranges. Holding fruit over a bowl to catch juice, cut between membranes of each peeled fruit to release segments into bowl. Set aside. Squeeze juice from remaining 2 oranges; set aside.

Toast almonds in a 2-quart pan over medium heat until golden (about 5 minutes), stirring often. Pour almonds out of pan and set aside. In same pan, heat 1 tablespoon of the oil; add ¼ cup of the shallots and cook, stirring, until soft but not browned (2 to 3 minutes). Add water, ¾ cup of the orange juice, and almond extract. Bring to a boil; stir in rice. Reduce heat to low, cover, and simmer until rice is tender to bite (20 to 25 minutes).

Meanwhile, rinse fish, pat dry, and cut into serving-size pieces. Coat lightly with cooking spray. Place fish on a lightly oiled rack in a broiler pan. Broil about 4 inches below heat, turning once, until fish is just opaque but still moist in thickest part; cut to test (about 10 minutes).

While fish is broiling, heat remaining 1 tablespoon oil in a wide nonstick frying pan over medium heat. Add vinegar, remaining 2 tablespoons shallots, any remaining orange juice, and citrus segments and their juices. Cook, swirling pan often, just until sauce is warm (about 2 minutes).

Stir almonds into rice; spoon onto 4 to 6 individual plates. Lift fish onto plates; spoon sauce over fish. Garnish with mixed citrus peels; season to taste with salt and pepper. Makes 4 to 6 servings.

Per serving: 527 calories (20% fat, 51% carbohydrates, 29% protein), 12 g total fat (2 g saturated fat), 67 g carbohydrates, 39 g protein, 94 mg cholesterol, 113 mg sodium

*****Shallots**, once considered an unusual ingredient used only in French cuisine, are now sold in most produce departments. Not to be confused with scallions (green onions or onion shoots), shallots are small, subtly flavored dry bulbs containing one or more cloves. Chop or sliver them to include in sauces and dressings.*

Rockfish & Tiny Potatoes with Mustard-Honey Glaze

Preparation time: About 15 minutes
Baking time: About 35 minutes

Azesty glaze gives mild rockfish fillets sparkling flavor. Accompany with tender-crisp green beans or broccoli.

1	tablespoon olive or salad oil
16	very small thin-skinned potatoes (*each* 1 to 1½ inches in diameter), scrubbed
¼	cup Dijon mustard
2	tablespoons honey
4	rockfish fillets (about 5 oz. *each*)
	Salt and pepper

Pour oil into a 10- by 15-inch rimmed baking pan. Add potatoes and turn to coat with oil. Bake in a 425° oven until potatoes are just tender when pierced (about 25 minutes).

Meanwhile, in a small bowl, stir together mustard and honey. Rinse fish, pat dry, and brush with about half the mustard mixture.

When potatoes are tender, push them to one end of pan and brush with remaining mustard mixture. Place fish in pan in a single layer. Bake until fish is just opaque but still moist in thickest part; cut to test (8 to 10 minutes).

To serve, transfer fish and potatoes to 4 individual plates. Stir pan juices and season to taste with salt and pepper; pour into a small bowl. Serve pan juices with fish and potatoes. Makes 4 servings.

Per serving: 366 calories (17% fat, 50% carbohydrates, 33% protein), 7 g total fat (1 g saturated fat), 45 g carbohydrates, 30 g protein, 50 mg cholesterol, 550 mg sodium

---

To soften corn or flour tortillas *for tacos and fajitas, heat them on the grill, turning often with tongs, for 15 to 20 seconds—just until they're speckled with brown and pliable enough to roll around the filling. Or stack the tortillas, wrap in foil, and heat in a 350° oven for about 10 minutes.*

Grilled Fish Tacos

Preparation time: About 30 minutes
Marinating time: At least 15 minutes
Grilling time: About 10 minutes

Lime- and tequila-marinated fish makes an unusual filling for warm tortillas. Crunchy cabbage slaw and your favorite salsa go into the tacos as well; alongside, you might serve simmered black beans.

1¾	to 2 pounds firm-textured white-fleshed fish fillets or steaks such as Chilean sea bass, swordfish, or sturgeon (1½ to 2 inches thick)
⅓	cup lime juice
3	tablespoons tequila (optional)
	Cilantro Slaw (recipe follows)
6	to 12 flour tortillas (*each* 7 to 9 inches in diameter) or corn tortillas (*each* about 6 inches in diameter)
	About 1 cup purchased or homemade salsa
	Reduced-fat sour cream or plain nonfat yogurt

Rinse fish, pat dry, and place in a wide, shallow bowl. Stir together lime juice and tequila (if used); pour over fish. Turn fish to coat; then cover and refrigerate for at least 15 minutes or up to 4 hours, turning occasionally. Meanwhile, prepare Cilantro Slaw.

Lift fish from marinade and drain briefly; discard any remaining marinade. Place fish on a lightly oiled grill 4 to 6 inches above a solid bed of medium-hot coals. Cook, turning once or twice, until fish is lightly browned on outside and just opaque but still moist in thickest part; cut to test (about 10 minutes).

Transfer fish to a platter. To assemble tacos, heat tortillas on grill, turning often with tongs, just until softened (15 to 20 seconds). Cut off chunks of fish (removing any bones and skin) and place in tortillas; add salsa, Cilantro Slaw, and sour cream to taste. Roll to enclose; eat out of hand. Also offer slaw as a side dish. Makes 6 servings.

Cilantro Slaw. In a large bowl, combine 3 cups *each* finely shredded **green cabbage** and **red cabbage;** 1 cup firmly packed **cilantro leaves,** minced;

cup **lime juice;** 1 tablespoon **salad oil;** ½ teaspoon **cumin seeds;** and 1 teaspoon **sugar.** Season to taste with **salt** and **pepper.** If made ahead, cover and refrigerate for up to 4 hours.

Per serving: 307 calories (23% fat, 37% carbohydrates, 40% protein), 8 g total fat (1 g saturated fat), 28 g carbohydrates, 30 g protein, 58 mg cholesterol, 518 mg sodium

South Seas Swordfish

. . . .

Preparation time: About 20 minutes
Cooking time: About 15 minutes

Fish, coconut, taro leaves—all three are popular ingredients in South Pacific cooking. Here, coconut extract and chicken broth substitute for rich coconut milk, while readily available spinach stands in for taro.

1	to 1¼ pounds **swordfish steaks** (cut about ¾ inch thick)
1½	cups **low-sodium chicken broth**
2	tablespoons minced **fresh ginger**
½	teaspoon **coconut extract**
1	pound **spinach,** stems removed, leaves rinsed and drained
3	cups hot cooked **rice**
1	tablespoon **cornstarch** blended with 1 tablespoon **cold water**
¼	cup **lemon juice** **Salt**

Rinse fish and pat dry; cut into 4 equal pieces, if necessary. In a wide frying pan, combine broth, ginger, and coconut extract. Bring to a boil over high heat; add fish. Reduce heat, cover, and simmer until fish is just opaque but still moist in thickest part; cut to test (about 10 minutes). Transfer fish to a platter; keep warm.

Increase heat to high. Add spinach to pan and cook, stirring, until wilted (about 3 minutes). With a slotted spoon, transfer spinach to platter alongside fish; then spoon rice onto platter. Stir cornstarch mixture into cooking liquid; bring to a boil, stirring. Stir in lemon juice, season to taste with salt, and pour over fish. Makes 4 servings.

Per serving: 380 calories (14% fat, 54% carbohydrates, 32% protein), 6 g total fat (2 g saturated fat), 50 g carbohydrates, 30 g protein, 45 mg cholesterol, 195 mg sodium

Broiled Fish Dijon

. . . .

3 0   M I N U T E S   O R   L E S S

Preparation time: About 5 minutes
Broiling time: About 10 minutes

A bold blend of garlic and mustard complements the rich flavor of swordfish. Broiling makes this dish especially quick and easy; you can be out of the kitchen and in the dining room in under half an hour.

6	**swordfish steaks,** cut about 1 inch thick (5 to 6 oz. *each*)
1½	pounds small **zucchini** (about 6 zucchini), cut lengthwise into halves
¼	cup **lemon juice**
2	tablespoons **Dijon mustard**
1	clove **garlic,** minced or pressed **Paprika**
2	tablespoons drained **capers**

Rinse fish and pat dry. Then arrange fish and zucchini (cut side up) in a single layer on an oiled rack in a large broiler pan. Drizzle with lemon juice. Broil 4 to 6 inches below heat for 5 minutes. Meanwhile, in a small bowl, stir together mustard and garlic.

Turn fish over; spread with mustard mixture. Then continue to broil until zucchini is lightly browned and fish is just opaque but still moist in thickest part; cut to test (about 5 more minutes). Sprinkle fish and zucchini with paprika and capers. Makes 6 servings.

Per serving: 193 calories (29% fat, 10% carbohydrates, 61% protein), 6 g total fat (2 g saturated fat), 5 g carbohydrates, 29 g protein, 54 mg cholesterol, 354 mg sodium

Grilled Soy-Lemon Halibut

. . . .

Preparation time: About 10 minutes
Marinating time: 1 to 2 hours
Cooking time: 8 to 10 minutes

A tart teriyaki marinade perfectly complements mild-tasting halibut.

2   **pounds halibut, shark, or sea bass steaks or fillets (¾ to 1 inch thick)**
2   **tablespoons butter or margarine, melted**
3   **tablespoons reduced-sodium soy sauce**
2   **tablespoons lemon juice**
1   **tablespoon *each* sugar and Worcestershire**
1   **tablespoon minced fresh ginger or ½ teaspoon ground ginger**
1   **clove garlic, minced or pressed**
⅛ **teaspoon pepper**
    Vegetable oil cooking spray

Rinse fish and pat dry; then cut into 6 equal pieces, if necessary. In a shallow dish, stir together butter, soy sauce, lemon juice, sugar, Worcestershire, ginger, garlic, and pepper. Add fish and turn to coat. Then cover and refrigerate for 1 to 2 hours, turning occasionally.

Coat grill of a covered barbecue with cooking spray. Lift fish from marinade and drain briefly; discard marinade. Place fish on grill 4 to 6 inches above a solid bed of hot coals. Cover barbecue, open vents, and cook, turning once, until fish is just opaque but still moist in thickest part; cut to test (8 to 10 minutes). Makes 6 servings.

Per serving: 194 calories (27% fat, 4% carbohydrates, 69% protein), 6 g total fat (2 g saturated fat), 2 g carbohydrates, 32 g protein, 54 mg cholesterol, 266 mg sodium

---

Fresh herbs *such as dill bring pleasing aroma and flavor to food—without adding fat or sodium. To prepare bunched herbs for use, rinse them under cold running water and shake off the excess moisture. Then wrap the herbs in a dry cloth or paper towel, enclose them in a plastic bag, and refrigerate.*

Halibut with Tomatoes & Dill

. . . .

Preparation time: About 10 minutes
Baking time: About 35 minutes

R oasted cherry tomatoes, seasoned with garlic and fresh dill, make a light and colorful sauce for thick halibut fillets or steaks that bake separately in the same oven. If you can't find halibut, choose another firm, mild-flavored, white-fleshed fish such as rockfish, lingcod, Pacific snapper, mahi mahi, or orange roughy.

1   **pound (about 3 cups) cherry tomatoes, cut into halves**
½   **cup thinly sliced green onions**
2   **cloves garlic, minced or pressed**
2   **tablespoons chopped fresh dill or ½ teaspoon dry dill weed**
2   **teaspoons olive oil**
2   **tablespoons water**
1½   **pounds halibut fillets or steaks (or rockfish or cod fillets)**
2   **tablespoons lemon juice**
     Dill sprigs (optional)

Arrange tomatoes, cut side up, in a 9- by 13-inch baking pan. In a small bowl, mix onions, garlic, chopped dill, oil, and water. Distribute onion mixture over tomatoes. Bake on top rack of a 425° oven for 25 minutes.

Rinse fish and pat dry; then cut into 4 equal pieces, if necessary. Place fish in a baking pan large enough to hold pieces in a single layer. Drizzle with lemon juice, cover, and place in oven, setting pan on bottom oven rack.

Continue to bake fish and tomatoes until tomatoes are lightly browned on top and fish is just opaque but still moist in thickest part; cut to test (8 to 10 minutes).

Transfer fish to a platter. Add fish cooking juices to tomato mixture and stir well; spoon over fish. Garnish with dill sprigs, if desired. Makes 4 servings.

Per serving: 239 calories (25% fat, 12% carbohydrates, 63% protein), 7 g total fat (0.9 g saturated fat), 7 g carbohydrates, 37 g protein, 54 mg cholesterol, 106 mg sodium

LOW-FAT SAUCES FOR FISH

A grilled fish steak or plateful of fresh cracked crab is often so inviting that the only accent needed is a squeeze of fresh lemon. If you crave further embellishment, however, try one of these appealing choices. The first two sauces are delicious with cold poached fish, while Tomato-Caper Sauce is excellent with hot broiled, grilled, or baked fish. Try our Cocktail Sauce with a favorite shellfish.

RADISH TARTAR SAUCE

Preparation time: About 20 minutes

- ¾ **cup plain nonfat or low-fat yogurt**
- 2 **tablespoons reduced-fat sour cream**
- ¾ **cup chopped radishes**
- ⅓ **cup thinly sliced green onions**
- 2 **tablespoons drained capers**
- 1 **tablespoon prepared horseradish**
  Salt

In a medium-size bowl, stir together yogurt, sour cream, radishes, onions, capers, and horseradish. Season to taste with salt. If made ahead, cover and refrigerate for up to 1 day. Stir before using. Serve with cold poached fish steaks or fillets. Makes about 1¾ cups.

Per tablespoon: 6 calories (23% fat, 49% carbohydrates, 28% protein), 0.2 g total fat (0.1 g saturated fat), 0.8 g carbohydrates, 0.4 g protein, 0.5 mg cholesterol, 22 mg sodium

COOL DILL SAUCE

Preparation time: About 10 minutes

- ⅔ **cup plain nonfat or low-fat yogurt**
- 1 **tablespoon *each* white wine vinegar and minced chives**
- 1 **tablespoon minced fresh dill or 1 teaspoon dry dill weed**
- ⅛ **teaspoon liquid hot pepper seasoning**
  Salt and pepper

In a small bowl, stir together yogurt, vinegar, chives, dill, and hot pepper seasoning. Season to taste with salt and pepper. If made ahead, cover and refrigerate for up to 1 day. Stir before using. Serve with cold poached or grilled salmon or white-fleshed fish. Makes about ¾ cup.

Per tablespoon: 8 calories (2% fat, 58% carbohydrates, 40% protein), 0 g total fat (0 g saturated fat), 1 g carbohydrates, 0.7 g protein, 0.3 mg cholesterol, 11 mg sodium

COCKTAIL SAUCE

Preparation time: About 5 minutes

- ½ **cup catsup**
- ¼ **cup *each* tomato-based chili sauce and grapefruit juice**
- 2 **tablespoons lemon juice**
- 1 **tablespoon thinly sliced green onion**
- 1 **teaspoon *each* prepared horseradish and Worcestershire**
- 2 **or 3 drops liquid hot pepper seasoning**

In a small bowl, stir together catsup, chili sauce, grapefruit juice, lemon juice, onion, horseradish, Worcestershire, and hot pepper seasoning. Serve with cold poached fish or cold shellfish. Makes about 1 cup.

Per tablespoon: 15 calories (2% fat, 92% carbohydrates, 6% protein), 0 g total fat (0 g saturated fat), 4 g carbohydrates, 0.2 g protein, 0 mg cholesterol, 151 mg sodium

TOMATO-CAPER SAUCE

Preparation time: 8 to 10 minutes
Cooking time: About 15 minutes

- 1 **teaspoon olive oil**
- 1 **medium-size onion, finely chopped**
- 1 **clove garlic, minced or pressed**
- 1 **can (about 14½ oz.) diced tomatoes**
- 2 **teaspoons drained capers**
- 1 **tablespoon lemon juice**
- 2 **tablespoons minced parsley**

Heat oil in a wide nonstick frying pan over medium heat. Add onion and garlic; cook, stirring often, until onion is soft (about 5 minutes). Add tomatoes and capers. Bring to a gentle boil. Cook, uncovered, stirring often, until thickened (about 10 minutes). Stir in lemon juice and parsley. Serve over hot cooked fish. Makes about 2 cups.

Per tablespoon: 6 calories (24% fat, 66% carbohydrates, 10% protein), 0.2 g total fat (0 g saturated fat), 1 g carbohydrates, 0.2 g protein, 0 mg cholesterol, 26 mg sodium

Orange Roughy with Polenta

Preparation time: About 10 minutes
Cooking time: About 20 minutes

Brighten up the dinner hour with this colorful, quick-to-fix combination. Red bell pepper and green cilantro are sprinkled over mild white fish fillets served on a bed of chile-flecked polenta.

1	cup polenta
4⅓	cups low-sodium chicken broth
½	teaspoon cumin seeds
1	large can (about 7 oz.) diced green chiles
1	pound orange roughy fillets, cut into 4 equal pieces
1	medium-size red bell pepper (6 to 7 oz.), seeded and minced
1	tablespoon cilantro leaves
	Salt
	Lime wedges

Pour polenta into a 3- to 4-quart pan; stir in broth and cumin seeds. Bring to a boil over high heat, stirring often with a long-handled wooden spoon (mixture will spatter). Reduce heat and simmer gently, uncovered, stirring often, until polenta tastes creamy (about 20 minutes). Stir in chiles.

While polenta is simmering, rinse fish and pat dry; then arrange in a 9- by 13-inch baking pan. Bake in a 475° oven until fish is just opaque but still moist in thickest part; cut to test (about 6 minutes).

To serve, spoon polenta onto 4 individual plates. Top each serving with a piece of fish; sprinkle with bell pepper and cilantro. Season to taste with salt; serve with lime wedges. Makes 4 servings.

Per serving: 326 calories (29% fat, 42% carbohydrates, 29% protein), 10 g total fat (0.7 g saturated fat), 34 g carbohydrates, 23 g protein, 23 mg cholesterol, 434 mg sodium

---

Discovered only in 1975, *orange roughy has achieved great popularity. A mild, tender-firm fish with pearly white flesh, it comes from the deep waters off New Zealand; the catch is frozen at sea.*

Curried Fish & Rice

Preparation time: About 20 minutes
Cooking time: About 20 minutes

A warm-and-cool fish salad is a pleasant dinner choice in any season. This one features good-tasting Chilean sea bass (richer than other sea bass). The sautéed fillets, cooked rice, and shredded lettuce are topped with a curry-seasoned sauce of tart yogurt and sweet red pepper.

1	small head romaine lettuce (8 to 10 oz.), separated into leaves, rinsed, and crisped
2	tablespoons salad oil
1	cup sliced green onions
1	large red bell pepper (about 8 oz.), seeded and finely chopped
2	teaspoons curry powder
1½	cups plain low-fat yogurt
⅓	cup water
2½	cups cooled cooked brown or white rice
4	Chilean sea bass fillets, ¾ to 1 inch thick (about 6 oz. *each*)

Finely shred about a third of the lettuce leaves. Cover a platter with remaining whole leaves; then mound shredded lettuce on one side of platter. Set aside.

Heat 1 tablespoon of the oil in a wide nonstick frying pan over medium-high heat. Add onions and bell pepper and cook, stirring often, until pepper is soft (8 to 10 minutes). Add curry powder; cook, stirring, for 1 more minute.

Transfer vegetable mixture to a large bowl and stir in yogurt and water. Set 1¼ cups of the mixture aside. Add rice to remaining vegetable mixture and stir to combine well; then mound on shredded lettuce. Set aside.

Heat remaining 1 tablespoon oil in pan over medium-high heat. Rinse fish and pat dry. Then add to pan and cook, turning once, until just opaque but still moist in thickest part; cut to test (8 to 10 minutes). Arrange fish on lettuce leaves; spoon reserved 1¼ cups yogurt mixture over fish. Makes 4 servings.

Per serving: 450 calories (26% fat, 37% carbohydrates, 37% protein), 13 g total fat (3 g saturated fat), 41 g carbohydrates, 41 g protein, 75 mg cholesterol, 192 mg sodium

Red Snapper & Shrimp

Preparation time: About 30 minutes
Cooking time: About 50 minutes

Two favorite kinds of seafood get together in this special-occasion entrée. Snapper fillets topped with shrimp simmer to succulence in a thick, chile-sparked tomato sauce.

1	tablespoon olive oil
1	medium-size onion, chopped
1	medium-size green bell pepper (about 6 oz.), seeded and chopped
2	cloves garlic, minced or pressed
1	can (about 4 oz.) diced green chiles
1	large can (about 28 oz.) tomatoes, drained and coarsely chopped
⅛	teaspoon *each* salt and pepper
1½	pounds red snapper fillets (½ inch thick)
8	ounces medium-size raw shrimp (about 36 per lb.), shelled and deveined
3	tablespoons lemon juice

Heat oil in a wide nonstick frying pan over medium heat. Add onion, bell pepper, and garlic; cook, stirring occasionally, until onion is soft (about 10 minutes). Add chiles, tomatoes, salt and pepper. Bring to a boil; reduce heat and simmer, uncovered, until sauce is thick (about 20 minutes).

Rinse fish and pat dry. Arrange fillets in a single layer in sauce; distribute shrimp evenly over fish. Drizzle with lemon juice. Cover and simmer until shrimp are just opaque in center and fish is just opaque but still moist in thickest part; cut to test (about 15 minutes).

To serve, transfer fish and shrimp to a serving dish. Bring sauce to a boil; then boil, uncovered, stirring often, until thickened (about 5 minutes). Pour sauce over fish and shrimp. Makes 8 servings.

Per serving: 163 calories (20% fat, 22% carbohydrates, 58% protein), 4 g total fat (0.6 g saturated fat), 9 g carbohydrates, 24 g protein, 67 mg cholesterol, 374 mg sodium

Whole Tilapia with Onion & Lemon

Preparation time: About 25 minutes
Baking time: About 20 minutes

Here's a dinner for two that's sure to please: whole tilapia baked on a bed of gingery onion and lemon slices. Moist and tender, the mild fish has a delicate flavor much like that of petrale sole.

1¼	pounds red onions, cut into ⅛-inch-thick slices
3	tablespoons lemon juice
1	tablespoon minced fresh ginger
1	whole tilapia (about 1½ lbs.), dressed (gutted, with head and tail attached)
1	tablespoon extra-virgin olive oil
2	large lemons
3	tablespoons minced cilantro
	Salt and pepper

In a large bowl, mix onions, lemon juice, and ginger. Set 1 or 2 onion slices aside, then spread remaining onion mixture in a 9- by 13-inch baking pan. Rinse fish, pat dry, and brush on both sides with oil; place on top of onion mixture.

Cut a ½-inch slice from both ends of each lemon. Stuff fish cavity with these lemon ends, reserved onion slices, and half the cilantro. Thinly slice remainder of each lemon; tuck lemon slices around fish. Sprinkle remaining cilantro over onion mixture and lemon slices. Bake in a 400° oven until fish is just opaque but still moist in thickest part; cut to test (about 20 minutes).

To serve, gently pull skin from fish; serve fish with onion-lemon mixture. Season to taste with salt and pepper. Makes 2 servings.

Per serving: 359 calories (22% fat, 40% carbohydrates, 38% protein), 10 g total fat (2 g saturated fat), 40 g carbohydrates, 38 g protein, 82 mg cholesterol, 177 mg sodium

Fish & Clams in Black Bean Sauce

30 MINUTES OR LESS

Preparation time: About 10 minutes
Cooking time: About 10 minutes

Mild, sweet rockfish and clams stand up well to a pungent black bean sauce. Since you steam this entrée right in a heatproof serving dish, there's almost no cleanup after dinner.

1	pound rockfish fillets
1½	tablespoons fermented salted black beans, rinsed and drained
2	cloves garlic, minced or pressed
1	tablespoon reduced-sodium soy sauce
2	tablespoons dry sherry
3	green onions
3	thin slices fresh ginger
12	small hard-shell clams in shell, scrubbed
1	tablespoon salad oil

Rinse fish, pat dry, and place in a heatproof, 1-inch-deep nonmetal dish that is at least ½ inch smaller in diameter than the pan you will use for steaming.

In a small bowl, mash black beans with garlic; stir in soy sauce and sherry. Drizzle mixture over fish. Cut one of the onions into thirds; place cut onion and ginger on top of fish. Cut remaining 2 onions into 2-inch lengths; then cut lengths into thin shreds and set aside. Arrange clams around fish.

Set dish on a rack in a pan above about 1 inch of boiling water. Cover and steam, keeping water at a steady boil, until fish is just opaque but still moist in thickest part; cut to test (about 5 minutes). If fish is done before clams pop open, remove fish and continue to cook clams for a few more minutes, until shells pop open; then return fish to dish.

Using thick potholders, lift dish from pan. Remove and discard ginger and onion pieces, then sprinkle onion slivers over fish. Heat oil in a small pan until it ripples when pan is tilted; pour over fish (oil will sizzle). Before serving, discard any unopened clams. Makes 2 servings.

Per serving: 365 calories (30% fat, 9% carbohydrates, 61% protein), 12 g total fat (2 g saturated fat), 7 g carbohydrates, 52 g protein, 98 mg cholesterol, 799 mg sodium

Seafood Linguine

Preparation time: About 25 minutes
Cooking time: About 25 minutes

Mussels and shrimp in a garlicky wine sauce are served over tender linguine in this classic dish. If you like, substitute clams for the mussels.

2	pounds mussels or small hard-shell clams in shell, scrubbed
1	bottle (about 8 oz.) clam juice
¼	cup butter or margarine
¾	cup sliced green onions
2	large cloves garlic, minced or pressed
½	cup dry white wine
1	pound medium-size raw shrimp (about 36 per lb.), shelled and deveined
12	ounces fresh linguine
½	cup chopped parsley

Pull beard from each mussel with a swift tug.

Pour clam juice into a 5- to 6-quart pan and bring to a boil over high heat. Add mussels; reduce heat, cover, and boil gently until shells pop open (5 to 10 minutes). Discard any unopened mussels. Drain mussels, reserving liquid; keep mussels warm. Strain cooking liquid to remove grit; reserve 1 cup of the liquid.

Melt 2 tablespoons of the butter in a wide frying pan over medium-high heat. Add onions and garlic and cook, stirring often, until onions are soft (about 3 minutes). Stir in wine and the 1 cup reserved cooking liquid. Increase heat to high and bring to a boil; then boil, uncovered, until reduced by about half (about 5 minutes). Stir in remaining 2 tablespoons butter. Add shrimp, then cover and remove from heat. Let stand until shrimp are opaque in center; cut to test (about 8 minutes).

Meanwhile, cook linguine in in a 5- to 6-quart pan in about 3 quarts boiling water until just tender to bite (1 to 2 minutes); or cook according to package directions. Drain well.

Add pasta and parsley to shrimp mixture and mix gently, lifting pasta with 2 forks. Mound on a platter; top with mussels. Makes 6 servings.

Per serving: 343 calories (29% fat, 42% carbohydrates, 29% protein), 11 g total fat (5 g saturated fat), 35 g carbohydrates, 25 g protein, 168 mg cholesterol, 400 mg sodium

Shrimp with Black Bean Sauce

Preparation time: About 30 minutes
Cooking time: About 10 minutes

This quick stir-fry is sure to win the approval of time-conscious cooks and discriminating diners alike. Sweet shrimp and vegetables in a savory black bean sauce are served on a crisp bed of shredded napa cabbage. Accompany the dish with Rosemary & Lemon Stretch Breadsticks (page 189) and iced tea.

3	tablespoons fermented salted black beans, rinsed and drained
4	ounces lean ground pork
1	large red bell pepper (about 8 oz.), seeded and finely chopped
12	ounces mushrooms, thinly sliced
3	cloves garlic, minced or pressed
1	tablespoon minced fresh ginger
1	cup low-sodium chicken broth
2	tablespoons oyster sauce
1	tablespoon cornstarch
1	tablespoon salad oil
12	ounces shelled, deveined medium-size raw shrimp (about 36 per lb.)
6	green onions, thinly sliced
6	cups finely shredded napa cabbage

In a large bowl, mix beans, pork, bell pepper, mushrooms, garlic, and ginger. In a small bowl, stir together broth, oyster sauce, and cornstarch; set aside.

Heat oil in a wide nonstick frying pan over high heat. Add shrimp and cook, stirring, until just opaque in center; cut to test (2 to 3 minutes). Remove from pan and set aside.

Add pork-mushroom mixture to pan and cook, stirring often, until meat is lightly browned (about 5 minutes). Add broth mixture and bring to a boil, stirring. Mix in shrimp and onions. Arrange cabbage on a platter; top with shrimp mixture. Makes 6 servings.

Per serving: 175 calories (29% fat, 27% carbohydrates, 44% protein), 6 g total fat (1 g saturated fat), 12 g carbohydrates, 20 g protein, 99 mg cholesterol, 576 mg sodium

Margarita Shrimp

NATURALLY LOW IN FAT

Preparation time: About 15 minutes
Cooking time: About 10 minutes

For an elegant, easy-to-fix main course, stir-fry shrimp in tequila and lime, then serve over thinly sliced red onions. Quick cooking keeps the shellfish tender and succulent.

¼	cup tequila
½	teaspoon grated lime peel
2	tablespoons *each* lime juice and water
2	tablespoons minced cilantro or parsley
1	tablespoon honey
⅛	teaspoon ground white pepper
1	pound extra-large raw shrimp (26 to 30 per lb.), shelled and deveined
2	teaspoons orange-flavored liqueur, or to taste (optional)
	Salt
2	large red onions, thinly sliced
	Cilantro sprigs
	Lime wedges

In a small bowl, stir together tequila, lime peel, lime juice, water, cilantro, honey, and white pepper. Pour mixture into a wide frying pan; add shrimp. Cook over medium-high heat, stirring, until shrimp are just opaque in center; cut to test (3 to 4 minutes). With a slotted spoon, transfer shrimp to a bowl and keep warm. Bring cooking liquid to a boil over high heat; boil, uncovered, until reduced to ⅓ cup. Remove pan from heat and stir in liqueur, if desired. Season to taste with salt.

To serve, arrange onion slices in a single layer on a rimmed platter. Spoon shrimp and cooking liquid over onions. Garnish with cilantro sprigs; serve with lime wedges. Makes 4 servings.

Per serving: 162 calories (10% fat, 40% carbohydrates, 50% protein), 2 g total fat (0.3 g saturated fat), 16 g carbohydrates, 21 g protein, 140 mg cholesterol, 150 mg sodium

__Tequila__ is a clear or pale golden liquor made from the fermented, distilled sap of the agave plant. To bring Mexican flavor to sautéed or grilled seafood, poultry, or meat, add just a splash of tequila.

Greek-style Shrimp on Zucchini

Preparation time: About 25 minutes
Cooking time: About 25 minutes

Serve these simmered shrimp in herb-seasoned tomato sauce over a bed of zucchini "noodles" —slender strands of blanched zucchini. Crumble a little feta cheese into the hot sauce for a Greek accent.

2	teaspoons olive oil
2	small carrots, sliced
1	stalk celery, chopped
1	medium-size onion, chopped
1	clove garlic, minced or pressed
1	can (about 14½ oz.) tomatoes
¼	cup dry white wine
¼	cup chopped fresh basil (or ¼ cup chopped parsley plus 2 teaspoons dry basil)
1	teaspoon dry oregano
	Pepper
	Zucchini Noodles (recipe follows)
1	pound medium-size raw shrimp (about 36 per lb.), shelled and deveined
⅓	cup crumbled feta cheese

Heat oil in a wide nonstick frying pan over medium-high heat. Add carrots, celery, and onion. Cook, stirring often, until vegetables are soft (about 5 minutes). Add garlic and cook, stirring, for 2 minutes.

Cut up tomatoes; then add tomatoes and their liquid, wine, basil, and oregano to vegetable mixture. Bring to a boil; then reduce heat and simmer, uncovered, until sauce is thickened (about 10 minutes). Season to taste with pepper.

While sauce is simmering, prepare Zucchini Noodles; pour onto a deep platter and keep warm.

Add shrimp to tomato sauce and cook, stirring, until just opaque in center; cut to test (about 5 minutes). Stir in cheese, then spoon shrimp and sauce over Zucchini Noodles. Makes 4 servings.

Zucchini Noodles. Cut 1 pound **zucchini** lengthwise into ⅛-inch-thick slices. Stack slices and cut lengthwise into ⅛-inch-thick strips. In a 2-quart pan, bring 4 cups **water** to a boil over high heat. Add zucchini and cook just until tender to bite (2 to 3 minutes). Drain well.

Per serving: 228 calories (27% fat, 31% carbohydrates, 42% protein), 7 g total fat (2 g saturated fat), 17 g carbohydrates, 24 g protein, 150 mg cholesterol, 453 mg sodium

Barbecued Crab with Spaghetti

Preparation time: About 20 minutes
Cooking time: About 55 minutes

Crab is at its messiest and most delicious in this dish, a wonderful choice for a winter feast. Start by simmering cracked crab in a spicy barbecue sauce, then serve it over hot spaghetti. You eat the crab legs and claws with your fingers, so be sure to provide plenty of big paper napkins. And don't forget a loaf of crusty sourdough bread to soak up the sauce!

2	tablespoons butter or margarine
1	large onion, finely chopped
3	cloves garlic, minced or pressed
1	can (about 14½ oz.) low-sodium chicken broth
1	can (about 8 oz.) tomato sauce
1	cup catsup
⅓	cup *each* white wine vinegar and firmly packed brown sugar
3	tablespoons Worcestershire
1	tablespoon reduced-sodium soy sauce
1½	teaspoons dry mustard
1	teaspoon liquid hot pepper seasoning
½	teaspoon *each* celery seeds, ground allspice, and dry thyme
2	dry bay leaves

2   **medium-size to large Dungeness crabs (3½ to 4 lbs. *total*), cooked, cleaned, and cracked**

12   **ounces to 1 pound dry spaghetti or spaghettini**
     Chopped parsley

Melt butter in a 5- to 6-quart pan over medium-low heat. Add onion and garlic; cook, stirring often, until onion is soft but not browned (8 to 10 minutes).

Stir in broth, tomato sauce, catsup, vinegar, sugar, Worcestershire, soy sauce, mustard, hot pepper seasoning, celery seeds, allspice, thyme, and bay leaves. Increase heat to high and bring to a boil; then reduce heat and boil very gently, uncovered, until sauce is reduced to 3 cups (about 45 minutes).

Meanwhile, remove body meat from crabs, discarding shells; set shelled body meat and cracked claws aside.

In a 6- to 8-quart pan, cook spaghetti in about 4 quarts boiling water until just tender to bite (8 to 10 minutes); or cook according to package directions. Drain well, pour into a large serving bowl, and keep warm.

While spaghetti is cooking, add all the crab to sauce and simmer, uncovered, stirring gently several times, just until crab is heated through (about 5 minutes). Pour crab sauce over spaghetti and sprinkle generously with parsley. Makes 4 to 6 servings.

Per serving: 573 calories (12% fat, 68% carbohydrates, 20% protein), 8 g total fat (3 g saturated fat), 99 g carbohydrates, 28 g protein, 61 mg cholesterol, 1,410 mg sodium

Crab Singapore

· ·

3 0   M I N U T E S   O R   L E S S

Preparation time: About 15 minutes
Cooking time: About 5 minutes

Bold Southeast Asian flavors set off the distinctive sweetness of Dungeness crab in a dish pungent with fermented black beans, garlic, and fiery hot chiles. If you buy your crab already cooked, freshen it before using by rinsing the pieces well with cool water.

    Singapore Chile Sauce (recipe follows)

1   **large Dungeness crab (2 to 2½ lbs.), cooked, cleaned, and cracked (including back shell if available)**

3   **cloves garlic, peeled**

1   **tablespoon chopped fresh ginger**

1   **tablespoon salad oil**
    Cilantro sprigs (optional)

2   **cups hot cooked long-grain white rice**

Prepare Singapore Chile Sauce; set aside. Rinse crab back shell (if available) and set aside with crab.

In a small bowl, pound together garlic and ginger with a mortar and pestle (or mince very finely with a knife).

Heat oil in a wok or 5- to 6-quart pan over high heat. Add garlic-ginger paste; cook, stirring, until golden (30 seconds to 1 minute). Add Singapore Chile Sauce and crab; cook, stirring with a wide spatula, until crab is hot and sauce comes to a boil (3 to 4 minutes).

To serve, turn crab and sauce out of pan onto a platter; place crab back shell atop crab pieces. Garnish with cilantro sprigs, if desired. Serve with rice. Makes 2 servings.

Singapore Chile Sauce. In a small bowl, smoothly blend 1 teaspoon **cornstarch**, ¾ cup **low-sodium chicken broth,** and ¼ cup **catsup.** Stir in 1 tablespoon **fermented salted black beans,** rinsed and drained (or 1 tablespoon reduced-sodium soy sauce), and 2 or 3 **small fresh hot red or green chiles** (such as Thai, serrano, Fresno, or jalapeño), seeded and minced.

Per serving: 503 calories (19% fat, 57% carbohydrates, 24% protein), 10 g total fat (1 g saturated fat), 70 g carbohydrates, 30 g protein, 109 mg cholesterol, 903 mg sodium

__Thai, serrano, Fresno, and jalapeño__ are just four of the many varieties of hot chiles in today's marketplace. When you handle fresh chiles, be aware that the cut surfaces release oils that can irritate the skin. Wear rubber gloves and avoid touching your face or eyes; if any skin does come in contact with chile oil, wash the affected areas thoroughly with soap and water.

Layered Cioppino

MODIFIED CLASSIC

Preparation time: About 1 hour
Cooking time: 25 to 40 minutes

San Francisco's famous *cioppino*, said to have been created by Italian immigrant fishermen, exists in innumerable versions. We especially like this rendition of the dish. Shrimp, clams, crab, and firm white fish are layered with a tomato-chard sauce in a heavy pan, then simmered to make a thick, savory stew.

If you like, substitute an equal weight of sea scallops for the fish chunks. You might also augment the sauce with up to a cup of chopped yellow or green onions. Or, for a spicier flavor, add two to four small fresh hot red or green chiles, seeded and minced.

2	large cans (about 28 oz. *each*) tomatoes
1	can (about 6 oz.) tomato paste
1	cup dry white wine
¼	cup olive oil
2	teaspoons pepper
4	cups coarsely chopped Swiss chard
2	large red bell peppers (about 1 lb. *total*), seeded and chopped
½	cup chopped parsley
¼	cup chopped fresh basil or 1 tablespoon dry basil
2	tablespoons *each* chopped fresh marjoram, rosemary, thyme, and sage; or 2 teaspoons *each* dry marjoram, rosemary, thyme, and sage

Select seafood for cioppino *with care. Truly fresh fish and shellfish have a clean aroma reminiscent of the ocean; if seafood smells offensive, it won't taste good. Fresh shrimp should be firm; their shells shouldn't be soft or slippery. Look for hard-shell clams with tightly closed shells; choose cooked crab with bright red shells. Buy fish fillets that look moist and freshly cut—avoid any with dry or discolored edges. If you buy packaged fish, reject packages in which cloudy liquid has collected.*

36	extra-jumbo raw shrimp (16 to 20 per lb.)
36	small hard-shell clams in shell, scrubbed
2	large Dungeness crabs (about 2 lbs. *each*), cooked, cleaned, and cracked
2	pounds firm-textured white-fleshed fish fillets such as rockfish, cut into 2-inch chunks
	Salt

Pour tomatoes and their liquid into a large bowl; coarsely mash tomatoes. Stir in tomato paste, wine, oil, pepper, chard, bell peppers, parsley, basil, marjoram, rosemary, thyme, and sage until well blended.

Devein shrimp by inserting tip of a slender skewer under vein between shell segments along back of each shrimp; gently pull to remove vein. Set shrimp aside.

Arrange clams over bottom of a heavy 12- to 14-quart pan. Spoon a fourth of the tomato mixture over clams. Top with shrimp, a third of the remaining tomato mixture, crab, half the remaining tomato mixture, fish, and remaining tomato mixture (a 12-quart pan may be full to rim).

Cover pan and bring seafood mixture to a boil over high heat (10 to 20 minutes). Then reduce heat and simmer gently, covered, until fish is just opaque but still moist in thickest part; cut to test (15 to 20 minutes). Season to taste with salt.

To serve, ladle cioppino into wide bowls, spooning down to bottom of pan to get some of each layer; discard any unopened clams. Makes 12 servings.

Per serving: 299 calories (26% fat, 18% carbohydrates, 56% protein), 8 g total fat (1 g saturated fat), 13 g carbohydrates, 40 g protein, 165 mg cholesterol, 609 mg sodium

Cajun Scallops & Brown Rice

Preparation time: About 10 minutes
Cooking time: About 45 minutes

Warm up appetites with this bay scallop dish. It's spicy, but a light cream sauce helps keep the heat under control. Serve on a bed of brown rice, with a medley of your favorite vegetables on the side.

4½	cups low-sodium chicken broth
1½	cups long-grain brown rice
1½	pounds bay scallops
1	teaspoon paprika
½	teaspoon ground white pepper
¼	teaspoon ground allspice
2	teaspoons salad oil
1½	tablespoons cornstarch blended with ⅓ cup cold water
½	cup reduced-fat sour cream
	Parsley sprigs

In a 3- to 4-quart pan, bring 3½ cups of the broth to a boil over high heat. Add rice; reduce heat, cover, and simmer until rice is tender to bite (about 45 minutes).

About 10 minutes before rice is done, rinse scallops and pat dry; then mix with paprika, white pepper, and allspice. Heat oil in a wide nonstick frying pan over high heat. Add scallops and cook, turning often with a wide spatula, until just opaque in center; cut to test (2 to 3 minutes). With a slotted spoon, transfer scallops to a bowl.

Bring pan juices to a boil over high heat; boil, uncovered, until reduced to ¼ cup. Add remaining 1 cup broth and return to a boil. Stir in cornstarch mixture; bring to a boil, stirring. Stir in sour cream and scallops. Serve over rice; garnish with parsley sprigs. Makes 6 servings.

Per serving: 350 calories (20% fat, 50% carbohydrates, 30% protein), 8 g total fat (2 g saturated fat), 43 g carbohydrates, 26 g protein, 44 mg cholesterol, 226 mg sodium

Stir-fried Scallops & Asparagus

. . . .

3 0   M I N U T E S   O R   L E S S

Preparation time: About 15 minutes
Cooking time: About 15 minutes

For an elegant, quick-to-fix main course, serve stir-fried scallops and asparagus atop thin pasta strands.

8	ounces bay or sea scallops
½	cup unseasoned rice vinegar or white wine vinegar

2	tablespoons sugar
1	teaspoon *each* Oriental sesame oil and reduced-sodium soy sauce
2	tablespoons salad oil
1	pound asparagus, tough ends removed, stalks cut into about ½-inch-thick slanting slices
3	tablespoons water
8	ounces dry vermicelli or spaghettini
1	clove garlic, minced or pressed
1	tablespoon minced fresh ginger
	Lemon slices

Rinse scallops and pat dry. If using sea scallops, cut into ½-inch pieces. Set aside. In a small bowl, stir together vinegar, sugar, sesame oil, and soy sauce. Set aside.

Heat 1 tablespoon of the salad oil in a wok or wide frying pan over high heat. Add asparagus and stir to coat; then add the 3 tablespoons water. Cover and cook until asparagus is tender-crisp to bite (3 to 5 minutes). Lift asparagus from pan and keep warm. Set pan aside.

In a 5- to 6-quart pan, cook vermicelli in about 3 quarts boiling water until just tender to bite (8 to 10 minutes); or cook according to package directions. Drain well, pour into a large bowl, and keep warm.

Heat remaining 1 tablespoon salad oil in frying pan over high heat. Add garlic, ginger, and scallops. Cook, turning often with a wide spatula, until scallops are just opaque in center; cut to test (2 to 3 minutes).

Return asparagus to pan and add vinegar mixture; stir just until sugar is dissolved. Pour scallop mixture over pasta and mix gently. Garnish with lemon slices. Makes 4 servings.

Per serving: 375 calories (23% fat, 57% carbohydrates, 20% protein), 9 g total fat (1 g saturated fat), 54 g carbohydrates, 19 g protein, 19 mg cholesterol, 147 mg sodium

Scallops &
Spinach Pasta

Preparation time: About 10 minutes
Cooking time: About 10 minutes

The white, red, and green colors of the Italian flag may have inspired this robust combination of snowy scallops, ripe tomatoes, and spinach fettuccine. Serve with crusty rolls and an Italian white wine such as Verdicchio, or with a California Sauvignon Blanc.

8	ounces dry green fettuccine or 1 package (about 9 oz.) fresh green fettuccine
2	tablespoons pine nuts
1	pound bay scallops
2	tablespoons olive oil
2	cloves garlic, minced or pressed
1	large tomato (about 8 oz.), seeded and chopped
¼	cup dry white wine
¼	cup chopped Italian parsley
	Salt and pepper

In a 5- to 6-quart pan, cook fettuccine in about 3 quarts boiling water until just tender to bite (8 to 10 minutes for dry pasta, 3 to 4 minutes for fresh); or cook according to package directions. Drain well.

While pasta is cooking, toast pine nuts in a wide nonstick frying pan over medium heat until golden (3 to 5 minutes), stirring often. Pour nuts out of pan and set aside.

Rinse scallops and pat dry. Heat oil in pan over medium-high heat. Add scallops and cook, turning often with a wide spatula, until just opaque in center; cut to test (2 to 3 minutes). With a slotted spoon, lift scallops to a plate; keep warm.

Add garlic to pan; cook, stirring, just until garlic begins to brown (1 to 2 minutes). Stir in tomato, then wine; bring to a boil. Remove pan from heat and add pasta, scallops, and parsley; mix gently. Season to taste with salt and pepper. Sprinkle with pine nuts. Makes 4 servings.

Per serving: 423 calories (27% fat, 45% carbohydrates, 28% protein), 13 g total fat (2 g saturated fat), 46 g carbohydrates, 29 g protein, 91 mg cholesterol, 231 mg sodium

Clam Paella for Two

Preparation time: About 15 minutes
Cooking time: About 30 minutes

Making traditional paella is a fairly complex undertaking, but this simplified version—starring just one kind of shellfish—is appealingly quick and easy to assemble. Serve it for supper on any night, accompanied with whole-grain bread and a crisp green salad.

1	tablespoon olive oil
1	clove garlic, minced or pressed
¼	teaspoon ground turmeric
⅔	cup long-grain white rice
2	tablespoons finely chopped parsley
8	ounces (about 1½ cups) cherry tomatoes, cut into halves
⅔	cup dry white wine
¾	cup bottled clam juice or low-sodium chicken broth
24	small hard-shell clams in shell, scrubbed

Heat oil in a wide frying pan over medium heat. Add garlic, turmeric, and rice. Cook, stirring often, until rice begins to look opaque (about 3 minutes). Stir in parsley, tomatoes, wine, and clam juice. Bring to a boil; then reduce heat, cover, and simmer for 15 minutes.

Arrange clams over rice. Cover and continue to cook until clams pop open and rice is tender to bite (8 to 10 more minutes). Discard any unopened clams; then spoon clams and rice into bowls. Makes 2 servings.

Per serving: 452 calories (19% fat, 55% carbohydrates, 26% protein), 9 g total fat (1 g saturated fat), 61 g carbohydrates, 29 g protein, 61 mg cholesterol, 313 mg sodium

Vermicelli with Sake Clam Sauce

. . . .

30 MINUTES OR LESS

Preparation time: About 10 minutes
Cooking time: About 10 minutes

Robust flavor and time-saving preparation make this supper dish a winner. Tender pasta in a sauce of sake and chopped clams is tossed with Parmesan cheese, hot red pepper, and minced parsley.

2	**cans (about 6½ oz.** *each***) chopped clams**
¾	**cup finely chopped onion**
2	**cloves garlic, minced or pressed**
1	**cup sake or dry vermouth**
2	**tablespoons drained capers**
10	**ounces dry vermicelli, linguine, or spaghetti**
¼	**cup finely chopped parsley**
¼	**cup grated Parmesan cheese (optional)**
	About ⅛ teaspoon crushed red pepper flakes
	Parsley sprigs (optional)

Drain clams, reserving ½ cup of the liquid. Pour reserved clam liquid into a wide frying pan; add onion, garlic, and ¼ cup of the sake. Bring mixture to a boil over high heat; then boil, uncovered, stirring often, until mixture is reduced by about three-fourths. Add remaining ¾ cup sake, clams, and capers; reduce heat and cook, stirring often, for about 3 minutes.

While you are preparing sauce, cook vermicelli in a 5- to 6-quart pan in about 3 quarts boiling water until just tender to bite (8 to 10 minutes); or cook according to package directions.

Drain pasta well, pour into a wide bowl, and add clam sauce. Mix with 2 forks, lifting and turning pasta until almost all liquid has been absorbed. Sprinkle with chopped parsley, cheese (if desired), and red pepper flakes; mix again. Garnish with parsley sprigs, if desired. Makes 4 servings.

Per serving: 411 calories (5% fat, 69% carbohydrates, 26% protein), 2 g total fat (0.3 g saturated fat), 59 g carbohydrates, 22 g protein, 32 mg cholesterol, 173 mg sodium

Steamed Clams with Garlic

. . . .

NATURALLY LOW IN FAT

Preparation time: About 25 minutes
Cooking time: About 25 minutes

Plenty of fresh garlic—up to ½ cup, if you like—gives these succulent steamed clams an assertive flavor and a wonderful perfume.

1	**teaspoon butter or margarine**
2	**medium-size onions, thinly sliced**
¼	**to ½ cup chopped garlic**
¼	**cup water**
2	**medium-size tomatoes (about 12 oz.** *total***), chopped**
1	**teaspoon** *each* **paprika, dry thyme, and black pepper**
⅛	**teaspoon ground red pepper (cayenne)**
1	**cup dry white wine**
36	**small hard-shell clams in shell, scrubbed**

Melt butter in a 5- to 6-quart pan over medium heat. Add onions, garlic, and water. Cook, stirring often, until liquid has evaporated and onions are soft (about 10 minutes).

Stir in tomatoes, paprika, thyme, black pepper, and red pepper; cook, uncovered, for 5 minutes. Add wine and bring to a boil over high heat.

Add clams; reduce heat, cover, and boil gently until shells pop open (about 10 minutes). Discard any unopened clams; then ladle clams and sauce into wide bowls. Makes 4 servings.

Per serving: 225 calories (13% fat, 45% carbohydrates, 42% protein), 3 g total fat (0.8 g saturated fat), 21 g carbohydrates, 20 g protein, 48 mg cholesterol, 102 mg sodium

*****Small hard-shell clams*** suitable for steaming include the littleneck and Manila clams of the Pacific coast and the little necks (spelled as two words) and cherrystones of the Atlantic coast. When you buy live clams, always make sure they're actually alive. The shells should be tightly closed—or, if gaping, they should close promptly when tapped.*

Mussels Provençal

Preparation time: About 15 minutes
Cooking time: About 30 minutes

Satisfy a hungry group of shellfish lovers with mussels steamed in an aromatic sauce of tomatoes, garlic, and wine. Offer plenty of crusty French bread to soak up the sauce.

3½	pounds mussels in shell, scrubbed
1	tablespoon olive oil
3	cloves garlic, minced or pressed
1	large onion, chopped
1	cup chopped celery
1	large can (about 28 oz.) tomatoes
1	cup dry white wine or low-sodium chicken broth
½	cup minced parsley
½	teaspoon pepper

Pull beard from each mussel with a swift tug. Set mussels aside.

Heat oil in a 6- to 8-quart pan over medium-high heat. Add garlic, onion, and celery. Cook, stirring often, until vegetables are soft (about 7 minutes). Cut up tomatoes; then add tomatoes and their liquid to pan. Bring to a boil; then reduce heat, cover, and simmer for 15 minutes. Add wine, parsley, and pepper. Cover and bring to a boil.

Add mussels, cover, and cook until shells pop open (7 to 9 minutes). Discard any unopened mussels. With a slotted spoon, transfer mussels to wide, shallow bowls; ladle sauce over each serving. Makes 4 to 6 servings.

Per serving: 194 calories (28% fat, 40% carbohydrates, 32% protein), 5 g total fat (0.8 g saturated fat), 17 g carbohydrates, 13 g protein, 26 mg cholesterol, 551 mg sodium

Mussels & Millet in Curry Sauce

Preparation time: About 25 minutes
Cooking time: 30 to 35 minutes

Millet is a major ingredient of most commercial bird-seed mixtures—but that doesn't mean people can't enjoy it, too. In fact, it's so rich in protein, B vitamins, and iron—and tastes so delicious—that it's a dietary mainstay in much of the world. Here, the grain cooks in a curry-spiced fresh tomato broth to make a fluffy setting for steamed mussels.

1	tablespoon salad oil
1	large onion, thinly sliced
1	tablespoon minced fresh ginger
1	teaspoon *each* mustard seeds and ground coriander
½	teaspoon *each* ground cumin and ground red pepper (cayenne)
¼	teaspoon ground turmeric
3	cups low-sodium chicken broth
2	small tomatoes (about 8 oz. *total*), chopped
1	cup millet, rinsed and drained
1½	pounds mussels in shell, scrubbed
	Salt and pepper
	Plain nonfat yogurt

Heat oil in a 5- to 6-quart pan over medium-high heat. Add onion and ginger; cook, stirring often, until onion is soft (about 5 minutes).

Stir in mustard seeds, coriander, cumin, red pepper, and turmeric. Add broth and tomatoes; bring mixture to a boil.

Add millet to pan. Reduce heat, cover, and simmer for 15 minutes. Meanwhile, pull beard from each mussel with a swift tug.

Add mussels to pan; cover and simmer until millet is tender to bite and mussels pop open (7 to 9 minutes). Season to taste with salt and pepper. Discard any unopened mussels; then ladle mussels and millet into bowls. Offer yogurt to add to taste. Makes 3 servings.

Per serving: 435 calories (23% fat, 59% carbohydrates, 18% protein), 11 g total fat (2 g saturated fat), 64 g carbohydrates, 20 g protein, 19 mg cholesterol, 257 mg sodium

COOKING SEAFOOD LIGHT

Fish and shellfish are naturally lean—and to keep them low in fat, select the lightest possible cooking styles. The recipes in this chapter include appetizing examples of many suitable methods, specifying one or more seafood choices for each.

Among the techniques you'll discover are grilling on the barbecue; broiling with little or no oil or butter; moist-heat methods such as poaching, steaming, and steeping; and baking whole fish, steaks, or fillets in a light sauce. Baking in a parchment or foil wrap to retain moisture is another superb low-fat technique.

On this page, we've highlighted two methods. These techniques are worthy of note because they work so well for a wide variety of seafood. Oven browning is perfect for many kinds of fish: start by dipping the fillets or steaks in buttermilk to keep them moist, then roll in a seasoned crumb coating and bake. Sesame-Soy Barbecued Seafood is a great all-purpose recipe for grilled seafood, adding flavor and a glossy finish to both fish and shellfish.

OVEN-BROWNED FISH

- - - - - - - - - - - - - - - - - -

Preparation time: About 10 minutes
Baking time: 10 to 20 minutes

Recommended fish: Halibut, lingcod, rockfish, snapper, mahi mahi, orange roughy, sea bass

Cheese-Crumb Coating
(recipe follows)

1 to 1½ pounds fish steaks or fillets (½ to 1 inch thick)

3 tablespoons low-fat buttermilk

Prepare Cheese-Crumb Coating. Rinse fish; pat dry. Pour buttermilk into a wide bowl. Dip fish in buttermilk; then dip in coating to coat thickly on all sides.

Place fish pieces at least 1 inch apart in a foil-lined shallow baking pan. Bake in a 425° oven until fish is browned on outside and just opaque but still moist in thickest part; cut to test (10 to 20 minutes). Makes 4 servings.

Cheese-Crumb Coating. On a square of wax paper, combine ¾ cup **soft bread crumbs,** 1 tablespoon grated **Parmesan cheese,** ¼ teaspoon **dry thyme,** and ½ teaspoon **paprika.**

Per serving (with halibut): 161 calories (20% fat, 13% carbohydrates, 67% protein), 3 g total fat (0.7 g saturated fat), 5 g carbohydrates, 26 g protein, 38 mg cholesterol, 139 mg sodium

SESAME-SOY BARBECUED SEAFOOD

- - - - - - - - - - - - - - - - - -

Preparation time: About 15 minutes
Grilling time: 5 to 15 minutes

Recommended seafood: Mahi mahi, orange roughy, sea bass, halibut, shark, swordfish, tuna, trout; skewered sea scallops or shelled, deveined shrimp

Sesame-Soy Baste (recipe follows)

1½ to 2 pounds fish steaks or fillets (½ to 1½ inches thick), cleaned whole trout, sea scallops, or shelled and deveined shrimp

Vegetable oil cooking spray

Prepare Sesame-Soy Baste. Rinse seafood and pat dry. If using scallops or shrimp, thread on serving-size skewers.

Position barbecue grill 4 to 6 inches above a solid bed of hot coals; coat grill with cooking spray. Place fish or skewered shellfish on grill and brush generously with Sesame-Soy Baste. Cook, turning once and brushing often with baste, until just opaque but still moist in thickest part; cut to test. For fish, allow about 10 minutes for each inch of thickness; for scallops, allow 5 to 8 minutes; for shrimp, allow 3 to 5 minutes. Makes 6 to 8 servings.

Sesame-Soy Baste. In a small bowl, mix 1 teaspoon **Oriental sesame oil;** ⅓ cup **reduced-sodium soy sauce;** 2 tablespoons minced **green onion;** 1 tablespoon **dry sherry** or sherry vinegar; 1 tablespoon minced **fresh ginger;** 2 teaspoons **sugar;** 2 cloves **garlic,** minced or pressed; and a dash of **ground red pepper** (cayenne).

Per serving (with mahi mahi): 110 calories (13% fat, 12% carbohydrates, 75% protein), 2 g total fat (0.3 g saturated fat), 3 g carbohydrates, 20 g protein, 74 mg cholesterol, 542 mg sodium

VEGETARIAN ENTREES

*B*ased on pasta, grains, hearty vegetables, and dried legumes, the entrées in this chapter offer satisfying flavor and great low-fat nutrition—and plenty of variety. If it's chili you hunger for, try making it with black beans and sprightly touches of fresh citrus. If this is a good day for Italian flavors, bring on a mushroom-studded risotto or a bright bowlful of polenta with vegetables. Because protein of vegetable origin is rarely complete (it lacks one or more of the essential amino acids), you'll find it useful to learn how to combine complementary grains and legumes. Recipes such as Wild Spanish Rice and Linguine with Lentils are delicious demonstrations of this technique, providing complete protein of the same quality as that found in higher-fat meats and poultry.

Black Bean Chili with Oranges

Preparation time: About 40 minutes
Cooking time: 2 to 2½ hours

Fresh oranges brighten this spicy meatless chili. Serve it with the Southwest Blue Cornbread Sticks on page 179.

1	pound dried black beans
1	tablespoon salad oil
2	large onions, chopped
2	cloves garlic, minced or pressed
8	cups canned or homemade (page 41) vegetable broth
1	tablespoon coriander seeds
1	teaspoon *each* whole allspice and dry oregano
¾	teaspoon crushed red pepper flakes
¼	teaspoon hulled cardamom seeds
4	to 6 medium-size to large oranges, mandarins, or tangelos (about 2½ lbs. *total*)
	Salt
	Cilantro sprigs
	Reduced-fat sour cream

Rinse and sort beans, discarding any debris. Drain beans; set aside.

Heat oil in a 5- to 6-quart pan over high heat. Add onions and garlic; cook, stirring often, until onions are tinged with brown (about 8 minutes). Stir in beans, broth, coriander seeds, allspice, oregano, red pepper flakes, and cardamom seeds. Bring to a boil; then reduce heat, cover, and simmer until beans are tender to bite (1½ to 2 hours).

Meanwhile, finely shred 2 teaspoons peel (colored part only) from oranges. Squeeze juice from enough oranges to make ½ cup. Cut remaining peel and all white membrane from remaining oranges; then thinly slice fruit crosswise.

Uncover beans, bring to a boil over high heat, and boil until almost all liquid has evaporated (10 to 15 minutes); as mixture thickens, reduce heat and stir occasionally. Stir in 1 teaspoon of the shredded orange peel and the ½ cup juice. Season to taste with salt.

To serve, ladle beans into bowls; top with orange slices. Garnish with cilantro sprigs and remaining 1 teaspoon shredded orange peel. Offer sour cream to add to taste. Makes 6 servings.

Per serving: 408 calories (11% fat, 72% carbohydrates, 17% protein), 5 g total fat (0.6 g saturated fat), 76 g carbohydrates, 18 g protein, 0 mg cholesterol, 1,357 mg sodium

Lean Mean Vegetable Chili

Preparation time: About 20 minutes
Cooking time: About 30 minutes

Because you start with canned beans, this all-vegetable chili is especially quick to prepare. (If you prefer, you can make the dish with home-cooked dried beans, following the instructions on page 149.)

3	large carrots, chopped
1	large onion, coarsely chopped
½	cup water
1	large can (about 28 oz.) tomatoes
1	can (about 15 oz.) *each* black beans, pinto beans, and red kidney beans (or 3 cans of 1 kind); or use 6 cups drained cooked beans (page 149) plus 1 cup canned or homemade (page 41) vegetable broth
3	tablespoons chili powder
	Reduced-fat sour cream or plain low-fat yogurt
	Crushed red pepper flakes

In a 4- to 5-quart pan, combine carrots, onion, and water. Cook over high heat, stirring occasionally, until liquid evaporates and vegetables begin to brown (about 10 minutes).

Cut up tomatoes; then add tomatoes and their liquid, beans and their liquid, and chili powder to onion mixture. Bring to a boil; then reduce heat and simmer, uncovered, until flavors are blended (about 15 minutes).

To serve, ladle chili into wide bowls; offer sour cream and red pepper flakes to add to taste. Makes 6 to 8 servings.

Per serving: 215 calories (6% fat, 73% carbohydrates, 21% protein), 1 g total fat (0.2 g saturated fat), 42 g carbohydrates, 12 g protein, 0 mg cholesterol, 930 mg sodium

Garlic-braised Eggplant & White Beans

Preparation time: About 15 minutes
Baking time: About 20 minutes
Cooking time: About 30 minutes

Serve this boldly seasoned eggplant-vegetable stew over pasta shells; accompany with green salad, a loaf of chewy Italian bread, and a bottle of full-bodied red wine.

	Olive oil cooking spray
1	**small eggplant (about 12 oz.), unpeeled, cut into ½-inch cubes**
6	**cloves garlic, peeled and thinly sliced**
2	**tablespoons olive oil**
½	**teaspoon fennel seeds**
⅛	**to ¼ teaspoon crushed red pepper flakes**
1	**teaspoon Italian herb seasoning; or ¼ teaspoon *each* dry basil, dry marjoram, dry oregano, and dry thyme**
2	**medium-size onions, thinly sliced**
1	**can (about 14½ oz.) pear-shaped tomatoes**
1	**can (about 15 oz.) cannellini (white kidney beans), drained and rinsed; or 2 cups cooked cannellini (page 149), drained and rinsed**
8	**ounces dry medium-size pasta shells**
½	**cup chopped Italian parsley**
	Salt and pepper
	Grated Parmesan cheese (optional)

Coat a shallow baking pan with cooking spray. Spread eggplant in pan; sprinkle with garlic, then coat with cooking spray. Bake in a 425° oven until golden brown (about 20 minutes).

When you cut fat, *add flavor to make up for it! Tips like this can help you make the transition to a leaner diet. When buying cheese, for example, keep in mind that stronger types give you more emphasis for each gram of fat. A light sprinkling of Parmesan doesn't add an unreasonable amount of fat to a bowlful of pasta, but you'll get more flavor if you choose sharper, tangier Romano cheese instead.*

Meanwhile, heat oil in a wide frying pan over medium heat. Add fennel seeds, red pepper flakes, herb seasoning, and onions; cook, stirring often, until onions are soft but not browned (6 to 8 minutes).

Cut up tomatoes; then add tomatoes and their liquid to onion mixture. Stir in baked eggplant. Reduce heat, cover, and simmer for 15 minutes. Stir in beans, cover, and continue to simmer until beans are heated through and flavors are blended (about 3 more minutes).

While eggplant mixture is simmering, in a 5- to 6-quart pan, cook pasta in about 3 quarts boiling water until just tender to bite (10 to 12 minutes); or cook according to package directions. Drain pasta well and divide among 4 to 6 wide, shallow individual bowls.

Stir parsley into eggplant mixture; season to taste with salt and pepper. Spoon equally over pasta. Offer cheese to add to taste, if desired. Makes 4 to 6 servings.

Per serving: 347 calories (18% fat, 67% carbohydrates, 15% protein), 7 g total fat (0.9 g saturated fat), 59 g carbohydrates, 13 g protein, 0 mg cholesterol, 254 mg sodium

Linguine with Lentils

Preparation time: About 15 minutes
Cooking time: About 55 minutes

Simple fare, but simply delicious! Lentils and Swiss chard, flavored in a spicy broth, combine with linguine and creamy Neufchâtel cheese for a satisfying main dish. Alongside, offer a plump loaf of whole-grain bread.

3	**cups canned or homemade (page 41) vegetable broth**
1	**cup lentils, rinsed and drained**
1	**teaspoon cumin seeds**
1	**pound Swiss chard**
2	**tablespoons olive oil**
1	**large onion, chopped**
2	**cloves garlic, minced or pressed**
½	**teaspoon crushed red pepper flakes**
12	**ounces dry linguine**
6	**ounces Neufchâtel cheese, diced**
	Salt and pepper

In a 5- to 6-quart pan, bring 2 cups of the broth to a boil over high heat. Add lentils and cumin seeds. Reduce heat, cover, and simmer until lentils are tender to bite (about 30 minutes). Drain, if necessary; then pour into a bowl.

While lentils are simmering, trim and discard stem ends from chard. Rinse chard well, drain, and cut stems and leaves crosswise into ¼-inch-wide strips (keep stems and leaves in separate piles).

Heat oil in lentil cooking pan over medium heat. Add chard stems, onion, garlic, and red pepper flakes. Cook, stirring often, until onion is lightly browned (about 15 minutes). Add chard leaves; cook, stirring, until limp (about 3 minutes). Add lentils and remaining 1 cup broth; cook just until hot (about 3 minutes).

Meanwhile, in another 5- to 6-quart pan, cook linguine in about 3 quarts boiling water until just tender to bite (8 to 10 minutes); or cook according to package directions. Drain well and pour into a warm wide bowl. Add lentil mixture and cheese; mix gently. Season to taste with salt and pepper. Makes 6 servings.

Per serving: 474 calories (25% fat, 58% carbohydrates, 17% protein), 13 g total fat (5 g saturated fat), 69 g carbohydrates, 21 g protein, 22 mg cholesterol, 777 mg sodium

Green & Red Lasagne

. . . .

MODIFIED CLASSIC

Preparation time: About 35 minutes
Cooking time: About 20 minutes
Baking time: About 1 hour

This colorful meatless lasagne is especially convenient, since you don't precook the pasta. Layered with cheese and a rich vegetable sauce, it cooks as the casserole bakes.

	Tomato-Mushroom Sauce (recipe follows)
1	**large egg**
1	**large egg white (about 2 tablespoons)**
1	**package (about 10 oz.) frozen chopped spinach, thawed and squeezed dry**
2	**cups low-fat cottage cheese**
⅓	**cup grated Romano cheese**
¼	**teaspoon pepper**
⅛	**teaspoon ground nutmeg**

8	**ounces dry lasagne noodles**
1½	**cups (about 6 oz.) shredded part-skim mozzarella cheese**

Prepare Tomato-Mushroom Sauce. Meanwhile, in a medium-size bowl, beat egg and egg white to blend; stir in spinach, cottage cheese, Romano cheese, pepper, and nutmeg.

Spread a fourth of the sauce in a 9- by 13-inch baking dish; top with a third of the uncooked lasagne noodles. Spoon on a third of the spinach mixture. Repeat layers of sauce, lasagne, and spinach mixture until all ingredients are used; end with sauce. Sprinkle with mozzarella cheese. Cover tightly. (At this point, you may refrigerate for up to 1 day.)

Bake, covered, in a 375° oven until lasagne noodles are tender to bite (about 1 hour; about 1½ hours if refrigerated). Let stand, covered, for about 10 minutes before cutting and serving. Makes 6 to 8 servings.

Tomato-Mushroom Sauce. Heat 1 teaspoon **olive oil** in a wide (at least 12-inch) nonstick frying pan over medium heat. Add 2 large **onions,** finely chopped; 1 large **red bell pepper** (about 8 oz.), seeded and finely chopped; 8 ounces **mushrooms,** thinly sliced; 3 cloves **garlic,** minced or pressed; 1 teaspoon **dry oregano;** and 2½ teaspoons **dry basil.** Cook, stirring often, until liquid has evaporated and onions are very soft (15 to 20 minutes).

Stir in 1 large can (about 15 oz.) **no-salt-added tomato sauce,** 1 can (about 6 oz.) **tomato paste,** 1 tablespoon **reduced-sodium soy sauce,** and ½ cup **dry red wine.** Cook, stirring, until mixture comes to a boil; use hot.

Per serving: 371 calories (20% fat, 52% carbohydrates, 28% protein), 8 g total fat (3 g saturated fat), 48 g carbohydrates, 25 g protein, 51 mg cholesterol, 766 mg sodium

Garden Patch Rigatoni

. . . .

Preparation time: About 20 minutes
Cooking time: About 25 minutes
Baking time: About 25 minutes

This homey, satisfying casserole combines plump tubular pasta and a host of vegetables in a savory Cheddar sauce nipped with hot pepper and Dijon mustard.

2	tablespoons butter or margarine
½	cup thinly sliced celery
2	tablespoons all-purpose flour
2	cups nonfat milk
½	cup *each* low-fat cottage cheese and shredded sharp Cheddar cheese
1	tablespoon Dijon mustard
½	teaspoon liquid hot pepper seasoning
⅛	teaspoon ground nutmeg
8	ounces dry rigatoni or other bite-size tube-shaped pasta
3	medium-size carrots, cut into thin slanting slices
2	cups broccoli flowerets
1	cup fresh yellow or white corn kernels (from about 1 large ear corn); or 1 cup frozen corn kernels, thawed
2	medium-size pear-shaped (Roma-type) tomatoes (about 6 oz. *total*), seeded and chopped
½	cup shredded reduced-fat Swiss cheese
2	tablespoons grated Parmesan or Romano cheese

Melt butter in a 2-quart pan over medium heat. Add celery and cook, stirring often, until soft but not browned (about 5 minutes). Add flour and cook, stirring, until bubbly. Remove from heat and gradually stir in milk; return to heat and continue to cook, stirring, until sauce comes to a boil (about 6 minutes). Add cottage cheese, Cheddar cheese, mustard, hot pepper seasoning, and nutmeg; stir until Cheddar cheese is melted. Remove from heat and set aside.

In a 5- to 6-quart pan, cook rigatoni in about 3 quarts boiling water just until almost tender to bite (10 to 12 minutes); or cook a little less than time specified in package directions. After pasta has cooked for 5 minutes, add carrots to pan; after 3 more minutes, add broccoli. Drain pasta and vegetables well; pour into a large bowl and add cheese sauce, corn, and tomatoes. Mix lightly.

Spread pasta mixture in an oiled 2- to 2½-quart casserole; sprinkle with Swiss and Parmesan cheeses. Bake in a 400° oven until lightly browned on top (about 25 minutes). Makes 4 to 6 servings.

Per serving: 435 calories (26% fat, 53% carbohydrates, 21% protein), 13 g total fat (7 g saturated fat), 58 g carbohydrates, 23 g protein, 37 mg cholesterol, 467 mg sodium

Asparagus & Pasta Stir-fry

. . . .

3 0 M I N U T E S O R L E S S

Preparation time: About 15 minutes
Cooking time: 10 to 15 minutes

Fresh ginger and garlic season this medley of vermicelli and tender asparagus. You might serve it with Basque Sheepherder's Bread (page 186) and Salad of Leaves & Fruit (page 46).

6	ounces dry vermicelli
2	teaspoons salad oil
1	clove garlic, minced or pressed
1	teaspoon minced fresh ginger
1	pound asparagus, tough ends removed, stalks cut diagonally into 1½-inch-long pieces
½	cup diagonally sliced green onions
2	tablespoons reduced-sodium soy sauce
⅛	teaspoon crushed red pepper flakes

In a 5- to 6-quart pan, cook vermicelli in about 3 quarts boiling water until just tender to bite (about 8 minutes); or cook according to package directions. Drain well and keep warm.

Heat oil in a wok or wide frying pan over high heat. Add garlic, ginger, asparagus, and onions. Cook, stirring, until asparagus is tender-crisp to bite (3 to 5 minutes). Add soy sauce and red pepper flakes; stir for 1 more minute. Add drained pasta to pan; cook, lifting and stirring, until hot. Makes 4 to 6 servings.

Per serving: 161 calories (13% fat, 71% carbohydrates, 16% protein), 2 g total fat (0.3 g saturated fat), 29 g carbohydrates, 6 g protein, 0 mg cholesterol, 245 mg sodium

COOKING LEGUMES

Low in cost, high in nutrition, and rich in good, earthy flavors, legumes are one of the best food bargains going. To begin with, they pack in a powerhouse of protein; a navy bean, for example, is a full 20 percent protein. Legumes also contain plenty of iron, calcium, potassium, and B vitamins. They're high in fiber and low in sodium—and they're cholesterol-free.

Ideal a food as they may sound, legumes do have a few minor drawbacks. Some people find them hard to digest at first, though adequate soaking and cooking usually help solve that problem. The long soaking and cooking times present another disadvantage, but you can always speed things up by using the quick-soaking method described below. Lentils and split peas, the quickest-cooking of all legumes, require no soaking at all.

Soaking Legumes

Before soaking, rinse and sort legumes, discarding any debris.

• **Quick soaking:** For each pound of dried legumes, bring 8 cups water to a boil. Add rinsed and sorted legumes and boil for 2 minutes. Remove from heat, cover, and let stand for 1 hour. Drain and rinse, discarding water.

• **Overnight soaking:** For each pound of dried legumes, dissolve 2 teaspoons salt in 6 cups water. Add rinsed and sorted legumes; soak until next day. Drain and rinse, discarding water.

Cooking Legumes

Cooking times printed on packages of legumes may differ from the times listed here. Always test for doneness after the minimum suggested cooking time; legumes should be tender to bite.

For each pound of dried legumes (weight before soaking), dissolve 2 teaspoons salt in 6 cups water; bring to a boil. Add soaked legumes; reduce heat, partially cover, and boil gently until tender to bite (individual cooking times are listed in chart below). Add more water, if needed, to keep legumes submerged. Drain cooked legumes. If desired, season to taste with salt. Each pound of dry legumes yields 6 to 7 cups cooked legumes.

A GUIDE TO LEGUMES

NAME	DESCRIPTION	SOAKING	COOKING TIME
Black beans	Robust flavor; popular in Caribbean, Central American, and South American cooking.	Yes	1–1½ hours
Black-eyed peas	Smooth texture, pealike flavor; good mixed with other vegetables.	Yes	About 1 hour
Garbanzo beans (chick peas, ceci beans)	Firm texture, nutlike flavor; popular in Middle Eastern and African cooking. Good in minestrone, salads.	Yes	2–2½ hours
Great Northern beans (white beans)	Mild flavor; good in soups or combined with other vegetables.	Yes	1–1½ hours
Kidney beans, red & white (cannellini)	Firm texture, hearty flavor. Hold shape well in chilis, casseroles. If you can't find the white type (cannellini), substitute Great Northerns.	Yes	1–1½ hours
Lentils	Mild flavor blends well with many foods and spices.	No	25–30 minutes
Lima beans, baby	Mild flavor; use like other white beans in soups, casseroles.	Yes	¾–1¼ hours
Pink, pinto & red beans	Hearty flavor; good in soups, casseroles, barbecue-style beans. Popular in Mexican cooking.	Yes	1¼–1½ hours
Soybeans	Strong flavor; ancient crop of Asia.	Yes*	3–3½ hours
Split peas, green & yellow	Earthy flavor; good in soups, side dishes.	No	35–45 minutes
White beans, small (navy beans)	Mild flavor. Hold shape well; classic for baked beans.	Yes	About 1 hour

*Soak soybeans overnight in the refrigerator.

Slim Red & Green Pasta

Preparation time: About 40 minutes
Cooling time: About 30 minutes
Cooking time: About 10 minutes

Scarlet peppers, garbanzos, and handfuls of fresh basil go into this lean but richly flavored sauce. Serve it over armoniche ("harmonicas") or another whimsically shaped pasta.

2½   **pounds red bell peppers or fresh pimentos; or use jars or cans (about 21 oz. *total*) of roasted red peppers or whole or sliced pimentos**

1   **cup thinly sliced green onions**

1   **can (about 15 oz.) garbanzo beans, drained and rinsed; or 2 cups cooked garbanzo beans (page 149), drained and rinsed**

¾   **cup chopped fresh basil or ¼ cup dry basil**

1½   **tablespoons chopped fresh tarragon or 1½ teaspoons dry tarragon**

3   **tablespoons drained capers**
     Salt and pepper

1   **pound dry armoniche, rotelle, or other bite-size pasta shapes**

If using fresh bell peppers, place in a 10- by 15-inch rimmed baking pan. Broil about 4 inches below heat, turning as needed, until charred all over (15 to 20 minutes). Cover with foil and let cool in pan for 30 minutes. Remove and discard stems, skins, and seeds; rinse peppers. (If using bottled or canned peppers, drain and seed them.)

In a food processor, whirl peppers until finely chopped (or chop with a knife). Place in a 3- to 4-quart pan and add onions, beans, basil, tarragon, and capers. Cook over medium-high heat, stirring often, until steaming (5 to 7 minutes). Season to taste with salt and pepper; keep warm.

Meanwhile, cook armoniche in a 6- to 8-quart pan in about 4 quarts boiling water until just tender to bite (8 to 10 minutes); or cook according to package directions. Drain well and pour into a wide, shallow bowl. Spoon pepper mixture over pasta and mix gently. Makes 8 servings.

Per serving: 289 calories (6% fat, 79% carbohydrates, 15% protein), 2 g total fat (0.2 g saturated fat), 58 g carbohydrates, 11 g protein, 0 mg cholesterol, 150 mg sodium

Mushroom & Barley Casserole with Fila Crust

Preparation time: About 50 minutes
Cooking time: About 35 minutes
Baking time: About 45 minutes

Crisp diamonds of fila pastry top savory layers of mushroom, barley, and cottage cheese fillings in this hearty vegetable pie.

     Cheese Filling (recipe follows)
     Barley Filling (recipe follows)
     Mushroom Duxelles (recipe follows)

4   **sheets fila pastry (*each* about 12 by 16 inches), thawed if frozen**

3   **tablespoons butter or margarine, melted**
     Reduced-fat sour cream or plain low-fat yogurt
     Prepared horseradish with beets

Prepare Cheese Filling and Barley Filling. While barley is simmering, prepare Mushroom Duxelles.

Spread duxelles evenly in a 2- to 2½-quart casserole (6 by 11 by 2 inches, to 8 by 11 by 1½ inches). Cover evenly with Barley Filling, then Cheese Filling.

Work with fila sheets one at a time, keeping remainder covered to prevent drying. Lay one fila sheet flat and brush lightly with about 1½ teaspoons of the butter. Top with remaining 3 fila sheets, brushing each with butter. Then fold stack in half, bringing short ends together. Place fila stack on top of Cheese Filling; fold ends of pastry under to fit flush with casserole rim. Brush pastry with remaining butter. With a sharp knife, cut diagonally through pastry sheets every 1½ to 2 inches to make a diamond pattern. (At this point, you may cover and refrigerate for up to 1 day.)

Bake, uncovered, in a 350° oven until pastry is a deep golden brown and filling is hot in center (about 45 minutes; 50 to 55 minutes if refrigerated). Serve with sour cream and horseradish. Makes 6 to 8 servings.

Cheese Filling. Pour 2 cups **nonfat or low-fat cottage cheese** into a fine strainer. Set strainer in a sink or over a bowl and let drain for at least 10 minutes or up to 1 hour. Transfer drained cheese to a bowl and stir in 1 tablespoon grated **lemon peel** and ½ teaspoon **pepper.**

Barley Filling. In a 5- to 6-quart pan, bring 3 cups **canned or homemade (page 41) vegetable broth** to a boil over high heat. Add 1 cup **pearl barley,** rinsed and drained; reduce heat, cover, and simmer until barley is tender to bite (about 30 minutes). Drain, reserving liquid for Mushroom Duxelles. To barley, add 1 tablespoon **tomato paste** and ¼ cup **reduced-fat sour cream;** mix well.

Mushroom Duxelles. In a 5- to 6-quart pan, combine 2½ pounds **mushrooms** (minced), ½ cup minced **shallots** or red onions, and ½ teaspoon **ground nutmeg.** Cook over high heat, stirring often, until liquid evaporates and mushrooms begin to brown (about 30 minutes). Add ⅓ cup of the **reserved barley liquid;** stir to scrape browned bits free. Then continue to cook, stirring often, until liquid has evaporated. Use warm or cold.

Per serving: 304 calories (24% fat, 56% carbohydrates, 20% protein), 8 g total fat (4 g saturated fat), 44 g carbohydrates, 16 g protein, 22 mg cholesterol, 795 mg sodium

Zucchini Polenta

. . . .
30 MINUTES OR LESS

Preparation time: About 10 minutes
Cooking time: 12 to 15 minutes

Flecks of zucchini add interest to golden polenta. Serve the dish with fresh ripe tomatoes, cut into thick slices and sprinkled with basil.

1	**cup polenta or yellow cornmeal**
3	**cups canned or homemade (page 41) vegetable broth**
2	**cups shredded zucchini**
½	**cup shredded reduced-fat jack cheese**

In a 3- to 4-quart pan, stir together polenta and broth. Bring to a boil over high heat, stirring. Stir in zucchini; reduce heat to low and simmer, uncovered, stirring often, until polenta tastes creamy (about 10 minutes). Stir in cheese. Makes 4 servings.

Per serving: 192 calories (19% fat, 65% carbohydrates, 16% protein), 4 g total fat (2 g saturated fat), 31 g carbohydrates, 8 g protein, 10 mg cholesterol, 853 mg sodium

Wild Spanish Rice

. . . .
MODIFIED CLASSIC

Preparation time: About 15 minutes
Cooking time: About 1¾ hours

Elegant wild rice is balanced by nutty-tasting brown rice in this tomato-sauced, olive-strewn casserole.

2	**cups canned or homemade (page 41) vegetable broth**
½	**cup wild rice, rinsed and drained**
1	**tablespoon olive oil or salad oil**
1	**medium-size red onion, thinly sliced**
2	**cloves garlic, minced or pressed**
1	**cup long-grain brown rice**
1	**teaspoon chili powder**
2½	**cups tomato juice**
1	**medium-size green bell pepper (about 6 oz.), seeded and chopped**
2	**medium-size pear-shaped (Roma-type) tomatoes (about 6 oz.** *total***), seeded and chopped**
½	**cup pimento-stuffed green olives, cut lengthwise into halves**
¼	**cup dry-roasted peanuts**

In a wide nonstick frying pan, bring broth to a boil over high heat. Add wild rice; then reduce heat, cover, and simmer until rice is tender to bite (about 45 minutes). Drain rice, reserving broth; set rice and broth aside.

In same pan, heat oil over medium heat. Add onion and garlic; cook, stirring often, until onion is soft and golden (6 to 8 minutes). Add brown rice, increase heat to medium-high, and cook, stirring, until rice looks opaque (about 3 minutes). Add chili powder, tomato juice, and reserved broth.

Bring mixture to a boil; then reduce heat, cover, and simmer until rice is tender to bite (45 to 50 minutes). Add drained wild rice, bell pepper, tomatoes, and olives; cook, stirring gently, until heated through (about 2 minutes).

Transfer to a serving dish and sprinkle with peanuts. Makes 4 to 6 servings.

Per serving: 337 calories (26% fat, 64% carbohydrates, 10% protein), 10 g total fat (1 g saturated fat), 56 g carbohydrates, 9 g protein, 0 mg cholesterol, 1,188 mg sodium

Risotto with Mushrooms

Preparation time: About 15 minutes
Cooking time: About 35 minutes

Served with bread and a crisp salad, this simple risotto is a lovely entrée for lunch or supper. To make it, you simmer rice and sliced mushrooms in vegetable broth until the grain is tender and creamy-textured.

2	teaspoons olive oil
1	clove garlic, minced or pressed
1	cup coarsely chopped onion
1	cup short-grain white rice
2¼	cups canned or homemade (page 41) vegetable broth
8	ounces mushrooms, thinly sliced
¼	cup grated Parmesan cheese
2	tablespoons dry white wine
	Parsley sprigs

Heat oil in a wide frying pan over medium heat. Add garlic and onion; cook, stirring often, until onion is soft but not browned (about 5 minutes). Add rice; cook, stirring, until grains look opaque (about 3 minutes).

Stir in broth and mushrooms. Bring to a boil over high heat, stirring often. Reduce heat and simmer, uncovered, until rice is tender to bite and almost all liquid has been absorbed (about 25 minutes); stir occasionally at first, then more often as mixture thickens.

Remove rice from heat and stir in cheese and wine. Pour into a serving dish and garnish with parsley sprigs. Makes 4 to 6 servings.

Per serving: 216 calories (17% fat, 73% carbohydrates, 10% protein), 4 g total fat (1 g saturated fat), 38 g carbohydrates, 6 g protein, 3 mg cholesterol, 534 mg sodium

Double Squash Stew with Cornmeal Dumplings

Preparation time: About 1 hour
Baking time: About 2 hours

Golden dumplings, crunchy with cornmeal, crown this tempting baked vegetable stew. As the name implies, it features two kinds of squash: sliced zucchini and cubes of nutty-tasting butternut squash.

5	cloves garlic, minced or pressed
1	large onion, chopped
1½	cups canned or homemade (page 41) vegetable broth
1	can (about 4 oz.) diced green chiles
2½	pounds pear-shaped (Roma-type) tomatoes, chopped
3	pounds butternut or banana squash, peeled, seeded, and cut into about 1-inch cubes
1½	teaspoons ground cumin
1	teaspoon ground cinnamon
	Cornmeal Dumplings (recipe follows)
1½	pounds zucchini, cut into ¼-inch-thick slices
⅓	cup minced fresh basil or 2 tablespoons dry basil
	Salt and pepper

In a shallow 10- by 15-inch (at least 4½-quart) casserole, combine garlic, onion, and ½ cup of the broth. Bake in a 400° oven until liquid evaporates and vegetables begin to brown (about 35 minutes). To deglaze, add ½ cup more broth and stir to scrape browned bits free. Then continue to bake until vegetables begin to brown again.

Add remaining ½ cup broth; stir to scrape browned bits free. Stir in chiles, tomatoes, butternut squash, cumin, and cinnamon. Cover tightly and bake until squash is tender when pierced— 45 to 50 minutes. (At this point, you may let cool, then cover and refrigerate for up to 1 day. Before continuing, bake, covered, in a 400° oven until hot—about 20 minutes.)

While squash mixture is baking, prepare Cornmeal Dumplings.

Mix zucchini and basil into hot vegetables, and season to taste with salt and pepper. Spoon dumpling batter onto vegetables in 6 to 8 equal mounds (or spoon batter in dollops around edge of casserole). Cover with a tent of foil (don't let foil touch dumplings). Bake until dumplings are firm and dry to the touch (about 20 minutes). Makes 6 to 8 servings.

Cornmeal Dumplings. In a bowl, combine 1½ cups **yellow cornmeal,** ½ cup **all-purpose flour,** 1½ teaspoons **baking powder,** and 1½ teaspoons **sugar.** Add 1 large **egg,** ¾ cup **nonfat or low-fat milk,** and 3 tablespoons **butter** or margarine, melted. Mix well. Let stand until batter is thick enough to hold its shape (at least 5 minutes).

Per serving: 359 calories (18% fat, 71% carbohydrates, 11% protein), 8 g total fat (4 g saturated fat), 68 g carbohydrates, 10 g protein, 44 mg cholesterol, 521 mg sodium

Chutney Burgers

. . . .

Preparation time: About 40 minutes
Cooking time: About 1 hour

These spicy all-vegetable patties are based on a mixture of potatoes, mushrooms, and carrots. Serve them in toasted rolls, accompanied with a tart-sweet chutney made from banana, ginger, and dried fruit.

	Ginger-Banana Chutney (recipe follows)
2	tablespoons butter or margarine
1	cup chopped onion
1	teaspoon minced garlic
½	teaspoon *each* ground cumin and ground ginger
1	cup *each* coarsely chopped mushrooms and cooked thin-skinned potatoes
1	cup diced carrots (¼-inch cubes)
2	tablespoons chopped cilantro
⅓	cup all-purpose flour
2	large eggs, lightly beaten
1	cup soft whole wheat bread crumbs
	Salt and pepper
1	to 2 teaspoons salad oil
4	kaiser rolls, split and warmed
	Rinsed and crisped lettuce leaves, sliced tomatoes, sliced onions, and cilantro sprigs

Prepare Ginger-Banana Chutney; set aside.

Melt butter in a wide nonstick frying pan over medium heat. Add chopped onion and garlic; cook, stirring often, until onion is golden (about 8 minutes). Add cumin and ginger; stir for 1 minute. Add mushrooms, potatoes, carrots, and chopped cilantro; cook, stirring often, until carrots are tender to bite (about 7 minutes). Add flour and cook, stirring, for 3 minutes. Remove from heat. Let cool slightly; then mix in eggs and bread crumbs. Season to taste with salt and pepper. Shape vegetable mixture into four ⅓-inch-thick patties.

Heat 1 teaspoon of the oil in a clean wide nonstick frying pan over medium heat. Place patties in pan; cook until deep golden brown on bottom (4 to 5 minutes). Turn patties over; add 1 more teaspoon oil to pan, if necessary. Then cook until patties are browned on other side (2 to 3 minutes).

Spread rolls with Ginger-Banana Chutney; serve patties in rolls. Offer lettuce, tomatoes, sliced onions, and cilantro sprigs to add to taste. Makes 4 servings.

Ginger-Banana Chutney. In a 1- to 2-quart pan, combine ½ cup **mashed banana;** ⅓ cup *each* chopped **onion,** chopped **pitted dates,** and **pineapple juice;** ¼ cup *each* **dried currants** and **cider vinegar;** 3 tablespoons minced **pickled ginger;** and ½ teaspoon **curry powder.** Bring to a gentle boil over medium heat; then reduce heat and simmer, uncovered, stirring often, until chutney has the consistency of thick jam (about 30 minutes). Remove from heat; use warm or cool. If made ahead, let cool; then cover and refrigerate for up to 3 days.

Per serving: 550 calories (27% fat, 63% carbohydrates, 10% protein), 17 g total fat (6 g saturated fat), 89 g carbohydrates, 14 g protein, 122 mg cholesterol, 513 mg sodium

***When you're building burgers** and other sandwiches, remember that whole-grain breads and rolls are nutritious choices. Be sure to read the new Nutrition Facts label (see page 31), though, before you buy these or any other breads. Added ingredients such as eggs, oil, nuts, and seeds sometimes bring unsuspected fat.*

Picadillo-stuffed Peppers

Preparation time: About 25 minutes
Cooking time: About 20 minutes
Baking time: About 45 minutes

Brown rice and black beans in a savory-sweet, raisin-dotted tomato sauce make a delicious filling for big, bright bell peppers.

6   **medium-size yellow bell peppers (about 2¼ lbs. *total*)**
1   **tablespoon olive oil**
2   **cloves garlic, minced or pressed**
1   **large can (about 15 oz.) tomato sauce**
¼   **cup dry white wine**
2   **tablespoons cider vinegar**
1½ **teaspoons ground cinnamon**
1   **teaspoon dry oregano**
½   **cup raisins**
3   **cups cooked brown rice**
1   **can (about 15 oz.) black beans, drained and rinsed; or 2 cups cooked black beans (page 149), drained and rinsed**
¼   **cup sliced almonds**
2   **tablespoons grated Parmesan cheese**

Cut off stem ends of peppers and remove seeds. If necessary, trim bases so peppers will stand upright. In a 6- to 8-quart pan, bring 3 to 4 quarts water to a boil over high heat. Add peppers; cook for 2 minutes. Using tongs, lift peppers from pan and plunge into cold water to cool; drain and set aside.

Heat oil in a wide nonstick frying pan over medium-high heat. Add garlic and cook, stirring, just until soft (about 2 minutes). Add 1 cup of the tomato sauce, wine, vinegar, cinnamon, oregano, and raisins; cook, stirring occasionally, for 15 minutes. Stir in rice, beans, and almonds.

Fill peppers equally with rice mixture; set upright in a shallow 1½-quart baking pan. Pour remaining tomato sauce into pan around peppers. Cover and bake in a 375° oven for 30 minutes. Uncover; sprinkle peppers evenly with cheese. Continue to bake until cheese is golden brown (about 15 more minutes). Makes 6 servings.

Per serving: 298 calories (18% fat, 70% carbohydrates, 12% protein), 6 g total fat (1 g saturated fat), 55 g carbohydrates, 9 g protein, 1 mg cholesterol, 585 mg sodium

Ratatouille-topped Baked Potatoes

Preparation time: About 25 minutes
Baking time: About 1½ hours

Fluffy baked potatoes are filled to overflowing with a medley of herb-seasoned garden vegetables—eggplant, summer squash, bell peppers, and tomatoes.

1   **medium-size eggplant (about 1 lb.), unpeeled, cut into ½- by 2-inch sticks**
8   **ounces *each* zucchini and crookneck squash, cut into ½-inch-thick slices**
1½ **pounds pear-shaped (Roma-type) tomatoes, cut into quarters**
1   ***each* large red and yellow bell pepper (about 1 lb. *total*), seeded and thinly sliced**
1   **large onion, chopped**
3   **garlic cloves, minced or pressed**
1   **dry bay leaf**
½   **teaspoon *each* dry thyme and dry rosemary**
1   **tablespoon olive oil**
6   **large red thin-skinned potatoes (about 8 oz. *each*), scrubbed**
    Pepper

In a 3- to 4-quart baking dish, mix eggplant, zucchini, crookneck squash, tomatoes, bell peppers, onion, garlic, bay leaf, thyme, rosemary, and oil. Cover and bake in a 400° oven for 1 hour. Uncover and continue to bake, stirring once or twice, until eggplant is very soft when pressed and only a thin layer of liquid remains in bottom of dish (about 30 more minutes).

After eggplant mixture has baked for 30 minutes, pierce each unpeeled potato in several places with a fork. Place potatoes on a baking sheet; bake until tender throughout when pierced (about 1 hour).

To serve, make a deep cut lengthwise down center of each potato; then make a second cut across center. Grasp each potato between cuts; press firmly to split potato wide open. Spoon eggplant mixture equally into potatoes; season to taste with pepper. Makes 6 servings.

Per serving: 294 calories (10% fat, 80% carbohydrates, 10% protein), 3 g total fat (0.4 g saturated fat), 61 g carbohydrates, 8 g protein, 0 mg cholesterol, 35 mg sodium

COOKING GRAINS

Rich in fiber and complex carbohydrates, grains are a great addition to almost any menu. Serve them as a bed for richly sauced meats, fish, or vegetables; or let them stand on their own as a side dish.

Here are some guidelines for cooking grains.

• **Yield:** 1 cup uncooked grain yields about 3 cups cooked grain.

• **Salt:** For each cup uncooked grain, add about ¼ teaspoon salt to the cooking water.

• **Cooking option:** For some grains—bulgur, buckwheat, millet and, of course, rice—one alternative to simple boiling is to cook the grain like a pilaf. Start by sautéing the dry grain in butter, margarine, or salad oil (about 1 tablespoon per cup); then, instead of water, add boiling broth. Cover and simmer until grain is done.

• **Doneness:** Grains, like pasta, are done when they're tender to bite. Each grain should be tender, yet still slightly resilient at the core.

A MEDLEY OF GRAINS

NAME	DESCRIPTION	HOW TO COOK
Barley	Mild, nutty flavor. Use in soups, stews, casseroles.	2 parts water to 1 part barley. Bring to a boil; reduce heat, cover, and simmer for 40–45 minutes. Let stand, covered, for 5–10 minutes.
Buckwheat (kasha)	Not a true grain, but a member of a herbaceous plant family. Available untoasted or toasted; strong, distinct flavor. Use in casseroles or serve with sauces.	Cook as directed for bulgur, but only for 10–12 minutes. Or, in an ungreased frying pan, mix 2 cups buckwheat and 1 large beaten egg; cook over high heat, stirring, for 2 minutes. Then add boiling broth or water; reduce heat, cover, and simmer for 12–15 minutes.
Bulgur	Wheat berries that have been steamed, dried, and cracked; delicate, nutty flavor. Use in casseroles, whole grain breads, salads.	1½ parts water to 1 part bulgur. Bring to a boil; reduce heat, cover, and simmer for 12–15 minutes. Or see "Cooking option," above.
Millet	Mild, nutty flavor. Use in stuffings, casseroles, whole-grain breads; serve with sauces.	2½ parts water to 1 part millet. Bring to a boil; reduce heat, cover, and simmer for 18–20 minutes. Or see "Cooking option," above.
Oats	Rolled, quick-cooking, or groats (steel-cut); mild flavor, creamy texture. Use as a cereal or in baked goods.	1 part boiling water to 1 part *rolled or quick-cooking oats* (or use up to 2 parts water for a creamier consistency). Reduce heat, cover, and simmer for 3–10 minutes. Soak 1 part *groats* in 2 parts water for 1 hour. Bring to a boil; reduce heat, cover, and simmer for 25–30 minutes.
Rice, brown	Unpolished, long or short grain; sweet, nutty flavor. Use in soups, stews, casseroles; serve with sauces.	2 parts water to 1 part brown rice. Bring to a boil; reduce heat, cover, and simmer for 35–40 minutes. Let stand, covered, for 5–10 minutes. Or see "Cooking option," above.
Rice, white	Long, medium, or short grain, polished or preprocessed (parboiled to remove surface starch); mild, delicate flavor. Use in soups, salads, casseroles, puddings; serve with sauces.	2 parts water to 1 part white rice. Bring to a boil; reduce heat, cover, and simmer for 15–20 minutes. Let stand, covered, for 5–10 minutes. Or see "Cooking option," above. For preprocessed rice, follow package directions.
Rice, wild	Not a true rice, but a grass seed. Nutty flavor, chewy texture. Use in salads, stuffings; serve with sauces.	Rinse in several changes of cold water. For cooking, use 4 parts water to 1 part wild rice. Bring to a boil; reduce heat, cover, and simmer for 45–50 minutes. If too moist, drain well.
Rye & triticale	Both have earthy flavor; triticale (a wheat-rye hybrid containing more protein than either parent grain) is slightly milder than rye. Use it in casseroles and whole-grain breads.	3 parts water to 1 part rye or triticale. Bring to a boil; reduce heat, cover, and simmer for 1–1¼ hours. If too dry, add water and continue to cook. If too moist, drain well.
Wheat, cracked	Similar to bulgur, but not steamed before being cracked. Same uses as bulgur.	See directions for bulgur.
Wheat, whole kernels (wheat berries)	Nutty, mild flavor; chewy texture. Use in sauces, casseroles, stews, whole-grain breads; serve with sauces.	3 parts water to 1 part whole wheat. Bring to a boil; reduce heat, cover, and simmer for 2 hours. If too dry, add water and continue to cook. If too moist, drain well.

ACCOMPANIMENTS

When you choose lighter servings of meat—or poultry or fish—there's plenty of room left on the plate for side dishes. Fresh vegetables are favorites for this role, whether you choose tender broccoli or snap beans, vitamin-rich greens, or sturdy root vegetables. Potato lovers can enjoy their preferred food in all sorts of low-fat guises: layered with tomatoes and eggplant, baked in cubes or shoestring-thin sticks, even shredded and made into risotto. Grains, too, are a superb accompaniment. Serve them plain or in combination (as in Wild Rice & Barley Pilaf); or team them with vegetables, as in Winter Flower Bud Rice. And don't forget fruits. Flavorful dishes like Broiled Pineapple with Basil provide the perfect complement to many a simple entrée.

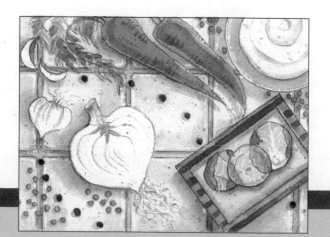

Tomato, Potato & Eggplant Gratin

Preparation time: About 45 minutes
Broiling time: About 15 minutes
Cooking time: About 15 minutes
Baking time: 1 to 1¼ hours

This hearty layered casserole, fragrant with herbs, is superb as a side dish for grilled lamb. It's good as a light main dish, too; try it for supper, with crusty bread and a crisp romaine salad.

Olive oil cooking spray

1 large eggplant (1¼ to 1½ lbs.), unpeeled, cut crosswise into ¼-inch-thick slices

3 tablespoons olive oil

1 large onion, thinly sliced

1 medium-size red bell pepper (about 6 oz.), seeded and finely chopped

3 large tomatoes (about 1½ lbs. *total*), peeled, seeded, and chopped

3 cloves garlic, minced or pressed

¼ teaspoon sugar

½ teaspoon dry thyme

5 large russet potatoes (about 2½ lbs. *total*)

Salt and pepper

Chopped parsley

Coat a large, shallow baking pan with cooking spray. Arrange eggplant slices in a single layer in pan; coat with cooking spray. Broil about 4 inches below heat until well browned (6 to 8 minutes). Turn eggplant slices over, coat other sides with cooking spray, and broil until browned (5 to 6 more minutes). Set aside.

Heat 2 tablespoons of the oil in a wide frying pan over medium heat. Add onion and bell pepper. Cook, stirring often, until vegetables are soft but not browned (8 to 10 minutes). Stir in tomatoes, garlic, sugar, and thyme. Cook, stirring often, until tomatoes are soft (3 to 5 minutes). Remove from heat.

Peel and thinly slice potatoes. Spread a third of the potatoes in an oiled shallow 3-quart casserole; sprinkle with salt and pepper. Top with half the eggplant, then half the tomato sauce. Cover with half the remaining potatoes, sprinkle with salt and pepper, and add remaining eggplant and tomato

sauce. Top with remaining potatoes; sprinkle with salt and pepper. Drizzle potatoes with remaining 1 tablespoon oil.

Bake in a 375° oven until potatoes are lightly browned on top and tender when pierced (1 to 1¼ hours). Sprinkle with parsley. Makes 6 servings.

Per serving: 277 calories (27% fat, 65% carbohydrates, 8% protein), 9 g total fat (1 g saturated fat), 47 g carbohydrates, 6 g protein, 0 mg cholesterol, 28 mg sodium

Garlic-roasted Potatoes & Greens

Preparation time: About 25 minutes
Baking time: About 1 hour

Contrasting flavors give this hot potato salad special appeal. To make it, you mix sweet, mellow roasted potato chunks with peppery watercress and a touch of red wine vinegar.

Olive oil cooking spray

2 pounds thin-skinned potatoes, scrubbed and cut into ¾-inch cubes

6 large cloves garlic, peeled and cut into quarters

3 tablespoons red wine vinegar

1 tablespoon olive oil

Salt and pepper

3 to 4 cups lightly packed watercress sprigs, rinsed and crisped

Coat a shallow baking pan with cooking spray. Place potatoes and garlic in pan; stir to mix, then coat with cooking spray. Bake in a 450° oven until well browned (about 1 hour), turning with a wide spatula every 15 minutes.

Drizzle vinegar and oil over potatoes. Turn potato mixture gently with spatula to loosen any browned bits. Season to taste with salt and pepper; transfer to a wide bowl.

Coarsely chop about half the watercress; mix lightly with potatoes. Tuck remaining watercress around potatoes. Serve hot or at room temperature. Makes 4 to 6 servings.

Per serving: 184 calories (16% fat, 75% carbohydrates, 9% protein), 3 g total fat (0.4 g saturated fat), 35 g carbohydrates, 4 g protein, 0 mg cholesterol, 27 mg sodium

Potato & Carrot Oven Fries

Preparation time: About 10 minutes
Baking time: About 45 minutes

Because they're baked rather than deep-fried, these crunchy potato and carrot sticks are pleasingly lean.

3 or 4 large white thin-skinned potatoes (about 2 lbs. *total*), scrubbed and cut into ½- by 4-inch sticks

2 pounds carrots, cut into ½- by 4-inch sticks

2 tablespoons salad oil
  Salt and pepper
  Cider vinegar (optional)

In a large bowl, mix potatoes, carrots, and 1½ tablespoons of the oil.

Grease two 10- by 15-inch rimmed baking pans with remaining 1½ teaspoons oil and place in a 425° oven for 5 minutes. Then spread vegetables evenly in pans. Bake, turning once with a wide spatula, until vegetables are lightly browned and tender when pierced (about 45 minutes); switch positions of pans halfway through baking.

To serve, transfer vegetables to a platter or a napkin-lined basket. Season to taste with salt and pepper. Sprinkle with vinegar, if desired. Makes 4 servings.

Per serving: 341 calories (20% fat, 73% carbohydrates, 7% protein), 8 g total fat (0.9 g saturated fat), 64 g carbohydrates, 7 g protein, 0 mg cholesterol, 97 mg sodium

Potato Risotto

MODIFIED CLASSIC

Preparation time: About 10 minutes
Cooking time: About 35 minutes

This rich-tasting dish has the creamy texture of the famous Italian rice specialty—but it's made with shredded potatoes, cooked gently in chicken broth and finished with evaporated skim milk and a touch of Parmesan cheese. Serve it with sizzling grilled chicken breasts or veal chops.

1 tablespoon butter or margarine

1 small onion, finely chopped

½ teaspoon minced fresh thyme or ¼ teaspoon dry thyme

1 clove garlic, minced or pressed

1 can (about 14½ oz.) low-sodium chicken broth

3 medium-size thin-skinned potatoes (about 1¼ lbs. *total*)

¼ cup *each* evaporated skim milk and grated Parmesan cheese
  Freshly grated nutmeg
  Thyme sprigs

Melt butter in a 2- to 3-quart pan over medium heat. Add onion and minced thyme; cook, stirring often, until onion is soft but not browned (about 5 minutes). Stir in garlic, then add broth. Bring to a boil over high heat; boil, uncovered, until reduced to 1½ cups (about 3 minutes).

Peel and shred potatoes; add to onion mixture. Reduce heat to medium-low and cook, uncovered, stirring often, until potatoes are tender to bite (about 25 minutes). Remove from heat and stir in milk and cheese. Season to taste with nutmeg.

To serve, spoon potatoes into a serving bowl; garnish with thyme sprigs. Makes 4 to 6 servings.

Per serving: 152 calories (25% fat, 60% carbohydrates, 15% protein), 4 g total fat (2 g saturated fat), 23 g carbohydrates, 6 g protein, 10 mg cholesterol, 140 mg sodium

Spicy Baked Potato Sticks

NATURALLY LOW IN FAT

Preparation time: About 10 minutes
Baking time: About 1 hour

We offer two tempting flavor variations for these easy oven-fried potato wedges. Try them both!

  Olive oil cooking spray

1½ pounds small russet potatoes, scrubbed and cut lengthwise into quarters

½ teaspoon ground cumin

⅛ teaspoon ground red pepper (cayenne)
  Salt

Coat a shallow baking pan with cooking spray. Arrange potatoes, skin side down, in a single layer in pan; coat cut surfaces with cooking spray. Mix cumin and red pepper; sprinkle over potatoes. Bake in a 400° oven until potatoes are golden brown and tender when pierced (about 1 hour). Season to taste with salt. Makes 4 servings.

Per serving: 142 calories (5% fat, 86% carbohydrates, 9% protein), 0.9 g total fat (0 g saturated fat), 31 g carbohydrates, 3 g protein, 0 mg cholesterol, 14 mg sodium

Mustard-baked Potato Sticks

Follow directions for **Spicy Baked Potato Sticks,** but omit cumin and ground red pepper. Instead, combine 1 tablespoon *each* **vegetable oil** and **Dijon mustard** with 1 teaspoon **lemon juice;** drizzle over cut surfaces of potatoes before baking. Omit salt. Makes 4 servings.

Per serving: 176 calories (23% fat, 70% carbohydrates, 7% protein), 4 g total fat (0.4 g saturated fat), 31 g carbohydrates, 3 g protein, 0 mg cholesterol, 126 mg sodium

Italian Oven-fried Potatoes

MODIFIED CLASSIC

Preparation time: About 20 minutes
Baking time: 35 to 45 minutes

Fresh herbs, garlic, and Parmesan cheese enliven these richly browned potato chunks. They're good with lemon-drizzled chicken breasts.

- 2 **pounds red thin-skinned potatoes, scrubbed and cut into 1-inch chunks**
- 1 **to 2 tablespoons olive oil**
- 2 **tablespoons *each* minced fresh oregano and minced fresh basil; or 2 teaspoons *each* dry oregano and dry basil**
- 1 **clove garlic, minced or pressed**
- ⅓ **cup grated Parmesan cheese**
  Salt
  Oregano and basil sprigs

In a 10- by 15-inch rimmed baking pan, mix potatoes and oil. Bake in a 475° oven until potatoes are richly browned (35 to 45 minutes). After potatoes

have begun to brown (but not before then), turn them over several times with a wide spatula.

Transfer potatoes to a serving bowl and sprinkle with minced oregano and basil, garlic, and 3 tablespoons of the cheese. Stir to mix; season to taste with salt. Top with remaining cheese and garnish with oregano and basil sprigs. Makes 4 servings.

Per serving: 264 calories (26% fat, 63% carbohydrates, 11% protein), 8 g total fat (2 g saturated fat), 42 g carbohydrates, 7 g protein, 5 mg cholesterol, 141 mg sodium

Baked New Potatoes & Apples

Preparation time: About 15 minutes
Baking time: About 50 minutes

Potatoes and apples are classic partners. Here, they bake together in a flavorful, allspice-scented sauce of beef broth and apple juice.

- 2 **pounds small thin-skinned potatoes (*each* 1½ to 2 inches in diameter), scrubbed**
- 2 **medium-size onions, cut into 1-inch-wide wedges**
- 2 **tablespoons olive oil**
- 1 **pound red-skinned apples**
- 1¼ **cups beef broth**
- ¾ **cup apple juice**
- 2 **tablespoons cornstarch**
- ¾ **teaspoon ground allspice**

Place potatoes in a 9- by 13-inch baking pan. Separate onion wedges into layers and sprinkle over potatoes. Add oil and mix well. Bake in a 400° oven for 25 minutes, stirring occasionally.

Meanwhile, core apples and cut into ¾-inch-wide wedges. Also, in a small bowl, stir together broth, apple juice, cornstarch, and allspice.

When potatoes have baked for 25 minutes, add apples and juice mixture to pan; stir to combine. Continue to bake, spooning juices over apples and potatoes several times, until potatoes are very tender when pierced and juices begin to form thick bubbles (about 25 minutes). Makes 8 servings.

Per serving: 191 calories (18% fat, 75% carbohydrates, 7% protein), 4 g total fat (0.5 g saturated fat), 37 g carbohydrates, 3 g protein, 0 mg cholesterol, 140 mg sodium

Mashed Parsnips & Sunchokes

Preparation time: About 35 minutes
Cooking time: 45 to 50 minutes

For a rich-tasting alternative to potatoes, rice, or noodles, try this unusual blend of parsnips and sunchokes (Jerusalem artichokes). You simmer the vegetables in nutmeg-spiced chicken broth, then mash them together with a touch of butter and sour cream.

3   tablespoons vinegar or lemon juice
4   cups water
1½   pounds sunchokes (Jerusalem artichokes)
2   cups low-sodium chicken broth
2   pounds parsnips, peeled and cut into
     1-inch chunks
¼   teaspoon *each* ground nutmeg and
     ground white pepper
1   tablespoon butter or margarine
2   tablespoons reduced-fat sour cream
     or whipping cream
     Salt
     Chopped parsley

Prepare acid water by combining vinegar and water in a large bowl. Peel sunchokes and cut them into ½-inch cubes; as you cut cubes, immediately immerse them in acid water to prevent browning.

Drain sunchokes and place in a 3- to 4-quart pan. Add broth, parsnips, nutmeg, and white pepper. Bring to a boil over high heat; then adjust heat so mixture boils gently. Cover and cook until parsnips are soft enough to mash easily (about 35 minutes). Uncover, bring to a boil over high heat, and boil until liquid has evaporated (10 to 15 minutes); as liquid boils down, stir often and watch mixture carefully to avoid scorching.

Smoothly mash vegetables with an electric mixer or a potato masher (sunchokes may retain a little texture). Mix in butter and sour cream. Season to taste with salt; sprinkle with parsley. Makes 6 servings.

Per serving: 193 calories (16% fat, 76% carbohydrates, 8% protein), 3 g total fat (2 g saturated fat), 38 g carbohydrates, 4 g protein, 7 mg cholesterol, 50 mg sodium

Honey Carrots with Currants

Preparation time: About 15 minutes
Cooking time: About 15 minutes

Thin carrot sticks are cooked with honey and lemon just until tender, then dressed up with a tangy-sweet topping of orange juice, chutney, and currants. Offer the dish warm; or prepare both carrots and topping ahead, then serve cold.

1½   cups water
1½   pounds large carrots, cut into ⅛-inch-thick,
     3- to 4-inch-long sticks
2   tablespoons *each* honey and lemon juice
¼   cup dried currants
¼   cup Major Grey's chutney, minced
¼   cup orange juice
     Salt
     Finely slivered orange peel

In a 4- to 5-quart pan, bring water to a boil over high heat; add carrots, honey, and lemon juice. Cook, stirring often, until carrots are barely tender to bite (about 3 minutes). Drain carrots, reserving liquid; place carrots in a rimmed serving dish and keep warm.

Return cooking liquid to pan; bring to a boil over high heat. Boil, uncovered, until reduced to about ¼ cup (about 10 minutes). Add currants; stir until liquid begins to caramelize and currants look puffy. Stir in chutney. (At this point, you may let

carrots and currant topping cool, then cover and refrigerate separately for up to 1 day.)

To serve, stir orange juice into currant topping, then spoon topping over carrots. Season to taste with salt; sprinkle with orange peel. Makes 6 to 8 servings.

Per serving: 108 calories (2% fat, 94% carbohydrates, 4% protein), 0.2 g total fat (0 g saturated fat), 27 g carbohydrates, 1 g protein, 0 mg cholesterol, 136 mg sodium

Wine-poached Carrots

NATURALLY LOW IN FAT

Preparation time: About 15 minutes
Cooking time: 20 to 25 minutes

To enhance the natural sweetness of tender young carrots, try simmering them in a fruity white wine; we suggest a number of types below. On Napa Valley tables, this dish might be served with poached salmon or roast lamb.

1¼	**cups slightly sweet, fruity wine, such as Sauvignon Blanc, Chenin Blanc, gewürztraminer, Johannisberg Riesling, or white Zinfandel**
¾	**cup low-sodium chicken broth**
1	**teaspoon butter or margarine**
1½	**pounds small carrots (*each* about 5 inches long)**
	Salt
	Chervil or Italian parsley sprigs (optional)

In a wide frying pan, combine wine, broth, and butter. Bring to a boil over high heat. Add carrots; reduce heat, cover, and simmer, shaking pan occasionally, until carrots are tender when pierced (10 to 15 minutes).

Uncover pan; bring cooking liquid to a boil over high heat. Then boil, uncovered, shaking pan often, until liquid evaporates and carrots begin to brown (about 10 minutes). Season carrots to taste with salt; garnish with chervil sprigs, if desired. Makes 6 servings.

Per serving: 60 calories (14% fat, 76% carbohydrates, 10% protein), 1 g total fat (0.5 g saturated fat), 12 g carbohydrates, 1 g protein, 2 mg cholesterol, 55 mg sodium

Broccoli with Sherry-glazed Onions

NATURALLY LOW IN FAT

Preparation time: About 20 minutes
Cooking time: 20 to 25 minutes

A great choice for a buffet, this pretty vegetable combination features emerald broccoli topped with tiny onions in a sweet-sour sauce.

2	**pounds broccoli**
1	**package (about 1 lb.) frozen tiny onions, thawed**
1	**teaspoon olive oil**
1	**cup dry sherry or Madeira**
1	**cup low-sodium chicken broth**
¼	**cup sherry vinegar or cider vinegar**
¼	**cup firmly packed brown sugar**
2	**tablespoons dried currants**
1	**tablespoon cornstarch blended with 1⅓ cups cold water**
	Salt

Trim tough ends from broccoli stalks; peel stalks, if desired. Cut broccoli heads crosswise into 3-inch lengths. Cut stalks lengthwise into ⅓-inch-thick slices. Cut flowerets in half if they are thicker than 1½ inches; leave smaller flowerets whole.

In a 5- to 6-quart pan, cook broccoli, uncovered, in about 3 quarts boiling water just until barely tender when pierced (5 to 6 minutes). Drain well and arrange on a platter or in a shallow 3- to 4-quart casserole. Keep warm.

Wipe pan dry and add onions and oil. Cook over high heat, shaking pan often, until onions are browned (6 to 8 minutes). Remove onions from pan and set aside. Add sherry, broth, vinegar, sugar, and currants to pan. Bring to a boil; then boil, uncovered, until mixture is reduced to 1⅓ cups (6 to 8 minutes). Stir in cornstarch mixture; bring to a boil, stirring. Season to taste with salt.

Stir onions into hot sauce; pour over broccoli. Serve warm or at room temperature. Makes 8 to 10 servings.

Per serving: 116 calories (8% fat, 81% carbohydrates, 11% protein), 0.9 g total fat (0.1 g saturated fat), 19 g carbohydrates, 3 g protein, 0 mg cholesterol, 32 mg sodium

Sweet & Sour Broccoli

Preparation time: About 10 minutes
Cooking time: 5 to 8 minutes

It takes next to no time to dress up broccoli deliciously for dinner. Just toss the flowerets and sliced stalks with rice vinegar, soy sauce, and a little sugar.

	About 1 pound broccoli
½	**cup unseasoned rice vinegar**
1	**tablespoon sugar**
½	**teaspoon reduced-sodium soy sauce**

Trim tough ends from broccoli stalks; peel stalks, if desired. Cut stalks into ¼-inch-thick slanting slices; cut flowerets into bite-size pieces. Arrange all broccoli on a rack in a pan above about 1 inch of boiling water. Cover and steam, keeping water at a steady boil, just until tender when pierced (5 to 8 minutes). Place broccoli in a large bowl.

In a small bowl, stir together vinegar, sugar, and soy sauce; pour over warm broccoli and mix well. Drain immediately and serve. Makes 4 servings.

Per serving: 36 calories (5% fat, 75% carbohydrates, 20% protein), 0.2 g total fat (0 g saturated fat), 8 g carbohydrates, 2 g protein, 0 mg cholesterol, 49 mg sodium

Creamed Spinach in a Squash Shell

Preparation time: About 30 minutes
Cooking time: About 30 minutes

If you've been seeing the new hard-shell squash varieties in the market and wondering how to serve them, you'll be interested in this recipe. A steamed kabocha or kuri squash makes a festive edible bowl for lean, lemony creamed spinach.

	Steamed Squash (recipe follows)
1	**large onion, finely chopped**
¼	**cup water**
1¼	**cups low-sodium chicken broth**
3	**tablespoons all-purpose flour**
1	**cup reduced-fat sour cream**
1	**teaspoon *each* freshly grated nutmeg and grated lemon peel**
3	**packages (about 10 oz. *each*) frozen chopped spinach, thawed and squeezed dry**
	Salt and pepper
	Finely slivered lemon peel (optional)

Prepare Steamed Squash. While squash is cooking, combine onion and water in a wide frying pan. Cook over high heat, stirring occasionally, until liquid evaporates and onion begins to brown (about 10 minutes). To deglaze, add ¼ cup of the broth and stir to scrape browned bits free. Then continue to cook, stirring occasionally, until onion begins to brown again. Remove from heat and stir in flour. Gradually stir in remaining 1 cup broth and ½ cup of the sour cream; add nutmeg and the 1 teaspoon lemon peel. Bring to a boil over high heat, stirring; then boil, stirring, for 3 minutes. Remove from heat and stir in spinach. Pour one-quarter to one-half of the spinach mixture into a food processor or blender; whirl until puréed. Return purée to pan. Stir in remaining ½ cup sour cream; season to taste with salt and pepper.

Reheat spinach, if necessary. Fill hollowed-out squash with spinach; sprinkle with slivered lemon peel, if desired. Set lid in place, if desired. To serve, remove lid; scoop squash from the shell as you spoon out spinach. Makes 8 servings.

Steamed Squash. Use 1 squat, round **red kuri squash** (orange in color) or kabocha squash (green in color); choose a 4-pound squash, 7 to 8 inches in diameter. Rinse squash and pierce through top to center in 2 or 3 places, using a metal skewer. For easy handling, set squash on a piece of cheesecloth large enough to enclose it. Tie cheesecloth loosely on top of squash (leave some access to squash for testing).

Choose a 5- to 6-quart pan at least 1 inch wider than squash. Set squash on a rack in pan above ¾ to 1 inch **boiling water** (water should not touch squash). Cover and steam over medium heat, keeping water at a steady boil, until squash is very tender when pierced (about 30 minutes).

Protecting your hands, use cheesecloth to lift squash from pan; untie cloth. Neatly slice off top quarter of squash to make a lid. With a small spoon, gently scoop out seeds and discard; take care not to tear or poke a hole in shell (some kinds are more fragile, so handle carefully).

Per serving: 189 calories (21% fat, 64% carbohydrates, 15% protein), 5 g total fat (2 g saturated fat), 34 g carbohydrates, 8 g protein, 10 mg cholesterol, 96 mg sodium

Spiced Spinach

NATURALLY LOW IN FAT

Preparation time: About 20 minutes
Cooking time: About 25 minutes

Here's a perfect companion for plain poached or broiled fish: vivid fresh spinach that's seasoned Indian-style, with ginger, aromatic spices, and red pepper flakes.

1	teaspoon salad oil
1	large onion, thinly sliced
2	tablespoons water
2	cloves garlic, minced or pressed
1	tablespoon minced fresh ginger
½	teaspoon *each* ground cumin and ground coriander
¼	teaspoon *each* ground turmeric and crushed red pepper flakes
2	pounds spinach, stems removed, leaves rinsed and drained
	Salt
	Lemon wedges

In a 5- to 6-quart pan, combine oil, onion, water, garlic, ginger, cumin, coriander, turmeric, and red pepper flakes. Cook over medium heat, stirring often, until onion is golden brown (about 15 minutes).

Add as much spinach to pan as will fit. Cook, stirring often, until spinach begins to wilt, adding remaining spinach as space permits. When all spinach has been added, increase heat to high and continue to cook, stirring, until all spinach is wilted and almost all liquid has evaporated (7 to 10 minutes). Season to taste with salt and serve with lemon wedges. Makes 4 servings.

Per serving: 73 calories (20% fat, 54% carbohydrates, 26% protein), 2 g total fat (0.2 g saturated fat), 12 g carbohydrates, 5 g protein, 0 mg cholesterol, 132 mg sodium

Green Pea Pods with Red Onions

NATURALLY LOW IN FAT

Preparation time: About 25 minutes
Cooking time: About 5 minutes

Red onions in a seed-sprinkled vinaigrette are a bright, tangy topping for snow peas served cold or at room temperature.

4	cups water
½	cup red wine vinegar
1	teaspoon *each* mustard seeds and cumin seeds
2	large red onions, thinly sliced
1	teaspoon sugar
	Salt
2	pounds Chinese pea pods (also called snow or sugar peas), ends and strings removed

In a 5- to 6-quart pan, bring the 4 cups water to a boil over high heat. Add 5 tablespoons of the vinegar, mustard seeds, cumin seeds, and onions. Cook just until onions are limp (about 2 minutes). Pour into a fine strainer; drain well. In a medium-size bowl, stir together sugar and remaining 3 tablespoons vinegar; stir in drained onion-seed mixture. Season to taste with salt and set aside.

Rinse pan well. Then cook pea pods, uncovered, in pan in about 3 quarts boiling water just until they turn a brighter green (about 2 minutes). Drain pea pods well and arrange in a shallow 3- to 4-quart casserole. Let cool.

Just before serving, spoon onion mixture over pea pods. Makes 8 to 10 servings.

Per serving: 68 calories (5% fat, 74% carbohydrates, 21% protein), 0.4 g total fat (0 g saturated fat), 13 g carbohydrates, 4 g protein, 0 mg cholesterol, 10 mg sodium

***Fresh spinach**, available in most markets throughout the year, is an excellent source of vitamin A and potassium and a good source of vitamin C, riboflavin, and (when cooked) iron. An average-size bunch—about 12 ounces— contains only 90 calories.*

Chilled Sugar Snap Peas with Mint-Bacon Topping

Preparation time: About 25 minutes
Cooking time: About 3 minutes
Cooling time: At least 10 minutes

This crisp vegetable medley adds a colorful note to a festive dinner. You can cook the peas and make the sauce ahead, then cover and chill them for up to a day; bring the sauce to room temperature before pouring it over the peas.

1½   to 2 pounds sugar snap peas or Chinese pea pods (also called snow or sugar peas), ends and strings removed

1   tablespoon sugar

2   teaspoons cornstarch

½   cup *each* low-sodium chicken broth and unseasoned rice vinegar

2   tablespoons minced fresh mint

4   or 5 thick slices bacon (about 4 oz. *total*), crisply cooked, drained, and crumbled

In a 5- to 6-quart pan, cook peas, uncovered, in about 3 quarts boiling water until tender-crisp to bite (about 2 minutes). Drain, immerse in cold water until cool, and drain again. Arrange in a serving bowl and set aside.

In a small pan, mix sugar and cornstarch; then blend in broth and vinegar. Bring to boil over high heat, stirring. Remove from heat and let stand until cool (at least 10 minutes).

To serve, stir mint into sauce; pour sauce over peas and sprinkle with bacon. Makes 8 servings.

Per serving: 77 calories (26% fat, 53% carbohydrates, 21% protein), 2 g total fat (0.7 g saturated fat), 10 g carbohydrates, 4 g protein, 3 mg cholesterol, 73 mg sodium

Brussels Sprouts with Mustard Glaze

Preparation time: About 10 minutes
Cooking time: About 10 minutes

Fresh Brussels sprouts, steamed until tender and coated with a shiny mustard and brown sugar glaze, are delicious alongside simple entrées such as broiled chops or chicken breasts.

4   cups (about 1¼ lbs.) Brussels sprouts

3   tablespoons firmly packed brown sugar

2   tablespoons cider vinegar

1   tablespoon Dijon mustard

2   teaspoons butter or margarine
     Salt

Remove and discard coarse outer leaves from Brussels sprouts. Then rinse sprouts, drain, and place on a rack in a large pan above 1 inch of boiling water. Cover and steam, keeping water at a steady boil, until sprouts are tender when pierced (about 10 minutes).

When sprouts are almost done, combine sugar, vinegar, mustard, and butter in a wide nonstick frying pan. Cook over medium-high heat, stirring, until mixture bubbles vigorously. Stir in sprouts; season to taste with salt. Makes 4 servings.

Per serving: 116 calories (18% fat, 69% carbohydrates, 13% protein), 3 g total fat (1 g saturated fat), 22 g carbohydrates, 4 g protein, 5 mg cholesterol, 168 mg sodium

Sherried Green Beans & Peas

Preparation time: About 15 minutes
Cooking time: 5 to 7 minutes

Tender-crisp green beans and tiny peas, cooled and tossed with a simple sherry-soy sauce, make a refreshing side dish you can easily prepare ahead. Add the garnish—a sprinkling of diced bell pepper—just before serving.

1½	pounds tender green beans, ends removed
1	package (about 10 oz.) frozen tiny peas
2	teaspoons cornstarch
1	tablespoon minced fresh ginger
2	tablespoons reduced-sodium soy sauce
¼	cup dry sherry
½	cup water
1	tablespoon Oriental sesame oil
¼	cup finely diced red bell pepper

In a 4- to 5-quart pan, cook beans, uncovered, in about 3 quarts boiling water just until tender to bite (4 to 5 minutes). Stir in peas, then drain vegetables well. Immerse in cold water until cool, then drain and pour into a wide serving bowl or onto a rimmed platter.

In same pan, blend cornstarch, ginger, soy sauce, sherry, and the ½ cup water; bring to a boil over high heat, stirring. Remove from heat and let cool; stir in oil. (At this point, you may cover and refrigerate vegetables and sherry sauce separately for up to 1 day.)

To serve, pour sherry sauce over vegetables; mix gently. Sprinkle with bell pepper. Makes 8 to 10 servings.

Per serving: 70 calories (22% fat, 61% carbohydrates, 17% protein), 2 g total fat (0.2 g saturated fat), 10 g carbohydrates, 3 g protein, 0 mg cholesterol, 181 mg sodium

Almond-Zucchini Stir-steam

Preparation time: About 15 minutes
Cooking time: About 15 minutes

Stir-frying is a fine low-fat cooking method—but stir-steaming in liquid might be even better. These crisp zucchini sticks are cooked briefly in water and soy sauce; for a good-looking side dish, spoon them over rice and top with almonds.

½	cup slivered almonds
2	pounds zucchini, cut into ¼- by 2-inch sticks
2	cloves garlic, minced or pressed
2	tablespoons water

2	tablespoons reduced-sodium soy sauce
3	cups hot cooked rice

Toast almonds in a wide frying pan over medium heat until golden (about 5 minutes), stirring often. Pour out of pan and set aside.

To pan, add zucchini, garlic, and water. Cook over high heat, turning zucchini often with a wide spatula, until zucchini is tender-crisp to bite and all liquid has evaporated (about 8 minutes). Add soy sauce and stir to combine.

To serve, spoon rice into a serving bowl and pour zucchini over it; sprinkle with almonds. Makes 6 servings.

Per serving: 224 calories (25% fat, 63% carbohydrates, 12% protein), 6 g total fat (0.7 g saturated fat), 36 g carbohydrates, 7 g protein, 0 mg cholesterol, 208 mg sodium

Pasta Risotto with Asparagus

Preparation time: About 5 minutes
Cooking time: About 15 minutes

Simmered in broth and dotted with sliced fresh asparagus, tiny pasta shapes make a tempting "risotto" to accompany poultry or fish.

3	cups low-sodium chicken broth
1	cup dry tiny pasta shapes, such as stars, rice, or letters of the alphabet
2	cups 1-inch-long pieces of asparagus
½	cup grated Parmesan cheese

In a 2- to 3-quart pan, bring broth to a boil over high heat. Add pasta, reduce heat, and boil gently for 8 minutes. Add asparagus and continue to cook, stirring often, until pasta and asparagus are just tender to bite and almost all liquid has been absorbed (5 to 7 more minutes). Stir in ¼ cup of the cheese.

To serve, spoon risotto into a serving dish; sprinkle with remaining ¼ cup cheese. Makes 4 to 6 servings.

Per serving: 172 calories (20% fat, 57% carbohydrates, 23% protein), 4 g total fat (2 g saturated fat), 24 g carbohydrates, 10 g protein, 6 mg cholesterol, 184 mg sodium

Cauliflower with Toasted Mustard Seeds

30 MINUTES OR LESS

Preparation time: About 15 minutes
Cooking time: About 15 minutes

Steamed just until tender, mild-tasting cauliflower makes a delicious foil for a sprightly mustard-spiked yogurt sauce. Serve this cold side dish with juicy grilled lamb chops or a roast leg of lamb.

3	tablespoons mustard seeds
1½	cups plain low-fat or nonfat yogurt
¼	cup minced fresh mint or 2 tablespoons dry mint
2	teaspoons sugar
1	teaspoon ground cumin
1	large cauliflower (about 2 lbs.), stem and leaves trimmed
1	small head romaine lettuce (8 to 10 oz.), separated into leaves, rinsed, and crisped
	Mint sprigs (optional)

Toast mustard seeds in a small frying pan over medium heat until seeds turn gray (about 5 minutes), stirring often.

Place 2 tablespoons of the mustard seeds in a large bowl; stir in yogurt, minced mint, sugar, and cumin. Set aside.

Cut cauliflower into bite-size flowerets. Place flowerets on a rack in a 5- to 6-quart pan above 1 inch of boiling water. Cover; cook over high heat until cauliflower is tender when pierced (about 8 minutes). Immerse in cold water until cool; drain well on paper towels. Add cauliflower to yogurt-mint mixture and stir gently to coat cauliflower with sauce. (At this point, you may cover and refrigerate for up to 4 hours.)

To serve, arrange lettuce leaves on a platter. Spoon cauliflower mixture evenly over lettuce leaves. Sprinkle with remaining 1 tablespoon mustard seeds; garnish with mint sprigs, if desired. Makes 4 servings.

Per serving: 134 calories (26% fat, 48% carbohydrates, 26% protein), 4 g total fat (1 g saturated fat), 17 g carbohydrates, 9 g protein, 5 mg cholesterol, 79 mg sodium

Red Cabbage with Apple

Preparation time: About 10 minutes
Cooking time: About 1 hour

Perfect fare for a cold winter evening, this tempting sweet-tart dish combines shredded cabbage and apples with brown sugar, vinegar, and caraway seeds.

1	tablespoon salad oil
1	large onion, thinly sliced
1	medium-size head red cabbage (about 1½ lbs.), shredded
1	medium-size tart apple (about 6 oz.), peeled, cored, and shredded
1	large clove garlic, minced or pressed
1	teaspoon caraway seeds
2	tablespoons firmly packed brown sugar
½	cup red wine vinegar
1	cup water

Heat oil in a wide frying pan over medium heat. Add onion and cook, stirring often, until soft (about 5 minutes). Add cabbage and apple; cook, stirring often, for 5 minutes. Stir in garlic, caraway seeds, sugar, vinegar, and water.

Bring cabbage mixture to a boil over high heat; then reduce heat, cover, and simmer, stirring occasionally, until cabbage is very tender to bite and almost all liquid has evaporated (about 45 minutes). Makes 4 servings.

Per serving: 151 calories (22% fat, 70% carbohydrates, 8% protein), 4 g total fat (0.5 g saturated fat), 29 g carbohydrates, 3 g protein, 0 mg cholesterol, 23 mg sodium

Golden Acorn Squash

Preparation time: About 5 minutes
Baking time: About 50 minutes

Sweet acorn squash halves filled with hot orange-brandy sauce offer a good-looking way to warm up a winter meal.

2	tablespoons butter or margarine
2	acorn squash (about 1¼ lbs. *each*), cut lengthwise into halves and seeded

3 tablespoons *each* **firmly packed brown sugar and frozen orange juice concentrate (thawed)**

3 tablespoons **brandy or water**
Orange slices (optional)

Place 1 tablespoon of the butter in a 9- by 13-inch baking pan. Place pan in a 350° oven to melt butter; when butter is melted, tilt pan to coat bottom. Place squash halves, cut side down, in pan; return to oven and bake until tender when pierced (about 35 minutes).

Meanwhile, in a small pan, mix remaining 1 tablespoon butter, sugar, orange juice concentrate, and brandy. Bring to a boil over high heat, stirring; then remove from heat.

Turn squash halves cut side up. Pour brandy-butter mixture evenly into each half. Continue to bake until edges of squash halves are browned (about 15 more minutes). Transfer squash halves to a platter or individual plates, taking care not to spill sauce. Garnish with orange slices, if desired. Makes 4 servings.

Per serving: 224 calories (25% fat, 71% carbohydrates, 4% protein), 6 g total fat (4 g saturated fat), 38 g carbohydrates, 2 g protein, 16 mg cholesterol, 69 mg sodium

Broiled Pineapple with Basil

NATURALLY LOW IN FAT

Preparation time: About 10 minutes
Broiling time: 3 to 4 minutes

Hot pineapple drizzled with honey and cider vinegar has a tart-sweet flavor that perfectly complements teriyaki-seasoned grilled poultry, lamb, or pork.

¼ cup **honey**
2 tablespoons **cider vinegar**
1 tablespoon **finely chopped crystallized ginger**
1 teaspoon **dry basil**
1 **medium-size pineapple (about 3 lbs.), peeled and cored**
Basil sprigs (optional)

In a small pan, combine honey, vinegar, ginger, and dry basil. Stir over low heat until warm (about 3 minutes); set aside.

Cut pineapple crosswise into ½-inch-thick slices (or cut lengthwise into ½-inch-thick wedges). Arrange pineapple pieces in a single layer in a shallow baking pan; drizzle with honey mixture. Broil about 4 inches below heat until pineapple is lightly browned (3 to 4 minutes).

Using a wide spatula, transfer pineapple to a platter or individual plates. Spoon pan juices over pineapple; garnish with basil sprigs, if desired. Makes 4 to 6 servings.

Per serving: 133 calories (4% fat, 94% carbohydrates, 2% protein), 0.6 g total fat (0 g saturated fat), 35 g carbohydrates, 0.6 g protein, 0 mg cholesterol, 4 mg sodium

Fruited Rice Pilaf

Preparation time: About 10 minutes
Cooking time: 35 to 40 minutes

This chewy, high-fiber blend of brown rice, dried fruit, and peanuts is just right on your holiday table. Try it with turkey or baked ham.

2¼ cups **low-sodium chicken broth**
1 cup **long-grain brown rice**
1 teaspoon **butter or margarine**
¼ cup **dry-roasted peanuts**
¼ cup *each* **water, raisins, coarsely chopped dried apricots, and chopped pitted dates**

In a 2- to 3-quart pan, bring broth to a boil over high heat. Add rice; reduce heat, cover, and simmer until rice is tender to bite and all liquid has been absorbed (35 to 40 minutes).

About 5 minutes before rice is done, melt butter in a small frying pan over medium heat. Add peanuts and cook, stirring often, until golden (about 3 minutes). Pour out of pan and set aside. Add water, raisins, apricots, and dates to pan; cook, stirring, until fruit is softened (about 2 minutes). Add fruit mixture and peanuts to rice; stir well. Makes 4 to 6 servings.

Per serving: 262 calories (21% fat, 70% carbohydrates, 9% protein), 6 g total fat (1 g saturated fat), 47 g carbohydrates, 6 g protein, 2 mg cholesterol, 37 mg sodium

Wild Rice & Barley Pilaf

Preparation time: About 20 minutes
Cooking time: 1½ to 1¾ hours

Hearty two-grain pilaf, savory with sliced mushrooms, is a satisfying partner for roast meats or poultry.

1	small onion, minced
8	ounces mushrooms, sliced
1	clove garlic, minced or pressed
1	cup wild rice, rinsed and drained
3½	cups low-sodium chicken broth
½	cup pearl barley, rinsed and drained
	Salt and pepper

In a wide frying pan or a 2- to 3-quart pan, combine onion, mushrooms, garlic, and ½ cup water. Cook over high heat, stirring occasionally, until liquid evaporates and vegetables begin to brown (about 15 minutes). To deglaze, add 2 to 3 tablespoons water and stir to scrape browned bits free. Then continue to cook, stirring occasionally, until vegetables begin to brown again.

Repeat deglazing and browning steps 4 or 5 times, using 2 to 3 tablespoons water each time; vegetables should be richly browned (about 15 minutes *total*).

Stir rice and broth into mushroom mixture. Bring to a boil over high heat; reduce heat, cover, and simmer for 30 minutes. Stir in barley; cover and continue to simmer until rice and barley are tender to bite but just slightly chewy (30 to 40 more minutes). Season to taste with salt and pepper. Makes 6 servings.

Per serving: 189 calories (7% fat, 77% carbohydrates, 16% protein), 2 g total fat (0.3 g saturated fat), 37 g carbohydrates, 8 g protein, 0 mg cholesterol, 37 mg sodium

---

One of the oldest *of cultivated grains, nutritious barley is sold today mostly in "pearled" form—milled to remove the hull. The plump grains have a chewy texture and a mild, nutty flavor.*

Oat Pilaf with Hazelnuts & Scotch

Preparation time: About 20 minutes
Baking time: About 1 hour and 50 minutes

Whole oats that have been dried, toasted, and hulled are called groats; they're sold in well-stocked supermarkets and health-food stores. Simmered in beef broth and accented with toasted hazelnuts and a little Scotch, they make a distinctive pilaf.

¾	cup hazelnuts
2	large onions, chopped
6½	cups beef broth
3	cups oat groats (uncut grains)
6	tablespoons Scotch whisky
⅓	cup thinly sliced green onions

Spread hazelnuts in a shallow 3- to 3½-quart casserole and toast in a 350° oven until pale golden beneath skins (about 10 minutes). Let nuts cool slightly; then rub off as much of skins as possible with your fingers. Chop nuts coarsely and set aside.

Increase oven temperature to 400°. In casserole, combine chopped onions and ½ cup water. Bake until liquid has evaporated and onions are browned at edges (about 30 minutes). To deglaze, add ¼ cup of the broth and stir to scrape browned bits free.

Continue to bake, stirring occasionally, until onions begin to brown and stick to casserole again (about 20 minutes). Then repeat deglazing step, using ¼ cup more broth and stirring to scrape browned bits free; continue to bake until onions begin to brown again (about 20 minutes).

In a 2- to 3-quart pan, combine oats and remaining 6 cups broth. Bring to a boil over high heat. Add to casserole; stir to combine with onions. Cover casserole tightly and bake until oats are tender to bite (about 30 minutes). Uncover; stir in whisky. Sprinkle with hazelnuts and green onions. Makes 6 to 8 servings.

Per serving: 414 calories (30% fat, 54% carbohydrates, 16% protein), 13 g total fat (1 g saturated fat), 53 g carbohydrates, 16 g protein, 0 mg cholesterol, 771 mg sodium

Oven Pumpkin Risotto

MODIFIED CLASSIC

Preparation time: About 10 minutes
Baking time: About 45 minutes

This creamy baked risotto gets its rich golden hue from canned pumpkin. Garnish the dish with shavings of Parmesan cheese and a grating of nutmeg.

5	cups low-sodium chicken broth; or use canned or homemade (page 41) vegetable broth
2	cups medium- or short-grain white rice
1	can (about 1 lb.) solid-pack pumpkin
1	tablespoon grated lemon peel
¼	teaspoon ground nutmeg
⅓	cup shredded Parmesan cheese
	Parmesan cheese curls, cut with a vegetable peeler
	Freshly grated nutmeg (optional)

In a shallow 3- to 4-quart casserole, combine broth, rice, pumpkin, lemon peel, and the ¼ teaspoon nutmeg. Stir to mix well. Bake in a 400° oven until liquid begins to be absorbed (about 20 minutes). Stir again; then continue to bake, stirring often, until rice is tender to bite and mixture is creamy (about 25 more minutes). Stir in shredded cheese.

To serve, transfer to a serving dish; garnish with cheese curls. If desired, sprinkle lightly with grated nutmeg. Makes 6 servings.

Per serving: 311 calories (10% fat, 78% carbohydrates, 12% protein), 3 g total fat (2 g saturated fat), 60 g carbohydrates, 9 g protein, 4 mg cholesterol, 149 mg sodium

Winter Flower Bud Rice

Preparation time: About 10 minutes
Cooking time: About 35 minutes

When fresh cauliflower and broccoli are at their seasonal peak, try this savory, vegetable-studded rice alongside your favorite veal and turkey entrées.

2	cups cauliflower flowerets
2	cups broccoli flowerets
1	tablespoon butter or margarine
1	large onion, finely chopped
2	cloves garlic, minced or pressed
1	cup short-grain white rice
½	cup dry white wine
3	to 3¼ cups low-sodium chicken broth
⅔	cup grated Parmesan or Romano cheese
	Pepper

In a 3- to 4-quart pan, cook cauliflower, uncovered, in about 8 cups boiling water for 3 minutes. Add broccoli and continue to cook until both vegetables are barely tender when pierced (about 2 more minutes). Drain, immerse in cold water until cool, and drain again.

Melt butter in a wide nonstick frying pan over medium heat. Add onion and garlic. Cook, stirring often, until onion is soft but not browned (about 5 minutes). Add rice and cook, stirring often, until rice begins to look opaque (about 3 minutes). Stir in wine and 3 cups of the broth. Bring rice mixture to a boil, stirring. Then reduce heat and boil gently, uncovered, stirring occasionally, for 10 more minutes.

Stir cauliflower and broccoli into rice mixture. Continue to cook until rice is tender to bite and almost all broth has been absorbed (8 to 10 more minutes); add more broth if rice becomes too dry. Stir in ⅓ cup of the cheese; season to taste with pepper.

To serve, spoon rice mixture into a serving bowl and sprinkle with remaining ⅓ cup cheese. Makes 6 servings.

Per serving: 243 calories (22% fat, 61% carbohydrates, 17% protein), 6 g total fat (3 g saturated fat), 35 g carbohydrates, 10 g protein, 12 mg cholesterol, 232 mg sodium

Green Rice with Pistachios

Preparation time: About 25 minutes
Baking time: About 1 hour

To complement baked turkey breast, choose a festive casserole like this one. White rice is mixed with parsley, spinach, and green peppercorns, then topped with roasted pistachios.

2	cups long-grain white rice
5½	cups low-sodium chicken broth
½	teaspoon ground nutmeg
1½	tablespoons canned green peppercorns in brine, rinsed and drained
12	ounces spinach leaves, stems removed, leaves rinsed, drained, and finely chopped
1	cup minced parsley
½	cup salted roasted pistachio nuts, coarsely chopped

Spread rice in a shallow 3- to 3½-quart casserole (about 9 by 13 inches) and bake in a 350° oven, stirring occasionally, until light brown (about 35 minutes).

In a 2-quart pan, combine 5 cups of the broth, nutmeg, and peppercorns. Bring to a boil over high heat. Stir broth mixture into toasted rice. Cover casserole tightly and continue to bake until rice is tender to bite and broth has been absorbed (about 20 more minutes); stir after 10 and 15 minutes.

Uncover casserole and stir in spinach, ¾ cup of the parsley, and remaining ½ cup broth; bake for 5 more minutes. Stir rice mixture; sprinkle with pistachios and remaining ¼ cup parsley. Makes 8 to 10 servings.

Per serving: 218 calories (20% fat, 68% carbohydrates, 12% protein), 5 g total fat (0.8 g saturated fat), 37 g carbohydrates, 7 g protein, 0 mg cholesterol, 126 mg sodium

---

Do you forget about sage *unless you're making poultry stuffing? If so, think again. Used fresh or dry, this agreeable Mediterranean herb brings an aromatic savor to pork, veal, chicken, and lamb; it provides a lively accent for meatless dishes, too.*

Corn Risotto with Sage

Preparation time: About 15 minutes
Cooking time: 35 to 40 minutes

Sweet corn kernels and aromatic fresh sage distinguish this luscious Italian-style treat. Imported arborio rice gives the dish an especially creamy texture.

3	medium-size ears yellow or white corn, husks and silk removed
1	tablespoon butter or margarine
1	large onion, finely chopped
1	cup arborio or short-grain white rice
3½	cups low-sodium chicken broth; or use canned or homemade (page 41) vegetable broth
¼	cup grated Parmesan cheese
¼	cup shredded fontina cheese
3	tablespoons chopped fresh sage or 2 teaspoons dry sage
	Sage sprigs

Cut corn kernels from cobs; set kernels and cobs aside separately.

Melt butter in a wide frying pan over medium heat. Add onion and cook, stirring often, until soft but not browned (about 5 minutes). Add rice and cook, stirring often, until it begins to look opaque (about 3 minutes). Stir in about three-fourths of the corn kernels.

Pour broth into pan. Bring to a boil over high heat, stirring often. Reduce heat to low and simmer, stirring occasionally, until rice is tender to bite and almost all liquid has been absorbed (20 to 25 minutes); as mixture thickens, reduce heat to very low and stir more often.

Remove pan from heat. Hold corn cobs over pan and use the dull side of a knife to scrape corn juices from cobs into pan. Gently stir in Parmesan cheese, fontina cheese, and chopped sage. Let stand until cheese is melted (about 2 minutes).

To serve, transfer to a serving dish. Sprinkle with remaining corn kernels and garnish with sage sprigs. Makes 6 servings.

Per serving: 241 calories (22% fat, 65% carbohydrates, 13% protein), 6 g total fat (3 g saturated fat), 39 g carbohydrates, 8 g protein, 13 mg cholesterol, 159 mg sodium

You'll relish the color and zesty flavor that simple entrées gain from fruit chutney or savory vegetable marmalade.

LEMON CHUTNEY

Preparation time: About 30 minutes
Standing time: At least 4 hours
Cooking time: About 1¼ hours

6	to 8 medium-size lemons (2 to 2¼ lbs. *total*), thinly sliced and seeded
2	large onions, chopped
3	tablespoons salt
2	cups water
2	cups distilled white vinegar
4	cups sugar
1	cup raisins
¼	cup mustard seeds
2	teaspoons ground ginger
¼	to ½ teaspoon ground red pepper (cayenne)

Cut lemon slices into halves; place in a large bowl and stir in onions and salt. Cover and let stand at room temperature for at least 4 hours or up to 1 day.

Pour lemon mixture into a colander and rinse well; let drain. Transfer drained lemon mixture to a 5- to 6-quart pan and add 2 cups water. Bring to a boil over high heat; reduce heat and boil gently, uncovered, until lemon peel is very tender when pierced (about 15 minutes).

Stir in vinegar, sugar, raisins, mustard seeds, ginger, and red pepper. Stir over low heat until sugar is dissolved; increase heat to high and bring mixture to a boil. Reduce heat and simmer, uncovered, stirring occasionally, until reduced to 8 cups (about 1 hour). Let cool. Serve with grilled fish, chicken, or lamb. To store, cover and refrigerate for up to 3 months. Makes 8 cups.

Per tablespoon: 33 calories (3% fat, 94% carbohydrates, 3% protein), 0.1 g total fat (0 g saturated fat), 9 g carbohydrates, 0.2 g protein, 0 mg cholesterol, 18 mg sodium

RED PEPPER RELISH WITH AROMATICS

Preparation time: About 20 minutes
Cooking time: 20 to 25 minutes

1	to 1¼ pounds red bell peppers, seeded and thinly sliced
1	lemon, sliced and seeded
1	cup *each* unseasoned rice vinegar and water
1	cup sugar
1	tablespoon mustard seeds
1	teaspoon coriander seeds
¼	teaspoon fennel seeds
⅛	teaspoon *each* ground nutmeg and hulled cardamom seeds
3	or 4 whole cloves

Cut bell pepper slices into 1- to 1½-inch lengths. Cut lemon slices into quarters. In a 4- to 5-quart pan, combine peppers, lemon, vinegar, water, sugar, mustard seeds, coriander seeds, fennel seeds, nutmeg, cardamom seeds, and cloves. Bring to a boil over high heat; boil rapidly, stirring often, until almost all liquid has evaporated (about 20 minutes). As mixture thickens, stir often to prevent scorching. Serve warm or cold, with roast turkey, chicken, or pork. If made ahead, let cool; then cover and refrigerate for up to 1 week. Stir before serving. Makes about 1½ cups.

Per tablespoon: 42 calories (4% fat, 93% carbohydrates, 3% protein), 0.2 g total fat (0 g saturated fat), 10 g carbohydrates, 0.3 g protein, 0 mg cholesterol, 2 mg sodium

RED ONION–HORSERADISH MARMALADE

Preparation time: About 10 minutes
Cooking time: About 15 minutes

1	pound red onions, diced
1	tablespoon olive oil
2	tablespoons firmly packed brown sugar
⅓	cup *each* red wine vinegar and dry white wine
2	teaspoons prepared horseradish

In a wide frying pan, combine onions, oil, and sugar. Cover and cook over medium-high heat, stirring occasionally, until liquid has evaporated and onions are golden brown (about 8 minutes). Add vinegar, wine, and horseradish. Cook, uncovered, stirring often, until liquid has evaporated (about 6 minutes). Serve warm or cool, with grilled or roast beef or lamb. If made ahead, let cool; then cover and refrigerate for up to 3 days. Makes about 1 cup.

Per tablespoon: 30 calories (28% fat, 65% carbohydrates, 7% protein), 0.9 g total fat (0.1 g saturated fat), 5 g carbohydrates, 0.5 g protein, 0 mg cholesterol, 5 mg sodium

BREADS

Muffins, biscuits, scones, bagels, challah, sweet or savory rolls, and sturdy rye or wheat loaves—all are breads of one kind or another. And all play an important role in a low-fat diet, providing essential nutrients as well as mealtime satisfaction. Adding new breads to your repertoire is easy—and it's bound to reap rewards, both in compliments and in good eating. Following our fat-reduced recipes, you can make moist muffins and coffeecakes to serve with fresh fruit or juice for an appealing breakfast. At lunchtime, use seeded bagels or hearty rye bread as a delicious foundation for sandwiches of tuna, chicken, or reduced-fat cheese. And to bring variety to the dinner table, offer a basket of fla-vorful popovers, crunchy breadsticks, or herbed scones.

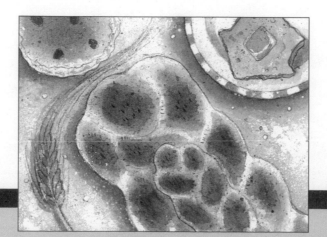

Whole-grain
Herb-Cheese Muffins

Preparation time: About 15 minutes
Baking time: About 20 minutes

Made with sautéed pepper and onion, these muffins are a savory choice for breakfast—and great for lunch and dinner, too.

2	tablespoons salad oil
1	large onion, minced
1	large green bell pepper (about 8 oz.), seeded and chopped
2	tablespoons honey
1	tablespoon Dijon mustard
1	cup nonfat milk
1	large egg
2	large egg whites (about ¼ cup)
6	tablespoons shredded Cheddar cheese
1	cup whole wheat flour
½	cup *each* all-purpose flour and yellow cornmeal
2	teaspoons baking powder
1	teaspoon dry thyme
⅛	teaspoon ground red pepper (cayenne)

Heat 1 tablespoon of the oil in a wide frying pan over medium heat. Add onion and bell pepper; cook, stirring often, until soft (8 to 10 minutes). Remove from heat and let cool.

In a large bowl, beat together remaining 1 tablespoon oil, honey, mustard, milk, egg, egg whites, and ¼ cup of the cheese; then stir in onion mixture. In another large bowl, stir together whole wheat flour, all-purpose flour, cornmeal, baking powder, thyme, and red pepper. Add milk mixture to flour mixture and stir just until dry ingredients are evenly moistened.

Spoon batter into 12 oiled or paper-lined 2½-inch muffin cups; cups will be about two-thirds full. Sprinkle with remaining 2 tablespoons cheese.

Bake in a 375° oven until muffins are well browned (about 20 minutes). Makes 12 muffins.

Per muffin: 159 calories (30% fat, 56% carbohydrates, 14% protein), 5 g total fat (1 g saturated fat), 23 g carbohydrates, 5 g protein, 22 mg cholesterol, 168 mg sodium

Oat Bran
Whole Wheat Muffins

MODIFIED CLASSIC

Preparation time: About 20 minutes
Baking time: 20 to 25 minutes

Applesauce, raisins, and cinnamon make these fiber-rich muffins moist and spicy.

3	cups oat bran
1	cup whole wheat flour
1	teaspoon ground cinnamon
1	tablespoon baking powder
1	teaspoon baking soda
¼	teaspoon salt
½	cup firmly packed brown sugar
1	cup raisins
½	cup chopped walnuts
4	large egg whites (about ½ cup)
½	cup honey
1¾	cups nonfat milk
½	cup unsweetened applesauce
¼	cup salad oil
1	teaspoon vanilla

In a large bowl, stir together oat bran, flour, cinnamon, baking powder, baking soda, and salt. Stir in sugar, raisins, and walnuts until evenly mixed.

In another bowl, beat egg whites, honey, milk, applesauce, oil, and vanilla until smoothly blended. Add milk mixture to bran mixture and stir just until dry ingredients are evenly moistened.

Spoon batter into 24 oiled or paper-lined 2½-inch muffin cups; cups will be full. Bake in a 400° oven until tops spring back when touched (20 to 25 minutes). Serve warm or cool. Makes 24 muffins.

Per muffin: 163 calories (28% fat, 62% carbohydrates, 10% protein), 6 g total fat (0.7 g saturated fat), 29 g carbohydrates, 4 g protein, 0.4 mg cholesterol, 158 mg sodium

When you bake muffins, *cut fat by using nonstick pans that need no oiling. If you use standard muffin pans, line them with paper baking cups or mist them with vegetable oil cooking spray.*

Coffee-Bran Muffins

Preparation time: About 15 minutes
Baking time: About 25 minutes

Wake up to the bracing flavor of hearty bran-raisin muffins made with dark corn syrup and a liberal measure of strong black coffee. Be sure you use unprocessed wheat bran (it's sold in health-food stores), *not* bran cereal.

1½	cups unprocessed wheat bran
1⅓	cups all-purpose flour
1	teaspoon baking soda
¼	cup butter or margarine, at room temperature
½	cup sugar
1	cup low-fat buttermilk
½	cup cold strong coffee
¼	cup dark corn syrup
1	large egg
¾	cup raisins

In a large bowl, stir together wheat bran, flour, and baking soda.

In a medium-size bowl, beat butter and sugar until smoothly blended. Add buttermilk, coffee, corn syrup, and egg; beat until blended. Add coffee mixture to flour mixture. Stir just until dry ingredients are evenly moistened, stirring in raisins with last few strokes (batter will be thin).

Spoon batter into 12 oiled or paper-lined 2½-inch muffin cups; cups will be full. Bake in a 375° oven until tops of muffins spring back when firmly pressed (about 25 minutes). Serve warm or cool. Makes 12 muffins.

Per muffin: 204 calories (25% fat, 68% carbohydrates, 7% protein), 6 g total fat (3 g saturated fat), 37 g carbohydrates, 4 g protein, 29 mg cholesterol, 183 mg sodium

Bran-Peach Muffins

Preparation time: About 15 minutes
Baking time: About 30 minutes

Tangy-sweet dried peach chunks stud these wholesome muffins. Bake them for a weekend breakfast or to serve alongside a salad at supper.

1	cup all-purpose flour
½	cup whole wheat flour
½	cup oat bran
2	teaspoons baking powder
¾	cup firmly packed brown sugar
1	teaspoon ground cinnamon
1½	cups firmly packed dried peaches, coarsely chopped
1	large egg white (about 2 tablespoons)
1¼	cups low-fat milk
2	tablespoons salad oil

In a large bowl, stir together all-purpose flour, whole wheat flour, oat bran, baking powder, sugar, and cinnamon. Add peaches and stir until evenly distributed.

In a medium-size bowl, beat egg white, milk, and oil until smoothly blended. Add milk mixture to flour mixture and stir just until dry ingredients are evenly moistened. Spoon batter into 12 oiled or paper-lined 2½-inch muffin cups.

Bake in a 350° oven until muffins are well browned (about 30 minutes). Serve warm or cool. Makes 12 muffins.

Per muffin: 218 calories (17% fat, 75% carbohydrates, 8% protein), 5 g total fat (0.8 g saturated fat), 44 g carbohydrates, 4 g protein, 2 mg cholesterol, 106 mg sodium

Spicy Zucchini Bran Muffins

Preparation time: About 15 minutes
Baking time: 25 to 30 minutes

These moist, distinctive muffins feature shredded zucchini, bran flakes, cinnamon, and ginger. You'll enjoy them warm or cool, at breakfast or with a bowl of soup at lunchtime.

2	cups bran flake cereal
1	cup shredded zucchini
¾	cup nonfat milk
1	large egg
⅔	cup sugar
¼	cup salad oil
1½	cups all-purpose flour
2½	teaspoons baking powder

2 teaspoons ground cinnamon
½ teaspoon ground ginger

In a large bowl, combine cereal, zucchini, milk, egg, sugar, and oil. Stir until cereal is moistened; set aside.

In a medium-size bowl, stir together flour, baking powder, cinnamon, and ginger. Add flour mixture to zucchini mixture and stir just until dry ingredients are evenly moistened.

Spoon batter into 12 paper-lined or oiled 2½-inch muffin cups. Bake in a 375° oven until muffins are browned and firm to the touch (25 to 30 minutes). Serve warm or cool. Makes 12 muffins.

Per muffin: 176 calories (26% fat, 66% carbohydrates, 8% protein), 5 g total fat (0.7 g saturated fat), 30 g carbohydrates, 4 g protein, 18 mg cholesterol, 176 mg sodium

Citrus Muffins
. . . .

Preparation time: About 25 minutes
Baking time: 18 to 20 minutes

These oatmeal-date muffins get their baked-in marmalade flavor from grapefruit juice and a generous amount of grated orange peel.

1 cup *each* all-purpose flour and quick-cooking rolled oats
¼ cup seven-grain cereal or quick-cooking rolled oats
2 teaspoons baking powder
½ teaspoon baking soda
¼ cup butter or margarine, at room temperature
¼ cup sugar
5 tablespoons grated orange peel
1 large egg
¾ cup grapefruit or orange juice
1 cup chopped pitted dates

In a large bowl, stir together flour, oats, cereal, baking powder, and baking soda. In a medium-size bowl, beat butter, sugar, and orange peel until smoothly blended. Beat in egg; then stir in grapefruit juice and dates. Add egg mixture to flour mixture and stir just until dry ingredients are evenly moistened.

Spoon batter into 10 oiled or paper-lined 2½-inch muffin cups. Bake in a 400° oven until muffins are deep golden brown (18 to 20 minutes). Serve warm or cool. Makes 10 muffins.

Per muffin: 229 calories (27% fat, 66% carbohydrates, 7% protein), 7 g total fat (3 g saturated fat), 39 g carbohydrates, 4 g protein, 34 mg cholesterol, 215 mg sodium

Apricot-Blackberry Cornmeal Kuchen
. . . .

Preparation time: About 15 minutes
Baking time: 30 to 35 minutes

Apricots and fresh ripe blackberries (or boysenberries, if you like) share the spotlight in a luscious coffeecake that's just right for a summertime brunch or breakfast.

½ cup *each* all-purpose flour and yellow cornmeal
1½ teaspoons baking powder
1 large egg
⅓ cup firmly packed brown sugar
½ cup low-fat buttermilk
2 tablespoons salad oil
5 medium-size apricots (about 12 oz. *total*), halved and pitted
10 blackberries or boysenberries
2 tablespoons granulated sugar

In a large bowl, stir together flour, cornmeal, and baking powder. In a medium-size bowl, beat egg, brown sugar, buttermilk, and oil until smoothly blended. Add egg mixture to flour mixture; stir just until dry ingredients are evenly moistened.

Spread batter in an oiled 8-inch-round baking pan or quiche pan. Gently press apricot halves, pitted side up, into batter. Place a berry in hollow of each apricot half.

Bake in a 350° oven until center of cake feels firm when lightly touched (30 to 35 minutes). Sprinkle with granulated sugar. Let cake cool slightly, then cut into wedges and serve warm. Makes 6 to 8 servings.

Per serving: 204 calories (25% fat, 67% carbohydrates, 8% protein), 6 g total fat (0.9 g saturated fat), 35 g carbohydrates, 4 g protein, 31 mg cholesterol, 137 mg sodium

Gingerbread-Apple Coffeecake

. . . .

Preparation time: About 25 minutes
Cooking time: About 12 minutes
Baking time: About 40 minutes

Great for a weekend brunch, this spicy coffeecake is good for dessert, too.

3	**tablespoons butter or margarine**
6	**cups peeled, sliced tart apples**
¼	**cup granulated sugar**
¼	**cup bourbon or apple juice**
1	**cup *each* dark molasses and water**
1	**teaspoon baking soda**
½	**cup (¼ lb.) butter or margarine, at room temperature**
1	**cup firmly packed brown sugar**
2	**large eggs**
2	**cups all-purpose flour**
1	**tablespoon baking powder**
2	**teaspoons *each* ground cinnamon and ground ginger**
¼	**teaspoon ground cloves**

Melt the 3 tablespoons butter in a wide frying pan over medium-high heat. Add apples and cook, turning often with a wide spatula, until just tender when pierced (about 5 minutes). Stir in granulated sugar and bourbon; cook until liquid evaporates and apples begin to brown (about 6 minutes). Spread apple mixture evenly in a well-buttered 9- by 13- inch baking pan; set aside.

In a 1- to 2-quart pan, combine molasses and water; bring to a boil over high heat. Stir in baking soda, remove from heat, and let cool.

In a large bowl, beat the ½ cup butter and brown sugar until smoothly blended. Beat in eggs. In another bowl, stir together flour, baking powder,

---

Quick fruit breads *like those on the facing page taste best—and slice most neatly—if you let them cool completely. For the fullest flavor, wrap the loaves airtight and let them stand at room temperature for up to a day before serving.*

---

cinnamon, ginger, and cloves. Stir flour mixture and molasses mixture alternately into egg mixture, blending well after each addition.

Spread batter evenly over apples in baking pan. Bake in a 350° oven until cake begins to pull away from sides of pan and center springs back when lightly pressed (about 40 minutes). Run a knife around sides of pan; invert cake onto a platter. Serve warm or cool. Makes 12 servings.

Per serving: 368 calories (29% fat, 67% carbohydrates, 4% protein), 12 g total fat (7 g saturated fat), 64 g carbohydrates, 3 g protein, 65 mg cholesterol, 371 mg sodium

Buttermilk Doughnut Coffeecake

. . . .

Preparation time: About 20 minutes
Baking time: About 20 minutes
Standing time: 5 to 10 minutes

This whimsical coffeecake looks like a big doughnut. It tastes like one, too: it's made with doughnut batter baked in a ring mold or tube pan. Soak the cake with a tangy orange syrup, then serve it fresh and warm.

2	**cups all-purpose flour**
2	**teaspoons baking powder**
½	**teaspoon baking soda**
1	**teaspoon ground cinnamon**
½	**teaspoon ground nutmeg**
1	**large egg**
⅓	**cup granulated sugar**
½	**cup low-fat buttermilk**
3	**tablespoons butter or margarine, melted**
	Orange Syrup (recipe follows)
⅓	**cup powdered sugar**

In a large bowl, stir together flour, baking powder, baking soda, cinnamon, and nutmeg. In a small bowl, beat egg, granulated sugar, buttermilk, and butter until smoothly blended. Add egg mixture to flour mixture and stir just until dry ingredients are evenly moistened (batter will be stiff).

Spread batter evenly in an oiled 4-cup (8-inch-diameter) metal ring mold or 8- to 9-inch tube pan. Bake in a 375° oven until richly browned (about 20 minutes). Meanwhile, prepare Orange Syrup.

Remove cake from oven. With a long, slender skewer, pierce cake at ½-inch intervals, piercing all the way through to pan each time. Immediately spoon Orange Syrup onto cake, letting syrup soak in completely between additions. Let stand for 5 to 10 minutes, then invert cake onto a platter. Ladle any free-flowing syrup back onto cake. Sift powdered sugar onto cake. Makes 6 to 8 servings.

Orange Syrup. In a small pan, combine 2 cups **orange juice** and ⅔ cup **sugar**. Bring to a boil over medium-high heat; then boil, uncovered, until reduced to 1½ cups (about 5 minutes).

Per serving: 364 calories (17% fat, 77% carbohydrates, 6% protein), 7 g total fat (4 g saturated fat), 71 g carbohydrates, 6 g protein, 44 mg cholesterol, 308 mg sodium

Apricot Tea Bread

Preparation time: About 15 minutes
Baking time: About 1 hour

Delicious at teatime, this quick loaf is packed with golden raisins, apricots, and almonds.

2	cups all-purpose flour
2	teaspoons baking powder
¼	teaspoon baking soda
1	large egg
2	large egg whites (about ¼ cup)
¾	cup sugar
¼	cup butter or margarine, at room temperature
1	tablespoon finely shredded orange peel
¼	cup orange juice
¾	cup reduced-fat sour cream
1½	cups dried apricots, cut into pieces
2	cups golden raisins
¼	cup sliced almonds

In a large bowl, stir together flour, baking powder, and baking soda. In a medium-size bowl, beat egg, egg whites, sugar, butter, and orange peel until smoothly blended. Stir in orange juice and sour cream. Add egg mixture to flour mixture and beat to blend. Stir in apricots, raisins, and almonds.

Pour batter into an oiled, floured 5- by 9-inch loaf pan (or use a nonstick pan). Spread batter evenly in pan and smooth top. Bake in a 350° oven until loaf begins to pull away from sides of pan and a wooden skewer inserted in center comes out clean (about 1 hour). Turn out of pan onto a rack; let cool completely. Makes 1 loaf (about 16 servings).

Per serving: 241 calories (21% fat, 72% carbohydrates, 7% protein), 6 g total fat (3 g saturated fat), 45 g carbohydrates, 5 g protein, 25 mg cholesterol, 124 mg sodium

Applesauce Raisin Bread

Preparation time: About 15 minutes
Baking time: About 1 hour

This moist, fragrant bread is so good that it's bound to disappear in a flash. If you can, though, try to save a few slices for tomorrow; the spicy bread makes wonderful toast.

1½	cups all-purpose flour
½	cup whole wheat flour
2	teaspoons baking powder
½	teaspoon *each* baking soda and ground cinnamon
1	teaspoon ground nutmeg
1	large egg
1	jar (about 15 oz.) unsweetened applesauce
2	tablespoons salad oil
½	cup granulated sugar
¼	cup firmly packed brown sugar
1	cup raisins
½	cup chopped walnuts

In a large bowl, stir together all-purpose flour, whole wheat flour, baking powder, baking soda, cinnamon, and nutmeg. In another large bowl, beat egg, applesauce, and oil until smoothly blended. Stir in granulated sugar and brown sugar until well blended. Add egg mixture to flour mixture and stir just until dry ingredients are evenly moistened. Stir in raisins and walnuts.

Spread batter in an oiled 5- by 9-inch loaf pan. Bake in a 350° oven until bread is richly browned and a wooden skewer inserted in center comes out clean (about 1 hour). Let cool in pan for 10 minutes; then turn out onto a rack and let cool completely. Makes 1 loaf (about 12 servings).

Per serving: 238 calories (23% fat, 70% carbohydrates, 7% protein), 6 g total fat (0.8 g saturated fat), 43 g carbohydrates, 4 g protein, 18 mg cholesterol, 144 mg sodium

Cornbread

Preparation time: About 5 minutes
Baking time: About 30 minutes

Especially easy to make, this mildly sweet buttermilk cornbread is a perfect accompaniment to chilis and other spicy dishes. Try it with Ground Turkey Chili Mole (page 115) or Cuban-style Mini-Roast with Black Beans & Rice (page 84). If you prefer bread with a nippier flavor, add diced green chiles to the batter.

1	cup *each* yellow cornmeal and all-purpose flour
4	teaspoons baking powder
¼	teaspoon salt
1	large egg
2	large egg whites (about ¼ cup)
1	cup low-fat buttermilk
2	tablespoons butter or margarine, melted
3	tablespoons honey

In a large bowl, stir together cornmeal, flour, baking powder, and salt. In a medium-size bowl, beat egg, egg whites, buttermilk, butter, and honey until blended. Add buttermilk mixture to flour mixture and stir just until dry ingredients are evenly moistened.

Spread batter in an 8-inch-square nonstick (or oiled regular) baking pan. Bake in a 375° oven until bread pulls away from sides of pan and a wooden pick inserted in center comes out clean (about 30 minutes). Serve warm or at room temperature. Makes 8 servings.

Per serving: 197 calories (19% fat, 69% carbohydrates, 12% protein), 4 g total fat (2 g saturated fat), 34 g carbohydrates, 6 g protein, 36 mg cholesterol, 396 mg sodium

Chile Cornbread

Follow directions for **Cornbread**, but stir 1 large can (about 7 oz.) **diced green chiles** into egg mixture before combining with flour mixture. Makes 8 servings.

Per serving: 203 calories (19% fat, 69% carbohydrates, 12% protein), 4 g total fat (2 g saturated fat), 36 g carbohydrates, 6 g protein, 36 mg cholesterol, 547 mg sodium

Apricot–Oat Bran Scones

Preparation time: About 15 minutes
Baking time: About 15 minutes

Fiber—both soluble and insoluble—adds substance to these updated scones. Split in half and spread with honey or preserves, they're nice with breakfast coffee or afternoon tea. Or serve them at lunch, perhaps alongside Pineapple, Strawberry & Apple Salad (page 47).

1	cup *each* all-purpose flour and whole wheat flour
¼	cup sugar
4	teaspoons baking powder
2	cups oat bran flake cereal
¼	cup cold butter or margarine, cut into pieces
1	large egg
⅔	cup low-fat milk
½	cup chopped dried apricots or pitted prunes

In a food processor or a large bowl, whirl or stir together all-purpose flour, whole wheat flour, sugar, baking powder, and cereal. Add butter; whirl (or cut in with a pastry blender or 2 knives) until mixture resembles coarse crumbs. Add egg and milk; whirl or stir just until dry ingredients are evenly moistened. Then stir in apricots until evenly distributed.

Turn dough out onto a lightly floured board and knead briefly. Divide into thirds. Pat each portion into a 5-inch round about ½ inch thick. With a floured knife, cut each round into 6 wedges.

Arrange wedges on an oiled baking sheet and

bake in a 400° oven until lightly browned (about 15 minutes). Transfer to a rack and let cool briefly. Makes 18 scones.

Per scone: 125 calories (25% fat, 65% carbohydrates, 10% protein), 4 g total fat (2 g saturated fat), 21 g carbohydrates, 3 g protein, 19 mg cholesterol, 201 mg sodium

Marjoram Scones

Preparation time: About 10 minutes
Baking time: About 25 minutes

Herb-seasoned, currant-flecked whole wheat triangles are a delightful accompaniment for soups, salads, or hearty stews. You'll enjoy them with Rich Brown Braised Beef (page 70).

1½	cups all-purpose flour
½	cup whole wheat flour
½	teaspoon *each* salt and baking soda
1	teaspoon dry marjoram
2	teaspoons baking powder
2	tablespoons sugar
¼	cup cold butter or margarine, cut into pieces
½	cup dried currants
¾	cup low-fat buttermilk

In a food processor or a large bowl, whirl or stir together all-purpose flour, whole wheat flour, salt, baking soda, marjoram, baking powder, and sugar. Add butter; whirl (or cut in with a pastry blender or 2 knives) until mixture resembles coarse crumbs.

Add currants; whirl or stir just until currants are evenly distributed. Add buttermilk; then whirl or stir just until dry ingredients are evenly moistened.

Turn dough out onto a lightly floured board and knead briefly; then pat dough into a 6½-inch round. Place dough round on an oiled baking sheet. With a knife, score dough into 8 equal wedges. Bake in a 425° oven until well browned (about 25 minutes). To serve, break or cut into wedges. Makes 8 scones.

Per scone: 214 calories (28% fat, 63% carbohydrates, 9% protein), 7 g total fat (4 g saturated fat), 35 g carbohydrates, 5 g protein, 16 mg cholesterol, 421 mg sodium

Southwest Blue Cornbread Sticks

Preparation time: About 20 minutes
Baking time: About 25 minutes

A staple in the Southwest, blue cornmeal is now available in other parts of the country, too; you'll find it in specialty food shops and many well-stocked supermarkets. Though interchangeable with familiar yellow or white cornmeal, it does add a distinctive parched-corn flavor to tortillas and baked goods—such as these chile-cheese cornsticks.

1	cup plus 2 tablespoons blue cornmeal
2	tablespoons salad oil
1	medium-size onion, finely chopped
1	small fresh jalapeño chile, seeded and finely chopped
1	cup all-purpose flour
1	tablespoon *each* sugar and baking powder
1	large egg
1¼	cups nonfat milk
½	cup shredded reduced-fat jack cheese

Use 2 tablespoons of the cornmeal to coat oiled cornstick pans or 1½-inch muffin pans; set pans aside.

Heat the 2 tablespoons oil in a medium-size nonstick frying pan over medium heat. Add onion and chile; cook, stirring often, until onion is lightly browned (6 to 8 minutes). Set aside.

In a large bowl, stir together flour, sugar, baking powder, and remaining 1 cup cornmeal. In a medium-size bowl, beat egg and milk until well blended. Add egg mixture, cheese, and onion mixture to cornmeal mixture; stir just until dry ingredients are evenly moistened.

Spoon batter into pans, filling almost to rims. Bake in a 375° oven until cornsticks are lightly browned and feel firm when lightly pressed (about 25 minutes). Let cool in pans on a rack for about 10 minutes, then loosen carefully and remove from pans. Serve warm. Makes 14 cornsticks.

Per cornstick: 132 calories (29% fat, 58% carbohydrates, 13% protein), 4 g total fat (0.9 g saturated fat), 19 g carbohydrates, 4 g protein, 18 mg cholesterol, 147 mg sodium

Irish Soda Bread

Preparation time: About 15 minutes
Baking time: About 40 minutes

This hearty round loaf, made with just 2 table-spoons of butter, is studded with currants and caraway seeds. For a satisfying afternoon snack, cut it into thick slices and serve with strong hot tea.

1	cup all-purpose flour
2	cups whole wheat flour
2	tablespoons firmly packed brown sugar
1	teaspoon *each* salt and baking soda
2	tablespoons cold butter or margarine, cut into pieces
1	cup dried currants
1	teaspoon caraway seeds
1¼	cups low-fat buttermilk
1	tablespoon milk

In a food processor or a large bowl, whirl or stir together all-purpose flour, whole wheat flour, sugar, salt, and baking soda. Add butter; whirl (or cut in with a pastry blender or 2 knives) until mixture resembles coarse crumbs. Add currants and caraway seeds; whirl or stir just until evenly distributed. Add buttermilk and whirl or stir just until dry ingredients are evenly moistened.

Turn dough out onto a lightly floured board and knead briefly; then pat into a 7-inch round. Place dough round on an oiled baking sheet. Brush with milk. With a sharp knife, cut a ½-inch-deep cross in top of dough.

Bake in a 375° oven until bread is golden all over and sounds hollow when tapped (about 40 minutes). Transfer to a rack and let cool. To serve, cut into thick slices. Makes 1 loaf (about 8 servings).

Per serving: 274 calories (15% fat, 74% carbohydrates, 11% protein), 5 g total fat (2 g saturated fat), 53 g carbohydrates, 8 g protein, 10 mg cholesterol, 508 mg sodium

---

Quick breads *made by the biscuit method— such as the Irish Soda Bread above and the scones on pages 178 and 179—require a light touch. Rough treatment will toughen these breads, especially if the dough is very low in fat.*

Whole Wheat Popovers

MODIFIED CLASSIC

Preparation time: 5 to 10 minutes
Baking time: 45 to 50 minutes

Made with broth instead of the usual milk, these popovers are good with breakfast, lunch, or dinner. The batter is easy to whirl together in the blender. For best results, prepare the pans before you mix up the batter, and serve the hot popovers as soon as they're done.

	Vegetable oil cooking spray
3	large eggs
1	cup low-sodium chicken broth
⅓	cup whole wheat flour
⅔	cup all-purpose flour

Coat six 6-ounce custard cups or 2¾-inch muffin cups with cooking spray.

In a blender or food processor, combine eggs, broth, whole wheat flour, and all-purpose flour. Whirl until smoothly blended. Immediately pour batter into prepared cups.

Bake in a 375° oven until popovers are very well browned and firm to the touch (45 to 50 minutes). Run a knife between each cup and popover; invert cups to remove popovers. Serve hot. Makes 6 popovers.

Per popover: 118 calories (26% fat, 54% carbohydrates, 20% protein), 3 g total fat (0.9 g saturated fat), 16 g carbohydrates, 6 g protein, 106 mg cholesterol, 41 mg sodium

Blueberry Whole Wheat Pancakes

30 MINUTES OR LESS

Preparation time: About 10 minutes
Cooking time: About 20 minutes

Fresh blueberries make these pancakes a sweet morning treat. They're marvelous plain, but you can top them with powdered sugar or your favorite syrup if you like.

- ¾ cup *each* all-purpose flour and whole wheat flour
- 2 teaspoons baking powder
- 4 teaspoons sugar
- 2 large egg whites (about ¼ cup)
- 1¼ cups nonfat milk
- 1½ tablespoons salad oil
- ¼ cup blueberries

In a small bowl, stir together all-purpose flour, whole wheat flour, baking powder, and sugar. In a large bowl, beat egg whites, milk, and oil until smoothly blended. Add flour mixture to milk mixture and stir until just dry ingredients are evenly moistened (batter will be lumpy). Then stir in blueberries.

Heat a wide nonstick frying pan over medium heat. Lightly oil pan, if necessary. For each pancake, spoon about 3 tablespoons batter into hot pan; spread to make a 4-inch circle (you can cook about 4 pancakes at a time).

Cook until pancakes are bubbly on top and browned on bottom (about 3 minutes); then turn and cook until browned on other side (about 2 more minutes). Makes 4 servings (about 16 pancakes *total*).

Per serving: 264 calories (20% fat, 65% carbohydrates, 15% protein), 6 g total fat (0.8 g saturated fat), 44 g carbohydrates, 10 g protein, 2 mg cholesterol, 314 mg sodium

Ginger Whole Wheat Pancakes

. . . .

Preparation time: About 25 minutes
Cooking time: 10 to 15 minutes

Crystallized ginger accents griddlecakes made with cider and yogurt. The topping is spicy, too; it's a simple blend of maple syrup and apple butter. (If you enjoy the flavors of ginger and apples, you might also try Gingerbread-Apple Coffeecake, page 176.)

- 1⅓ cups all-purpose flour
- 1 cup whole wheat flour
- ⅓ cup powdered sugar
- 3 tablespoons minced crystallized ginger
- 1½ teaspoons baking soda
- 1 teaspoon *each* baking powder and ground cinnamon
- 1 cup *each* apple cider and vanilla low-fat yogurt
- 2 large eggs
- 2 tablespoons butter or margarine, melted
    Salad oil
    Spiced Apple Syrup (recipe follows)

In a large bowl, stir together all-purpose flour, whole wheat flour, sugar, ginger, baking soda, baking powder, and cinnamon. In a medium-size bowl, beat cider, yogurt, eggs, and butter until smoothly blended. Add to flour mixture and stir just until dry ingredients are evenly moistened.

Heat a regular or nonstick griddle or wide frying pan over medium heat. Lightly oil griddle, if necessary. For each pancake, spoon about ¼ cup batter onto hot griddle; spread to make a 4-inch circle. Cook until pancakes are bubbly on top and browned on bottom (about 1 minute); then turn and cook until browned on other side (about 1 more minute). Meanwhile, prepare Spiced Apple Syrup.

Serve pancakes with Spiced Apple Syrup to add to taste. Makes 6 servings (about 24 pancakes *total*).

Spiced Apple Syrup. In a small pan, combine ½ cup **apple butter** and 1 cup **maple syrup.** Cook over medium heat, stirring often, until smoothly blended and heated through (3 to 5 minutes). Makes about 1½ cups.

Per serving of pancakes: 333 calories (18% fat, 71% carbohydrates, 11% protein), 7 g total fat (3.2 g saturated fat), 60 g carbohydrates, 10 g protein, 83 mg cholesterol, 489 mg sodium

Per tablespoon of Spiced Apple Syrup: 45 calories (1% fat, 99% carbohydrates, 0% protein), 0 g total fat (0 g saturated fat), 12 g carbohydrates, 0 g protein, 0 mg cholesterol, 1 mg sodium

LIGHT BREAKFASTS

A good breakfast starts the day right! That may not be new advice, but it's still sound. Here are a few tasty ways to vary your morning routine.

PEACH SMOOTHIE

Preparation time: About 15 minutes
Freezing time: About 2 hours

3   medium-size peaches (about 1 lb. *total*), peeled and pitted
    Lemon juice
⅓   cup low-fat buttermilk
2   to 4 teaspoons sugar, or to taste

Cut peaches into about ¾-inch chunks (you should have 1½ to 2 cups). Dip peach chunks in lemon juice to coat, then set slightly apart in a single layer in a shallow metal pan.

Cover pan and freeze until fruit is solid (about 2 hours). With a wide spatula, slide peach chunks from pan into freezer containers; return to freezer until ready to use.

To prepare smoothie, use 1½ cups of the frozen peaches. Let peaches stand at room temperature until slightly softened (about 5 minutes). Pour buttermilk into a blender or food processor. With motor running, add peach chunks, a few at a time (keep top of blender covered to prevent splashing); whirl until mixture is slushy. Blend in sugar. Pour into a glass and serve at once. Makes 1 serving.

Per serving: 229 calories (4% fat, 88% carbohydrates, 8% protein), 1 g total fat (0.5 g saturated fat), 55 g carbohydrates, 5 g protein, 3 mg cholesterol, 85 mg sodium

WILD RICE BREAKFAST

Preparation time: About 10 minutes
Standing time: At least 4 hours
Cooking time: 20 to 35 minutes

Quick-simmered Wild Rice (recipe follows)
1   tablespoon butter or margarine
1   teaspoon ground cinnamon
2   to 4 tablespoons firmly packed brown sugar
1   large Golden Delicious apple (about 8 oz.), peeled, cored, and thinly sliced
1   medium-size banana, sliced
    About 1½ cups warm low-fat or nonfat milk

Prepare Quick-simmered Wild Rice.

Melt butter in a wide frying pan over medium heat; add cinnamon and 2 tablespoons of the sugar. Add apple and cook, turning with a wide spatula as needed, until translucent (3 to 4 minutes). Add banana and heat until warm, turning slices with spatula once (about 3 minutes).

Spoon rice into bowls and top with fruit mixture; offer milk and more sugar to add to taste. Makes 4 to 6 servings.

Quick-simmered Wild Rice. Place 1 cup **wild rice** in a fine wire strainer; rinse with **cold water.**

In a 1½- to 2-quart pan, bring 2 cups **water** to a boil over high heat. Add drained rice; cover, remove from heat, and let stand for at least 4 hours or up to 12 hours. Bring rice mixture to a boil over high heat; reduce heat and simmer, covered, until grains begin to split and are tender to bite yet slightly chewy (10 to 25 minutes). Remove from heat.

Per serving: 246 calories (15% fat, 73% carbohydrates, 12% protein), 4 g total fat (2 g saturated fat), 47 g carbohydrates, 7 g protein, 12 mg cholesterol, 66 mg sodium

BRUNCH PAELLA

Preparation time: About 20 minutes
Cooking time: About 35 minutes

1   pound Italian turkey sausages, cut into ½-inch-thick slices
1   cup long-grain white rice
2   cups low-sodium chicken broth
1   can (about 14½ oz.) stewed tomatoes
1   teaspoon caraway seeds
    Condiments (optional): Shredded reduced-fat jack cheese, plain nonfat or low-fat yogurt, chopped cilantro, lime wedges

In a wide frying pan, cook sausage over medium-high heat, stirring often, until browned (about 10 minutes). Spoon off and discard fat. Add rice; cook, stirring, until grains begin to look opaque (about 3 minutes). Add broth, tomatoes, and caraway seeds. Increase heat to high and bring mixture to a boil. Then reduce heat, cover, and simmer, stirring occasionally, until rice is tender to bite (about 20 minutes). Offer condiments to add to taste, if desired. Makes 4 to 6 servings.

Per serving: 316 calories (29% fat, 46% carbohydrates, 25% protein), 10 g total fat (4 g saturated fat), 36 g carbohydrates, 20 g protein, 54 mg cholesterol, 790 mg sodium

QUICK FRUIT & RICOTTA PIZZA

Preparation time: About 20 minutes
Baking time: About 13 minutes

1   package (about 10 oz.) refrigerated pizza dough
2   ounces paper-thin slices prosciutto
1   cup part-skim ricotta cheese
2   teaspoons grated lemon peel
2   tablespoons sugar
¼   teaspoon ground cinnamon
2   medium-size nectarines (10 to 11 oz. *total*), pitted and thinly sliced
¾   cup seedless red grapes, halved

Unroll pizza dough and press into an oiled 14-inch-round pizza pan or 10- by 15-inch rimmed baking pan. Bake on bottom rack of a 425° oven until well browned (about 8 minutes).

Meanwhile, cut enough prosciutto into ¼-inch-wide strips to make ¼ cup; set remainder aside. In a small bowl, mix ricotta cheese and lemon peel. In another small bowl, mix sugar and cinnamon.

Drop ricotta mixture in 1-tablespoon portions over crust. Arrange nectarines, grapes, and prosciutto strips over ricotta; sprinkle with sugar mixture.

Return pizza to oven and continue to bake until fruit is hot to the touch (about 5 more minutes). Cut pizza into wedges and serve hot; offer remaining prosciutto to add to taste. Makes 6 servings.

Per serving: 242 calories (23% fat, 57% carbohydrates, 20% protein), 6 g total fat (3 g saturated fat), 35 g carbohydrates, 12 g protein, 20 mg cholesterol, 458 mg sodium

BRUSCHETTA WITH TOMATO, BASIL & FRESH MASCARPONE

Preparation time: About 25 minutes
Chilling time: At least 12 hours
Broiling time: About 4 minutes

     Herbed Nonfat Mascarpone (recipe follows)
4   slices crusty bread (*each about ½ inch thick*)

1¼   pounds pear-shaped (Roma-type) tomatoes, finely chopped
1   cup lightly packed fresh basil leaves
     Salt

Prepare Herbed Nonfat Mascarpone.

Place bread slices slightly apart on a baking sheet. Broil about 5 inches below heat, turning once, until slices are golden brown on both sides (about 4 minutes).

Top each hot toast slice with a fourth each of the tomatoes and basil and 3 tablespoons of the Herbed Nonfat Mascarpone. Serve at once. Eat with a knife and fork; season to taste with salt and remaining mascarpone. Makes 4 servings.

Herbed Nonfat Mascarpone. Line a fine strainer with muslin or a double layer of cheesecloth. Set strainer over a deep bowl (bottom of strainer should sit at least 2 inches above bottom of bowl).

Mix 4 cups **plain nonfat yogurt** and ¼ cup minced **fresh basil;** spoon mixture into cheesecloth-lined strainer. Cover airtight and refrigerate until yogurt is firm (at least 12 hours) or for up to 2 days; occasionally pour off liquid that drains into bowl. Makes about 1½ cups.

Per serving: 195 calories (7% fat, 66% carbohydrates, 27% protein), 1 g total fat (0.2 g saturated fat), 32 g carbohydrates, 13 g protein, 0 mg cholesterol, 247 mg sodium

Orange Yogurt Waffles

Preparation time: About 20 minutes
Cooking time: About 15 minutes

Crisp waffles bursting with orange flavor are sure winners for a leisurely breakfast or brunch.

2	large egg yolks
2	cups plain low-fat yogurt
¼	cup nonfat milk
1	tablespoon grated orange peel
¼	cup orange juice
2	tablespoons sugar
¼	teaspoon ground nutmeg
2	tablespoons butter or margarine, melted
1	cup all-purpose flour
¾	cup whole wheat flour
1	teaspoon baking powder
2	teaspoons baking soda
4	large egg whites (about ½ cup)

In a large bowl, beat egg yolks, yogurt, milk, orange peel, orange juice, sugar, nutmeg, and butter until smoothly blended. In another bowl, stir together all-purpose flour, whole wheat flour, baking powder, and baking soda. Add flour mixture to egg mixture and stir just until dry ingredients are evenly moistened (do not overmix).

Beat egg whites until they hold stiff, moist peaks; fold into batter. Cook in a preheated waffle iron according to manufacturer's directions. Makes 6 servings (6 large or 12 small waffles *total*).

Per serving: 265 calories (24% fat, 58% carbohydrates, 18% protein), 7 g total fat (4 g saturated fat), 39 g carbohydrates, 12 g protein, 86 mg cholesterol, 639 mg sodium

Yeasted Corn Loaf

NATURALLY LOW IN FAT

Preparation time: About 50 minutes
Standing time: About 24 hours
Rising time: 2 to 2 ½ hours
Baking time: 35 to 40 minutes

An award-winning Seattle bakery gave us the recipe for this long oval loaf. To achieve a thick, crisp crust like that of the professional product, you can use a preheated baking stone in a water-misted oven—but even when baked on a standard baking sheet, the bread is delicious.

1½	teaspoons active dry yeast
1½	cups cool water
3¼	to 3½ cups unbleached bread flour
1	tablespoon extra-virgin olive oil
1	teaspoon salt
1	cup polenta or yellow cornmeal

In a large bowl, combine ¾ teaspoon of the yeast and ¾ cup of the water. Let stand until yeast is softened (about 5 minutes). Add 1 cup of the flour. Beat until smooth, using a heavy spoon or an electric mixer. Cover tightly with plastic wrap and let stand at 70° to 75°F until sponge bubbles actively and smells like alcohol (about 24 hours). Or let sponge stand at 70° to 75°F for 2 hours, then cover and refrigerate for about 3 days; bring to room temperature before using.

In a small bowl, combine remaining ¾ teaspoon yeast and remaining ¾ cup water; let stand until yeast is softened (about 5 minutes). Add to sponge mixture. Stir in oil, salt, and polenta; beat until blended. Then mix in 2¼ cups more flour.

To knead by hand, turn dough out onto a lightly floured board and knead until smooth and elastic (10 to 15 minutes), adding more flour as needed to prevent sticking.

To knead with a dough hook, beat on high speed until dough pulls cleanly from sides of bowl and no longer feels sticky (about 8 minutes). If necessary, add more flour, 2 tablespoons at a time, until dough pulls free from bowl.

Place dough (kneaded by either method) in an oiled bowl and turn over to oil top. Cover with plastic wrap and let rise at 70° to 75°F until doubled (1 to 1¼ hours). Punch dough down and knead briefly on a lightly floured board to release air; then return to bowl and let rise again until doubled (30 to 45 minutes).

Punch dough down and knead briefly on floured board; then shape dough into a smooth, 10-inch-long loaf with pointed ends. Place loaf on a well-floured baking sheet. Cover lightly and let rise until loaf is puffy and holds a faint impression when lightly pressed (25 to 30 minutes).

At least 30 minutes before baking, place a 14- by 16-inch baking stone or 12- by 15-inch baking sheet in oven and heat to 425°. With a razor blade or very sharp knife, cut 4 lengthwise, ¼-inch-deep slashes in loaf; space slashes slightly apart and start them 1 inch in from each long side of loaf and 2 inches in from ends. Using a spray bottle, mist loaf and walls of oven with water (avoid light bulb). Slide bread onto baking stone or sheet, mist oven with water again, and bake until bread is deep golden (35 to 40 minutes). Transfer to a rack and let cool. Makes 1 large loaf (about 24 servings).

Per serving: 99 calories (9% fat, 79% carbohydrates, 12% protein), 1 g total fat (0.1 g saturated fat), 19 g carbohydrates, 3 g protein, 0 mg cholesterol, 92 mg sodium

Scandinavian Rye Bread

· ·

NATURALLY LOW IN FAT

Preparation time: About 35 minutes
Standing time: 6 to 24 hours
Rising time: 1 to 1¼ hours
Baking time: About 40 minutes

This crusty bread begins with a yeasty sponge— or starter dough—for sour flavor.

1	**package active dry yeast**
1¼	**cups warm water (about 110°F)**
1½	**cups coarsely ground or regular rye flour**
1½	**tablespoons butter or margarine, melted and cooled**
1	**teaspoon *each* crushed caraway seeds, cumin seeds, and fennel seeds**
2	**teaspoons grated orange peel**
¾	**teaspoon salt**
2¼	**to 2½ cups all-purpose flour**
1	**tablespoon beaten egg**

In a large bowl, mix yeast, warm water, and ¾ cup of the rye flour. Cover tightly with plastic wrap and let stand at room temperature for 6 to 24 hours; the longer the standing time, the more sour the flavor.

To sponge, add remaining ¾ cup rye flour, butter, caraway seeds, cumin seeds, fennel seeds, orange peel, and salt. Stir in 1 cup of the all-purpose flour; beat with a heavy spoon or an electric mixer until dough is stretchy (about 5 minutes). Then mix in 1¼ cups more all-purpose flour.

To knead by hand, turn dough out onto a lightly floured board and knead until smooth and elastic (8 to 10 minutes), adding more all-purpose flour as needed to prevent sticking.

To knead with a dough hook, beat on high speed until dough pulls cleanly from sides of bowl and no longer feels sticky (about 8 minutes). If necessary, add more all-purpose flour, 1 tablespoon at a time, until dough pulls free from bowl.

Place dough (kneaded by either method) in an oiled bowl and turn over to oil top. Cover with plastic wrap and let rise in a warm place until doubled (45 minutes to 1 hour). Punch dough down and knead briefly on a lightly floured board to release air; then shape into a smooth, 10-inch-long loaf and place on an oiled baking sheet. Dust with 1 teaspoon all-purpose flour; cover lightly and let rise in a warm place until puffy (15 to 20 minutes).

With a razor blade or very sharp knife, cut 4 equally spaced, ½-inch-deep diagonal slashes across top of loaf. Brush loaf with beaten egg; bake in a 400° oven until deep brown (about 40 minutes). Transfer to a rack and let cool. Makes 1 large loaf (about 24 servings).

Per serving: 80 calories (14% fat, 75% carbohydrates, 11% protein), 1 g total fat (0.5 g saturated fat), 15 g carbohydrates, 2 g protein, 5 mg cholesterol, 78 mg sodium

---

__To give rye yeast breads__ a lofty volume and pleasing texture, the rye flour is usually combined with all-purpose flour. That's because rye is low in gluten—the protein in grains that gives bread dough its elastic structure.

Basque Sheepherder's Bread

Preparation time: About 45 minutes
Rising time: 1½ to 2 hours
Baking time: 45 to 50 minutes

We continue to receive requests for this huge, dome-shaped loaf, a bread featured on our June 1976 cover. To achieve the characteristic shape, you will need a 5-quart cast-iron or cast-aluminum Dutch oven with a lid.

2	packages active dry yeast
3	cups warm water (about 110°F)
⅓	cup sugar
2	teaspoons salt
½	cup (¼ lb.) butter or margarine, melted and cooled
8½	to 9¾ cups all-purpose flour
	Salad oil

In a large bowl, combine yeast, warm water, and sugar. Let stand until yeast is softened (about 5 minutes). Add salt, butter, and 5 cups of the flour; beat with a heavy spoon until dough is stretchy (about 5 minutes). Then stir in about 3½ cups more flour.

Turn dough out onto a floured board; knead until smooth and satiny (10 to 20 minutes), adding more flour as needed to prevent sticking. Place dough in an oiled bowl; turn over to oil top. Cover and let rise in a warm place until doubled (1 to 1¼ hours).

Punch dough down and knead briefly on a lightly floured board to release air. Shape into a smooth ball. Line inside bottom of a 5-quart (about 10-inch) cast-iron or cast-aluminum Dutch oven with a circle of foil. Grease foil, inside of Dutch oven, and underside of lid with oil.

Place dough in Dutch oven and cover with lid. Let rise in a warm place until dough just begins to push against lid (30 to 40 minutes—watch closely).

Bake, covered with lid, in a 375° oven for 12 minutes. Remove lid and continue to bake until loaf is deep golden brown and sounds hollow when tapped (30 to 35 more minutes). Slide a knife between Dutch oven sides and bread. Tip loaf onto a rack (this job will be easier if you have a helper) and peel off foil. Turn loaf upright; let cool for at least 45 minutes. Makes 1 very large loaf (24 to 30 servings).

Per serving: 199 calories (19% fat, 72% carbohydrates, 9% protein), 4 g total fat (2 g saturated fat), 35 g carbohydrates, 5 g protein, 9 mg cholesterol, 199 mg sodium

Easy Corn-Cheese Bread

Preparation time: About 15 minutes
Rising time: About 45 minutes
Baking time: About 45 minutes

This hearty no-knead yeast bread gets its pleasantly moist texture from cottage cheese. Bake it for a simple breakfast, to serve with salad at lunch, or for a filling snack.

1	cup fresh yellow or white corn kernels (from about 1 large ear corn); or 1 cup frozen corn kernels, thawed
1	cup beer
½	cup low-fat cottage cheese
¼	cup sugar
1	package active dry yeast
¼	cup grated Parmesan cheese
½	teaspoon *each* salt and pepper
	About 3¼ cups bread flour or all-purpose flour

Place corn kernels in a fine wire strainer and press them with the back of a spoon to express liquid; discard liquid and let corn drain well.

In a small pan, combine beer and cottage cheese. Heat over low heat until warm (about 110°F). Stir in sugar and yeast; let stand until yeast is softened (about 5 minutes).

In a food processor or a large bowl, combine corn, yeast mixture, Parmesan cheese, salt, and pepper. Gradually add 3¼ cups of the flour, about 1 cup at a time, to make a soft dough; after each addition, whirl or beat to combine thoroughly. If necessary, stir in more flour, 1 tablespoon at a time. Whirl or beat until dough is stretchy (about 3 minutes in a food processor, about 5 minutes by hand). Dough will be soft.

Transfer dough to an oiled 6-cup soufflé dish or 8-inch-round baking pan with a removable rim. Cover with oiled plastic wrap and let rise in a warm place until almost doubled (about 45 minutes).

Bake in a 350° oven until deep golden brown (about 45 minutes). Let cool in dish on a rack for at least 15 minutes. Run a knife between loaf and sides of dish; then turn loaf out of dish onto rack. Makes 1 loaf (16 to 20 servings).

Per serving: 125 calories (10% fat, 75% carbohydrates, 15% protein), 1 g total fat (0.4 g saturated fat), 23 g carbohydrates, 5 g protein, 1 mg cholesterol, 110 mg sodium

Holiday Challah

. . . .

MODIFIED CLASSIC

Preparation time: About 45 minutes
Rising time: About 1½ hours
Baking time: 30 to 35 minutes

Fat, round, and coiled to symbolize whole-ness—this is the shape challah takes in honor of the Jewish high holidays. Our version of this golden egg bread is exceptionally tender and fine-textured, superb served warm or cool with butter and honey. (If you prefer, you can shape the dough into a braid rather than a coil.)

1	package active dry yeast
¾	cup warm water (about 110°F)
¼	cup honey
1	cup hot water
⅓	cup golden raisins
2	large eggs
½	teaspoon salt
2	tablespoons salad oil
	About 3½ cups all-purpose flour

In a large bowl, combine yeast, the ¾ cup warm water, and honey; let stand until yeast is softened (about 5 minutes). Meanwhile, in a small bowl, combine the 1 cup hot water and raisins; set aside to soak. In another small bowl, beat eggs to blend; measure out 1 tablespoon of the beaten eggs, cover, and refrigerate.

To yeast mixture, add remaining beaten eggs, salt, oil, and 1½ cups of the flour. Beat with a heavy spoon or an electric mixer until dough is stretchy (about 5 minutes). Drain raisins well and mix into dough. Add 2 cups more flour; beat with a heavy spoon until dough is evenly moistened.

To knead by hand, turn dough out onto a lightly floured board and knead until smooth and elastic (about 10 minutes), adding more flour as needed to prevent sticking.

To knead with a dough hook, beat on high speed until dough pulls cleanly from sides of bowl and no longer feels sticky (5 to 8 minutes). If necessary, add more flour, 1 tablespoon at a time, until dough pulls free from bowl.

Place dough (kneaded by either method) in an oiled bowl and turn over to oil top. Cover with plastic wrap and let rise in a warm place until doubled (about 1 hour).

Punch dough down and knead briefly on a lightly floured board to release air. Then shape dough into a 32-inch-long rope, tapered at one end. If dough is so elastic it shrinks back, let it rest for a few minutes; then continue.

Place thick end of dough rope in center of an oiled 9- to 10-inch spring-form pan; then coil dough around itself from center out to pan rim. Tuck end of rope beneath loaf. Cover lightly and let rise in a warm place until puffy (20 to 30 minutes). Meanwhile, position oven rack about one-third of the way from bottom of oven.

Brush loaf gently with reserved beaten egg and bake in a 325° oven until deep golden brown (30 to 35 minutes). Check after 20 minutes; if top is browning too fast, drape loaf with foil. Let cool in pan on a rack for about 10 minutes; then remove pan rim. Makes 1 large loaf (20 to 24 servings).

Per serving: 114 calories (18% fat, 72% carbohydrates, 10% protein), 2 g total fat (0.4 g saturated fat), 21 g carbohydrates, 3 g protein, 19 mg cholesterol, 56 mg sodium

---

***Active dry yeast** is granular in form; it's sold either in envelopes (each containing a scant tablespoon of yeast) or in small jars. You can usually store it in a cool, dry place for about a year, but be sure to heed the expiration date printed on the package.*

Fragrant Greek Seed Bread

Preparation time: About 20 minutes
Rising time: 40 to 45 minutes
Baking time: About 30 minutes

This big braided loaf is topped with sesame seeds and nigella—small black seeds that taste both slightly sweet, like anise, and somewhat bitter. Look for nigella (also called kalonji and, incorrectly, black onion seeds) in Indian and Middle Eastern groceries.

2	loaves (about 1 lb. *each*) frozen whole wheat bread dough, thawed and kneaded together
1	tablespoon beaten egg
1½	tablespoons sesame seeds
1½	teaspoons nigella (kalonji), optional
¾	teaspoon anise seeds

Knead dough briefly on a floured board, then cut into 3 equal pieces. Roll each piece to make an 18-inch-long rope; transfer ropes to an oiled baking sheet. Pinch top ends of ropes together, then braid ropes, positioning braid diagonally across baking sheet. Pinch other ends of ropes to secure; tuck underneath loaf. Brush loaf with beaten egg.

Combine sesame seeds, nigella, and anise seeds; sprinkle over loaf. Cover loaf lightly and let rise in a warm place until puffy (40 to 45 minutes). Then bake in a 375° oven until deep golden (about 30 minutes). Transfer to a rack and let cool. Makes 1 large loaf (about 24 servings).

Per serving: 108 calories (20% fat, 69% carbohydrates, 11% protein), 2 g total fat (0.5 g saturated fat), 18 g carbohydrates, 3 g protein, 5 mg cholesterol, 183 mg sodium

---

No time to bake from scratch? *Frozen bread dough, white or whole wheat, is a convenient shortcut to yeasty treats like the seeded loaf above and the Yellow Bell Pizza on page 193. Before you begin, thaw the dough in the refrigerator or at room temperature, following package directions.*

Portuguese Sweet Bread

Preparation time: About 40 minutes
Rising time: 1¾ to 2 hours
Baking time: About 25 minutes

Portuguese immigrants first popularized this tender, egg-rich bread in Hawaii during the late 19th century. We published the version below in 1980; it's flavored with lemon and vanilla and shaped into a golden coil.

⅓	cup milk
2	tablespoons instant mashed potato granules or flakes
⅓	cup sugar
¼	cup butter or margarine, cut into pieces
1	package active dry yeast
¼	cup warm water (about 110°F)
2	large eggs
½	teaspoon *each* salt and grated lemon peel
¼	teaspoon vanilla
2¼	to 2⅔ cups all-purpose flour

In a small pan, bring milk to a boil. Remove from heat and immediately stir in potato granules, sugar, and butter. Let cool (butter need not melt completely).

In a large bowl, combine yeast and warm water; let stand until yeast is softened (about 5 minutes). In a small bowl, beat eggs to blend; measure out 1 tablespoon, cover, and refrigerate. Add remaining beaten eggs to yeast mixture along with salt, lemon peel, vanilla, and potato mixture. Beat to blend well. Add 1 cup of the flour and beat with a heavy spoon or an electric mixer until dough is stretchy (about 5 minutes). Then mix in 1 cup more flour.

To knead by hand, turn dough out onto a lightly floured board and knead until smooth, satiny, and no longer sticky (10 to 20 minutes), adding more flour as needed to prevent sticking.

To knead with a dough hook, add ¼ cup more flour and beat on low speed until combined. Then beat on high speed until dough pulls cleanly from sides of bowl and no longer feels sticky (about 8 minutes). If necessary, add more flour, about

1 tablespoon at a time, until dough pulls free from bowl.

Place dough (kneaded by either method) in an oiled bowl and turn over to oil top. Cover with plastic wrap and let rise in a warm place until doubled (1¼ to 1½ hours).

Punch dough down and knead briefly on a lightly floured board to release air. Then shape dough into a 30-inch-long rope. Coil dough rope into an oiled 9-inch pie pan, starting at outside edge and ending in center; twist rope slightly as you coil it. Cover lightly and let rise in a warm place until puffy (about 30 minutes).

Brush loaf with reserved beaten egg and bake in a 350° oven until deep golden brown (about 25 minutes). Lift loaf from pan to a rack to cool. Makes 1 loaf (16 to 18 servings).

Per serving: 130 calories (29% fat, 61% carbohydrates, 10% protein), 4 g total fat (2 g saturated fat), 20 g carbohydrates, 3 g protein, 33 mg cholesterol, 103 mg sodium

Rosemary & Lemon Stretch Breadsticks

Preparation time: About 20 minutes
Rising time: About 45 minutes
Baking time: About 20 minutes

Shaping this rosemary-accented bread into sticks is easy, since there's no rolling involved. Just cut the dough into strips, then pull and stretch each one into a long, skinny baton.

1	package active dry yeast
1	cup warm water (about 110°F)
1	teaspoon sugar
1	teaspoon *each* grated lemon peel and salt
1½	teaspoons chopped fresh rosemary; or 1½ teaspoons dry rosemary, crumbled
2	tablespoons plus 1 teaspoon olive oil
2½	to 3 cups all-purpose flour

In a large bowl, combine yeast, warm water, and sugar; let stand until yeast is softened (about 5 minutes). Add lemon peel, salt, rosemary, 2 tablespoons of the oil, and 1½ cups of the flour. Beat with a heavy spoon or an electric mixer until

dough is stretchy and glossy (3 to 5 minutes). Then mix in about 1 cup more flour to make a soft dough.

To knead by hand, turn dough out onto a lightly floured board and knead until smooth and elastic (about 10 minutes), adding more flour as needed to prevent sticking.

To knead with a dough hook, beat dough on high speed until it pulls cleanly from sides of bowl and no longer feels sticky (5 to 7 minutes). If necessary, add more flour, about 1 tablespoon at a time, until dough pulls free from bowl.

Generously flour board; on board, pat dough into a 6-inch square. Brush dough with remaining 1 teaspoon oil, cover lightly with plastic wrap, and let rise at room temperature until puffy (about 45 minutes).

Oil 3 large baking sheets. Gently coat dough with 2 tablespoons flour. With a floured sharp knife, cut dough lengthwise into quarters. Working with one quarter at a time, cut it lengthwise again into 8 equal pieces. Pick up one piece and stretch it to about 15 inches long; place on a baking sheet. Repeat to shape remaining breadsticks, spacing them at least ½ inch apart on baking sheets.

Bake breadsticks in a 350° oven until golden brown (about 20 minutes), switching positions of baking sheets halfway through baking. (If using one oven, refrigerate one sheet of breadsticks, lightly covered, while baking the other two.) Lift breadsticks from sheets. Serve; or let cool on racks. Makes 32 breadsticks.

Per breadstick: 56 calories (25% fat, 66% carbohydrates, 9% protein), 2 g total fat (0.2 g saturated fat), 9 g carbohydrates, 1 g protein, 0 mg cholesterol, 69 mg sodium

Whole Wheat Poppy Seed Bagels

Preparation time: About 1 hour
Rising time: 1 hour and 5 to 10 minutes
Baking time: 30 to 35 minutes

Chewy, shiny-crusted bagels are a popular low-fat alternative to breakfast muffins. These hearty whole wheat bagels, low in sugar and salt, are topped with a generous sprinkling of poppy seeds.

2	packages active dry yeast
2	cups warm water (about 110°F)
2	tablespoons sugar
1	teaspoon salt
2½	cups whole wheat flour
3	to 3½ cups all-purpose flour
1	large egg, lightly beaten
¼	cup poppy seeds

In a large bowl, combine yeast and warm water; let stand until yeast is softened (about 5 minutes). Add 1 tablespoon of the sugar, salt, whole wheat flour, and 2 cups of the all-purpose flour; beat with a heavy spoon or an electric mixer until dough is stretchy (about 5 minutes). Then mix in 1 cup more all-purpose flour.

To knead by hand, turn dough out onto a lightly floured board and knead until smooth and satiny (10 to 20 minutes), adding more flour as needed to prevent sticking (dough should be firm).

To knead with a dough hook, beat on high speed until dough pulls cleanly from sides of bowl and no longer feels sticky (about 8 minutes). If necessary, add more all-purpose flour, about 1 tablespoon at a time, until dough pulls free from bowl.

Place dough (kneaded by either method) in an oiled bowl; turn over to oil top. Cover with plastic wrap and let rise in a warm place until doubled (about 45 minutes).

Punch dough down and knead briefly on a lightly floured board to release air. Cut into 12 equal pieces. To shape each bagel, gently knead one piece into a ball. Holding ball with both hands, poke your thumbs through center. With thumbs in hole, pull dough gently to shape an evenly thick ring, 3 to 3½ inches in diameter. Set shaped bagels on a lightly floured board. Cover lightly and let rise until puffy (20 to 25 minutes).

In a 5- to 6-quart pan, combine 3 quarts water and remaining 1 tablespoon sugar. Bring to a boil over high heat; adjust heat so water boils gently. Lightly oil two 12- by 15-inch baking sheets.

As bagels get puffy, lift them with your fingers and drop gently, 3 or 4 at a time, into boiling water. Cook, turning often, for 5 minutes. Lift out with a slotted spoon and drain briefly on a cloth towel. Place bagels slightly apart on baking sheets. Brush with beaten egg; sprinkle with poppy seeds.

Bake in a 400° oven until well browned (30 to 35 minutes), switching positions of baking sheets after 15 minutes. Transfer to racks and let cool. Makes 12 bagels.

Per bagel: 254 calories (13% fat, 74% carbohydrates, 13% pratein), 4 g total fat (0.5 g saturated fat), 48 g carbohydrates, 9 g protein, 18 mg cholesterol, 192 mg sodium

Pita Bread

Preparation time: About 45 minutes
Rising time: About 1 hour
Baking time: 5 to 6 minutes

Steam makes the hollow in the middle of these small Mideastern loaves. They're ideal for filling with sliced meats, tuna, and other light sandwich fixings.

1	package active dry yeast
1½	cups warm water (about 110°F)
½	teaspoon salt
2	tablespoons olive oil
1	cup whole wheat flour
3	to 3½ cups all-purpose flour

In a large bowl, combine yeast and warm water; let stand until yeast is softened (about 5 minutes). Add salt, oil, whole wheat flour, and 1½ cups of the all-purpose flour. Beat with a heavy spoon or an electric mixer until dough is stretchy (about 5 minutes). Then mix in 1 cup more all-purpose flour.

To knead by hand, turn dough out onto a lightly floured board and knead until smooth and elastic (8 to 10 minutes), adding more all-purpose flour as needed to prevent sticking.

To knead with a dough hook, add ½ cup more all-purpose flour and beat on low speed until combined. Then beat on high speed until dough pulls cleanly from sides of bowl and no longer feels sticky (about 8 minutes). If necessary, add more all-purpose flour, about 1 tablespoon at a time, until dough pulls free from bowl.

Place dough (kneaded by either method) in an oiled bowl and turn over to oil top. Cover with plastic wrap and let rise in a warm place until doubled (about 1 hour).

Punch dough down and knead briefly on a lightly floured board to release air. Cut dough into 12 equal pieces. Roll out each piece to make a ⅛-inch-thick round. Place rounds 2 inches apart on oiled baking sheets. (If using one oven, cover unbaked rounds while baking others.)

Bake on bottom rack of a 500° oven until rounds are puffed and speckled with brown (5 to 6 minutes). Transfer to racks; let cool for 1 minute, then seal in a plastic bag to soften. Makes 12 pita breads.

Per bread: 194 calories (18% fat, 71% carbohydrates, 11% protein), 4 g total fat (0.5 g saturated fat), 34 g carbohydrates, 5 g protein, 0 mg cholesterol, 93 mg sodium

Cinnamon Slashed Flatbread

Preparation time: About 30 minutes
Rising time: About 1 hour and 20 minutes
Baking time: 20 to 25 minutes

Slashes in this sweet cinnamon bread catch and hold the buttery topping, letting it sink into the bread during baking.

1	package active dry yeast
¼	cup warm water (about 110°F)
1	cup evaporated skim milk
½	cup sugar
¾	teaspoon salt
1	large egg
½	cup (¼ lb.) butter or margarine, melted and cooled
4¼	to 4¾ cups all-purpose flour
1	teaspoon ground cinnamon

In a large bowl, combine yeast and warm water; let stand until yeast is softened (about 5 minutes). Add milk, 5 tablespoons of the sugar, salt, egg, 2 tablespoons of the butter, and 2½ cups of the flour. Beat with a heavy spoon or an electric mixer until dough is stretchy (about 5 minutes). Then mix in 1 cup more flour.

To knead by hand, turn dough out onto a lightly floured board and knead until smooth and springy (about 10 minutes), adding more flour as needed to prevent sticking.

To knead with a dough hook, beat on medium speed until dough pulls cleanly from sides of bowl and no longer feels sticky (6 to 8 minutes). If necessary, add more flour, about 1 tablespoon at a time, until dough pulls free from bowl.

Place dough (kneaded by either method) in an oiled bowl and turn over to oil top. Cover with plastic wrap and let rise in a warm place until doubled (about 1 hour).

Punch dough down and knead briefly on a lightly floured board to release air. Pat and stretch dough to fit an oiled 10- by 15-inch rimmed baking pan. With a sharp knife, slash dough diagonally to make a diamond pattern, making cuts about ½ inch deep and 1 inch apart.

In a small bowl, mix cinnamon, remaining 6 tablespoons butter, and 2 tablespoons of the sugar. Drizzle mixture over dough. Let rise, uncovered, in a warm place until almost doubled (about 20 minutes). Sprinkle with remaining 1 tablespoon sugar. Bake in a 400° oven until browned (20 to 25 minutes). Serve warm. Makes 12 to 15 servings.

Per serving: 263 calories (27% fat, 63% carbohydrates, 10% protein), 8 g total fat (4 g saturated fat), 41 g carbohydrates, 6 g protein, 33 mg cholesterol, 211 mg sodium

Christmas Tree Bread

Preparation time: About 1 hour
Rising time: About 1½ hours
Baking time: 40 to 45 minutes

In the midst of the Christmas morning excitement, offer this showy bread, sliced to display the spiraled fruit filling. For a festive breakfast, accompany the bread with a fresh fruit compote and mugs of hot chocolate, coffee, or Mocha au Lait (page 19).

2	**packages active dry yeast**
½	**cup warm water (about 110°F)**
½	**cup (¼ lb.) butter or margarine, cut into pieces**
1	**cup milk**
3	**large eggs**
¼	**cup sugar**
2	**teaspoons vanilla**
1	**teaspoon grated lemon peel**
½	**teaspoon ground cardamom or ground mace**
½	**teaspoon salt**
	About 5½ cups all-purpose flour
	Fruit Filling (recipe follows)
1	**large egg yolk beaten with 1 tablespoon water**
	Orange Glaze (recipe follows)

In a large bowl, combine yeast and warm water; let stand until yeast is softened (about 5 minutes). In a small pan, combine butter and milk. Heat over medium heat to 110°F (butter need not melt completely).

Add milk mixture, whole eggs, sugar, vanilla, lemon peel, cardamom, salt, and 3 cups of the flour to yeast mixture. Beat with an electric mixer on medium speed until dough is stretchy and glossy (5 to 8 minutes). Mix in 2¼ cups more flour.

To knead by hand, turn dough out onto a lightly floured board and knead until smooth and elastic (about 10 minutes), adding just enough additional flour to prevent sticking.

To knead with a dough hook, beat on high speed until dough pulls cleanly from sides of bowl and no longer feels sticky (5 to 8 minutes). If necessary, add more flour, about 1 tablespoon at a time, until dough pulls free from bowl.

Place dough (kneaded by either method) in an oiled bowl and turn over to oil top. Cover with plastic wrap and let rise in a warm place until doubled (about 1 hour). Meanwhile, prepare Fruit Filling.

Punch dough down and knead briefly on a lightly floured board to release air. Cut off ⅓ cup of the dough and set aside. On board, roll remaining portion of dough out to make a 10- by 36-inch rectangle. Spread with Fruit Filling to within ½ inch of long sides. Starting at a long side, roll up dough jelly roll style; pinch seam to seal.

Place rolled dough, seam side down, on an oiled 14- by 17-inch baking sheet; arrange in a zigzag pattern (like stacked S's) to make a tree shape, narrow at top and broad at base. Shape reserved ⅓ cup dough into a ball; attach to base of tree to form a trunk.

Cover loaf lightly and let rise in a warm place until puffy (about 25 minutes). Brush with egg yolk mixture and bake in a 350° oven until golden brown (40 to 45 minutes). Let bread cool on baking sheet for 15 minutes. Meanwhile, prepare Orange Glaze.

Spoon glaze over warm bread; transfer bread to a platter. Makes 1 loaf (12 to 16 servings).

Fruit Filling. In a small bowl, soak 1 cup **golden raisins** in 3 tablespoons **orange juice** and 2 tablespoons **brandy** or vanilla until plump (about 30 minutes). Meanwhile, toast ¾ cup **slivered almonds** in a wide frying pan over medium heat until golden (about 5 minutes), stirring often. Remove from heat.

In a food processor, combine raisin mixture, almonds, 1 cup *each* coarsely chopped peeled **apple** and coarsely chopped **dried apricots,** 2 teaspoons **ground cinnamon,** and 1 teaspoon grated **orange peel.** Whirl until finely chopped.

Orange Glaze. In a small bowl, stir together 1¼ cups **powdered sugar** and 2 tablespoons **orange juice** until smooth.

Per serving: 446 calories (27% fat, 64% carbohydrates, 9% protein), 14 g total fat (5 g saturated fat), 71 g carbohydrates, 10 g protein, 81 mg cholesterol, 172 mg sodium

LOW-FAT PIZZAS

Cutting down on fat doesn't mean going without pizza. When the craving strikes, enjoy one of these two choices.

YELLOW BELL PIZZA

Preparation time: About 20 minutes
Rising time: About 20 minutes
Baking time: About 16 minutes

1   loaf (about 1 lb.) frozen white bread dough, thawed

1   cup (about 4 oz.) shredded part-skim mozzarella cheese

2   medium-size yellow bell peppers (about 12 oz. *total*), seeded and thinly sliced

4   teaspoons grated Parmesan cheese

1   tablespoon chopped fresh basil or 1 teaspoon dry basil

Cut dough into quarters. Shape each piece into a ball; on a floured board, roll each ball into a 6-inch round. Place rounds, 1 inch apart, on 2 lightly oiled 12- by 15-inch baking sheets. With your hands, flatten rounds to ¼ inch thick (make edges slightly thicker) and 7 inches wide. Let stand, uncovered, at room temperature until puffy (about 20 minutes).

Sprinkle each round to within ¼ inch of edges with 2 tablespoons of the mozzarella cheese. Top rounds with bell pepper. Sprinkle with remaining ½ cup mozzarella cheese, Parmesan cheese, and basil.

Bake pizzas in a 400° oven until crust is browned on bottom; lift to check (about 16 minutes; switch positions of baking sheets after 8 minutes). Serve hot. Makes 4 servings.

Per serving: 431 calories (27% fat, 57% carbohydrates, 16% protein), 13 g total fat (5 g saturated fat), 61 g carbohydrates, 17 g protein, 23 mg cholesterol, 712 mg sodium

NO-SAUCE PIZZA

Preparation time: About 20 minutes
Rising time: 45 minutes to 1 hour
Cooking time: About 30 minutes
Baking time: About 20 minutes

1   package active dry yeast

¾   cup warm water (about 110°F)

1   teaspoon *each* sugar and salt

2   to 2½ cups all-purpose flour

1½ tablespoons olive oil

3   large onions, thinly sliced

2   medium-size pear-shaped (Roma-type) tomatoes (about 6 oz. *total*), thinly sliced

¼   cup grated Parmesan cheese

1   tablespoon dry oregano or 2 tablespoons fresh oregano leaves

In a large bowl, combine yeast and warm water; let stand until yeast is softened (about 5 minutes). Add sugar, salt, and 1 cup of the flour; beat with a heavy spoon or an electric mixer until smooth. Then mix in 1 cup more flour.

To knead by hand, turn dough out onto a lightly floured board and knead until smooth and elastic (about 5 minutes), adding more flour as needed to prevent sticking.

To knead with a dough hook, beat on medium speed until dough pulls cleanly from sides of bowl and no longer feels sticky (about 3 minutes); if necessary, add more flour, 1 tablespoon at a time, until dough pulls free.

Place dough (kneaded by either method) in an oiled bowl and turn over to oil top. Cover with plastic wrap and let rise in a warm place until doubled (45 minutes to 1 hour).

Meanwhile, in a wide frying pan, heat 1 tablespoon of the oil over medium-low heat. Add onions; cook, stirring occasionally, until soft and golden (about 30 minutes). Let cool.

Punch dough down; knead briefly on a floured board to release air. Roll dough into a 15-inch round. Transfer to an oiled 14-inch-round pizza pan; roll edge up and over to form a rim.

Cover dough with onions and tomatoes; sprinkle with cheese and oregano. Brush crust with remaining 1½ teaspoons oil.

Bake in a 425° oven until crust is golden (about 20 minutes). Serve hot. Makes 8 servings.

Per serving: 222 calories (20% fat, 68% carbohydrates, 12% protein), 5 g total fat (1 g saturated fat), 38 g carbohydrates, 6 g protein, 2 mg cholesterol, 327 mg sodium

DESSERTS

*E*nding a festive meal with something sweet is a pleasant tradition, one you can happily enjoy even if you've decided to emphasize lower-fat foods. As our pared-down desserts demonstrate, you can eat crisp or chewy cookies, comforting puddings, juicy pies, even fudge brownies and cakes. Our recipe secrets include extending whole eggs with egg whites (the fat is in the yolk) and cooking with reduced-fat dairy products, such as nonfat and low-fat milk and yogurt. Of course, ripe fruit is a classic finale, and in these pages we've gathered an array of fresh fruit creations. When you opt for treats such as Apricot-Blueberry Cobbler or Peach & Berry Bake, you'll be rewarded with vitamins and fiber as well as sweet and refreshing flavor.

Orange-tipped Walnut Biscotti

. . . .

Preparation time: About 35 minutes
Baking time: 25 to 28 minutes

In this adaptation of our favorite lemon-pistachio biscotti, the cookies are studded with walnuts and accented with orange and spices.

2	cups all-purpose flour
2	teaspoons baking powder
¾	teaspoon ground cinnamon
¼	teaspoon ground nutmeg
⅛	teaspoon ground allspice
¼	cup butter or margarine, at room temperature
⅔	cup sugar
1	teaspoon grated orange peel
1	large egg
2	large egg whites (about ¼ cup)
1	teaspoon vanilla
½	cup coarsely chopped walnuts
	Orange Icing (recipe follows)

In a medium-size bowl, stir together flour, baking powder, cinnamon, nutmeg, and allspice; set aside. In a large bowl, beat together butter, sugar, and orange peel until well blended. Beat in egg, then egg whites. Beat in vanilla. Gradually add flour mixture, beating until blended. Stir in walnuts.

Divide dough in half. On a lightly floured board, shape each portion into a long loaf about 1½ inches in diameter. Place loaves about 3 inches apart on an oiled baking sheet; flatten each loaf to a thickness of about ½ inch. Bake in a 350° oven until firm to the touch (15 to 18 minutes).

Remove baking sheet from oven; cut hot loaves crosswise into about ½-inch-thick slices. Turn slices cut sides down and spread out slightly on baking sheets (you will need at least 2 baking sheets). Return to oven and continue to bake until cookies look dry and are lightly browned (about 10 more minutes). Transfer cookies to racks and let cool.

Prepare Orange Icing; spread icing over about 1 inch of one end of each cookie. Let stand until icing is firm (about 15 minutes). Store airtight. Makes about 54 cookies.

Orange Icing. In a small bowl, stir together 1 cup sifted **powdered sugar** and 1 teaspoon grated **orange peel.** Stir in 1 to 1½ tablespoons **orange juice,** using just enough to give icing a good spreading consistency.

Per cookie: 52 calories (28% fat, 65% carbohydrates, 7% protein), 2 g total fat (0.6 g saturated fat), 9 g carbohydrates, 0.9 g protein, 6 mg cholesterol, 30 mg sodium

Graham Cracker Crackle Cookies

. . . .

30 MINUTES OR LESS

Preparation time: About 20 minutes
Baking time: About 7 minutes

Dotted with semisweet chocolate chips, these crunchy cookies get their pleasant flavor from malted milk powder and golden graham cracker crumbs.

1	large egg white (about 2 tablespoons)
⅛	teaspoon cream of tartar
1¼	cups powdered sugar
2	tablespoons malted milk powder
½	cup graham cracker crumbs
¼	cup semisweet chocolate chips

In a large bowl, combine egg white, cream of tartar, sugar, and malted milk powder. Beat with an electric mixer on high speed until thick and smooth. Stir in graham cracker crumbs.

Drop dough in 1½-teaspoon mounds 3 inches apart on 3 oiled, floured 12- by 15-inch nonstick baking sheets (or use regular baking sheets, lightly coated with vegetable oil cooking spray, then floured). Lightly press chocolate chips equally into mounds.

Bake cookies in a 375° oven until golden brown (about 7 minutes; switch positions of baking sheets after 4 minutes). Transfer baking sheets to racks and let cookies cool for 1 minute; then transfer cookies to racks with a wide spatula. If made ahead, let cool completely; store airtight. Makes about 18 cookies.

Per cookie: 76 calories (20% fat, 75% carbohydrates, 5% protein), 2 g total fat (0.5 g saturated fat), 14 g carbohydrates, 0.8 g protein, 0.3 mg cholesterol, 35 mg sodium

Oatmeal Raisin Cookies

3 0   M I N U T E S   O R   L E S S

Preparation time: About 15 minutes
Baking time: About 10 minutes

Spicy, cakelike cookies filled with golden raisins are sure to satisfy the cookie crowd. We've used both oat bran and rolled oats in the dough.

1	cup all-purpose flour
½	cup oat bran
½	teaspoon ground allspice
1	teaspoon baking soda
½	teaspoon salt
1	cup firmly packed brown sugar
½	cup salad oil
½	cup nonfat milk
2	large egg whites (about ¼ cup)
1	teaspoon vanilla
3	cups rolled oats
1	cup golden raisins

In a small bowl, stir together flour, oat bran, all-spice, baking soda, and salt; set aside. In a large bowl, beat sugar and oil with an electric mixer until creamy. Add milk, egg whites, and vanilla; beat until blended. Gradually add flour mixture, beating until blended. Stir in oats and raisins.

Drop rounded tablespoonfuls of dough about 2 inches apart on ungreased baking sheets. Bake in a 375° oven until cookies are light golden (about 10 minutes). Let cookies cool on baking sheets on racks for about 2 minutes; then transfer to racks and let cool completely. Store airtight. Makes about 48 cookies.

Per cookie: 80 calories (29% fat, 63% carbohydrates, 8% protein), 3 g total fat (0.3 g saturated fat), 13 g carbohydrates, 2 g protein, 0 mg cholesterol, 55 mg sodium

---

__Oat bran__ has garnered lots of attention in recent years—but in fact, all forms of oats are very nutritious simply because they aren't refined. Both oat bran and rolled oats are high in soluble fiber, which—as part of a low-fat diet— may help reduce cholesterol.

Fudgy Brownies

M O D I F I E D   C L A S S I C

Preparation time: About 15 minutes
Baking time: About 35 minutes

To enhance the fudge flavor and cut the fat, we made these irresistible brownies with cocoa in place of the usual chocolate. Using egg whites in place of whole eggs streamlines the recipe further.

7	tablespoons butter or margarine
¾	cup unsweetened cocoa
2	cups sugar
1½	teaspoons vanilla
1	large egg
5	large egg whites (about 10 tablespoons)
1	cup all-purpose flour
2	tablespoons finely chopped walnuts

In a 2- to 3-quart pan, combine butter and cocoa; stir over medium-low heat until butter is melted and mixture is well blended. Remove from heat and stir in sugar and vanilla. Add egg and egg whites; beat until blended. Stir in flour until well blended.

Spread batter evenly in an oiled 9-inch-square baking pan. Sprinkle walnuts evenly over batter. Bake in a 325° oven until brownies feel dry on top (about 35 minutes). Let cool in pan on a rack; then cut into 2¼-inch squares. Store airtight. Makes 16 brownies.

Per brownie: 199 calories (29% fat, 65% carbohydrates, 6% protein), 7 g total fat (4 g saturated fat), 34 g carbohydrates, 3 g protein, 27 mg cholesterol, 74 mg sodium

Whole Wheat Orange Bars

Preparation time: About 25 minutes
Baking time: About 35 minutes

Served with tall glasses of milk, these hearty bars are super for after-school snacking. Chopped dates and juicy chunks of fresh orange make them especially moist. Before cooling and cutting the cookies, spread them with an easy orange frosting.

1 large orange (about 10 oz.)
1 cup *each* whole wheat flour and all-purpose flour
½ cup chopped pitted dates
2 tablespoons sugar
1 teaspoon baking soda
½ teaspoon baking powder
1 can (about 6 oz.) frozen orange juice concentrate, thawed
¼ cup butter or margarine, melted
2 large eggs, lightly beaten
   Orange Frosting (recipe follows)

Cut peel and all white membrane from orange; then cut fruit into ½-inch chunks and remove seeds. Set aside.

In a medium-size bowl, stir together whole wheat flour, all-purpose flour, dates, sugar, baking soda, and baking powder; set aside. Reserve 1 tablespoon of the orange juice concentrate for frosting; pour remaining concentrate into a large bowl and stir in butter and eggs.

Add flour mixture and orange chunks to egg mixture; stir just until dry ingredients are evenly moistened. Spread batter in an oiled 9-inch-square baking pan and bake in a 350° oven just until cookies pull away from sides of pan (about 35 minutes).

Prepare Orange Frosting and spread over hot cookies; let cool. To serve, cut into 12 rectangles. Makes 12 cookies.

Orange Frosting. In a small bowl, combine ¾ cup **powdered sugar,** the 1 tablespoon **reserved orange juice concentrate,** and 1 tablespoon **water.** Stir until smooth.

Per cookie: 215 calories (22% fat, 70% carbohydrates, 8% protein), 5 g total fat (3 g saturated fat), 39 g carbohydrates, 4 g protein, 46 mg cholesterol, 176 mg sodium

Warm Gingerbread

Preparation time: About 20 minutes
Baking time: About 25 minutes

A bowl of hearty vegetable soup, a leafy salad, and a big square of warm, spicy gingerbread add up to a satisfying midwinter lunch. If you like, decorate the gingerbread with a snowy powdered-sugar pattern: place a doily on the uncut cake, then sift on a little sugar and carefully lift off the doily.

¼ cup butter or margarine, at room temperature
¼ cup granulated sugar
1 large egg, lightly beaten
½ cup light molasses
1¼ cups all-purpose flour
1 teaspoon baking soda
¼ teaspoon *each* ground nutmeg and salt
1 teaspoon ground ginger (or 1 tablespoon minced fresh ginger; or 3 tablespoons minced crystallized ginger)
½ cup hot water
   About 1 tablespoon powdered sugar (optional)

In a medium-size bowl, beat butter, granulated sugar, and egg until smoothly blended. Beat in molasses. In another bowl, stir together flour, baking soda, nutmeg, salt, and ginger; add to egg mixture alternately with hot water, stirring until smooth after each addition. Pour batter into an oiled, floured 8- or 9-inch-round baking pan and spread evenly.

Bake gingerbread in a 350° oven until a wooden pick inserted in center comes out clean (about 25 minutes). Let cool in pan on a rack until just warm to the touch (about 15 minutes), then turn out onto rack. Invert a serving plate over gingerbread; holding rack and plate together, invert both. Lift off rack.

Serve gingerbread warm or cool. Just before serving, place a doily or other pattern on gingerbread, if desired; then sift powdered sugar over it. Lift off doily. Makes 6 servings.

Per serving: 293 calories (29% fat, 66% carbohydrates, 5% protein), 10 g total fat (5 g saturated fat), 48 g carbohydrates, 4 g protein, 56 mg cholesterol, 400 mg sodium

Carrot Cake

Preparation time: About 20 minutes
Baking time: About 45 minutes

Here's a welcome contribution to your next potluck supper. Crushed pineapple, golden raisins, and plenty of shredded carrots give this generous cake an appealing texture; a simple glaze of pineapple juice and powdered sugar replaces the traditional cream cheese frosting.

1	cup *each* all-purpose flour and whole wheat flour
1½	tablespoons ground cinnamon
1	teaspoon ground nutmeg
2	teaspoons *each* baking soda and baking powder
½	teaspoon salt
1	cup firmly packed brown sugar
½	cup granulated sugar
1	can (about 8 oz.) crushed pineapple packed in its own juice
¾	cup salad oil
6	large egg whites (about ¾ cup)
1	teaspoon vanilla
3	cups finely shredded carrots
1½	cups golden raisins
	Pineapple Glaze (recipe follows)

In a large bowl, stir together all-purpose flour, whole wheat flour, cinnamon, nutmeg, baking soda, baking powder, salt, brown sugar, and granulated sugar. Set aside.

Drain pineapple, reserving juice for Pineapple Glaze. In another large bowl, combine pineapple, oil, egg whites, vanilla, and carrots; beat with an electric mixer until well blended. Add pineapple-carrot mixture and raisins to flour mixture; stir until dry ingredients are evenly moistened. Spread batter evenly in an oiled, floured 9- by 13-inch baking pan.

Bake in a 350° oven until a wooden pick inserted in center of cake comes out clean (about 45 minutes). Let cool in pan on a rack. Before serving, prepare Pineapple Glaze and pour evenly over cake. Makes 24 servings.

Pineapple Glaze. In a small bowl, combine 1½ cups sifted **powdered sugar** and about ¼ cup of the **reserved pineapple juice.** Stir until glaze is smooth and has a good pouring consistency.

Per serving: 219 calories (29% fat, 67% carbohydrates, 4% protein), 7 g total fat (0.9 g saturated fat), 38 g carbohydrates, 3 g protein, 0 mg cholesterol, 215 mg sodium

Spiced Pumpkin Roll

Preparation time: About 1 hour
Baking time: About 15 minutes
Freezing time: About 3 hours

This frozen cake roll has the same flavors as pumpkin pie à la mode, but far fewer calories. Its elegant appearance makes it a fitting finale for a holiday meal.

	Vegetable oil cooking spray or salad oil
¾	cup all-purpose flour
2	teaspoons ground cinnamon
1	teaspoon *each* baking powder and ground ginger
½	teaspoon *each* ground nutmeg and salt
3	large eggs
1	cup granulated sugar
⅔	cup canned solid-pack pumpkin
⅓	cup powdered sugar
1	quart vanilla low-fat frozen yogurt, slightly softened
	Shredded orange peel (optional)

Lightly coat a 10- by 15-inch rimmed baking pan with cooking spray; line with wax paper and spray again. Set aside. In a small bowl, stir together flour, cinnamon, baking powder, ginger, nutmeg, and salt; set aside.

In a large bowl, beat eggs with an electric mixer on high speed until thick and lemon-colored. Gradually add granulated sugar; continue to beat, scraping bowl often, until mixture is creamy and pale in color. With mixer on low speed, beat in pumpkin, then flour mixture. Pour batter into pan and spread evenly.

Bake in a 375° oven until top of cake springs back when lightly pressed (about 15 minutes). Immediately invert cake onto a dishtowel sprinkled with 3 tablespoons of the powdered sugar. Peel off wax paper. Starting with a long side, immediately roll cake and towel into a cylinder. Let cool completely on a rack.

Carefully unroll cooled cake and remove towel. Spread cake evenly with frozen yogurt; reroll. Wrap in plastic wrap and freeze until firm (about 3 hours).

To serve, unwrap cake, place on a platter, and let stand at room temperature for about 10 minutes. Sift remaining powdered sugar over top. Cut cake crosswise into slices; if desired, garnish each serving with orange peel. Makes 14 servings.

Per serving: 170 calories (10% fat, 80% carbohydrates, 10% protein), 2 g total fat (0.4 g saturated fat), 34 g carbohydrates, 4 g protein, 48 mg cholesterol, 159 mg sodium

Liqueur Pound Cake

MODIFIED CLASSIC

Preparation time: About 30 minutes
Baking time: About 40 minutes

Fine-textured and tender, this syrup-soaked loaf is almost devoid of fat—it's made with egg whites only, and contains no shortening at all.

    Vegetable oil cooking spray
    Cake flour to dust pan
1   **cup sifted cake flour**
1   **teaspoon baking soda**
½   **teaspoon baking powder**
6   **large egg whites (about ¾ cup), at room temperature**
1¼   **cups sifted powdered sugar**
1   **teaspoon vanilla**
    Apple-Liqueur Syrup (recipe follows)

Coat a 4½- by 8½-inch loaf pan with cooking spray; dust pan with flour, then tap to remove excess. Set pan aside.

In a medium-size bowl, stir together the 1 cup flour, baking soda, and baking powder; set aside. In a large bowl, beat egg whites with an electric mixer on high speed until foamy. Gradually add sugar, beating until mixture barely holds soft peaks; beat in vanilla. Add flour mixture; beat just until well blended. Spread batter in pan.

Bake in a 300° oven until cake is golden brown and just beginning to pull away from sides of pan (about 40 minutes). Meanwhile, prepare Apple-Liqueur Syrup.

Use a slender spatula to loosen hot cake from pan. Carefully invert pan and turn cake out onto a rack. Pour ¼ cup of the Apple-Liqueur Syrup into pan, then return cake to pan. Using a slender skewer, pierce cake all over at 1-inch intervals (pierce all the way through to pan bottom). Slowly pour 6 to 7 tablespoons more syrup over top of cake; pour remaining syrup into a small pitcher or serving bowl. Let cake cool in pan to room temperature. If made ahead, cover and refrigerate cake and syrup separately for up to 2 days; reheat syrup before serving, if desired.

To serve, invert cake onto a platter; cut into about ½-inch-thick slices. Offer remaining syrup to add to taste. Makes 16 servings.

Apple-Liqueur Syrup. In a 2-quart pan, combine 1 can (about 6 oz.) **frozen apple juice concentrate,** ½ cup **rum,** 2 tablespoons **amaretto,** 1 tablespoon **lemon juice,** and 1 teaspoon **coriander seeds.** Bring to a boil over high heat; then boil, uncovered, until reduced to 1 cup (5 to 8 minutes). Use hot or cool.

Per serving: 105 calories (2% fat, 89% carbohydrates, 9% protein), 0.2 g total fat (0 g saturated fat), 19 g carbohydrates, 2 g protein, 0 mg cholesterol, 118 mg sodium

---

__Fresh seasonal fruits__ are a perfect, pretty complement to plain cakes made with egg whites and little if any shortening. Top each slice with plump, juicy raspberries or strawberries, golden peaches, tart-sweet pineapple, or crisp melon balls—and you'll forget all about buttery icings.

Orange Cake

Preparation time: About 40 minutes
Baking time: About 20 minutes

If you like oranges, you'll definitely want to add this moist cake to your file of favorites. Baked in a single layer, it's soaked with an orange-liqueur syrup while still warm from the oven.

2	**large eggs, at room temperature**
½	**cup sugar**
¾	**cup all-purpose flour**
1½	**teaspoons baking powder**
2	**tablespoons grated orange peel**
¼	**cup butter or margarine, melted and cooled**
	Spirited Orange Syrup (recipe follows)

In a large bowl, beat eggs and sugar with an electric mixer on high speed until thick and lemon-colored. Add flour, baking powder, orange peel, and butter; continue to beat until well blended. Spread batter evenly in an oiled, floured 9-inch-round baking pan.

Bake in a 375° oven until cake just begins to pull away from sides of pan and center springs back when lightly pressed (about 20 minutes). Meanwhile, prepare Spirited Orange Syrup.

Transfer cake (in pan) to a rack. Then pierce cake all over with a fork. Slowly pour warm Spirited Orange Syrup over warm cake; let cool. If made ahead, cover airtight and hold at room temperature for up to 1 day.

To serve, invert a rimmed serving plate over cake in pan; holding plate and pan together, invert both. Lift off pan. Makes 8 servings.

Spirited Orange Syrup. In a 1½- to 2-quart pan, stir together ⅓ cup *each* **sugar** and **water** and 2 cups **orange juice.** Bring to a boil over high heat; then boil, uncovered, until reduced to about 1½ cups (about 10 minutes). Remove from heat and stir in 2 tablespoons **orange-flavored liqueur.** Use syrup warm.

Per serving: 241 calories (29% fat, 65% carbohydrates, 6% protein), 8 g total fat (4 g saturated fat), 39 g carbohydrates, 3 g protein, 69 mg cholesterol, 167 mg sodium

Old-fashioned Apple Cake

MODIFIED CLASSIC

Preparation time: About 20 minutes
Standing time: 15 minutes
Baking time: About 50 minutes

Hearty spice cake, thick with walnuts, raisins, and crisp shredded apples, makes a satisfying snack or dessert. Serve the cake in big squares, perhaps with mugs of hot cider or glasses of frosty-cold milk.

1½	**pounds tart green-skinned apples, such as Granny Smith or Newtown Pippin, cored and coarsely grated**
1½	**cups sugar**
2½	**cups all-purpose flour**
1½	**teaspoons baking soda**
1	**tablespoon baking powder**
2	**teaspoons ground cinnamon**
1	**large egg**
2	**large egg whites (about ¼ cup)**
¼	**cup salad oil**
½	**cup low-fat buttermilk**
2	**teaspoons vanilla**
1	**cup raisins**
½	**cup chopped walnuts**
	Vegetable oil cooking spray or salad oil

In a large bowl, stir together apples and sugar; let stand for 15 minutes.

In a medium-size bowl, stir together flour, baking soda, baking powder, and cinnamon; add to apple mixture and stir to blend. In another bowl, beat egg, egg whites, oil, buttermilk, and vanilla until blended; add to apple mixture and stir well. Stir in raisins and walnuts.

Lightly coat a 9- by 13-inch baking pan with cooking spray. Pour batter into pan and spread evenly. Bake in a 350° oven until a wooden pick inserted in center of cake comes out clean (about 50 minutes). Let cool in pan on a rack. Makes 15 servings.

Per serving: 279 calories (22% fat, 72% carbohydrates, 6% protein), 7 g total fat (1 g saturated fat), 52 g carbohydrates, 4 g protein, 14 mg cholesterol, 246 mg sodium

Summer Hazelnut Torte with Berries

Preparation time: About 20 minutes
Baking time: About 15 minutes

For a summer dessert, spoon fresh berries over wedges of nut-flavored sponge cake. The cake is best if served the same day it's baked.

⅔	cup all-purpose flour
½	teaspoon baking powder
1	large egg, at room temperature
2	large egg whites (about ¼ cup)
⅓	cup granulated sugar
⅛	teaspoon salt
½	teaspoon vanilla
2	teaspoons hazelnut oil or salad oil
	Berry Medley (recipe follows)
2	to 3 tablespoons hazelnut-flavored liqueur or amaretto
⅓	cup coarsely chopped hazelnuts
1	to 2 tablespoons powdered sugar

Sift flour and baking powder into a small bowl; set aside. In a large bowl, combine egg, egg whites, granulated sugar, and salt. Beat with an electric mixer on high speed until mixture is thick and tripled in volume (about 5 minutes). Beat in vanilla. Using a rubber spatula, fold in flour mixture until almost blended. Drizzle with oil; continue to fold gently until all flour is mixed in. Spread batter in an oiled, floured 8-inch-round baking pan.

Bake in a 350° oven until top of cake is golden brown and a wooden pick inserted in center comes out clean (about 15 minutes). Let cake cool in pan on a rack for 5 minutes; then carefully invert cake from pan onto rack and let stand until barely warm to the touch (about 10 minutes). Meanwhile, prepare Berry Medley.

To serve, transfer cake to a serving plate; drizzle with liqueur. Sprinkle with hazelnuts, then dust with powdered sugar. Cut cake into wedges; top each serving with Berry Medley. Makes 6 servings.

Berry Medley. In a medium-size bowl, lightly mix 1 cup *each* **raspberries** and **blackberries** with 1 to 2 tablespoons **sugar** and 2 teaspoons **kirsch** or lemon juice.

Per serving: 241 calories (28% fat, 63% carbohydrates, 9% protein), 7 g total fat (0.8 g saturated fat), 37 g carbohydrates, 5 g protein, 35 mg cholesterol, 116 mg sodium

Crazy Cocoa Cake

Preparation time: About 10 minutes
Baking time: About 30 minutes

This moist, fluffy chocolate cake is one of the easiest desserts you'll ever make. A long-time favorite of busy cooks, it fits right in with today's lighter menus.

1½	cups all-purpose flour
1	cup granulated sugar
3	tablespoons unsweetened cocoa
1	teaspoon baking soda
½	teaspoon salt
5	tablespoons salad oil
1	tablespoon vinegar
1	teaspoon vanilla
1	cup cold water
2	tablespoons powdered sugar

Sift flour, granulated sugar, cocoa, baking soda, and salt into a 9-inch-square baking pan. Make 3 depressions in flour mixture and evenly distribute oil, vinegar, and vanilla among them. Pour cold water over all.

With a rubber spatula, combine ingredients, scraping sides and bottom of pan to mix thoroughly (a few lumps may remain in batter).

Bake in a 350° oven until a wooden pick inserted in center of cake comes out clean (about 30 minutes). Let cool in pan on a rack. Sift powdered sugar over cake before serving. Makes 8 servings.

Per serving: 271 calories (29% fat, 67% carbohydrates, 4% protein), 9 g total fat (1 g saturated fat), 46 g carbohydrates, 3 g protein, 0 mg cholesterol, 295 mg sodium

Mexican Cocoa Cake

Preparation time: About 10 minutes
Baking time: 30 to 40 minutes

Delicious with hot coffee, this rich cocoa cake features the cinnamon and almond flavors of traditional Mexican chocolate. For an extra treat, top the cake with Spiced Cream.

	Spiced Cream (optional; recipe follows)
1	**cup sifted cake flour**
⅓	**cup unsweetened cocoa**
1	**teaspoon** *each* **baking soda, baking powder, and ground cinnamon**
6	**large egg whites (about ¾ cup)**
1⅓	**cups firmly packed brown sugar**
1	**cup plain nonfat yogurt**
2	**teaspoons vanilla**
¼	**teaspoon almond extract**
2	**tablespoons powdered sugar**

Prepare Spiced Cream, if desired; refrigerate.

In a small bowl, stir together flour, cocoa, baking soda, baking powder, and cinnamon. In a large bowl, beat egg whites, brown sugar, yogurt, vanilla, and almond extract until well blended. Stir in flour mixture and beat until dry ingredients are evenly moistened.

Pour batter into an 8-inch-square nonstick (or oiled regular) baking pan; spread evenly. Bake in a 350° oven until center of cake springs back when lightly pressed (30 to 40 minutes).

Let cake cool in pan on a rack for 15 minutes; then invert from pan onto a serving plate. Serve warm or cool. Just before serving, sift powdered sugar over top. Serve with Spiced Cream, if desired. Makes 8 servings.

Spiced Cream. Pour ¼ cup **nonfat milk** into a small bowl. Cover bowl; then freeze beaters of an electric mixer and bowl of milk until milk is slushy (30 to 45 minutes). In a small pan, sprinkle ½ teaspoon **unflavored gelatin** over ¼ cup **cold water;** let stand until gelatin is softened (about 5 minutes). Then stir over low heat just until gelatin is dissolved. Remove from heat.

To slushy milk, add gelatin mixture, ⅔ cup

instant nonfat dry milk, 2 tablespoons **sugar,** 1 teaspoon **vanilla,** and ½ teaspoon **ground cinnamon.** Beat on high speed until mixture holds soft peaks (5 to 10 minutes). Cover and refrigerate for at least 15 minutes or for up to 2 days. If needed, whisk or beat again before serving until cream holds soft peaks. Serve cold. Makes about 2 cups.

Per serving of cake: 230 calories (2% fat, 88% carbohydrates, 10% protein), 0.6 g total fat (0.3 g saturated fat), 52 g carbohydrates, 6 g protein, 0.6 mg cholesterol, 297 mg sodium

Per tablespoon of Spiced Cream: 9 calories (1% fat, 73% carbohydrates, 26% protein), 0 g total fat (0 g saturated fat), 2 g carbohydrates, 0.6 g protein, 0.3 mg cholesterol, 9 mg sodium

Black Forest Cocoa Angel Food Cake

MODIFIED CLASSIC

Preparation time: About 40 minutes
Baking time: About 35 minutes
Cooking time: About 10 minutes

Just a little unsweetened cocoa gives this lofty angel food cake its tempting chocolate flavor. Fill the cake with cherries, spread with a fluffy icing—and you have a dazzling low-fat dessert.

¾	**cup sifted cake flour**
¼	**cup unsweetened cocoa**
1½	**cups powdered sugar**
12	**large egg whites (about 1½ cups), at room temperature**
1½	**teaspoons cream of tartar**
⅛	**teaspoon salt**
1	**cup granulated sugar**
1½	**teaspoons vanilla**
¼	**teaspoon almond extract**
	Tart Cherry Filling (recipe follows)
	Fluffy Frosting (recipe follows)
2	**tablespoons kirsch**
	Chocolate curls (optional)

Sift flour, cocoa, and powdered sugar into a small bowl; set aside. In a large bowl, beat egg whites, cream of tartar, and salt with an electric mixer on high speed until foamy. Gradually add granulated sugar, about 2 tablespoons at a time, beating until mixture holds stiff peaks. Gently fold in vanilla and almond extract. Sprinkle flour-cocoa mixture, ¼ cup at a time, over meringue; using a rubber spatula, fold in gently after each addition just until flour mixture disappears. Turn batter into an ungreased 10-inch tube pan with a removable bottom; gently smooth top. Gently draw spatula through batter to eliminate large air bubbles.

Bake in a 375° oven until top of cake springs back when lightly touched (about 35 minutes). Invert pan on a funnel to keep cake from shrinking; let cool completely.

Meanwhile, prepare Tart Cherry Filling. Just before assembling dessert, prepare Fluffy Frosting.

Remove cake from pan. Using a serrated knife, cut cake horizontally into 3 layers. Sprinkle bottom layer with 1 tablespoon of the kirsch; spread with a very thin layer of Fluffy Frosting, then with half the Tart Cherry Filling. Add middle layer. Sprinkle with remaining 1 tablespoon kirsch; spread thinly with frosting, then spread with remaining filling. Cover with top layer; spread sides and top of cake with remaining frosting. If made ahead, let stand, uncovered, at room temperature for up to 6 hours. Decorate with chocolate curls before serving, if desired. Makes 12 servings.

Tart Cherry Filling. Drain 1 can (about 1 lb.) **pitted tart red cherries,** reserving liquid. Measure ½ cup of the liquid and set aside; discard remainder. In a small pan, mix ½ cup **sugar** and 2 tablespoons **cornstarch.** Stir in cherries and the ½ cup **reserved cherry liquid.** Bring to a boil over medium heat, stirring. Boil, stirring, until thickened and clear; then boil for 1 more minute. Remove from heat and stir in 1 tablespoon **kirsch.** Let cool.

Fluffy Frosting. In top of a double boiler, combine 2 large **egg whites** (about ¼ cup), at room temperature; ½ cup **light corn syrup;** ½ cup **sugar;** and a pinch of **salt.** Beat with an electric mixer on high speed until blended. Place over rapidly boiling water and cook, beating constantly, until frosting holds stiff peaks (about 4 minutes). Remove from heat and beat for 1 more minute. Beat in ½ teaspoon **vanilla** and 1 to 2 drops **red food coloring,** if desired. Use while warm.

Per serving: 319 calories (1% fat, 93% carbohydrates, 6% protein), 0.3 g total fat (0.1 g saturated fat), 75 g carbohydrates, 5 g protein, 0 mg cholesterol, 118 mg sodium

Low-fat Cheesecake

. . . .

MODIFIED CLASSIC

Preparation time: About 15 minutes
Baking time: About 1 hour
Chilling time: At least 8 hours

Cheesecake lovers take heart! This light interpretation tastes so creamy-rich it's bound to earn a place on your roster of favorites. Our fat-cutting tactics are simple: we use low-fat cottage cheese and nonfat yogurt, and substitute extra egg whites for some of the eggs.

1½	**cups graham cracker crumbs**
3	**tablespoons butter or margarine, melted**
1	**cup low-fat cottage cheese**
2	**cups plain nonfat yogurt**
½	**cup sugar**
1	**tablespoon all-purpose flour**
1	**large egg**
2	**large egg whites (about ¼ cup)**
2	**teaspoons vanilla**
2	**cups raspberries, strawberries, or other fresh fruit (hulled and/or sliced, if necessary)**

In a small bowl, mix graham cracker crumbs and butter until well combined. Press crumb mixture firmly over bottom and part of the way up sides of an 8-inch spring-form pan. Bake in a 350° oven for 7 minutes. Let cool on a rack. Reduce oven temperature to 300°.

In a food processor or blender, whirl cottage cheese and yogurt until smooth and glossy (at least 1 minute). Add sugar, flour, egg, egg whites, and vanilla; whirl until smooth.

Pour filling into crust and bake until top feels dry when lightly touched and center jiggles only slightly when pan is gently shaken (about 55 minutes). Let cool completely on a rack. Cover airtight and refrigerate for at least 8 hours or for up to 1 day.

To serve, cut cheesecake into slices and top with raspberries. Makes 10 servings.

Per serving: 212 calories (24% fat, 60% carbohydrates, 16% protein), 6 g total fat (2 g saturated fat), 31 g carbohydrates, 8 g protein, 32 mg cholesterol, 287 mg sodium

Orange Blossom Strawberry Pie

Preparation time: About 15 minutes
Baking time: 12 to 15 minutes
Cooking time: About 5 minutes
Chilling time: At least 1 hour

Cutting down on shortening gives the low-fat pastry for this pie a crisper texture; adding a little sugar makes it tender. Bake the crust first, then fill it with whole ripe strawberries and an orange-accented fresh strawberry glaze.

	Low-fat Pastry (recipe follows)
6	to 7 cups strawberries, hulled
6	tablespoons water
¾	cup sugar
2	tablespoons cornstarch
1	teaspoon grated orange peel
2	to 3 tablespoons orange-flavored liqueur; or 2 tablespoons frozen orange juice concentrate, thawed

Prepare Low-fat Pastry. Pierce all over with a fork to prevent puffing, then bake in a 425° oven until golden (12 to 15 minutes). Let cool in pan on a rack.

Measure 2 cups of the least perfect strawberries. Place in a blender or food processor, add water, and whirl until puréed. In a 1½-quart pan, stir together sugar, cornstarch, and orange peel. Stir in strawberry purée. Place over medium-high heat and bring to a full boil (about 5 minutes), stirring often. Remove from heat and stir in liqueur.

Arrange remaining 4 to 5 cups berries, tips up, in cooled pastry shell. Evenly spoon hot cooked berry purée over whole berries to cover completely. Refrigerate, uncovered, until purée is cool and set (at least 1 hour). If made ahead, cover lightly and refrigerate for up to a day. Makes 8 servings.

Low-fat Pastry. In a medium-size bowl or a food processor, combine 1 cup **all-purpose flour** and 1½ teaspoons **sugar.** Stir or whirl until well blended. Add ¼ cup cold **butter** or margarine, cut into pieces; cut in with a pastry blender or 2 knives (or whirl) until mixture resembles coarse crumbs. Gradually add 2 to 3 tablespoons **cold water,** mixing lightly with a fork (or whirling briefly) until

mixture begins to hold together. Pat into a flat, smooth round.

On a lightly floured board, roll out pastry to make a 12-inch round. Fit pastry into a 9-inch pie pan. Trim edge, fold under, and flute decoratively.

Per serving: 245 calories (23% fat, 73% carbohydrates, 4% protein), 6 g total fat (4 g saturated fat), 44 g carbohydrates, 3 g protein, 16 mg cholesterol, 60 mg sodium

Amaretti-topped Fresh Pineapple Pie

Preparation time: About 25 minutes
Standing time: At least 20 minutes
Baking time: About 50 minutes

Crushed almond macaroons stand in for a top crust in this juicy pie. The filling is a simple blend of pineapple chunks, sugar, and tart lime.

	Low-fat Pastry (at left)
¼	cup quick-cooking tapioca
¾	cup sugar
5	cups ½-inch chunks fresh pineapple
½	teaspoon grated lime peel
1	tablespoon lime juice
1¼	cups coarsely crushed almond macaroons (about 24 cookies, *each* 1¾ inches in diameter)

Prepare Low-fat Pastry and set aside in pie pan.

In a large bowl, stir together tapioca and sugar. Add pineapple, lime peel, and lime juice; mix gently. Let stand, stirring gently several times, until tapioca is softened (at least 20 minutes).

Spoon pineapple filling into pastry shell; place pan on a baking sheet to catch drips. Bake in a 400° oven for 30 minutes. Sprinkle crushed macaroons over filling; continue to bake until filling is bubbly all over and pastry is golden brown (18 to 20 more minutes). Let cool slightly on a rack before cutting. Makes 8 servings.

Per serving: 316 calories (18% fat, 79% carbohydrates, 3% protein), 6 g total fat (4 g saturated fat), 64 g carbohydrates, 3 g protein, 16 mg cholesterol, 83 mg sodium

Berry Yogurt Cheese Pie
. . . .

Preparation time: About 35 minutes
Chilling time: At least 16 hours
Baking time: About 10 minutes

Tangy homemade yogurt cheese and plenty of cottage cheese go into the smooth, lime-accented filling for this berry-topped pie.

	Yogurt Cheese (page 7)
	Graham Crust (recipe follows)
1	**envelope unflavored gelatin**
¼	**cup cold water**
2	**cups nonfat or low-fat cottage cheese**
½	**cup sugar**
1½	**teaspoons grated lime peel**
2	**tablespoons lime juice**
2	**cups raspberries or hulled, sliced strawberries**

Prepare Yogurt Cheese. Prepare Graham Crust; set aside. In a 1- to 1½-quart pan, sprinkle gelatin over water; let stand until gelatin is softened (about 5 minutes). Then stir over low heat just until gelatin is dissolved.

Turn Yogurt Cheese out of strainer into a food processor or blender. Add gelatin mixture, cottage cheese, sugar, lime peel, and lime juice; whirl until smooth. Pour into Graham Crust, cover, and refrigerate until firm (at least 4 hours) or for up to 1 day. Top pie with raspberries before serving. Makes 8 servings.

Graham Crust. In a 9-inch pie pan, mix 1⅓ cups **graham cracker crumbs,** 3 tablespoons **sugar,** and ⅓ cup **butter** or margarine (melted). Press crumb mixture evenly over bottom and sides of pan. Bake in a 350° oven for 10 minutes.

Per serving: 318 calories (26% fat, 56% carbohydrates, 18% protein), 9 g total fat (5 g saturated fat), 43 g carbohydrates, 14 g protein, 25 mg cholesterol, 440 mg sodium

Creamy Peach-Yogurt Pie
. . . .

Preparation time: About 30 minutes
Baking time: About 50 minutes
Freezing time: About 8 hours

When peaches are at their best, enjoy this creamy frozen pie. The honey-sweetened filling is enclosed in an airy meringue shell.

½	**teaspoon butter or margarine, at room temperature**
2	**large egg whites (about ¼ cup), at room temperature**
½	**teaspoon cream of tartar**
½	**cup sugar**
1	**large package (about 8 oz.) Neufchâtel cheese, at room temperature**
1	**cup plain low-fat yogurt**
⅓	**cup instant nonfat dry milk**
½	**cup honey**
1	**teaspoon almond extract**
1½	**cups coarsely chopped peeled peaches**
2	**large firm-ripe peaches (about 12 oz. *total*)**
1	**tablespoon lemon juice**

Coat bottom and sides of a 9-inch pie pan with butter. Set aside.

In a large bowl, beat egg whites and cream of tartar with an electric mixer on high speed until frothy. Beat in sugar, 1 tablespoon at a time; continue to beat until meringue holds stiff, glossy peaks. Spread meringue in pan, pushing it up pan sides to resemble a pie shell and smoothing with a spatula dipped in cold water. Bake in a 275° oven until lightly browned and dry to the touch (about 50 minutes). Transfer pan to a rack; let crust cool.

In a food processor or blender, whirl Neufchâtel cheese, yogurt, dry milk, honey, and almond extract until smooth. Add chopped peaches and whirl just until blended. Spread mixture in crust, cover airtight, and freeze until firm (about 8 hours).

To serve, let pie stand at room temperature for 15 minutes. Meanwhile, peel and slice whole peaches (you should have about 2 cups). Arrange peaches on pie; brush with lemon juice. Makes 8 servings.

Per serving: 251 calories (26% fat, 64% carbohydrates, 10% protein), 7 g total fat (5 g saturated fat), 42 g carbohydrates, 7 g protein, 24 mg cholesterol, 166 mg sodium

Orange-Apple Strudel

MODIFIED CLASSIC

Preparation time: About 45 minutes
Baking time: About 45 minutes

Layers of crisp, delicate fila pastry enclose a spicy apple filling accented with orange peel. Serve the dessert warm or cooled, with a sweet orange sauce.

2	**pounds tart green-skinned apples, such as Granny Smith or Newtown Pippin**
2	**teaspoons grated orange peel**
½	**cup firmly packed brown sugar**
¼	**cup all-purpose flour**
1	**teaspoon ground cinnamon**
½	**teaspoon ground nutmeg**
3	**sheets fila pastry (*each* about 12 by 16 inches), thawed if frozen**
2	**tablespoons butter or margarine, melted Orange Sauce (recipe follows)**

Peel and core apples, then thinly slice them into a large bowl. Add orange peel, sugar, flour, cinnamon, and nutmeg; mix gently but thoroughly.

Place one sheet of fila pastry on a baking sheet; lightly brush with 1½ teaspoons of the butter. Stack remaining 2 fila sheets atop the first, brushing each with 1½ teaspoons butter. Then spoon apple mixture in a strip down one long side of stacked fila sheets, 1½ inches in from side and extending to about 1 inch of ends. Fold ends of pastry over filling, then roll up pastry and filling jelly roll style, starting at side nearest filling. Brush pastry roll with remaining 1½ teaspoons butter.

Bake in a 375° oven until pastry is a rich golden brown (about 45 minutes). Meanwhile, prepare Orange Sauce.

Let strudel cool on baking sheet on a rack. Serve warm or at room temperature. To serve, cut crosswise into slices; offer Orange Sauce to spoon over slices. Makes 10 servings.

Orange Sauce. In a 1- to 2-quart pan, stir together 1 tablespoon *each* **cornstarch** and **cold water.** Add 1 cup **orange juice** and ¼ cup **orange marmalade.** Bring to a boil over high heat, stirring. Serve hot or at room temperature.

Per serving: 170 calories (15% fat, 83% carbohydrates, 2% protein), 3 g total fat (2 g saturated fat), 37 g carbohydrates, 1 g protein, 6 mg cholesterol, 60 mg sodium

Bourbon Bread Pudding

MODIFIED CLASSIC

Preparation time: About 20 minutes
Standing time: At least 10 minutes
Baking time: About 1 hour
Broiling time: 2 to 3 minutes

For a spirited twist on tradition, try this distinctive version of familiar bread pudding. The homey treat features a buttery bourbon topping, poured over the baked dessert and glazed under the broiler.

3	**large egg whites (about 6 tablespoons)**
3	**large eggs**
3	**cups sugar**
2	**teaspoons vanilla**
4	**cups low-fat milk**
1	**loaf (about 1 lb.) day-old French bread, cut into ½-inch cubes**
1	**cup raisins**
¼	**cup unsalted butter or margarine**
½	**cup bourbon**
	Vanilla low-fat frozen yogurt or ice cream (optional)

In a large bowl, beat egg whites and 2 of the eggs until blended. Then beat in 2 cups of the sugar, vanilla, and milk. Add bread and raisins; let stand for at least 10 minutes, stirring often to saturate bread with milk mixture.

Spoon bread mixture into a buttered 9- by 13-inch baking pan. Set pan of pudding in a larger baking pan that is at least 2 inches deep; then set pans on middle rack of a 350° oven. Pour boiling water into larger pan to a depth of about 1 inch. Bake until center of pudding feels firm when lightly pressed (about 1 hour).

About 5 minutes before pudding is done, melt butter in a 1½-quart pan over medium-high heat. Add remaining 1 cup sugar and bourbon; stir until sugar is dissolved. Reduce heat to low.

In a small bowl, beat remaining egg until blended. Stir a little of the hot butter mixture into egg, then return egg mixture to pan; cook, stirring, for about 1 minute.

Pour hot bourbon mixture over warm pudding. Broil about 8 inches below heat until top of pudding is glazed and sauce is bubbly all over (2 to 3 minutes). Spoon pudding into bowls; top with frozen yogurt, if desired. Makes 12 to 14 servings.

Per serving: 424 calories (17% fat, 75% carbohydrates, 8% protein), 8 g total fat (4 g saturated fat), 77 g carbohydrates, 8 g protein, 65 mg cholesterol, 280 mg sodium

Raisin Rice Pudding

Preparation time: About 5 minutes
Cooking time: 50 to 65 minutes

This creamy rice pudding is flavored in the classic manner, with cinnamon and vanilla. It's delicious warm or chilled.

3½   cups nonfat milk
½   cup short- or medium-grain white rice
¼   teaspoon salt
3   large eggs
¼   cup sugar
2   teaspoons vanilla
    About ¼ teaspoon ground cinnamon
¼   cup golden or dark raisins
1   tablespoon honey

In a 1½- to 2-quart pan, combine 3 cups of the milk, rice, and salt. Bring just to a very gentle boil over medium heat, stirring. Reduce heat to low, cover, and simmer, stirring occasionally, until mixture is reduced to about 2¾ cups (45 minutes to 1 hour).

In a small bowl, beat eggs, sugar, remaining ½ cup milk, vanilla, and ¼ teaspoon of the cinnamon until blended. Stir in raisins.

Stir egg mixture into rice mixture. Bring just to a boil; then reduce heat and simmer, uncovered, until thickened (about 5 minutes). Stir in honey. Serve warm or chilled. Sprinkle with cinnamon just before serving. Makes 6 servings.

Per serving: 213 calories (12% fat, 70% carbohydrates, 18% protein), 3 g total fat (1 g saturated fat), 37 g carbohydrates, 9 g protein, 109 mg cholesterol, 196 mg sodium

Light Chocolate Mousse

MODIFIED CLASSIC

Preparation time: About 15 minutes
Freezing time: About 45 minutes

The intense flavor of this silky, gelatin-thickened mousse will please true chocolate lovers.

1   envelope unflavored gelatin
⅓   cup granulated sugar
⅓   cup unsweetened cocoa
½   cup water
½   cup evaporated skim milk
2   teaspoons vanilla
1   tablespoon amaretto (optional)

In 1- to 1½-quart pan, stir together gelatin, sugar, ¼ cup of the cocoa, and water. Bring to a boil over high heat, stirring constantly. Pour into a deep 2-quart metal bowl and stir in milk. Cover and freeze until firm (about 45 minutes).

Beat frozen mixture with an electric mixer on high speed until fluffy and thick enough to hold peaks (about 3 minutes); stir in vanilla and amaretto, if desired. Divide mousse among four ½-cup ramekins or bowls; smooth tops. If made ahead, cover (do not let wrapping touch mousse) and refrigerate for up to 1 day. Dust with remaining cocoa before serving. Makes 4 servings.

Per serving: 118 calories (7% fat, 77% carbohydrates, 16% protein), 1 g total fat (0.6 g saturated fat), 25 g carbohydrates, 5 g protein, 1 mg cholesterol, 42 mg sodium

***Cocoa can replace** higher-fat chocolate in dessert recipes. For each ounce of unsweetened chocolate, substitute 3 tablespoons unsweetened cocoa plus 1 tablespoon salad oil.*

Bing Cherry Flan

Preparation time: About 15 minutes
Baking time: About 45 minutes

In central France, this custardy fruit dessert is known as a *clafoutis*. It can be made with a variety of fresh fruits, but plump, glossy dark sweet cherries are the traditional first choice.

	Vegetable oil cooking spray
2	cups dark sweet cherries, stemmed and pitted
2	tablespoons kirsch or brandy
2	tablespoons all-purpose flour
⅓	cup granulated sugar
⅛	teaspoon ground nutmeg
1	large egg
2	large egg whites (about ¼ cup)
1½	cups evaporated skim milk
1	teaspoon vanilla
2	tablespoons powdered sugar

Coat a 10-inch quiche dish or other shallow 1½-quart baking dish with cooking spray. Spread cherries in dish; drizzle with kirsch and set aside.

In a medium-size bowl, mix flour, granulated sugar, and nutmeg. Beat in egg, then egg whites; gradually stir in milk and vanilla. Pour egg mixture over cherries. Bake in a 350° oven until custard is puffed and golden brown, and a knife inserted in center comes out clean (about 45 minutes). Let cool slightly, then sift powdered sugar over top. Cut into wedges and serve warm. Makes 6 servings.

Per serving: 174 calories (8% fat, 74% carbohydrates, 18% protein), 2 g total fat (0.4 g saturated fat), 33 g carbohydrates, 8 g protein, 38 mg cholesterol, 102 mg sodium

__Fragrant vanilla sugar__ offers a sweet accent for cakes, puddings, and fresh fruit.
To make it, embed a vanilla bean in a small jar of powdered or granulated sugar; seal and let stand for a day or two. As you use the sugar replenish the supply. The vanilla bean will continue to provide flavor for several months.

Strawberry Cream

Preparation time: About 25 minutes
Cooling and chilling time: At least 4½ hours

This cold dessert serves up a double dose of strawberries, blending the fresh fruit with flavored yogurt. Present it in clear dessert glasses to show off the pretty layers of pink berry cream and deep red strawberry purée.

	Strawberry Purée (recipe follows)
2	cups sliced hulled strawberries
½	cup sugar
1	envelope unflavored gelatin
¾	cup cold water
2	large egg whites (about ¼ cup)
2	cups part-skim ricotta cheese
1	cup strawberry low-fat yogurt
8	whole unhulled strawberries

Prepare Strawberry Purée; refrigerate. Place sliced strawberries and sugar in a bowl. Partially crush berries with a fork or potato masher (there should still be some berry chunks); set aside.

In a small pan, sprinkle gelatin over cold water; let stand until gelatin is softened (about 5 minutes). Stir in berry-sugar mixture. Bring just to a boil, stirring constantly; then pour into a large bowl and let cool until thick but not set (about 20 minutes).

In a small bowl, beat egg whites with an electric mixer on high speed until they hold stiff peaks. Fold into berry mixture. Place ricotta cheese and yogurt in bowl; beat with mixer until blended, then fold into berry mixture.

Divide mixture among eight 1-cup dessert glasses. Cover and refrigerate until set (at least 4 hours) or for up to 1 day. To serve, pour an eighth of the Strawberry Purée into each glass; top each serving with a whole strawberry. Makes 8 servings.

Strawberry Purée. In a blender or food processor, whirl 1 cup hulled **strawberries** until puréed. Sweeten purée with about 1 tablespoon **powdered sugar** (or to taste). Cover and refrigerate for at least 4 hours or until next day.

Per serving: 191 calories (25% fat, 54% carbohydrates, 21% protein), 5 g total fat (3 g saturated fat), 26 g carbohydrates, 10 g protein, 20 mg cholesterol, 109 mg sodium

FRESH FRUIT FINALES

Perfectly ripe seasonal fruit is always a treat. Select the best, then present it stylishly—as we do in the elegant desserts on this page.

PEARS WITH RED WINE SYRUP

Preparation time: About 20 minutes
Cooking time: 12 to 15 minutes

1 **cup dry red wine, such as Cabernet Sauvignon, Merlot, Petite Sirah, or Zinfandel**
½ **cup *each* sugar and water**
¼ **cup lemon juice**
1 **tablespoon chopped fresh mint or ½ teaspoon dry mint**
1 **teaspoon whole black peppercorns**
1 **teaspoon chopped fresh tarragon or ¼ teaspoon dry tarragon**
3 **large firm-ripe Bartlett or Comice pears (about 1½ lbs. *total*)**
  Tarragon or mint sprigs (optional)

In a 1½- to 2-quart pan, combine wine, sugar, water, lemon juice, mint, peppercorns, and chopped tarragon.

Bring to a boil over high heat; then boil, uncovered, until syrup is reduced to ½ cup (12 to 15 minutes).

Pour wine syrup through a fine strainer into a bowl; discard residue. Use syrup warm or cool.

Cut pears in half lengthwise; remove and discard cores. Place each half cut side down; then, starting at blossom end, make lengthwise cuts about ¼ inch apart to within about ½ inch of stem end. Place each pear half on an individual plate and press down gently to fan out slices.

Pour wine syrup equally over pear halves. Garnish with tarragon sprigs, if desired. Makes 6 servings.

Per serving: 158 calories (3% fat, 96% carbohydrates, 1% protein), 0.4 g total fat (0 g saturated fat), 34 g carbohydrates, 0.6 g protein, 0 mg cholesterol, 4 mg sodium

GINGERED CHERRIES ON HONEYDEW MELON

Preparation time: About 15 minutes

⅓ **cup preserved ginger in syrup, chopped**
1 **tablespoon lemon juice**
1 **large honeydew melon (about 4 lbs.)**
4 **cups light or dark sweet cherries (with stems)**

In a small bowl, stir together ginger and lemon juice; set aside. Cut melon into 6 wedges; remove seeds from wedges, then place each wedge on an individual plate. Scatter cherries over melon; spoon ginger mixture evenly over all. Makes 6 servings.

Per serving: 132 calories (7% fat, 88% carbohydrates, 5% protein), 1 g total fat (0.2 g saturated fat), 32 g carbohydrates, 2 g protein, 0 mg cholesterol, 19 mg sodium

HOT PAPAYA SUNDAES

Preparation time: About 15 minutes
Baking time: About 15 minutes

1 **tablespoon butter or margarine, melted**
¼ **cup lime juice**
⅓ **cup rum or water**
½ **teaspoon grated lime peel**
3 **tablespoons honey**
2 **medium-size firm-ripe papayas (about 1 lb. *each*)**
2 **cups vanilla low-fat frozen yogurt**

In a 9- by 13-inch baking dish, stir together butter, lime juice, rum, lime peel, and honey. Cut unpeeled papayas in half lengthwise; scoop out and discard seeds. Place papaya halves, cut side down, in honey mixture.

Bake in a 375° oven until papayas are heated through and sauce is beginning to bubble (about 15 minutes).

Carefully transfer hot papaya halves, cut side up, to individual plates; let stand for about 5 minutes. Meanwhile, stir pan juices in baking dish to blend; pour into a small pitcher. Fill each papaya half with small scoops of frozen yogurt; offer pan juices to pour over sundaes to taste. Makes 4 servings.

Per serving: 279 calories (15% fat, 77% carbohydrates, 8% protein), 4 g total fat (2 g saturated fat), 47 g carbohydrates, 5 g protein, 13 mg cholesterol, 92 mg sodium

Lemon Pudding Cake with Berries

. . . .

Preparation time: About 30 minutes
Baking time: About 1 hour

A perfect example of a timeless sweet treat, lemon pudding cake is simple, quick, and reasonably low in fat. The pudding that forms on the bottom is still a delicious surprise. To make the dessert even tastier, serve it with fresh berries and a smooth, sweet raspberry sauce.

3	large eggs, separated
¾	cup sugar
2	tablespoons butter or margarine, at room temperature
1	tablespoon grated lemon peel
1	cup low-fat buttermilk
⅓	cup lemon juice
¼	cup all-purpose flour
	Berry Sauce (recipe follows)
3	cups raspberries, blueberries, or hulled strawberries (or a combination)

Set a buttered 5- to 6-cup soufflé dish or other straight-sided baking dish in a larger baking pan that is at least 2 inches deep; set aside.

In a deep bowl, beat egg whites with an electric mixer on high speed until foamy. Gradually beat in ¼ cup of the sugar; continue to beat until whites hold short, distinct peaks. Set aside.

In another bowl, combine butter, remaining ½ cup sugar, lemon peel, and egg yolks. Beat (no need to wash beaters) on high speed until mixture is thick and lighter in color. Stir in buttermilk, lemon juice, and flour. Add about a fourth of the egg whites to batter; stir to mix well. Gently but thoroughly fold in remaining whites.

Pour batter into soufflé dish. Set dish (in baking pan) on middle rack of a 350° oven. Pour boiling water into baking pan up to level of batter. Bake until top of pudding is a rich brown and center feels firm when lightly pressed (about 1 hour). Meanwhile, prepare Berry Sauce.

Serve pudding hot or cool, spooning portions up from bottom of dish to get the lemon sauce that has formed beneath pudding. Accompany with Berry Sauce and raspberries. Makes 6 servings.

Berry Sauce. Place 2 cups **raspberries** or 1 package (about 10 oz.) frozen sweetened raspberries (thawed) in a blender or food processor. Add 1 tablespoon **berry-flavored liqueur** such as Chambord or framboise (optional). Whirl until puréed. To remove seeds, rub purée through a fine strainer into a bowl. If using fresh berries, sweeten purée with 3 tablespoons **sugar** (or to taste).

Per serving: 294 calories (24% fat, 68% carbohydrates, 8% protein), 8 g total fat (4 g saturated fat), 51 g carbohydrates, 6 g protein, 120 mg cholesterol, 123 mg sodium

Baked Apples & Figs with Cassis

. . . .

30 MINUTES OR LESS

Preparation time: About 15 minutes
Baking time: About 15 minutes

End a special meal with tart apples and plump, supple figs baked in liqueur. The dessert's sophisticated flavor belies its simple preparation.

2	large tart apples, such as Granny Smith or Gravenstein (about 1 lb. *total*)
1	tablespoon lemon juice
6	large ripe figs (about 12 oz. *total*)
¼	cup cassis (black currant–flavored liqueur) or black raspberry–flavored liqueur
1	tablespoon sugar
2	teaspoons butter or margarine
	Vanilla low-fat yogurt

Peel, core, and thinly slice apples. Overlap slices in a 9-inch pie pan; drizzle with lemon juice. Thinly slice figs crosswise and arrange over apples. Pour liqueur over fruit, sprinkle with sugar, and dot with butter.

Bake in a 400° oven until fruit is bubbly (about 15 minutes). Spoon onto individual plates and top each serving with a dollop of yogurt. Makes 4 servings.

Per serving: 189 calories (12% fat, 86% carbohydrates, 2% protein), 2 g total fat (1 g saturated fat), 38 g carbohydrates, 0.8 g protein, 5 mg cholesterol, 21 mg sodium

Aunt Martha's Raspberry Cobbler

Preparation time: About 20 minutes
Baking time: 35 to 40 minutes

Crowned with golden drop biscuits, this old-fashioned dessert celebrates summer-perfect raspberries. Serve it hot from the oven.

¾	cup sugar
1	tablespoon cornstarch
¾	teaspoon ground cinnamon
½	cup water
6½	cups raspberries
1	cup all-purpose flour
1	teaspoon baking powder
¼	teaspoon baking soda
¼	cup butter or margarine, at room temperature
½	cup low-fat milk

In a shallow 2-quart casserole, mix ½ cup of the sugar, cornstarch, cinnamon, water, and 6 cups of the raspberries.

In a small bowl, stir together flour, baking powder, and baking soda. In a medium-size bowl, beat butter and remaining ¼ cup sugar until smoothly blended. Add milk and flour mixture; stir until dry ingredients are evenly moistened.

Drop batter in 8 equal spoonfuls onto raspberry mixture, spacing mounds of batter slightly apart. Bake in a 400° oven until topping is a deep golden brown and berry mixture is bubbly in center (35 to 40 minutes). Top cobbler with remaining ½ cup raspberries; spoon into bowls. Makes 8 servings.

Per serving: 242 calories (24% fat, 71% carbohydrates, 5% protein), 7 g total fat (4 g saturated fat), 44 g carbohydrates, 3 g protein, 17 mg cholesterol, 167 mg sodium

Apricot-Blueberry Cobbler

Preparation time: About 1 hour
Standing time: At least 20 minutes
Baking time: 40 to 50 minutes

Combine two fresh summertime fruits to make this familiar biscuit-topped dessert.

¼	cup quick-cooking tapioca
1	cup plus 2 tablespoons sugar
8	cups sliced apricots
1⅓	cups blueberries
2	tablespoons lemon juice
	Biscuit Topping (recipe follows)
1	large egg white (about 2 tablespoons), lightly beaten

In a shallow 3-quart casserole, stir together tapioca and 1 cup of the sugar. Add apricots, blueberries, and lemon juice; mix gently. Let stand, stirring gently several times, until tapioca is softened (at least 20 minutes). Meanwhile, prepare Biscuit Topping.

On a lightly floured board, roll or pat out Biscuit Topping about ½ inch thick. Cut into circles with a 2½-inch cookie cutter; reroll scraps and cut. Place biscuits slightly apart on fruit mixture. Brush biscuits with egg white, then sprinkle with remaining 2 tablespoons sugar.

Bake in a 400° oven until fruit is bubbly in center (40 to 50 minutes). Serve warm or at room temperature. Makes 10 to 12 servings.

Biscuit Topping. In a food processor or a large bowl, whirl or stir together 1½ cups **all-purpose flour,** 3 tablespoons **sugar,** 1½ teaspoons **baking powder,** and ½ teaspoon **salt.** Add ½ cup (¼ lb.) cold **butter** or margarine, cut into pieces; whirl or rub with your fingers until mixture resembles coarse crumbs. Add ⅓ cup **low-fat milk;** whirl or stir with a fork just until evenly moistened. Shape dough into a ball.

Per serving: 314 calories (25% fat, 70% carbohydrates, 5% protein), 9 g total fat (5 g saturated fat), 56 g carbohydrates, 4 g protein, 23 mg cholesterol, 280 mg sodium

Apple Cobbler with Oatmeal Cookie Crust

Preparation time: About 40 minutes
Baking time: About 1 hour

To make this hearty home-style dessert, slice tart apples into a big, shallow casserole; then blanket the fruit with a spicy oatmeal crust.

10	large tart apples, such as Granny Smith or Gravenstein (about 5 lbs. *total*)
1¾	cups sugar
1	tablespoon cornstarch
1½	teaspoons ground cinnamon
½	teaspoon ground allspice
5	tablespoons butter or margarine, at room temperature
1	large egg white (about 2 tablespoons)
1	teaspoon vanilla
1	cup all-purpose flour
¾	cup regular rolled oats
¾	teaspoon ground cardamom or ground cinnamon
	Vanilla low-fat frozen yogurt (optional)

Peel and core apples, then slice into a shallow 3- to 3½-quart casserole. Add ¾ cup of the sugar, cornstarch, the 1½ teaspoons cinnamon, and allspice; mix gently but thoroughly. Set aside.

In a large bowl, beat butter and remaining 1 cup sugar until smoothly blended. Add egg white and vanilla; beat until blended. Stir in flour, oats, and cardamom. Crumble flour mixture over apple mixture. Bake in a 350° oven until topping is richly browned (about 1 hour). Serve hot or at room temperature; top with frozen yogurt, if desired. Makes 8 servings.

Per serving: 466 calories (16% fat, 81% carbohydrates, 3% protein), 9 g total fat (5 g saturated fat), 98 g carbohydrates, 4 g protein, 19 mg cholesterol, 81 mg sodium

---

Fresh berries *are fragile. Because they deteriorate so quickly, it's best to use them within a day or two of purchase. Refrigerate them, unwashed, in a shallow pan lined with paper towels until you're ready to serve them.*

Sherry-Plum Crisp

Preparation time: About 20 minutes
Standing time: At least 20 minutes
Baking time: About 45 minutes

Tender fruit and a crunchy cereal-and-walnut topping add up to an irresistible warm dessert.

¼	teaspoon *each* ground allspice and ground nutmeg
¼	cup *each* quick-cooking tapioca and cream sherry
12	large firm-ripe plums (about 3½ lbs. *total*), sliced
½	cup firmly packed brown sugar
½	cup *each* all-purpose flour and granulated sugar
¼	cup cold butter or margarine, cut into pieces
¾	cup crunchy wheat and barley cereal
⅓	cup finely chopped walnuts

In a 9- by 13-inch baking pan, mix allspice, nutmeg, tapioca, sherry, plums, and brown sugar. Let mixture stand, stirring gently several times, until tapioca is softened (at least 20 minutes).

In a food processor or a medium-size bowl, whirl or stir together flour and granulated sugar. Add butter; whirl or rub with your fingers until mixture resembles fine crumbs. Stir in cereal and walnuts. Squeeze mixture into large lumps and coarsely crumble over plum mixture.

Bake in a 350° oven until topping is golden brown and fruit is bubbly in center (about 45 minutes). Serve warm or at room temperature. Makes 8 to 10 servings.

Per serving: 342 calories (23% fat, 73% carbohydrates, 4% protein), 9 g total fat (4 g saturated fat), 64 g carbohydrates, 4 g protein, 14 mg cholesterol, 135 mg sodium

Peach & Berry Bake

Preparation time: About 15 minutes
Baking time: About 45 minutes

Down-home delicious! This crumb-topped fresh fruit casserole boasts some of the best of summer's bounty.

1	tablespoon cornstarch
1	teaspoon ground cinnamon
½	teaspoon ground nutmeg
½	cup sugar
4	cups peeled, sliced peaches
1	cup blueberries
1	cup all-purpose flour
1	teaspoon baking powder
¼	cup cold butter or margarine, cut into pieces
1	large egg
¾	cup orange juice
2	tablespoons lemon juice

In a shallow 1½- to 2-quart casserole, mix cornstarch, cinnamon, nutmeg, and ¼ cup of the sugar. Stir in peaches and blueberries.

In a food processor or a medium-size bowl, whirl or stir together flour, baking powder, and remaining ¼ cup sugar. Add butter; whirl or rub with your fingers until mixture resembles fine crumbs. Add egg; whirl or stir just until well blended. Sprinkle mixture evenly over fruit. In a small bowl, stir together orange juice and lemon juice; pour evenly over crumbs.

Bake in a 375° oven until topping is golden brown and fruit is bubbly in center (about 45 minutes). Serve warm or cool. Makes 8 servings.

Per serving: 229 calories (26% fat, 69% carbohydrates, 5% protein), 7 g total fat (4 g saturated fat), 41 g carbohydrates, 3 g protein, 42 mg cholesterol, 130 mg sodium

Raspberries in Meringue

. . . .

NATURALLY LOW IN FAT

Preparation time: About 1 hour
Chilling time: At least 4 hours
Baking time: 1 hour
Drying time: 3 to 4 hours

Just right for a special occasion are these delicate meringue shells, filled with juicy raspberries and crowned with lightly sweetened raspberry purée. To keep the meringues crisp, avoid making them in humid weather (they absorb moisture easily) and fill them just before serving.

4	large egg whites (about ½ cup)
½	teaspoon cream of tartar
1	cup sugar
1	teaspoon vanilla
	Raspberry Purée (recipe follows)
2	cups raspberries

Cover a large baking sheet with ungreased plain brown paper or parchment paper. Trace eight 3½-inch circles on paper, spacing circles about 1½ inches apart.

In a large bowl, beat egg whites and cream of tartar with an electric mixer on high speed until foamy. Gradually add sugar, about 1 tablespoon at a time; continue to beat, scraping sides of bowl often, until mixture holds stiff, glossy peaks. Fold in vanilla.

Spoon about ½ cup of the meringue onto each circle on prepared baking sheet. Using back of spoon, spread mixture to cover each circle; then build up a 1½-inch-high rim, creating a hollow in each shell. (Or spoon mixture into a pastry bag fitted with a large star tip; pipe onto traced circles, building up a rim as directed.)

Position oven rack just below center of a 250° oven. Then place baking sheet on rack and bake meringues for 1 hour. Turn off oven and let meringues stand in closed oven until they are completely dry to the touch (3 to 4 hours). Meanwhile, prepare Raspberry Purée.

Remove baking sheet from oven. Let meringues cool completely on baking sheet on a rack. Then carefully peel off paper backing from meringues. If made ahead, store in an airtight container for up to 5 days.

To serve, fill meringue shells with raspberries; pour an eighth of the Raspberry Purée over each serving. Makes 8 servings.

Raspberry Purée. In a blender or food processor, whirl 3 cups **raspberries** until puréed. To remove seeds, rub purée through a fine strainer into a bowl. Sweeten purée with about 2 tablespoons **powdered sugar** (or to taste). Cover and refrigerate for at least 4 hours or up to 2 days.

Per serving: 152 calories (2% fat, 92% carbohydrates, 6% protein), 0.4 g total fat (0 g saturated fat), 36 g carbohydrates, 2 g protein, 0 mg cholesterol, 28 mg sodium

Wine & Berry Compote

Preparation time: About 10 minutes
Cooking time: 15 to 20 minutes

For an elegant dessert, spoon this berry compote into goblets and top with vanilla yogurt. Or use the compote as a sauce for frozen yogurt, sponge cake, or angel food cake.

1	cup *each* dry red wine and water
¾	cup sugar
6	tablespoons lemon juice
1	teaspoon vanilla
1½	pounds mixed berries, such as strawberries, raspberries, blackberries, or blueberries (hulled, if necessary)
	Vanilla low-fat yogurt (optional)

In a 4- to 5-quart pan, combine wine, water, sugar, and lemon juice. Bring to a boil over high heat; then boil, stirring, until sugar is dissolved. Continue to boil, uncovered, until mixture is reduced by about half (about 15 minutes). Stir in vanilla. (At this point, you may let cool, then cover and refrigerate for up to 3 weeks. Reheat to a simmer before continuing.)

Gently stir berries into hot syrup; let cool briefly. Spoon into individual goblets; top each serving with a dollop of yogurt, if desired. Makes 6 to 8 servings.

Per serving: 143 calories (3% fat, 95% carbohydrates, 2% protein), 0.4 g total fat (0 g saturated fat), 33 g carbohydrates, 0.8 g protein, 0 mg cholesterol, 5 mg sodium

Minted Raspberries with White Chocolate

Preparation time: About 15 minutes
Cooling & chilling time: At least 2½ hours

For a lovely summer dessert, embellish plump ripe raspberries with a refreshing mint syrup and a light shower of grated white chocolate. You can make the syrup well in advance, if you like.

	Mint Syrup (recipe follows)
6	cups raspberries
1	ounce white chocolate, grated

Prepare Mint Syrup; let cool and refrigerate as directed.

Shortly before serving, divide raspberries among 4 dessert dishes; drizzle each serving with a fourth of the syrup, then sprinkle each with a fourth of the chocolate. Makes 4 servings.

Mint Syrup. In a 1-quart pan, bring ⅓ cup **water** to a boil over high heat. Stir in 6 tablespoons **sugar** and ¼ cup firmly packed chopped **fresh mint.** Return to a boil; then boil syrup, uncovered, until reduced to ⅓ cup (2 to 3 minutes). Remove from heat and let stand for 30 minutes. Pour syrup through a fine wire strainer into a jar; discard mint. Cover and refrigerate for at least 2 hours or up to 1 month.

Per serving: 202 calories (13% fat, 83% carbohydrates, 4% protein), 3 g total fat (1 g saturated fat), 45 g carbohydrates, 2 g protein, 0 mg cholesterol, 6 mg sodium

Cherries, Berries & French Cream

Preparation time: About 10 minutes

This smooth, lightly sweetened blend of low-fat cottage cheese and sour cream is reminiscent of the French dessert cheese called *coeur à la crème.* For a pretty presentation, center the bowl of cheese on a platter or in a flat basket; then surround with whole strawberries and cherries for dipping.

½	cup low-fat cottage cheese
1	to 2 tablespoons reduced-fat sour cream
1½	tablespoons powdered sugar
¼	teaspoon vanilla
⅛	teaspoon ground nutmeg
2	cups whole unhulled strawberries
2	cups dark or light sweet cherries (with stems)

In a blender or food processor, combine cottage cheese, 1 tablespoon of the sour cream, sugar, vanilla, and nutmeg. Whirl until smooth, adding more sour cream as necessary to give cheese mixture a good dipping consistency. (At this point, you may cover and refrigerate for up to 1 day.)

To serve, mound cheese mixture in a small bowl; place bowl on a platter and arrange strawberries and cherries around it. To eat, dip fruit into cheese mixture. Makes 4 to 6 servings.

Per serving: 98 calories (16% fat, 67% carbohydrates, 17% protein), 2 g total fat (0.7 g saturated fat), 17 g carbohydrates, 4 g protein, 3 mg cholesterol, 92 mg sodium

Island Fruit Platter with Mango Velvet

NATURALLY LOW IN FAT

Preparation time: About 35 minutes

Simple yet elegant, this pretty fruit platter is the perfect light conclusion for a summer barbecue supper.

1	piece honeydew melon (about 2 lbs.)
1	large ripe papaya (about 1¼ lbs.), peeled, halved, and seeded
1	medium-size pineapple (about 3 lbs.), peeled, cored, and cut crosswise into ½-inch-thick slices
	Mint sprigs (optional)
	Mango Velvet (recipe follows)

Remove seeds and cut rind from melon; cut melon into thin wedges. Thinly slice papaya halves crosswise. Arrange pineapple slices, overlapping them slightly, down center of a large platter. Arrange papaya and melon on either side. Garnish with mint sprigs, if desired.

Prepare Mango Velvet and serve with fruit. Makes 6 servings.

Mango Velvet. Peel 1 large ripe **mango** (about 1 lb.) and slice fruit from pit into a food processor or blender. Whirl until puréed. Add ¼ cup **frozen orange juice concentrate** and 2 tablespoons **lime juice.** Whirl until blended. Spoon purée into a small bowl.

Per serving: 161 calories (4% fat, 92% carbohydrates, 4% protein), 0.8 g total fat (0.1 g saturated fat), 41 g carbohydrates, 2 g protein, 0 mg cholesterol, 12 mg sodium

Dessert Nachos with Fruit Salsa

Preparation time: About 25 minutes
Baking time: About 10 minutes

Nachos and salsa for dessert? Yes—when the crisp chips are dusted with cinnamon sugar and the salsa is a sweet blend of diced fruits. Offer a honey-orange cream cheese sauce alongside, too.

	Fruit Salsa (recipe follows)
⅓	cup sugar
1	teaspoon ground cinnamon
10	flour tortillas (*each* 7 to 9 inches in diameter)
1	large package (about 8 oz.) Neufchâtel cheese
½	cup orange juice
3	tablespoons honey

Prepare Fruit Salsa; cover and refrigerate until ready to serve or for up to 4 hours.

In a shallow bowl, mix sugar and cinnamon. Working with one tortilla at a time, brush both sides lightly with water; then cut tortilla into 6 equal wedges. Dip one side of each wedge in sugar mixture. Arrange wedges in a single layer, sugared sides up, on oiled foil-lined baking sheets. Bake, one sheet at a time, in a 500° oven until tortilla wedges are crisp and golden (about 4 minutes). Remove wedges from baking sheets and let cool slightly on racks.

While tortillas are baking, in a 1- to 2-quart pan, combine Neufchâtel cheese, orange juice, and honey. Whisk over low heat until sauce is smooth (about 3 minutes).

To serve, mound warm tortilla wedges on a platter. Offer sauce and Fruit Salsa to spoon onto wedges. Makes 10 to 12 servings.

Fruit Salsa. Hull 2 cups **strawberries;** dice into a bowl. Add 2 large **kiwi fruit** (about 8 oz. *total*), peeled and diced, and 1 can (about 11 oz.) **mandarin oranges,** drained.

Per serving: 240 calories (27% fat, 64% carbohydrates, 9% protein), 7 g total fat (3 g saturated fat), 40 g carbohydrates, 5 g protein, 16 mg cholesterol, 238 mg sodium

Mango Sorbet in Cookie Tulips

· ·

Preparation time: About 1 hour
Freezing time: Depends on type of ice cream maker
Baking time: About 30 minutes

A special meal deserves a dramatic finale: scoops of vivid mango sorbet served in crisp cookie shells and garnished with your choice of fresh fruit. (When you plan your cooking schedule, be sure to allow time for freezing the sorbet.)

4	**medium-size ripe mangoes (about 2¾ lbs. total)**
⅔	**cup light corn syrup**
½	**cup lemon juice**
	Cookie Tulips (recipe follows)
	Fresh fruit (optional)

Peel mangoes; slice fruit from pits into a food processor or blender. Add corn syrup and lemon juice; whirl until smooth. Pour mixture into container of a 1-quart or larger ice cream maker and freeze according to manufacturer's directions. If made ahead, store in freezer in an airtight container for up to 1 week.

While sorbet is freezing, prepare Cookie Tulips.

To serve, scoop sorbet into Cookie Tulips; garnish with fruit, if desired. Makes 6 servings.

Cookie Tulips. In a medium-size bowl, beat ¼ cup **butter** or margarine (at room temperature) and ½ cup **sugar** until smoothly blended. Add 7 tablespoons **all-purpose flour**, 1 teaspoon **vanilla**, and 2 large **egg whites** (about ¼ cup); beat until smooth.

Bake cookies 2 at a time. Coat a 12- by 15-inch baking sheet with **vegetable oil cooking spray**. With fingertip, draw a 7-inch circle in one corner

─────────

Virtually any frozen dessert is more dramatic when scooped into attractive Cookie Tulips (recipe above). Especially in rainy or humid weather, be sure to seal the crisp cookies well in moisture-proof wrapping after baking; dampness causes them to droop and eventually collapse.

─────────

of sheet; repeat in opposite corner. Place 3 tablespoons of the batter in each circle and spread to fill evenly. Bake cookies in a 350° oven until golden (about 9 minutes). At once, using a wide spatula, lift cookies, one at a time, from sheet; drape each over a clean 1-pound food can and gently pinch sides to form a fluted cup. Let cookies cool until firm; then carefully lift from cans.

Repeat to bake 4 more cookies. If made ahead, let cool completely; store airtight for up to 1 day. Makes 6 cookies.

Per serving: 378 calories (19% fat, 78% carbohydrates, 3% protein), 9 g total fat (5 g saturated fat), 78 g carbohydrates, 3 g protein, 21 mg cholesterol, 148 mg sodium

Oranges in Ginger Champagne

· ·

NATURALLY LOW IN FAT

Preparation time: About 20 minutes
Cooking time: 6 to 8 minutes
Chilling time: At least 4 hours

Part beverage and part dessert, this stylish offering is well suited to elegant occasions.

¾	**cup *each* sugar and water**
2	**tablespoons minced crystallized ginger**
4	**medium-size oranges (about 2 lbs. *total*)**
1	**bottle (about 750 ml.) dry champagne or 4 cups ginger ale**

In a 2- to 3-quart pan, combine sugar, water, and ginger. Stir over medium heat until sugar is dissolved. Increase heat to high and bring to a boil. Boil, uncovered, without stirring, for 5 minutes. Pour into a bowl; let cool, then cover and refrigerate until cold (at least 1 hour) or for up to 1 day.

Cut peel and all white membrane from oranges. Holding oranges over bowl of ginger syrup, cut between membranes to release segments; add segments to syrup and stir gently. Cover and refrigerate for 3 hours.

To serve, spoon oranges and syrup into champagne or wine glasses. Fill glasses with champagne. Makes 8 servings.

Per serving: 188 calories (1% fat, 97% carbohydrates, 2% protein), 0.2 g total fat (0 g saturated fat), 33 g carbohydrates, 0.7 g protein, 0 mg cholesterol, 7 mg sodium

LOW-FAT FROZEN DESSERTS

These cooling treats are delightful at any time of year. The sherbet can be made in the freezer, while the other two recipes require an ice cream maker. You may use a frozen cylinder, self-refrigerated, or ice- and salt-cooled machine; follow the manufacturer's directions for each type.

BROWN SUGAR PEACH ICE CREAM

Preparation time: About 20 minutes
Cooking time: About 25 minutes
Chilling time: At least 4 hours
Freezing time: Depends on type of ice cream maker

1½	cups low-fat milk
1	cup half-and-half
1	cup firmly packed light brown sugar
3	large egg yolks
1	teaspoon vanilla
9	medium-size ripe peaches (about 3 lbs. *total*)
½	cup reduced-fat sour cream
2	tablespoons lemon juice

In a 3- to 4-quart pan, combine milk, half-and-half, and sugar. Cook over medium heat, stirring often, until sugar is dissolved.

In a bowl, beat egg yolks to blend. Whisk some of the milk mixture into yolks, then stir mixture back into pan. Cook over medium heat, stirring, until mixture is thick enough to coat a metal spoon in a smooth layer (about 20 minutes). At once, set pan in ice water. Add vanilla; let mixture stand until cool, stirring often. Lift from water, cover, and refrigerate until cold (at least 4 hours) or for up to 1 day.

Peel and pit peaches; then slice into a food processor or blender. Add sour cream and lemon juice; whirl until smooth. Stir peach purée into milk mixture; pour into container of a 2-quart or larger ice cream maker. Freeze according to manufacturer's directions until softly frozen. If made ahead, store in freezer in an airtight container for up to 1 week. Makes 16 servings (about ½ cup *each*).

Per serving: 135 calories (27% fat, 66% carbohydrates, 7% protein), 4 g total fat (2 g saturated fat), 23 g carbohydrates, 3 g protein, 50 mg cholesterol, 25 mg sodium

BLUEBERRY BUTTERMILK SHERBET

Preparation time: About 20 minutes
Chilling & freezing time: At least 5½ hours

2	cups fresh or frozen blueberries
2	teaspoons grated lemon peel
2	tablespoons lemon juice
¼	cup sugar
1	cup low-fat buttermilk

In a 2-quart pan, mix blueberries, lemon peel, lemon juice, and sugar. Cook over medium-high heat, stirring often, until berries begin to pop (about 6 minutes). Cover; refrigerate until cool (at least 1 hour) or for up to 1 day.

In a blender or food processor, combine blueberry mixture and buttermilk; whirl until smooth. Pour into a 9- or 10-inch-square metal pan, cover, and freeze until solid (at least 4 hours).

Break mixture into chunks; whirl in a food processor (or beat with an electric mixer) until smooth. Return to pan, cover, and freeze until firm (at least 30 minutes) or for up to 1 week. Let hard-frozen sherbet soften slightly before serving. Makes 6 servings (about ½ cup *each*).

Per serving: 77 calories (6% fat, 86% carbohydrates, 8% protein), 0.6 g total fat (0.2 g saturated fat), 18 g carbohydrates, 2 g protein, 2 mg cholesterol, 47 mg sodium

WINE SLUSH

Preparation time: About 10 minutes
Freezing time: Depends on type of ice cream maker

1½	cups chilled sweet, fruity wine, such as late-harvest wines made from Riesling, gewürztraminer, or Zinfandel grapes
2	to 3 cups melon cubes or peach slices

Pour wine into container of a 2-cup or larger ice cream maker. Freeze according to manufacturer's directions until softly frozen. Divide melon among 4 chilled bowls; top with wine slush. Makes 4 servings.

Per serving: 96 calories (4% fat, 89% carbohydrates, 7% protein), 0.2 g total fat (0 g saturated fat), 10 g carbohydrates, 0.8 g protein, 0 mg cholesterol, 14 mg sodium

METRIC CONVERSION TABLES

TEMPERATURES

U.S. TEMPERATURES	APPROXIMATE CELSIUS EQUIVALENT
32°F	0°C
100°F	38°C
110°F	43°C
125°F	52°C
150°F	66°C
175°F	80°C
200°F	95°C
212°F	100°C
225°F	110°C
250°F	120°C
275°F	135°C
300°F	150°C
325°F	165°C
350°F	175°C
375°F	190°C
400°F	205°C
425°F	220°C
450°F	230°C
475°F	245°C
500°F	260°C
525°F	275°C
550°F	290°C

To change Fahrenheit to Celsius: subtract 32, multiply by 5, divide by 9. Celsius equivalents have been rounded for convenience.

LENGTHS

U.S. MEASUREMENT	APPROXIMATE METRIC EQUIVALENT
⅛ inch	3 mm
¼ inch	6 mm
½ inch	1 cm
¾ inch	2 cm
1 inch	2.5 cm
2 inches	5 cm
3 inches	8 cm
4 inches	10 cm
5 inches	12.5 cm
6 inches	15 cm
7 inches	18 cm
8 inches	20 cm
9 inches	23 cm
10 inches	25 cm
11 inches	28 cm
12 inches/1 foot	30 cm
13 inches	33 cm
14 inches	35.5 cm
15 inches	38 cm
17 inches	43 cm
18 inches	46 cm
24 inches/2 feet	61 cm

To change inches to centimeters: multiply by 2.54. Metric equivalents have been rounded to the nearest whole or half millimeter or centimeter.

VOLUME

U.S. MEASUREMENT	APPROXIMATE METRIC EQUIVALENT
1 teaspoon	5 ml
3 teaspoons/1 tablespoon	15 ml
2 tablespoons	30 ml
4 tablespoons/¼ cup	60 ml
⅓ cup	80 ml
8 tablespoons/½ cup	120 ml
⅔ cup	160 ml
¾ cup	180 ml
16 tablespoons/1 cup	240 ml
1¼ cups	300 ml
1⅓ cups	320 ml
1½ cups	360 ml
1⅔ cups	400 ml
1¾ cups	420 ml
2 cups/1 pint	470 ml
2½ cups	590 ml
3 cups	710 ml
3½ cups	830 ml
4 cups/2 pints/1 quart	950 ml
5 cups	1.2 liters
6 cups/1½ quarts	1.4 liters
8 cups/2 quarts	1.9 liters
3 quarts	2.8 liters
4 quarts/1 gallon	3.8 liters

To change cups to liters: multiply by 0.24. Metric equivalents have been rounded for convenience.

FLOUR

U.S. MEASUREMENT	APPROXIMATE GRAM EQUIVALENT
1 tablespoon	8 g
4 tablespoons / ¼ cup	30 g
5⅓ tablespoons / ⅓ cup	40 g
½ cup	60 g
⅔ cup	85 g
¾ cup	95 g
1 cup	125 g
1¼ cups	155 g
1⅓ cups	165 g
1½ cups	185 g
1⅔ cups	210 g
1¾ cups	220 g
2 cups	250 g
2¼ cups	280 g
2⅓ cups	290 g
2½ cups	310 g
2⅔ cups	335 g
2¾ cups	345 g
3 cups	375 g
3¼ cups	405 g
3⅓ cups	415 g
3½ cups	435 g
3⅔ cups	460 g
3¾ cups	470 g
4 cups	500 g

Based on 1 cup unsifted all-purpose flour = 4.4 oz. Gram equivalents have been rounded for convenience.

SUGAR

U.S. MEASUREMENT	APPROXIMATE GRAM EQUIVALENT
1 teaspoon	4 g
1 tablespoon	12 g
4 tablespoons / ¼ cup	50 g
5⅓ tablespoons / ⅓ cup	70 g
½ cup	100 g
⅔ cup	135 g
¾ cup	150 g
1 cup	200 g
1¼ cups	250 g
1⅓ cups	270 g
1½ cups	300 g
1⅔ cups	335 g
1¾ cups	350 g
2 cups	400 g
2½ cups	500 g
3 cups	600 g
3½ cups	700 g
4 cups	805 g

Based on 1 cup granulated sugar = 7.1 oz. Gram equivalents have been rounded for convenience.

WEIGHTS

U.S. MEASUREMENT	APPROXIMATE METRIC EQUIVALENT
1 oz.	30 g
2 oz.	55 g
3 oz.	85 g
4 oz. / ¼ lb.	115 g
5 oz.	140 g
6 oz.	170 g
7 oz.	200 g
8 oz. / ½ lb.	230 g
9 oz.	255 g
10 oz.	285 g
12 oz. / ¾ lb.	340 g
14 oz.	400 g
16 oz. / 1 lb.	455 g
1¼ lbs.	565 g
1½ lbs.	680 g
1¾ lbs.	795 g
2 lbs.	905 g
2½ lbs.	1.15 kg
3 lbs.	1.35 kg
3½ lbs.	1.6 kg
4 lbs.	1.8 kg
5 lbs.	2.3 kg
6 lbs.	2.7 kg
8 lbs.	3.6 kg
10 lbs.	4.5 kg
12 lbs.	5.5 kg
15 lbs.	6.8 kg
18 lbs.	8.2 kg
20 lbs.	9.1 kg

To change ounces to grams: multiply by 28.35. Metric equivalents have been rounded for convenience.

INDEX